THEORY, METHOD, SUSTAINABILITY, AND CONFLICT

THEORY, METHOD, SUSTAINABILITY, AND CONFLICT

AN OXFORD HANDBOOK OF APPLIED ETHNOMUSICOLOGY

VOLUME 1

Edited by

SVANIBOR PETTAN

and

JEFF TODD TITON

OXFORD
UNIVERSITY PRESS

OXFORD
UNIVERSITY PRESS

Oxford University Press is a department of the University of Oxford. It furthers
the University's objective of excellence in research, scholarship, and education
by publishing worldwide. Oxford is a registered trade mark of Oxford University
Press in the UK and certain other countries.

Published in the United States of America by Oxford University Press
198 Madison Avenue, New York, NY 10016, United States of America.

Library of Congress Cataloging-in-Publication Data
Names: Pettan, Svanibor, 1960– | Titon, Jeff Todd, 1943–
Title: Theory, method, sustainability, & conflict : an Oxford handbook of
applied ethnomusicology, volume 1 / edited by Svanibor Pettan and Jeff Todd Titon.
Description: New York : Oxford University Press, 2019. |
Series: Oxford handbooks | Includes bibliographical references and index.
Identifiers: LCCN 2018023120 | ISBN 9780190885694 (pbk. : alk. paper) |
ISBN 9780190885717 (epub)
Subjects: LCSH: Applied ethnomusicology.
Classification: LCC ML3799.2 .T54 2019 | DDC 780.89—dc23
LC record available at https://lccn.loc.gov/2018023120

1 3 5 7 9 8 6 4 2

Printed by WebCom, Inc., Canada

CONTENTS

PART I AN INTRODUCTION TO APPLIED ETHNOMUSICOLOGY

Sections

PART II THEORETICAL AND METHODOLOGICAL CONSIDERATIONS

Chapters

PART III CONFLICTS

Figures and Tables

Figures

TABLES

CONTRIBUTORS

Dan Bendrups is an ethnomusicologist who investigates the role of music in sustaining cultural heritage. His research spans communities and cultures in the Americas and the Asia-Pacific, as well as migrant communities in Australia and New Zealand. He lectures in research education and development at La Trobe University, Australia, where he is also a member of the La Trobe University Institute of Latin American Studies.

Klisala Harrison (University of Helsinki, Finland) has served as Chairperson and founding Vice-Chairperson of the ICTM Study Group on Applied Ethnomusicology. She has edited and co-edited three anthologies and published six international, peer-reviewed articles on applied ethnomusicology method, theory and practice. Her areas of research include music, health and well-being; music and poverty; music for theatre and film; and indigenous musics of Canada, Greenland and northern Europe. Currently she works as an Academy of Finland Research Scholar investigating music for health and well-being of Arctic Indigenous people.

Erica Haskell is an Associate Professor of ethnomusicology at the University of New Haven, USA. She holds a Ph.D. and MA in ethnomusicology from Brown University. In her research, she has explored the politics of music, applied ethnomusicology, the involvement of international humanitarian organizations in cultural events and projects in Bosnia-Herzegovina, and the humanitarian intersections between postwar and post-catastrophe environments.

Svanibor Pettan is Professor and Chair of the ethnomusicology program at the University of Ljubljana, Slovenia. Initiator and first Chair of the ICTM Study Group Applied Ethnomusicology and a founding member of the SEM Section on Applied Ethnomusicology, he contributes to the advancement of the field in the global arena with studies in various formats, addressing war-peace continuum, minorities, conflicts and education. He currently serves as Vice-President of the International Council for Traditional Music and as Chair of its Study Group Music and Minorities.

Joshua D. Pilzer is Associate Professor of ethnomusicology in the Faculty of Music at the University of Toronto, Canada, and a specialist in the anthropology of music in modern Korea and Japan. His interests embrace the relationships between music, survival, memory, traumatic experience, marginalization, violence, and social movements. He is the author of *Hearts of Pine: Songs in the Lives of Three Korean Survivors of the Japanese "Comfort Women"* (Oxford University Press, 2012).

Huib Schippers has a long and diverse history of research into music education, community music, artistic practice, arts policy, and music industry. He was the driving force behind the World Music and Dance Centre in Rotterdam (1996–2003), and Founding Director of the innovative Queensland Conservatorium Research Centre in Brisbane, Australia (2003–2015), from where he led a major international research collaboration into musical ecosystems: "Sustainable futures for music cultures" (Oxford University Press, 2016). Currently, Schippers is Director/Curator of the iconic label Smithsonian Folkways in Washington DC.

Britta Sweers is Professor of cultural anthropology of music at the Institute of Musicology and Director of the Center for Global Studies at the University of Bern (Switzerland). Having studied at Hamburg University and Indiana University (Bloomington), she was Junior Professor at the Hochschule für Musik und Theater, Rostock (Germany), from 2003 to 2009. Her research interests include the transformation of traditional musics (particularly on the British Isles and the Baltic Countries) in global contexts, music and nationalism, and applied ethnomusicology.

Tan Sooi Beng is Professor of ethnomusicology at the School of Arts, Universiti Sains Malaysia, Penang. She is the author of *Bangsawan: A Social and Stylistic History of Popular Malay Opera* (Oxford University Press, 1993) and coauthor of *Music of Malaysia: Classical, Folk and Syncretic Traditions* (Ashgate Press, 2004). Tan is actively involved in engaged theater combining music, dance, and drama, aimed at educating young people and revitalizing traditions among the multiethnic communities of Penang.

Jeff Todd Titon is Professor of Music, Emeritus, at Brown University, Providence, Rhode Island, USA, where for 27 years he directed the Ph.D. program in ethnomusicology. The author or editor of eight books and numerous essays, he is known for developing phenomenological and ecological approaches to ethnographic fieldwork, for theorizing and practicing an applied ethnomusicology based in reciprocity and friendship, and for introducing the concepts of cultural and musical sustainability to the fields of folklore and ethnomusicology. His current research on a sound ecology may be tracked at https://sustainablemusic.blogspot.com

ABOUT THE COMPANION WEBSITE

www.oup.com/us/ohaev1

Oxford has created a website to accompany *The Oxford Handbook of Applied Ethnomusicology*. Audio recordings and color photographs, which cannot be made available in a book, are provided here. The reader is encouraged to consult this resource in conjunction with the chapters. Examples available online are indicated in the text with Oxford's symbol ⊙.

THEORY, METHOD, SUSTAINABILITY, AND CONFLICT

PART I

AN INTRODUCTION TO APPLIED ETHNOMUSICOLOGY

Our Introduction to this volume consists of three sections. Although applied ethnomusicology is practiced now in many regions of the world, it has developed differently in various times and places, just as ethnomusicology itself has. We begin in Section 1 (by Titon) with a focused statement on applied ethnomusicology as it has developed from a single representative area (the United States), and then broaden out in Section 2 (by Pettan) to a global perspective, where a greater plurality of voices and viewpoints may be observed, so that we may end with the understanding that applied ethnomusicology is no single field but is instead an ever-emergent movement, responding differently at various times and places, by means of music-centered interventions, to different cultures, histories, needs, and conditions. Indeed, this volume as a whole offers just such a plurality of voices and viewpoints. In addition to discussing histories and developments in national and global perspectives, particularly in the contexts of the US-based Society for Ethnomusicology (SEM) as well as the UNESCO-affiliated International Council for Traditional Music (ICTM), the co-editors also each offer personal perspectives, based in many years of involvement. Section 3, jointly written by Titon and Pettan, offers an introduction to the chapters that follow.

We wish to thank many people who have made this work possible. Suzanne Ryan, music editor at Oxford University Press, supported this project from the outset and helped us to understand how to shape the volume in conformity with *Handbook* expectations. The anonymous external reviewers read perceptively and made many useful comments and suggestions. For guidance, vision, and support along the path to applied ethnomusicology, Titon would like to thank colleagues and teachers Alan Kagan, Mulford Sibley, Charlotte Heth, David McAllester, Dennis Tedlock, Burt Feintuch, Erma Franklin, Loyal Jones, Elwood Cornett, Kenneth Irby, Maryanne Wolf, Sandy Ives, Archie Green, Bess Lomax Hawes, Daniel Sheehy, and Robert Baron.

Pettan would like to single out Samuel Araújo, Anthony Seeger, and Kjell Skyllstad, three important visionaries in applied ethnomusicology (among many more), who continue to inspire his own thinking and doing. Both editors thank the contributors to this volume, with whom it was a true honor and pleasure to join forces in creating this essentially important *Handbook*.

APPLIED ETHNOMUSICOLOGY

A Descriptive and Historical Account

JEFF TODD TITON

ETHNOMUSICOLOGY AND APPLIED ETHNOMUSICOLOGY

I like to think of *ethnomusicology* as the study of people making music (Titon, 1989, 1992b: xxi–xxii). People make sounds they call music, and they also make ideas about music. Those ideas form the cultural domain called music. They include what music is and is not; what it does and cannot do; how it is acquired and how it should be transmitted; what value it has; what it should (and should not) be used for; what it has been in the past and what it will be in the future; whether it should be encouraged and supported, or discouraged and repressed; and so forth. Just as music differs among individuals and social groups throughout the world, so do people's ideas about it differ, and this has been so throughout history.

Applied ethnomusicology puts ethnomusicological scholarship, knowledge, and understanding to practical use. That is a very broad definition. More specifically, as it has developed in North America and elsewhere, applied ethnomusicology is best regarded as a music-centered intervention in a particular community, whose purpose is to benefit that community—for example, a social improvement, a musical benefit, a cultural good, an economic advantage, or a combination of these and other benefits. It is music-centered, but above all the intervention is people-centered, for the understanding that drives it toward reciprocity is based in the collaborative partnerships that arise from ethnomusicological fieldwork. Applied ethnomusicology is guided by ethical principles of social responsibility, human rights, and cultural and musical equity. Although some ethnomusicologists regard applied ethnomusicology as a career alternative to academic work—and indeed, it can be—it's not always helpful to make that distinction, because ethnomusicologists who do applied work are employed both inside academic institutions, such as universities and museums, and outside them in government agencies, nongovernmental organizations (NGOs), and client organizations directly. In other words, the place of employment does not determine whether the ethnomusicology has any application outside the world of scholarship. What matters is the work itself: how, where, and why the intervention occurs, and the communities to whom we feel responsible (Titon, 2003; Dirksen, 2012).

Putting ethnomusicological scholarship, knowledge, and understanding to practical use and terming it *applied* implies the usual distinction made in the sciences between pure research, or the pursuit of knowledge for its own sake (as it is often called), and applied research, or knowledge put to practical use. It is possible to minimize this distinction, claiming that the moment a researcher circulates knowledge within a scholarly community it is being put to beneficial use. Classroom teaching is of course another kind of use. Besides, the phrase knowledge for its own sake appears oxymoronic, for in what sense can knowledge possibly be for its own sake if knowledge cannot logically be an agent or a self? If all ethnomusicological knowledge is put to use in one way or another, then the term applied ethnomusicology is redundant. All of this may be so, but for strategic reasons the editors of this volume find the term useful, in order to highlight a certain kind of activity and distinguish an ethnomusicology based in social responsibility where knowledge is intended for beneficial use in communities outside the academic world from an ethnomusicology which is meant to increase and improve the storehouse of knowledge about music and circulate it among scholars. In the absence of this distinction, as I will argue later (see below, "Applied Ethnomusicology in the United States: A Brief History"), applied ethnomusicology has been marginalized or ignored in the definitions and histories of our field that circulate among ethnomusicologists. Indeed, examination of ethnomusicology curricula reveals very few, if any, courses devoted to applied work at the doctoral level. The Ph.D. is a research degree, after all, and the chief criterion for career advancement in the university remains research that enjoys a high intellectual reputation among scholars. Fortunately, however, a sense of social responsibility motivates an increasing number of ethnomusicologists, employed inside and outside the academic world, who find ways to integrate it into their scholarly research, and to apply it in the public arena. Readers who wish to know more about my personal involvement with, and views on, applied ethnomusicology are invited to consult Titon 2003 and various entries on applied ethnomusicology on my blog at http://sustainablemusic.blogspot.com.

This volume is not meant as a "how-to" handbook, like the *Girl Scout Handbook*. Rather, in keeping with the other Oxford Handbooks in this series, it offers a sampling of current scholarship related to its subject, with contributions from some leading exponents. Applied ethnomusicology is a field of practice and theory, rather than a discipline with a bounded subject and an established, universally agreed-upon methodology. A branch of the academic discipline of ethnomusicology, its scope is still expanding. While its practitioners are in broad agreement over putting ethnomusicological knowledge to use rather than simply pursuing it as an end in itself, we differ in emphasis, whether in definition, method, or purpose (Harrison, 2012). Readers may look here for a variety of subjects, approaches and models.

APPLIED ETHNOMUSICOLOGY IN CONTEMPORARY NORTH AMERICA: A BRIEF OVERVIEW

What kinds of activities are applied ethnomusicologists involved in? Where, typically, do we intervene in the public arena? The co-editors of this volume, one active in North America, the other in Europe, have determined to write about these activities in the areas they know best. As I am most familiar with activities in the United States, and the professional organization based there (the *Society for Ethnomusicology*, or SEM), what follows in my part of this Introduction highlights US-based applied ethnomusicology. I will discuss the history (and prehistory) of applied ethnomusicology, and its reception, in the United States since the late 1800s. But before sketching that history, I describe applied ethnomusicology as it is practiced today. What are applied ethnomusicologists doing now? What are our goals, and how are we positioned within the larger world both within and outside the academy?

First, we are involved in promoting traditional music, dance, and other cultural expressions in order to benefit artists, traditions, and communities. Whether undertaken by ethnomusicologists acting primarily on their own behalf, or whether supported by cultural organizations, these *cultural policy interventions* are among the oldest types of applied ethnomusicology and remain one of the most common, particularly as directed toward minority, immigrant, and otherwise underserved populations within developed nations, and among indigenous peoples throughout the world. Sometimes, but not always, these musics are considered threatened or even endangered. Lately, sustainability has become the generally accepted policy goal, whether the musics are endangered or not (see Schippers, Chapter 4, and Titon, Chapter 5, in this volume). Cultural trauma has often been an important motivating factor, particularly when cultural renewal appears important in the face of political and economic stress (see Haskell, Chapter 6, in this volume). Examples of these interventions include the settlement schools in the southern Appalachian mountains, begun more than a century ago to promote the arts and crafts of mountain folk culture; the immigrant folk music and dance programs for children and adults in large cities such as New York and Chicago, which involved settlement schools and included festivals as well as adult recreation groups and additions to the public school curriculum; national radio broadcasts undertaken by Alan Lomax shortly before World War II to bring the songs and stories of ordinary citizens into media circulation; regional and national festivals such as the Smithsonian Folklife Festival, begun in the 1960s; policymaking and granting agencies that promote community arts, such as historical societies, arts councils, and the National Endowments; and NGOs devoted to expanding the creative economy through musical heritage and cultural tourism, sometimes with a view to recovering from ecological disasters such as hurricanes, urban blight, and mountaintop removal. In the twenty-first century, UNESCO has become the major international force in cultural policy, with its treaties encouraging the preservation of what it calls intangible cultural heritage. The United States has not signed these treaties, but outside the United States many ethnomusicologists are involved with UNESCO activities and indeed, some North American ethnomusicologists participated in the planning and ongoing review stages. Ethnomusicologists have worked as consultants, arts administrators, ethnographic fieldworkers, festival presenters, radio and television producers, podcasters and internet site developers, educators, facilitators, mediators, writers, expert witnesses, and in various other capacities formulating and administering cultural policies whose purpose is sociocultural, economic, and musical benefit. Ethnomusicologists also have been among those theorizing cultural policy interventions, and have contributed to a growing critical literature evaluating these practices. Many of the chapters in this volume comprise a part of this ongoing scholarship concerning applied ethnomusicology.

Another area of practice is *advocacy*, either on behalf of particular music-makers or a music community as a whole. Rather than adopting the role of the neutral, objective, scientific observer gathering information, the applied ethnomusicologist assumes the role of a partisan, working in partnership toward goals that are mutually understood and agreed upon. Indeed, the most successful advocacy usually arises after ethnomusicologists have visited and listened to the musicians articulate their concerns and what they would like to achieve. Seldom has partnership worked when the ethnomusicologist plays the role of expert and imposes solutions to problems perceived from a distance, or fails to understand the musical community's perspective. Advocacy includes grant-writing on behalf of individuals and communities; writing promotional and press materials; acting as an agent to arrange performances; facilitating community self-documentation initiatives; repatriation of recordings and musical artifacts from museums and archives; political lobbying for arts spaces; facilitating community arts education projects; researching the history of musical traditions for the community; acting as an intermediary between cultural insiders and outsiders; long-term planning for the sustainability of community music cultures; and in general working in partnership and on behalf of musicians and their communities. Advocacy usually arises from relationships developed over time, when an ethnomusicologist is attracted to particular musicians or music cultures, visits them for research purposes and returns, and determines to make a commitment that goes beyond mere study. Academic ethnomusicologists undertaking long-term fieldwork in a community are well-positioned for this, but while an increasing number do become advocates, some prefer to remain neutral observers.

A third area of practice involves *education*. Often educators themselves, applied ethnomusicologists work with other educators designing curricula, and to bring musicians into the schools to demonstrate, teach, and perform; they also facilitate visits to performance spaces where youngsters may observe and participate in music-making activities. Music education once prepared youth to participate mainly in the culture of classical music, or as US academics call it these days, Western art music. As cultural pluralism and multicultural initiatives in North American schools gained traction in the last third of the twentieth century, musical pluralism increased, introducing popular music, jazz, and the music and dance of ethnic communities to the school curricula. Ethnomusicologists have been active in making musical activities more inclusive, fostering interest in local musical artists and traditions, particularly from newly arrived cultural and ethnic groups. In this way, music is viewed as a way to increase intercultural understanding.

Other areas of contemporary practice include *peace and conflict resolution; medicine; law and the music industry; libraries, museums, and sound archives; journalism;* and *environmental sound activism and ecojustice.* Peace-related applications are more frequent outside North America, but work of this sort has been done in Canada in disputes between First Nations communities and the Canadian government, while music has been an important part of labor and civil rights movements in the United States since the nineteenth century. Among the projects of medical ethnomusicology are HIV-AIDS work in Africa, therapeutic work with post-traumatic stress survivors, and music within the autism community. Legal applications have involved ethnomusicologists testifying as expert witnesses, particularly in music copyright infringement cases, and work on copyright and intellectual property issues as the question "who owns culture" becomes increasingly important when money is to be made and cases of exploitation have been documented. Ethnomusicologists have served as advisors to the World Intellectual Property Organization (WIPO), a UNESCO-sponsored group attempting to arrive at laws for protecting intellectual property rights in the international arena. Ethnomusicologists are contributing to ecological studies of the soundscape, and of the effects of environmental noise on physiological and psychological health. We are involved in political action opposing sound pollution, such as noise from ocean vessels and military activities that affects whales, dolphins, and other sea mammals. Applied ethnomusicologists are contributing to the new discipline of ecomusicology, which involves music and sound in a time of environmental crisis. Journalists educated in ethnomusicology bring to world music a broadly informed historical and geographical perspective. Some are writing for newspapers, magazines, and online publications; many are active in promoting music, and some are performing musicians ourselves. Ethnomusicologists working in the music industry serve as consultants, ethnographers, technical assistants, and producers. Many libraries, museums, universities, and other institutions maintain sound archives where archivists with ethnomusicological training offer expertise in acquisition, cataloging, grant-writing, preservation, and outreach.

Since the 1990s, when applied ethnomusicology became a recognizable force within ethnomusicology, other names have been advanced to describe some of the work that applied ethnomusicologists do; but they ought not to be confused with applied ethnomusicology, which is the covering term.[1] *Public-sector ethnomusicology* describes applied ethnomusicology that is practiced by people employed by public-sector, taxpayer-funded (i.e., government) institutions such as (in the United States) the Library of Congress, the Smithsonian Institution, the National Endowment for the Arts, and state arts councils; and whose efforts are directed to the public at large while often targeted at particular communities within it. By definition, "public-sector ethnomusicology" is unable to include applied ethnomusicology as practiced by those who work in the private sector, in NGOs such as museums, historical societies, foundations, and various non-profit organizations, even when part of their funding comes from government grants; nor does it describe the work of applied ethnomusicologists in corporations and client organizations. *Public ethnomusicology* is a better name for this activity, insofar as it focuses on applications in the public arena. But both terms, public sector and public, neglect the private sphere and perpetuate an unhelpful distinction between academia and the world outside of colleges and universities. As I have pointed out, applied ethnomusicology is practiced by those employed inside the academic world as well as outside of it. Ethnomusicology appears to be in danger of replicating the same terminological virus that has infected American folklore studies since the 1980s, one which American Folklore Society President Barbara Kirshenblatt-Gimblett labeled a "mistaken dichotomy" (Kirshenblatt-Gimblett, 1988).

APPLIED ETHNOMUSICOLOGY: BEING, KNOWING, AND DOING

Some ethnomusicologists are attracted to applied work, and others not so much. Most ethnomusicologists, I've observed, do share certain characteristics, however. Sound and music are immensely important to the way we orient ourselves. As humans, we are beings "in the world" through all of our senses, but we are particularly aware of vibrations that come to us as sound. Epistemologically, we feel that knowing sound—and knowing by means of sound—is essential to being human in the world and is one of the most important avenues through which to understand the human condition. Certainly it is our special avenue. Where we diverge, somewhat, is in what we *do* as a result of this ontological and epistemological orientation. Some of us are most interested in pursuing and increasing knowledge about sound and music in the world, the music of the world's peoples. This is the usual end of scholarship. Scholars feel a special responsibility to present, discuss, debate, and circulate this knowledge among colleagues and students in the institutional world of universities and professional associations of ethnomusicologists. Others, those of us who practice applied ethnomusicology, also feel a responsibility to help put this knowledge to practical use in the public arena; and so either in addition to our research, scholarship, and teaching within the university world, or instead of it, we also involve ourselves in interventions into musical communities, for public benefit.

Some 45 years ago Mantle Hood wrote a textbook about the nature of ethnomusicology, but instead of titling it *Ethnomusicology* he named it *The Ethnomusicologist* (Hood, 1971). In the Introduction he described an ideal ethnomusicologist's background, education, skills and aptitudes, and personality. It was an unusual emphasis for a graduate textbook in ethnomusicology, but then this was an unusual book, often written in the first person, and to some extent reflecting, I think, the California social and intellectual atmosphere of the 1960s that had also produced public figures like Stewart Brand and Jerry Brown. Although the influence of personality on an ethnomusicologist's accomplishments is not often written about, it is sometimes discussed among ethnomusicologists, especially when we reflect on ethnographic fieldwork, that rite of passage in which ethnomusicologists (like their counterparts in cultural anthropology) traditionally travel to a different, and sometimes strange, culture and while there, try to learn something of the musical universe among that group of people. It is difficult, sometimes alienating, even psychologically traumatic, work (Wengle, 1988); and ethnomusicologists tend to think that certain personality types are better able to accomplish it than others. Applied ethnomusicologists like to interact with our field subjects, not just observe them. We feel a desire to give something back in exchange for what we are learning, and this impulse leads us not only to research but to work directly for the benefit of those we visit. And so although most ethnomusicologists are in the world ontologically and epistemologically in similar ways, we differ somewhat over what we should be doing with those ways of being and knowing. It should go without saying that applied ethnomusicologists engage in research and contribute to the growth of knowledge. Our Ph.D.s are research degrees, after all, and many of us have made substantial scholarly contributions to the flow of knowledge inside academia. But we also feel a social responsibility to put that knowledge to use in the public arena.

APPLIED ETHNOMUSICOLOGY IN THE UNITED STATES: A BRIEF HISTORY

As the co-editors worked on this volume and saw it through an eight-year period of invitations, proposals, abstracts, essays, reviews, revisions, and yet more reviews and more revisions, it became increasingly and unsettlingly clear that many US contributors thought of their work within a local and national context but knew relatively little about the history, ideas, and accomplishments of applied ethnomusicologists living outside the United States. Non-US contributors were similarly knowledgeable about applied work in their spheres of activity outside North America, but generally unaware of the history, projects, scholarship, and cultural policies generated by applied ethnomusicology in North America. Ideas that had been theorized, practiced, and thoroughly critiqued in some localities were being introduced in others as if they were newly discovered. More than once, contributors seemed to be reinventing wheels. Many whose work would benefit from an exchange of ideas with others involved in similar projects elsewhere were not taking advantage of that possibility. Although we believe that the reasons for this insularity have more to do with institutional histories and geography than with any serious divergence over assumptions, approach, and goals, one of the happy consequences of this volume, we hope, will be to increase the dialogue among practitioners of applied ethnomusicology no matter where they work, so that each becomes aware of the ways in which similar problems have been faced, and solutions attempted, elsewhere, while problems and issues that had not even occurred to some will become apparent after reading about the work of others. Another consequence of this insularity, however, was that it became impossible to sketch a unified history and description of applied ethnomusicology apart from those considerations. For that reason, in this section I construct a history of applied ethnomusicology in the United States, related to the growth of ethnomusicology and its professional organization, SEM, founded in 1955. (Svanibor Pettan writes in Section 2 of this Introduction about the communities of applied ethnomusicologists associated with the International Council on Traditional Music [ICTM], and its earlier incarnation, the International Folk Music Council [IFMC, founded in 1947].) In doing so, I draw on a graduate seminar in the history of ethnomusicological thought which I led at Brown University from 1988 until 2013. Reflexivity, postcolonial ethnomusicology, efforts to sustain musical genres and cultures, collaborative ethnography and advocacy, tourism and the creative economy, archival stewardship and repatriation of field recordings, applications to medicine and to peace and conflict resolution, proper roles for government in the arts, the place of · world music in education—these are not new themes in our field, but the timing of their entrances, their reception, and their use in applied work has not been uniform among the North American, European, Asian, African, Australian, and Latin American communities of applied ethnomusicologists.

Strictly speaking, the history of ethnomusicology began in 1950, when Jaap Kunst invented the term and it entered scholarly discourse (Kunst, 1950). I prefer to think of the pre-1950 period as ethnomusicology's prehistory, paying particular attention to the two disciplines, comparative musicology and cultural anthropology, that combined in the 1950s as ethnomusicology.[2] I find prototypes of US applied ethnomusicology among nineteenth-century ethnologists and folklorists whose field research in music exhibited both social responsibility and collaborative involvement with musical communities for their benefit. Music was an integral part of early folklore and anthropology, not an afterthought. From the very beginning, scholars writing for the *American Anthropologist* and the *Journal of American Folklore* showed much interest in people making music. The second issue of the former contained an essay by Washington Matthews (1843–1905) on a Navajo sung prayer (Matthews, 1888), for example, while the inaugural issue of the latter featured an article on Kwakiutl music and dance by Franz Boas (1858–1942), the most influential North American anthropologist of his generation (Boas, 1888). Boas's article described some of the group's music, stories, and their ideas and behavior in relation to them; it contained musical transcriptions, and mentioned his 1886 music collecting trip with the German comparative musicologist and music psychologist Carl Stumpf among the Bella Coola. Nothing in Boas's article might be considered applied ethnomusicology per se, but Boas undertook a public anthropology project of enormous import in the early twentieth century when he opposed so-called scientific racism and helped establish the idea that differences in human behavior result from learned cultural, rather than fixed biological, traits.

Matthews's work was aided by a deeply collaborative relationship in which he underwent Native rituals and may have married a Hidatsa woman. Collaborative relationships in which the parties work toward mutually agreed-upon goals became a hallmark of applied ethnomusicology, but their roots may be found in people like Matthews, as well as Alice Cunningham Fletcher (1838–1923), whose collaborative work moved more clearly in the direction of social and economic benefits that would be recognized today as applied ethnomusicology. Fletcher, who became President of both the American Anthropological Association and the American Folklore Society, as well as Vice President of the American Association for the Advancement of Science, lived with the Sioux in 1881, and collaborated with an Omaha, Frances La Flesche, whom she took into her household from 1890 on. Falling ill with a severe case of rheumatoid arthritis in 1883, she was nursed back to health by her Native American friends, who sang to her while she lay recovering. Then, she wrote, "the sweetness, the beauty and meaning of these songs were revealed to me" (Fletcher, 1994: 8). Like the others, Fletcher undertook ethnographic studies of Native music; but she also worked tirelessly on behalf of Native American education, integration, and advancement into mainstream culture.

. "Giving back" is the usual term North American ethnomusicologists employ to identify this reciprocity, which has taken various forms over the decades. However, Fletcher's efforts at aiding Native Americans are characterized today as attempts to Americanize them, a "grievous error in the administration of Native American lands and peoples" according to a Smithsonian Institution author (Smithsonian: Fletcher). Ethnomusicologists consider it unfortunate that the Omaha songs she collected were published with Western harmonization, added to them by the musician John Comfort Fillmore, who convinced Fletcher that these harmonies were implicit in the Omaha melodies (Fletcher, 1994). Nonetheless, Fletcher may be understood in her time as a progressive. The principal alternative to Americanization (or Christianization), after all, had for nearly three centuries been genocide. And prominent American composers such as Edward MacDowell were quoting, transforming, and harmonizing Native American melodies in their musical compositions.

Daniel Sheehy and Anthony Seeger trace the history of twentieth-century pioneers in applied ethnomusicology, such as Robert Winslow Gordon, Alan Lomax, and Charles Seeger (Sheehy, 1992; Seeger, 2006). In terming them applied ethnomusicologists, Seeger, Sheehy, and others combine ethnomusicology's historical and pre-historical periods. Certainly, these ancestors would have been called applied ethnomusicologists if ethnomusicology proper had come into being prior to 1950. To some extent their work was related to that of early anthropologists such as A. L. Kroeber and others on endangered Native American languages. The Lomaxes' folk music collections were meant for the general public, to supply a kind of people's alternative to the art music that was being taught in the public schools. Alan Lomax insisted that the treasure trove of folk music should be made accessible through media production, which in the 1940s and 1950s meant radio programs—he produced dozens of them for national broadcast. He issued an appeal for "cultural equity" that articulated many of the principles under which he had been operating for decades (Lomax, 1972). Lomax's "Appeal" may be the single most often-cited document in the literature of US applied ethnomusicology. Charles Seeger, Anthony Seeger's grandfather, had issued a call in 1939 for an applied musicology that would follow from government involvement in the arts, a vision in some ways similar to the situation in China today (Seeger, 2006: 227–228; also see Zhang, Chapter 6 of Volume 3). Seeger and his wife Ruth Crawford Seeger, John and Alan Lomax, Herbert Halpert, Zora Neale Hurston, and others were involved in efforts to encourage folk music (as the authentic popular music of a democratic society) during the Roosevelt administration. These activities, of course, diminished greatly as the United States concentrated during the 1940s on mobilization for World War II. But Sheehy concludes that "there is a tradition of applied thought and purpose that should be included in the history of ethnomusicology," as well as "an evolving sense of strategy and techniques for action that has flowed through this thought and that demands our attention as ethnomusicologists" (Sheehy, 1992: 329). Anthony Seeger entitled his 2006 essay "Lost Lineages" in the history of ethnomusicology and, like Sheehy, called for a more inclusive history of the field.

The usual historical accounts of ethnomusicology in the United States are not so inclusive: applied ethnomusicology is treated either as a peripheral activity or, more often, ignored entirely. These mainstream accounts trace ethnomusicology's roots to comparative musicology, a scientific project of the European Enlightenment. They do not pay much attention to its roots in folklore and cultural anthropology. In 1885 Guido Adler defined comparative musicology as "the comparison of the musical works . . . of the various peoples of the earth for ethnographical purposes, and the classification of them according to their various forms" (Haydon, 1941: 117). Comparative musicology began in the latter part of the nineteenth century with the systematization of music knowledge, which proceeded with the measurable, classificatory, and comparative procedures borrowed from philology, embryology, and other sciences, generating various hypotheses concerning origins, growth, diffusion, and function. Aided by the recording phonograph and efforts of various music collectors, it included the comparative work on the musical scales of various nations accomplished by the Englishman Alexander Ellis, and the research of the German Carl Stumpf and others in music psychology (or psychophysical science, as it was then called). Comparative musicology was further developed as a research discipline in early twentieth-century Berlin by Stumpf's younger colleague Erich von Hornbostel, Curt Sachs, and others, with related scholarship accomplished by Béla Bartok in Hungary, Constantin Brailliou in Rumania, and others in the fields of comparative musical folklore and the sociology of music.

Comparative musicology arrived in the United States in 1925 in the person of George Herzog, who had been von Hornbostel's assistant in Berlin. He went on to study anthropology with Franz Boas at Columbia University, specializing in "primitive music," as it was then called. Herzog received his doctorate in 1931 under Boas's supervision and pursued an academic career at Yale, Columbia, and Indiana University that lasted until the mid-1950s. He was recognized during this period as the leading authority on "primitive music." Among his students were two of the founders of SEM, David McAllester and Willard Rhodes. Bruno Nettl, who has written knowledgeably about Herzog's contributions to comparative musicology, was another of his students (Nettl and Bohlman, 1991: 270–272; Nettl, 2002: 90–92; Nettl, 2010: 168). Herzog's writings exhibited an empirical, scientific method that required large amounts of reliable data, a high standard to which he held himself and others. "All evidence," he wrote, "points to the wisdom of dispensing with sweeping theoretical schemes and of inquiring in each case into the specific historical processes that have molded the culture and musical style of a nation or tribe . . . So little is actually known . . . that the main attention of this field [of comparative musicology] is devoted to increasing that little, and collecting more material before it all disappears under the impact of Western civilization" (Herzog, 1936: 3). He had learned the importance of fieldwork and data-gathering from his teacher Boas, and he insisted on that, as well as musical transcription and analysis, from his students. His methods added Boas-styled ethnographic research to the comparative analysis that characterized the work of Horbostel and the Berlin school.

A useful summary of comparative musicology, with due attention to Herzog's prominence in the United States, appeared in Glen Haydon's graduate-level textbook, *Introduction to Musicology* (Haydon, 1941). As outlined there, its purpose was to increase knowledge of the music of the world's peoples. Academic research was the means to that end. The work of numerous comparative musicologists, chiefly European, was described, and their most important publications referenced. But comparative musicology soon underwent a facelift. Historical accounts date this to Jaap Kunst's book *Ethno-Musicology* (Kunst, 1950, and two subsequent editions), which defined *ethnomusicology* as the study of "all tribal and folk music and every kind of non-Western art music. Besides, it studies as well the sociological aspects of music . . . " (ibid., 1950: 1). Although he is usually credited with inventing the term *ethnomusicology*, Kunst's argument for the name change rested chiefly on redundancy of the word "comparative." All good science, he argued, is comparative in nature; disciplines like linguistics and embryology had, after all, dropped the adjective for the time being. His argument was persuasive, and some comparative musicologists began to adopt the new name, while others who wished to place more emphasis on the cultural study of music and less on musical analysis welcomed the name change and saw opportunity in it. However, comparative musicology remained the ancestral predecessor for Kunst and in later US historical accounts of the discipline, chiefly by Bruno Nettl (1956, 1964, 1983, 2002, 2005, 2010) as well as others. For nearly 60 years these historical accounts have informed generations of ethnomusicology professors and graduate students, in the United States and elsewhere. Despite increased theoretical sophistication and a growing recognition of historical relativism (e.g., Nettl and Bohlman, eds., 1991; Nettl, 2010; Rice, 2014), different subject emphases by other authors (e.g., Hood, 1971; Merriam, 1964), and an enlarged cast of characters (McLean, 2006), these mainstream histories continue to construct ethnomusicology as a research discipline almost exclusively centered in the academic world. Applied ethnomusicology seldom appears; when it does, it usually is treated with some reservations. As long as comparative musicology remained ethnomusicology's central occupation, applied work would be marginal at best.

The founding of the Society for Ethnomusicology (SEM) in 1955 not only provided an opportunity for a new emphasis on the cultural study of music, but might also have moved applied ethnomusicology to a more central position. Why it did not do so, at a time when applied anthropology was becoming important within US cultural anthropology, is an interesting question. In large part, as this brief history will show, the answer has to do with the founding generation's desire to establish and expand ethnomusicology as an academic discipline, on a firm institutional footing, throughout the university world. In so doing, they missed an opportunity to integrate applied work into the agenda of the new Society. It was left for the next generation to do so.

The early period of SEM was, predictably, taken up with debate over the direction of the discipline. In its first 15 years or so, the SEM journal, *Ethnomusicology*, was filled with essays by many leading practitioners who attempted to define the discipline and influence its course. Research in ethnomusicology's first two decades (ca. 1950–1975) has been characterized as falling broadly into two approaches, one musicological and the other anthropological (Kerman, 1986: 155–181). This is an oversimplification, but it is useful in highlighting the legacies of Hornbostel and Herzog, which in SEM could be seen in the work of Herzog's former colleague Kolinski, William Malm, George List, Mantle Hood, and Nettl, among others. Their focus was on collecting, recording, transcribing, describing, classifying, analyzing, and comparing music in order to increase the music knowledge-base and to test theories concerning musical distribution, diffusion, and acculturation. Like Herzog, most were interested also in the ethnographic study of cultural contexts for music ("music in culture") and in comparing and contrasting music's functions within cultures. Unless one thinks of the polymath Seeger as a comparativist, these comparative musicologists were not represented among the four SEM founders; but their work was prominent in monographs and in *Ethnomusicology*, where they advanced their scholarship and their view of what ethnomusicology ought to be. They also played a major role in establishing ethnomusicology as an academic discipline at the graduate level in US universities during the first 20 years of SEM.

On the other side of the debate over the future of ethnomusicology were the anthropologists, dance ethnologists, folklorists, and various other scholars who shared an interest in music and had been attracted to the new field. Most prominent among these were the anthropologists Alan Merriam and David McAllester, both among the four founders of SEM. Herzog was noticeably absent from SEM's origins, and it is worth asking why. Nettl, who writes movingly and generously about Herzog, observed that Herzog already was behaving erratically in 1952 (he would be hospitalized from the mid-1950s onward, with occasional time off, until his death in 1983, for what we would now call a bipolar disorder) and attributes his absence to this (Nettl, 2002: 90–92; Nettl, 2010: 168; Nettl and Bohlman, 1991: 271–272). No doubt this is correct; but it appears that the founders also wished to escape Herzog's dominance over the field. McAllester reported that as far as he knew, he was the only student ever to complete the doctorate under Herzog's supervision. "The campus was littered with the bodies of failed Herzog students," McAllester said. Herzog's habit was to demonstrate to them time after time that they could not meet his standards. "He never failed them in so many words," McAllester continued, "but they had a very hard time ever getting an appointment with him, and when they finally did, it was all at such a high level that they felt sort of defeated. If they brought in a transcription, it was so bad that he went over it note by note to show them and said, now see if you can't, now that you've had this practice, do better next time. Then a month or so later, when they caught up with him again, then the same thing would happen again." Rhodes was one of the dropouts, but he was already a full professor at Columbia and did not need the degree; yet it remained a sore point with him and his friend McAllester both. Even before Herzog moved from Columbia to Indiana University in 1948, he had been showing signs of the mental instability that would institutionalize him (Memorial Resolution, 1983). Herzog was Nettl's dissertation supervisor at Indiana, but before Nettl could complete his doctorate, Herzog's erratic behavior forced him to move to a different supervisor. "Bruno studied with him [Herzog] when he went out to Indiana, and he [Nettl] had a professor for a father, and so he had a strong position," McAllester said. (Paul Nettl, Bruno's father, was a professor of musicology at Indiana University.) "And he [Nettl] demanded another teacher, and he finished his Ph.D. with Carl Voegelin, the linguist. He left Herzog, but most of us couldn't do that. We were with Herzog and it was do or die, and many died" (McAllester, 1989).

No wonder then, given McAllester's and Rhodes's opinion of him, that Herzog was not invited into the inner circle of SEM founders. At that time they may have been less aware of Herzog's illness and decline than Nettl and the others who worked with Herzog at Indiana. But that must be only part of the answer. The other part is that McAllester, Merriam, Rhodes, and Seeger wanted to take a new direction, to move away from comparative musicology and Boasian ethnography, and toward an ethnomusicology that would make room not only for a greater variety of authoritative voices but also for more emphasis on the cultural study of music. Reaching out to scholars throughout the world, in 1953 the four founders initiated an ethnomusicology *Newsletter*, and two years later they founded the Society for Ethnomusicology (SEM), designed to foster communication and research in the field. SEM immediately began publishing a journal, *Ethnomusicology*, which since its inception has served as the flagship research periodical for the discipline. It is worth pausing for a moment to examine what the founders themselves thought they were up to. Nettl, reminiscing about this early period, the name change from "comparative musicology" to "ethnomusicology," and the founding of SEM, recalls that he (and others, he thinks) regarded these events more as a "revival" of a great scholarly tradition (comparative musicology, which had been all but eliminated in Europe during the Nazi era) than as a revolution (Nettl, 2010: 160–162). Inclined toward his teacher Herzog's understanding of that tradition, Nettl's subject position is understandable. Still a graduate student at the time and not directly involved as a founder, he had nevertheless set his course and was already a major stakeholder in the new field. His memoirs (Nettl, 2002, 2010, 2013) of this transitional period are both charming and invaluable, filled with information unavailable elsewhere and required reading for anyone interested in the history of ethnomusicology. In these memoirs, he tries to deconstruct the "myth" of SEM's "grand entrance," as he puts it, arguing that its historical significance and the importance of the four founders has been overrated (Nettl, 2010: 160–165). In retrospect, it is apparent that comparative musicology continued to exert a strong influence upon ethnomusicology during its first few decades (ca. 1950–1980). But the new Society, the new name, and its founders' orientation toward anthropology is a historical fact that signaled a significant and enduring new direction for the field.

Let me try to reconstruct something of that significance as I believe it to have appeared to the founders at the time. (In so doing, I rely in part on my conversations with Rhodes, Merriam, Seeger, and especially McAllester about that period.) McAllester recalled that after Herzog was finally confined to a mental hospital, he could no longer exercise his former control over degrees, grants, and publications in the field. "He became so ill that he had to be in an institution, and then the lid was off and the Society [SEM] could be established" (McAllester, 1989). For the four founders, SEM represented a move away from comparative musicology, not simply as an escape from Herzog's iron grip, but in establishing a new interdisciplinary field: ethnomusicology. The founders resisted efforts from other Societies who tried to dissuade them from starting a new Society. The American Musicological Society sent representatives to their early meetings and "announced that we should not be a splinter group, but that we should be part of the American Musicological Society . . . . And we said, if we joined them, the AMS, there were a whole bunch of people that would not be any longer members. We had folklorists, anthropologists, ethnologists, acousticians, physicists. . . and they would have dropped out if we had become a part of the American Musicological Society." These same scholars likewise would have left SEM had they allied themselves with the IFMC, McAllester reported. "Maud Karpeles came and pleaded with us to become a wing of the International Folk Music Council. . . . Alan Merriam particularly, well, Charlie Seeger too, they were both very insistent that it not get into the hands of. . . the International Folk Music [Council]. So when we started the society, they [the IFMC] soon got wind of it, and they were very upset because they had their American branch and they were afraid we would simply split their society and draw membership away from them. . . . There were scholars among them, great scholars among them, but they were not anthropologically oriented. And it just happened by the way we operated, that the Society for Ethnomusicology began with an anthropological orientation" (McAllester, 1989). Nettl agreed: "The beginning of the SEM was deeply rooted in the anthropological background of its most influential leaders" (Nettl, 2010: 143).

McAllester recalled the excitement that accompanied the founding of SEM, along with the possibilities of new directions for the Society. For Merriam even more than for McAllester, that direction was to be cultural anthropology. Eventually he termed this direction "the anthropology of music" rather than "comparative musicology," and he lobbied hard for the study of music, not in culture, but as culture, a phrase ("music as culture") that Merriam referenced to his earlier "unpublished thoughts" (Merriam, 1977: 204). According to Merriam, music was not something that existed within a cultural context; it was culture in the anthropological sense itself, with its own domain of ideas, behavior, and sonic dimension. Obtaining a full professorship in anthropology at Indiana University in 1962, Merriam was not only a founder but a forceful presence in SEM from the very beginning until his untimely death in an airplane crash in 1980. His area interests were in indigenous musics primarily, Native American and African. A former jazz musician, he had little use for the study of folk music, and even less for bi-musicality, about which more shortly. When I taught a summer session in Indiana's Folklore Institute in 1977, he invited me to his home a number of times. He had just remarried, and was in an expansive mood. Relevant for this historical sketch is the attitude he expressed toward the IFMC. He affirmed that the founders had refused Maud Karpeles's invitation to join the International Folk Music Council rather than form their own Society. Nettl attributed Merriam's reasons for objecting to the IFMC to "his perception of the IFMC as specifically interested in music alone, the notion that folk-music scholars were interested in only a small segment of the music of any society; and the idea that the IFMC included a substantial practical component, that is, was in large measure a society of folksingers and dancers" (Nettl, 2010: 143). Merriam's views had evolved since then, for in 1977 he told me the IFMC as a group was insufficiently objective and scientific about music as a human phenomenon. If they had been, they would have been concerned with all music, not mainly the oldest layers of music in what were then regarded as folk societies (Redfield, 1947). And if they had been, they would not have been so concerned with authenticity and so worried about salvaging this music for archival preservation; or worse yet, reviving it for a sophisticated urban audience. Merriam took some pleasure in noting that Indiana University's Folklore Institute did not share this attitude toward musical revivalism; indeed, Richard Dorson, the head of the Institute, had coined the term "fakelore" to describe it, and on the advice of George List, the senior ethnomusicologist in the Folklore Institute, Dorson would not permit amateur folk musicians in their doctoral program to undertake music research unless they had had sufficient formal training in Western music theory and history to be admitted to ethnomusicology courses. As Indiana was one of only a very few universities in the US granting doctoral degrees in folklore, the amount of academic research in US folk music during the Dorson-List-Merriam era was severely diminished as a consequence. For Merriam, ethnomusicology was revolutionary insofar as it elevated anthropology to a position of equality with musicology in birthing the new offspring, ethnomusicology. The *ethno-* prefix (derived from the Greek *ethnos* [= people with a common culture]) firmly established it as a new discipline that was properly part of "the scientific study of man," as anthropology had long been defined. Merriam assiduously pursued this goal, which he called "sciencing about music" (Merriam, 1964: 25 et passim).

With SEM established on the promise of interdisciplinarity and new directions, particularly from anthropology, one might have expected that the new organization would have been hospitable to applied ethnomusicology. Anthropologists had by then started putting their knowledge to use in solving social problems. John Van Willigen dates the rise of a socially committed applied or "action" anthropology to 1945, although he notes that anthropologists had for decades previously taken on community consultantship roles (van Willigen, 2002). But this exciting, albeit controversial, development in anthropology did not cross over into SEM with any success until decades later. The reasons, in retrospect, are not entirely surprising. To establish ethnomusicology within the most secure of institutional bases, that is, within universities, it was necessary to position it as a research science, aiming to increase knowledge of the music of the world's peoples. Musicological and anthropological ethnomusicologists might disagree over the discipline's emphasis, but they agreed that scholarship and the production of knowledge were its goals. Applications of that research in the public arena might be well and good, but the pursuit of knowledge for its own sake had always been valued most highly in university settings, where it could be protected from outside forces. In 1950 ethnomusicology itself was a fringe discipline in the United States, with only a few courses being offered (sometimes in anthropology departments, sometimes music) and only a few professors available to advise doctoral dissertations. For ethnomusicology to expand inside the university world, professors must succeed in establishing courses, programs (especially graduate programs), tenure tracks, and recognition of the discipline as a legitimate academic pursuit. The proven strategy to advance the discipline in the university world would be through research, emphasizing that study of the music of the world's peoples would add to the store of knowledge about human behavior and achievement. Research "for its own sake" was then, and remains, regarded in the academy as more elegant, of higher and "purer" disinterested purpose than research driven by applications. In the arts and humanities, where contemplation of the pure aesthetic object was required for philosophy, literary criticism, and art history, disinterested acts of scholarship were experienced as pleasurable in themselves. Eventually, one could hope, every music department, every music school or conservatory, and every anthropology department would have at least one ethnomusicologist doing research and offering music courses with a worldwide scope; and some would have more than one and would establish graduate programs training future generations of ethnomusicologists as the discipline would expand. Professionalization of ethnomusicology as a research discipline, and with that a need to distance it from well-meaning amateurs who also engaged in music research, was a second reason. Applied work might be done by those who lacked the proper scientific attitude and scholarly training to conduct credible research: missionaries, for example, who had historically put music to use in attempting to convert indigenous peoples, or amateur collectors who became partisans on behalf of those whose music they recorded. I believe that a third reason was the distrust, among this generation of scholars who came of age during or soon after World War II, of social engineering, whether for political, cultural, or musical ends. Applied research put to practical use in musical or cultural interventions, despite intended benefits, was something Americans might well oppose, particularly given the uses to which music had been put during the Nazi regime, and was still being put in the Soviet sphere. Many in the previous generation of US music scholars had been born in Europe and had fled to North America to escape Nazi persecution and establish musical scholarship inside a university world where they would be free from political interference. I do not mean to suggest that a cabal of ethnomusicology professors drew up such a plan, but rather that they were inclined by personality and training to move in that direction. Partly as a result, in its first two decades, ethnomusicology became more firmly established as a scholarly discipline; but applied ethnomusicology languished inside the US academic world.

Merriam was perhaps the first US ethnomusicologist to recognize an applied ethnomusicology by that name, although he did not favor it. The phase "applied ethnomusicology" did not appear in the SEM *Newsletter* or journal until Merriam's 1963 review of Henry Weman's *African Music and the Church in Africa*. Merriam wrote that this book is "perhaps most accurately described as a study in applied ethnomusicology, for his principal concern is how African music can be used . . . " in missionary work (Merriam, 1963b: 135). Merriam expanded on his comments a year later in *The Anthropology of Music*, and it is worth looking at them in detail:

> . . . the ultimate aim of the study of man. . . involves the question of whether one is searching for knowledge for its own sake, or is attempting to provide solutions for practical applied problems. Ethnomusicology has seldom been used in the same manner as applied or action anthropology, and ethnomusicologists have only rarely felt called upon to help solve problems in manipulating the destinies of people, but some such studies have been made [here he references Weman's book] and it is quite conceivable that this may in the future be of increased concern. The difficulty of an applied study is that it focuses the attention of the investigator upon a single problem which may cause or force him to ignore others of equal interest, and it is also difficult to avoid outside control over the research project. Although this problem is not yet of primary concern, it will surely shape the kinds of studies carried out if it does draw the increased attention of ethnomusicologists.
>
> (Merriam, 1964: 42–43)

Here, as elsewhere, Merriam privileges "knowledge for its own sake." In criticizing applied work for its narrow focus, Merriam is appealing to the idea that ethnomusicology should be the study of music as a whole; but "outside control" may be viewed as a threat to academic freedom, while the phrase "manipulating the destinies of people" expresses that distrust of and distaste for the political and cultural interventions of applied anthropology and, by extension, of applied ethnomusicology.

Several books and articles critique recent interventions, especially those resulting from UNESCO initiatives to preserve intangible cultural heritage (e.g., Weintraub and Yung, 2009). But this tradition of critique may be traced to Merriam's "white knight" label for those ethnomusicologists who feel called to "function as knights in shining armor riding to the defense of non-Western music" (Merriam, 1963a: 207). Skepticism toward applied ethnomusicology is also evident in Bruno Nettl's histories and descriptions of the field. Nettl, more than anyone else among the founding generation of SEM, shouldered the responsibility to construct a history of ethnomusicology, something which he has come to call his "elephant" (Nettl, 2010). The sole active survivor of his generation of ethnomusicologists, Nettl early on assumed the mantle of spokesperson for the discipline, and today he is recognized in the United States and elsewhere as its elder statesman. As intellectual history is his central concern, he devotes relatively little attention to applied ethnomusicology. His most influential book, *The Study of Ethnomusicology*, treats applied ethnomusicology within the context of applied anthropology: "In the course of the 1950s there developed a concept and a subdiscipline, 'applied anthropology,' whose task it was to use anthropological insight to help solve social problems, particularly those occasioned by rapid culture change in the wake of modernization and Westernization." Applied anthropologists also were consulted in attempts to solve economic problems such as third-world poverty. They advised government organizations such as the United States Agency for International Development (USAID), on interventions involving democratization, agricultural modernization, and economic development. Rapid social change and cultural upheaval was the result of the intervention, not the original problem to be solved. No wonder then, as Nettl continues, that although "Anthropologists wanted to help [they] frequently ended up offending the local population and doing what was perceived as harmful. As a result, in the late 1960s and early 1970s they were widely attacked for doing work of no relevance to social problems, of mixing in local politics, of spying. Ethnomusicologists shared in this criticism. . . ." Here, applied ethnomusicologists' efforts to conserve traditional music and culture are conflated with applied anthropologists' efforts meant to aid in the modernization of traditional culture. The implication is that, like applied anthropologists, applied ethnomusicologists were criticized as offensive, harmful, and irrelevant; and that they barged into local politics and were accused of being spies. But if this critique of anthro-colonialism is accurate about interventions meant to bring about modernization and development, it does not follow that it applies to interventions by applied ethnomusicologists meant to conserve traditional music. Nettl then balances the critique with a somewhat more positive view:

> the picture [of applied anthropology and ethnomusicology] is not entirely negative. Some societies are happy to have outsiders come, appreciate their efforts, their respect for the traditions, and their help in restoring vigor to rapidly disappearing musics. Persian and Indian music masters are proud to have Western scholars as students, for it raises their prestige locally and legitimizes their traditional art in the face of modernizing doubters. Even so, there is often the feeling that members of the society itself, given the right training, equipment, and time, could do it better.
>
> (Nettl, 1983: 297; repeated in the 2nd edition, 2005: 206)

Nettl points out that some ethnomusicologists "espouse fieldwork in which informants become collaborators, the members of a community being studied in effect becoming co-collaborators" (ibid.). Yet Nettl's deep unease with applied work as social engineering is embedded in the tone and weight of his discussion and in the examples he offers; and it is apparent where he thinks the majority of ethnomusicologists stand. For the first edition of this book (1983) this was a correct assessment, but by the second edition (2005) it was not. Indeed, in a recent interview he acknowledged applied ethnomusicology's considerable appeal to a new generation (Fouce, 2014: 1).[3]

A few ethnomusicologists in SEM's founding generation were involved in applied projects during the 1960s and 1970s, yet they did not call it applied ethnomusicology. No doubt they thought of these as proper activities for an ethnomusicologist, but to my knowledge they did not think of them as part of a subfield where research was directed toward the public interest. Some, most prominently SEM founder David McAllester, took an advocacy role in educating music teachers and broadening the kindergarten-through-high school curricula to include examples of the musics of the world's peoples. McAllester worked through the Music Educators' National Conference to accomplish this goal, and he advised several graduate students in the Wesleyan University world music program who went in this direction, among them Patricia Shehan Campbell (see her Chapter 3, coauthored with Lee Higgins, in Volume 3). Another prominent ethno-musicologist in the founding generation, Mantle Hood, undertook applied ethnomusi-cology projects in Indonesia. He related the story of his successful intervention to revive Javanese gamelan gong-making (for the large gong *ageng*), which had nearly gone extinct. However, he also reported that his intervention resulted in some unintended, negative consequences. He offered another example, when he was called on for suggestions to improve gamelan educational practice—what innovations would he recommend? But here he stepped back from applied ethnomusicology and refused to interfere, thinking that Western influence would not be good for the tradition (Hood, 1971: 358–371). His major work on ethnomusicology ends with a section on cultural exchange through music and the arts as part of a program to further international understanding—putting ethnomusicological knowledge to practical use for a clear and intended social benefit.

Thus it could be fairly said that SEM's founding generation concentrated their US efforts in two areas: first, on research in order to increase knowledge about music and to circulate it among scholars; and second, to secure an institutional base for ethnomusi-cology within the academic world. In the latter, they were more successful in the music divisions of the universities and colleges (variously called music departments, schools of music, conservatories, and the like) than in anthropology departments. Growth within music divisions allied the discipline more closely with musicology than anthropology, and although the SEM founders envisioned a broadly interdisciplinary field with a new emphasis on the cultural study of music—and achieved this at SEM conferences and to some extent in the SEM journal, *Ethnomusicology*—the institutional growth of the discipline favored the musicologically oriented scholars.

Ironically, however, it was not by positioning ethnomusicology as a research science that institutional growth was achieved; rather, in the last half of the twentieth century ethnomusicology benefited from a combination of external circumstances that the founding generation did not foresee. The most important of these were, first, the meteoric rise in the popularity of world music among the general public, and especially the young, which began in the 1960s. Second was the reversal, in US cultural mythology, from the idea that the nation was a melting pot that produced a single American type, to the acceptance of cultural diversity and pluralism, which in the field of education broke the Eurocentric hold on curricula and opened it to a variety of minority voices in the humanities: literature, fine arts, music, and history. Youth cultures became deeply involved in alternative musics, including folk music, blues, and bluegrass. World music began to enjoy widespread popularity, as George Harrison of the Beatles studied sitar in India, and Hindustani musicians Ali Akbar Khan and Ravi Shankar went on extended annual tours throughout the United States. Recording companies such as Nonesuch released world music recordings and targeted both indigenous as well as Asian art musics to an appreciative public. Young men and women turned to world music as one of many paths toward personal growth. Fueled by the rising popularity of world music, master musicians from Ghana, North and South India, the Arab world, China, Japan, and Indonesia soon were in residence as world music performance ensemble directors at American colleges and universities where ethnomusicologists were already teaching. Performance was attracting students into the field. Mantle Hood, director of the Ethnomusicology Institute at UCLA, spearheaded this movement, advocating on behalf of what he called bi-musicality. Just as serious study of a foreign language could turn a person bilingual, so serious study of a foreign music could make one bi-musical and impart a knowledge of that music that was otherwise unavailable. Some senior ethnomusicologists tempered their enthusiasm for world music performance ensembles, however, and for decades they were conspicuously absent at the University of Illinois and Indiana University. Nonetheless, the possibility that world music might be learned intrigued many, and some went on to enroll in graduate programs in ethnomusicology, resulting in more degrees, professors, and programs. By 1970 it was possible to study ethnomusicology and obtain the doctorate by studying with Hood at UCLA, Fredric Lieberman at Brown, George List and Merriam at Indiana, Nettl at Illinois, Robert Garfias at Washington, William Malm at Michigan, and McAllester at Wesleyan, among other universities. Moreover, those with doctoral training in ethnomusicology had begun teaching at other colleges and universities, and SEM's US membership had increased.

Diversification and expansion of the US college and university music curriculum created a demand for professors who could teach the new courses. Within music divisions, this meant the end of the near-complete domination of Western art music (or classical music, as the American public calls it). Now popular music, jazz, and the music of the world's peoples took their place among the course offerings. Gradually, ethnomusicologists began to realize that they could take a proactive role and convince university administrators that one way to accomplish their goal of affirmative action toward so-called American minority groups (something which ethnomusicologists by and large supported) was through greater diversity of music offerings, which would also mean more ethnomusicology hires. As programs and departments were established in African American studies, Native American studies, Asian American studies, Hispanic American studies, and the like, it became apparent that the music of American minorities, along with world music, had an important role to play in the expanded curricula. Of course, ethnomusicologists were far from the only ones to benefit from diversity, cultural pluralism, and affirmative action in the academic world; but while the popularity of world music has ebbed and flowed since the 1960s, the movement toward greater cultural diversity within US higher education has been persistent.

The folk music revival, rising popularity of world music, and the positive value now attached to ethnic roots and cultural pluralism brought about a renewed emphasis in applied ethnomusicology outside the academic world before it had much impact inside it. Because Alan Lomax embodied this public work in applied ethnomusicology—not only as a collector, writer, and promoter, but also as an advocate for cultural democracy and musical pluralism—it is instructive to ponder his encounter with none other than George Herzog, who also believed in the value of musical diversity and had devoted his life to the study of folk and "primitive" music. Herzog, as noted, embodied comparative musicology in the United States during the 1930s and 1940s. After Lomax had been "Assistant in Charge" of the Archive of American Folk Song at the Library of Congress for several years—field-collecting, acquiring from others, and curating recordings—he decided to move his base of operations, from February through June of 1939, to Manhattan to obtain "more systematic academic training in anthropology and in the anthropological approach to primitive and folk music." He hoped to study with Herzog and other anthropologists at Columbia, and also "to study music with private instructors" (Cohen, 2010: 115). A recently published collection of Lomax's correspondence reveals the encounter with Herzog—from Lomax's viewpoint, of course—to have been less than successful. Herzog would not let Lomax into his course, insisting that he must take his two courses in sequence—primitive music (offered in the fall) followed by folk music (in the spring). Herzog would not budge from the requirement. To Harold Spivacke, his supervisor at the Library of Congress, Lomax then wrote, "I met a very much surprised Dr. Herzog at Columbia this morning, a Dr. Herzog who told me that I had made a great mistake in coming to school to take his course this term, that I should have come next term, should have come next year and for a whole year. Such a neurotic little academic man you never saw before" (Cohen, 2010: 121). Although Lomax had a marvelous ear, outstanding musical taste, and broad knowledge of folk music, he had little formal musical education and could be regarded as a well-meaning amateur in search of professional training. In some scientific disciplines, such as ornithology and astronomy, serious work by amateur researchers is highly valued; and in the early history of science, the majority of natural historians and natural philosophers were amateurs and proud of it. But Herzog was wary of amateur music research. Their confrontation, exacerbated by their prickly personalities and strong convictions, can be understood as a sign of incompatibility between public and academic ethnomusicologies in an earlier era; today, as mentioned earlier, more practitioners of applied ethnomusicology are employed within academia than outside it.

Indeed, the growth of US applied ethnomusicology from the 1960s through the 1980s owed much to Alan Lomax's continuing influence, his call for cultural equity, the work of public folklorists, and the establishment of government institutions that supported cultural pluralism within the arts. At the federal level were the Office of Folklife Studies at the Smithsonian Institution, the Folk Arts Division of the National Endowment for the Arts, and the Archive of Folk Culture at the Library of Congress, enlarged from the former Archive of American Folk Song, which Lomax had directed, and under the aegis of a new Library unit, the American Folklife Center. Regional, state, and, in some cases, city arts councils also were established, funded in part by the National Endowment for the Arts, and by the end of the 1980s most of the state arts councils employed at least one folklorist and a few employed ethnomusicologists (see Murphy, Chapter 5 of Volume 3). Folklore in the United States, while conservative in the academic world, enjoyed a tradition of populist activism outside it. Each of these government agencies employed scholars as consultants, and some employed them as arts and humanities administrators; thus, a large public outreach and concern for the health of expressive culture within various US communities was put in place, with a growing number of ethnomusicologists involved in public folklore, most often as consultants, but sometimes as advocates and collaborators, doing applied work. Several ethnomusicologists worked as presenters at folk festivals, their prior fieldwork having identified and documented some of the musicians who performed there. Music was the most prominent among the arts singled out by public folklorists for identification, documentation, and presentation. As arts administrators, ethnomusicologists were employed by the Smithsonian Institution (Thomas Vennum, Charlotte Heth) and by the Folk Arts Division of the National Endowment for the Arts (NEA; Daniel Sheehy), which also hired numerous ethnomusicologists as consultants to sit on panels recommending funding for various community music projects as well as for apprenticeships and heritage awards (see Titon, Chapter 5 of this volume). Bess Lomax Hawes, director of the NEA's Folk Arts Division, held an informal session at the SEM conference most years during the 1980s to inform ethnomusicologists of the opportunities for submitting applied ethnomusicology project proposals to the NEA. This activity, known in the 1970s and 1980s as public-sector folklore, in the 1990s became known simply as "public folklore," and influenced the course of applied ethnomusicology in the United States profoundly.

Academic ethnomusicologists involved in public folklore thus began to think of their work as applied ethnomusicology, but SEM remained chiefly an organization devoted to communicating research among scholars. It was not until most of the founding generation aged and gradually relinquished leadership that applied ethnomusicology was able to enter SEM in a significant way. But it was not merely a changing of the generations. A significant change within academia resulted from the growing critique of science, fomented by post-structuralist and critical cultural theory, and culminating in the so-called "science wars" of the 1980s. North American graduate students in ethnomusicology during this period—beginning in the late 1960s—could not help being affected, as were cultural anthropologists and folklorists. The result, particularly among those attracted to the study of music as culture, was a turn in ethnomusicology from science toward cultural critique, from the musical object to the musical experience, from analysis to interpretation, from explanation to understanding. As a result, US ethnomusicology took a humanistic turn, and the cultural study of music moved to the forefront until, by the end of the 1980s, ethnomusicology had assimilated the humanistic cultural anthropology of Clifford Geertz, Dennis Tedlock, James Clifford, George Marcus, Vincent Crapanzano, Paul Rabinow, and others, a far cry from the empirical anthropology Herzog had championed. Much of this ethnomusicological humanism eventually achieved theoretical expression in the "new fieldwork" (Barz and Cooley, 1996) of reflexivity, reciprocity, and advocacy. Meanwhile, the scientific ethnomusicologists were in gradual retreat. A review of the essays in *Ethnomusicology* since about 1976 shows the balance point moving in the direction of music as culture rather than as form and structure. In 2010 the musicological ethnomusicologists came together outside SEM to form their own scholarly association (Analytical Approaches to World Music) with its own journal.[4]

Ethnomusicology's humanistic turn led a growing number of North American ethnomusicologists toward applied ethnomusicology in one form or another—advocating on behalf of individual musicians, musical communities, and musical life in particular places. The new fieldwork had become experience-centered, with ethnomusicological monographs such as those by Berliner (1978) and Keil (1979) reflecting this first-person turn to reflexivity. Kenneth Gourlay's 1982 essay in SEM's journal, "Towards a Humanizing Ethnomusicology," offered a theoretical basis for the new direction, along with a strongly worded critique of Merriam's insistence on science (Gourlay, 1982). In that same issue of *Ethnomusicology*, Charles Keil's essay, "Applied Ethnomusicology and a Rebirth of Music from the Spirit of Tragedy," charted a path toward work that "can make a difference" through "an insistence on putting music into play wherever people are resisting their oppression" (Keil, 1982: 407). Keil's 1982 essay caught the spirit of the postcolonialism that was central to cultural critique in the new anthropology, and to critical theory in cultural studies. And because applied ethnomusicology did not become a movement until the era of decolonization, it could (and did) oppose colonialism, orientalism, and other manifestations of the arrogance of Western power, while answering (if not avoiding) the critiques of colonialism that were being (and that continue to be) leveled at applied anthropology. Meanwhile, an ever-increasing number of US ethnomusicologists were becoming involved in public folklore and were realizing that there was much good work to be done for music in the public arena.

A humanized ethnomusicology thus made it possible for a resurgence of a postcolonial applied ethnomusicology, manifesting itself not only in a new fieldwork based in reciprocity leading to advocacy, but also through institutional gains within SEM. Applied ethnomusicology went mainstream within SEM during the 1990s. As the program chair for the 1989 SEM conference, I invited colleagues from my years in the early 1980s as a consultant for the NEA Folk Arts Division to present papers on a preplanned panel. Entitled "From Perspective to Practice in 'Applied Ethnomusicology,'" the panel included the following presenters and papers: Robert Garfias, "What an Ethnomusicologist Can Do in Public Sector Arts"; Daniel Sheehy, "Applied Ethnomusicology as a State of Mind"; Charlotte Heth, "Getting It Right and Passing It On: The Ethnomusicologist and Cultural Transmission"; and Bess Lomax Hawes, "Practice Makes Perfect: Lessons in Active Ethnomusicology." When in 1990 I became editor of *Ethnomusicology*, this panel formed the starting point for a special issue entitled "Ethnomusicology and the Public Interest," which featured articles by Daniel Sheehy, Bess Lomax Hawes, Martha Ellen Davis, and Anthony Seeger. This was the first time that applied ethnomusicology was featured in the SEM journal. In my introductory article for that special issue, I wrote that ethnomusicology in the public interest "is work whose immediate end is not research and the flow of knowledge inside intellectual communities but, rather, practical action in the world outside of archives and universities" and that "as a way of knowing and doing, fieldwork [which is constitutive of ethnomusicology] at its best is based on a model of friendship between people rather than on a model involving antagonism, surveillance, the observation of physical objects, or the contemplation of abstract ideas" (Titon, 1992a: 315, 321). Sheehy's article there began the process of constructing an alternative history for ethnomusicology in the United States, one in which applied work was more central (Sheehy, 1992). Hawes was invited to give the plenary Seeger Lecture at the 1993 SEM conference, and this autobiographical talk, meant in part to attract listeners to applied work as a calling, was published two years later in *Ethnomusicology* (Hawes, 1995). In 1998 Keil, continuing in the vein of postcolonial critique, and ever-prophetic, called in the SEM journal for an "applied sociomusicology" that, by reclaiming participatory music-making "for the vast majority," would help engender a revolution in consciousness that would overturn the global corporate capitalist world order and reverse the coming eco-catastrophe as we move toward "sustainable futures" (Keil, 1998: 304).

At the 1998 SEM Conference, Doris Dyen and Martha Ellen Davis convened a meeting to assess interest in proposing a standing Committee on Applied Ethnomusicology to the SEM Board. Until that meeting, a single name for this activity had not yet risen to the surface; among those in circulation then were "applied," "active," "action," "practice," "public," and "public sector" (Titon, 1992a: 320–321). As applied ethnomusicologists themselves, with experience in the public sector and in the academic world, Davis and Dyen felt the time was opportune for organizing something more formal to bring together those with common interests in working for the benefit of musical communities in the public arena. Thirty-eight hopeful founders (the editors of this volume among them) attended, their proposal was accepted by the SEM Board of Directors, and the Committee was established, with a variety of definitions of applied ethnomusicology. In 2000, Dyen and Davis, who had taken on the role of chairs of the Committee, appointed a deputy chair, Tom Van Buren, and successfully petitioned the Board to recognize the group as the Applied Ethnomusicology Section. Dyen and Davis stood aside in 2002 while appointing co-chairs Ric Alviso and Miriam Gerberg to join Van Buren, who stepped down in 2004 in favor of Mark Puryear. Alviso was succeeded in 2008 by Jeff Todd Titon, Gerberg in 2009 by Kathleen Noss Van Buren, Puryear in 2010 by Maureen Loughran, Noss Van Buren in 2014 by Michael Bakan, Loughran in 2015 by Erica Haskell, and Haskell in 2018 by Klisala Harrison.

During the Committee and Section's first decade, the co-chairs worked to make the group a comfortable space within SEM for ethnomusicologists employed outside of the academic world. To that end, they organized practical panels on non-academic careers for ethnomusicologists, such as the "Ethnomusicologists at Work" series, organized by Gerberg; and on strategies for survival both inside and outside official institutions. Co-chairs Gerberg, Puryear, and Alviso established Section prizes for outstanding presentations at SEM, and awards for travel grants to the conference. In the new millennium, as applied ethnomusicology has become increasingly popular among graduate students and welcomed inside academic institutions, the Section has become an SEM meeting-place and platform for applied ethnomusicologists based both within and outside academia. Most recently, the Section has sponsored panels involving themes such as music and politics, community advocacy, activism and "giving back," conflict resolution, ethics, repatriation of artifacts from archives and museums, medicine, the environment, and social justice. It also sponsors presentations from guests who do not normally attend the SEM conferences but who have worked in applied ethnomusicology either independently or in extra-academic institutions. For example, at the 2011 conference, Debora Kodish, public folklorist and director of the Philadelphia Folklore Project, led a Section-sponsored discussion among traditional music and dance activists and community scholar-practitioners from the African-American and Asian-American communities in Philadelphia, showcasing a model for ethnomusicologists seeking strategies for work in community-based institutions. With an excess of 300 members, Applied Ethnomusicology is now one of the largest and most active among the SEM Sections, exceeded in membership only by the student and the popular music Sections.

As might be expected of a practical endeavor, theorization of applied ethnomusicology lagged behind practice, but recent years have witnessed an increasing number of publications and events centered on applied ethnomusicology itself. These included an international conference on applied ethnomusicology organized by Erica Haskell and Maureen Loughran, at Brown University (Invested in Community, 2003), a special issue of *Folklore Forum* devoted to applied ethnomusicology (Fenn, 2003), a section to devoted to applied ethnomusicology in an issue of *Ethnomusicology Review* (2012), and a book of essays, *Applied Ethnomusicology: Historical and Contemporary Approaches* (Harrison, Mackinlay, and Pettan, 2010). Rebecca Dirksen authored an excellent overview of contemporary practice, with an emphasis on work by US-based ethnomusicologists, while Timothy Rice's book-length "very short introduction" to the discipline devotes the last two of nine chapters to what is in effect applied ethnomusicology (Dirksen, 2012; Rice, 2014). This *Oxford Handbook*, first published in a one-volume clothbound edition in 2015, continued in this vein, offering a cross-section of contemporary international work in the field. In 2017, one entire day's programming of the annual SEM conference was devoted to public, public-sector, and applied ethnomusicology. In response to the continued use of those three terms (public, public sector, and applied), Klisala Harrison argued that "applied" was the most appropriate term, particularly in the international context; and that "public" and "public sector" were best understood as sub-areas of "applied" that made sense only in certain national contexts (Harrison, 2016).

Concluding this sketch of applied ethnomusicology in the United States, I do not mean to dismiss entirely the critique that applied ethnomusicology may be used for undesirable ends. Knowledge is not innocent; cultural information has a long history of being put to use for military purposes and colonial conquest. Music used in the service of a social or musical benefit may turn out to have negative consequences, or what looks like a benefit to one political entity may be a harm to another. Merriam's charge that applied ethnomusicologists are engaged in "manipulating people's destinies" is one way of looking at missionary work, for example, and it is a fact that missionaries have put their knowledge of music to use for that purpose for many centuries. Today, faith-based organizations such as SIL International put ethnomusicological knowledge to use in aiding local artists in indigenous communities, with the goal of a "better future: one of justice, peace, joy, physical safety, social continuity and spiritual wholeness" (SIL International). Other forces are intervening: corporations, governments, technology, the law, and so forth. Social responsibility requires social justice, cultural equity, and de-colonization. I believe there is no self-correcting "invisible hand" in the marketplace or anywhere else that would permit scholars the luxury of research without social respon-sibility. Nor would scholars be well advised to accumulate knowledge and then supply it to those who in their ignorance would put it to use.

SEM had been slow to adopt a more active role, but recognition of the need for the or-ganization to enter the larger political sphere has gradually come. For many years, SEM took the position that while ethnomusicologists were of course free to express their per-sonal political views, the organization itself must not take a public political stand. But in 1976 the SEM *Newsletter* editor refused to print an employment advertisement from a university representing a government that practiced apartheid, an early harbinger of change. Not long afterward, SEM began endorsing resolutions supporting the rights of scholars detained by governments for political reasons, and the rights of musicians to travel freely internationally. It has passed position statements on rights and discrimi-nation, copyright ownership and sound recordings, and ethical considerations. Finally, in 2007, in response to a request from the SEM Ethics Committee, the SEM Board of Directors approved a "Position Statement against the Use of Music as Torture." Arising in response to numerous reports of music as part of the torture arsenal employed by US military and intelligence agencies and their allies against suspected terrorist detainees, it reads in part that the Society for Ethnomusicology "calls for full disclosure of US government-sanctioned and funded programs that design the means of delivering music as torture; condemns the use of music as an instrument of torture; and demands that the US government and its agencies cease using music as an instrument of physical and psychological torture" (SEM Torture). The position statement on music as torture was a significant step in SEM's evolution. It recognizes that ethnomusicologists are citi-zens of the world with social responsibilities, and that our professional organization has not only the right but also the duty to represent the profession's ethical beliefs and act upon them.

During the second decade of the twenty-first century, the SEM leadership's rec-ognition of the ethnomusicologist's social responsibility continued to grow, fueled by increased interest in applied ethnomusicology among graduate students, many of whom were contemplating careers outside the academic world. At the University of Limerick, Ireland, in the same year that the clothbound, one-volume edition of this *Oxford Handbook of Applied Ethnomusicology* was published (2015), SEM and ICTM sponsored a joint, three-day Forum on the subject of an activist, community-engaged ethnomusi-cology, attended by more than 100 ethnomusicologists from all over the world, at which the editors of this volume were among the keynote speakers.[5] As of 2018 a book of essays from that Forum remained in preparation under the editorship of forum conveners Beverley Diamond and Salwa El Shawan Castelo-Branco; upon publication it will move both SEM and ICTM yet further towards *Transforming Ethnomusicology* (forthcoming) in an applied direction.

NOTES

1. Its recognition was signaled in 1992 when the Journal of the Society for Ethnomusicology devoted a special issue to the subject (*Ethnomusicology* 36[2]).
2. In Kunst's definition ethnomusicology was chiefly a new name for the discipline of comparative musicology. But as we shall soon see, US cultural anthropologists interested in music saw opportunity in the new name, founded the international Society for Ethnomusicology in 1955, and were prominent among its leaders. Thus by 1955 ethnomusicology could be described as a new and interdisciplinary field, not just a new name for an older academic discipline.
3. In a 2013 interview he characterized as one of four "new, or newish developments in ethnomusicology" a "widespread concern with the need to do things that benefit the peoples whose music and musical culture are studied" (Nettl, 2014: 1).
4. In the new millennium, science is making a small comeback as music theory and comparative studies are applied in these analytical approaches to structural features of world musics. Science is manifest also in a growing interest among ethnomusicologists in neuroscience and music psychology, and questions concerning music and human evolution.
5. The Forum was titled Transforming Ethnomusicological Practice Through Activism and Community Engagement, and was held in Limerick City, Ireland, September 13–16, 2015. Further information about it may be found at https://www.ictmusic.org/joint-sem-ictm-forum-2015.

SECTION 2

....

APPLIED ETHNOMUSICOLOGY IN THE GLOBAL ARENA

....

SVANIBOR PETTAN

AN INTRODUCTORY VIGNETTE

....

IN 1975, a documentary film about hunting, *Ultime grida dalla savana* (internationally known as *Savage Man Savage Beast*) was released. The authors intended to document the phenomenon of hunting in different spatial and cultural contexts. The viewers can see not only animals hunting animals and humans hunting animals, but also animals hunting humans, and finally, humans hunting humans. The scenes in which lions eat a tourist and in which humans mutilate the bodies of caught humans were received with particular controversy. The filmmakers Antonio Climati and Mario Morra were filming all the scenes with the clear attitude of detached observers, documenting the multi-faceted footage in the domain of their professional interest and showing no intention whatsoever to intervene. The basic symbolic standpoint of this film brings up a number of useful questions concerning the attitudes in the field of ethnomusicology in its both temporal and spatial contexts, and highlights the stance of intervention in positioning applied ethnomusicology.[1]

The stance of the above-mentioned filmmakers reflects the attitude prevalent in the ethnomusicological mainstream within the past decades, which can be summarized in the following way: studying music as it is, not as a researcher or anybody else would want it to be. I vividly recall an example from my doctoral studies at the University of Maryland Baltimore County, in which the professor pointed out a music producer of an African music CD, who insisted on removal of those parts from the musical instrument that were responsible for the production of a buzzing sound. The producer's opinion was that the recording without them would be more pleasing to the ears of international audiences, which would consequently increase the profit expected from the final product. Of course, such an uninformed and disrespectful intervention into the aesthetics of the musicians invoked laughter and criticism among the students, with no need for further discussion.

The question, which I considered essential, that is, whether "those who know" (us, the ethnomusicologists) would actually consider making a step beyond the level of an academic debate and try to intervene, by providing the ignorant producer who misused his power over the musicians with arguments against his action, was left unanswered.

The two cases (the film and the CD producer), extreme as they are, raise at least two useful points:

a. The decision whether to intervene or not has moral implications.
b. In order to be successful, intervention has to be based on knowledge, understanding, and skills.

WHAT IS APPLIED ETHNOMUSICOLOGY, AND WHAT ISN'T IT?

As will be discussed later, definitions may vary according to the parameters such as time, place, research tradition, and individual preference, but the essence is captured in the wording created and accepted at the 39th World Conference of the International Council for Traditional Music (ICTM) in Vienna in 2007, suggesting that "[a]pplied ethnomusicology is the approach guided by principles of social responsibility, which extends the usual academic goal of broadening and deepening knowledge and understanding toward solving concrete problems and toward working both inside and beyond typical academic contexts." Characterization of the ICTM Study Group on Applied Ethnomusicology that follows provides further clarification, suggesting that it "advocates the use of ethnomusicological knowledge in influencing social interaction and course of cultural change."

The introduction to the book *Applied Ethnomusicology: Historical and Contemporary Approaches* (Harrison, Mackinlay, and Pettan, 2010) analyzes this definition part by part and also addresses three common misconceptions about applied ethnomusicology, which are worth mentioning in this context:

1. Applied ethnomusicology does *not* stand in opposition to the academic domain, but should be viewed as its extension and complement.[2]
2. Applied ethnomusicology is *not* an opposition to the theoretical (philosophical, intellectual) domain, but its extension and complement.[3]
3. Applied ethnomusicology is *not* an opposition to ethnographic, artistic, and scientific research, but their extension and complement.[4]

The introductory article to the above-mentioned volume ends with a quotation of Michael Birenbaum Quintero: "Apply your ethnomusicology or someone else will apply it for you," which once again points to intervention as a key notion.

There is a rich myriad of opinions about applied ethnomusicology among ethnomusicologists worldwide, from those who claim that all ethnomusicology is in fact applied, to those who feel that applied ethnomusicology does not enjoy necessary respect within the academic discipline and therefore should not be discussed at all. It is easy to agree with Daniel Sheehy's belief that "all ethnomusicologists have at one time or another been applied ethnomusicologists" (Sheehy, 1992: 323). But "applied ethno-musicology as a *conscious practice*," says Sheehy, "begins with a sense of purpose, a pur-pose larger than the advancement of knowledge about the music of the world's peoples" (ibid.). This is why I started my part of this Introduction with the crucial question of *intervention*, or in other words, with the conscious decision-making of a researcher whether or not to step beyond the mere study of the selected phenomenon and af-fect the researched circumstances. It is the sense of purpose, rather than any specific topic, that defines applied ethnomusicology. There are "sensitive" topics, such as, for in-stance, the roles of music in the Israeli/Palestinian divide, in which the author of the book (for whatever reason) does not mention applied ethnomusicology (see Brinner, 2009); and there are seemingly "neutral" topics, for instance the lullabies in Slovenia, which are from their initial conceptualization framed as "applied" by the author (see Juvančič, 2010).

There are many more or less known individuals, organizations, projects, and publications known for promoting the use of music for the betterment of human condi-tion. Their work, though inspiring, if not rooted in ethnomusicological research should not be considered "applied ethnomusicology." Venezuelan musician, activist, econo-mist, and politician José Antonio Abreu and his El Sistema, Argentinian/Israeli/German pianist and conductor Daniel Barenboim and his West-Eastern Divan Orchestra, Irish musicians and activists Bob Geldof (Live Aid) and Bono (ONE Campaign), Musicians Without Borders, Young at Heart, Studio MC Pavarotti, most articles in the journals such as *Music and Arts in Action* and *Sounds in Europe* are just a few examples, among many more.

Some ethnomusicologists express concern about the power imbalance in projects that fit within the realm of applied ethnomusicology (e.g., Hofman, 2010). The title of my first conference paper on the topic, presented in 1995, started exactly with the same notion: "Ethnomusicologist as a Power Holder?" The sentence with the ques-tion mark looks even more bizarre in the light of Deborah Wong's reminder that "[e]thnomusicology is marginalized in most music departments because its radical rela-tivism challenges logocentric thinking about music" (2013: 348). In my conference pres-entation, based on the work with Bosnian refugees in Norway (see below), I addressed the issue of power share with the participants in, to the extent possible, equal, horizontal terms. The (later) article by Samuel Araújo and members of the Grupo Musicultura (2006), inspired by Paolo Freire's dialogical pedagogy (1970), is a good example of the same intention. There is, however, the other side of the coin, which should not be overlooked. If a certain kind of knowledge and/or access to power holders in a society for the benefit of the people in need is the comparative advantage of an ethnomusicolo-gist, and there is a consensus between the interlocutors and the ethnomusicologist that he or she should use it, I can hardly think of counterarguments. This is how Anthony Seeger benefited the Suyá community in Brazil and Ursula Hemetek the Roma people in Austria. In Harris M. Berger's words, one should be aware of the dual nature of power:

> Power is, in one sense, the power to act, the ability to bring forth events in the world. But because our action is always social—always something we achieve because of and with others, past, present, future—the potential for domination is inherent, even ripe, in the entirety of social life, and even the most mundane, equitable, or convivial practice is informed by larger social contexts and the legacies of domination that they entail. This is as true of practices of music making, teaching, research or public sector work as it is of any other kind of activity. Seeing the social life of music as a domain of coordinated practice that is inherently, rather than contingently, political is one way of coming to terms with these difficult issues.

(Berger, 2014: 319).

A PERSONAL STANCE

Just as Salwa El-Shawan Castelo-Branco did in her Epilogue to the seminal volume *Music and Conflict* (O'Connell and Castelo-Branco, 2010), let me add to this Introduction a personal stance that should define my own position.

In my opinion, every scholar should be free to decide whether to make a step beyond the usual goal of deepening and broadening knowledge, understanding, and skills, and consciously intervene into the human and cultural environment of his or her research interest. While doing fieldwork in the 1980s on the East African islands of Zanzibar and Pemba for my B.A. thesis (University of Zagreb, Croatia) and in Egypt for my M.A. thesis (University of Ljubljana, Slovenia), my clear intention was to affect the self-focused folk music research in what was Yugoslavia at the time and to relate it to the much larger international community of ethnomusicologists, which I was learning about mainly from the periodicals (*Yearbook for Traditional Music, Ethnomusicology, the world of music*). My goal was clearly not the mere scholarly work based on the data from elsewhere in the world, but the conscious intervention into the essence of the discipline as it was understood in my home country at that time.

Between my B.A. and M.A. studies, I was obliged to serve for a year in the Yugoslav People's Army. Following my research interests, I asked the military authorities in Croatia to be sent to serve in the multicultural city of Prizren in far-away Kosovo, which was the most politically unstable part of what was Yugoslavia in the early 1980s. After becoming the instructor for cultural affairs, I came to the position not only to conduct fieldwork (by using a military tape recorder), but also to take it a step further: to bring regularly together youngsters from different ethnic communities and fellow soldiers into a choir. Obviously, research was beneficial to the work with the choir, and contacts established through the choir activities had a positive impact on my research.

Following the end of my doctoral studies (University of Maryland) in 1992, I was faced with the dilemma of whether to try to find a position in the safety of American academia or to return to my disintegrating, war-torn country. I decided once again to cross the boundary of intervention and use my capacities not only to study "music and war at home," but also to explore whether my knowledge, understanding, and skills could in any way confront the growing hatred and help reducing the suffering of the people affected by the war. My interlocutors in Croatia were highly unusual for any type of ethnomusicological inquiry known to me at that time: they included refugees and internally displaced people, soldiers, people in shelters, representatives of nongovernmental organizations (NGOs), radio editors, producers and sellers of music cassettes under both official and black market circumstances, members of the diasporas, and nonetheless musicians—amateur and professional, representatives of diverse musical genres and with diverse political orientations. Popular music was at the forefront, but my research encompassed folk and art music, as well. What was the essence of my intervention beyond the limits of research? My ethnomusicology students in both Zagreb and Ljubljana received assignments to work on joint performances with refugees in refugee camps in order to develop a sense of compassion and togetherness, and their seminar projects—for instance, one about music in various local religious communities at the time of political calls for unification (one ethnicity, one religion, one language, one territory)—clearly aimed for more than a mere broadening and deepening of knowledge.

Invited to teach for a term at the University of Oslo in Norway in the mid-1990s, I took the opportunity to implement a project, together with my senior host Professor Kjell Skyllstad. A few years earlier he envisioned and carried out a project named *The Resonant Community* (Skyllstad, 1993), the first case in my experience that had all elements of an applied ethnomusicology project. In the period from 1989 to 1992 music of various origins (African, Asian, European, and Latin American) had been successfully used in some elementary schools in Norway in order to foster "interracial understanding." Included and affected by this project were the teachers, pupils, and their parents, for whom teaching kits were created; some of the best musicians from four continents shared their arts with them. The evaluated and confirmed impact of *The Resonant Community* inspired us to put together the Azra project, an innovative proactive attempt, with the focus on Bosnian refugee musicians and Norwegian music students, which has been already presented elsewhere (e.g., Pettan, 1996; Skyllstad, 1997; Pettan, 2010), and thus not need to be described here. Therefore, I will dedicate just a few words to its methodological aspects.

I believe the Azra project fits into what Sheehy refers to as "conscious practice" and "sense of purpose." It is a "horizontal" (not "top-down") project, driven by the clear wish for intervention by well-intended scholars and their collaborators who together, in Angosino's words, "had a concern for using their knowledge for the betterment of the human condition" (Angrosino, 1990: 106). The goals of the project were as follows: (1) strengthening Bosnian cultural identity among the refugees from Bosnia-Herzegovina in Norway, and (2) stimulating mutually beneficial cross-cultural communication between the Bosnians and the Norwegians involved. The project was envisioned as a triangle consisting of three principal domains: research, education, and music-making. Its realization was carried on in four stages: (1) recognition of the problem and definition of the goals and basic strategies; (2) collection and analysis of data, plus refinement of the strategies; (3) intervention; and (4) evaluation of the results.

Work on this project made me aware of two distinctive types of mediation, which I termed *indirect* and *direct*. *Indirect mediation* means that the scholar gives the results of his or her research to those in a position to apply them. *Direct mediation* means that scholar himself or herself actively participates in the application of scholarly knowledge, understanding, and skills. Skyllstad and I used both categories in the Azra project. While mediating indirectly through conference papers, lectures, articles, and interviews, using the synthesis of empirical fieldwork and relevant literature to encourage other people to act, we reached the limits with no insight into the consequences of our involvement. Direct mediation proved to be more useful and far-reaching. For instance, within the Azra project, Skyllstad and I were able to shape its goals and contents, observe its flow and modify it when needed, and evaluate all its stages, including the final results.

My series of publications in different formats (books, articles, CD-ROM, film), accompanied by proactive lectures and picture exhibitions—all dedicated to Roma people, largely silenced victims of the war in Kosovo in the 1990s—can be seen as yet another application of ethnomusicological knowledge, understanding, and skills. The publications include those with scholarly rigor and those aimed at communication with general audiences (more in Pettan, 2010). One of the professional involvements that I highly value, but have never written an article about, is my role in the advisory committee at the Slovenian annual state review titled "Let's sing, let's play musical instruments, let's dance" for children and youngsters with special needs.

To summarize, like many other fellow ethnomusicologists, I am involved in projects of public interest. Not everything I do in ethnomusicology has an applied extension. In my invited lectures on applied ethnomusicology, I often encourage scholars in the audience to think of research that goes beyond the broadening and deepening of knowledge in the direction of benefiting the people they study. Some become inspired, while others simply do not want to think in these terms. And it is right to be so. For me, this is the clear line between ethnomusicology and applied ethnomusicology.

"APPLIED" IN OTHER DISCIPLINES

It is a common practice that scientific and scholarly disciplines have their applied domains. To mention just some, there are applied mathematics, applied physics, applied biology, applied geography, applied sociology, applied anthropology, and then (surprisingly seldom) applied musicology, partly substituted by the category of applied music. If hydrology, for instance, is the study of water and encompasses "the interrelationships of geologic materials and processes of water" (Fetter, 2001: 3), then "applied hydrogeologists are problem solvers and decision makers. They identify a problem, define the data needs, design a field program for collection of data, propose alternative solutions to the problem, and implement the preferred solutions" (ibid.: 11). Applied sociology refers to "any use of the sociological perspective and/or its tools in the understanding of, intervention in, and/or enhancement human social life" (Price and Steele, 2004), while applied anthropology refers to "any use of anthropological knowledge to influence social interaction, to maintain or change social institutions, or to direct the course of cultural change" (Spradley and McCurdy, 2000: 355).

Curiously, neither the International Musicological Society nor the American Musicological Society have sections focused on applied musicology. UCLA musicologist Elisabeth Le Guin points out that the reason might be that "in the institutional structure of the discipline's most prestigious academic society,[5] a stigma lingers around the idea of 'putting music to use', as the SEM describes applied ethnomusicology: a ghost of the old idea, coeval in its origins with my undergraduates' obdurately anti-verbal Romanticism, that music should amount to something more than its use-value" (LeGuin, 2012).

A recent book with applied musicology in its title refers to "using zygonic theory to inform music education, therapy, and psychology research" (Ockelford, 2013). According to *The Oxford Companion to Music*, applied music is an American term for a study course in performance, as opposed to theory.

It is worth inquiring about the independent scientific and scholarly societies that have the adjective "applied" in their names, which implies that they have already answered the "ultimate aim" in Merriam's terms, that is, whether "one is searching out knowledge for its own sake, or is attempting to provide solutions to practical applied problems" (Merriam, 1964: 42–43) in favor of the latter. In general, "applied societies" are international and are far from being small outfits of the main disciplinary bodies; some count their members in the thousands.[6] Although the aims of these societies are defined in the disciplinarily determined ways, the great majority of them make clear that they promote the outcomes of their disciplines with the intention that the public benefits from their efforts.[7] This is particularly clearly emphasized by the Society for Applied Anthropology, active since 1941, whose "unifying factor is a commitment to making an impact on the quality of life in the world" (www.sfaa.net).

A Brief Worldwide Overview

It is quite fascinating to observe engaged scholarship within the Australian ethnomusicological realm, from Catherine Ellis (1985) to the studies of Grace Koch (2013), Catherine Grant (2014), Huib Schippers and Catherine Grant (2016), Aaron Corn, Muriel Swijghuisen Reigersberg, Sally Treloyn and several others. High ethical stands and participatory work promoted by the research institutions focused on indigenous people of Australia, such as Australian Institute of Aboriginal and Torres Strait Islander Studies (AIATSIS), as well as the active/activist involvement in Aboriginal rights issue by several leading Australian ethnomusicologists, provide inspiring lessons for applied ethnomusicologists worldwide (see Newsome, 2008). The contributions by Dan

Bendrups and Huib Schippers in this volume and by Elizabeth Mackinlay in Volume 2, make a strong Australian contribution to the applied work with the Aborigines, other minorities, and carriers of music cultures in various parts of the globe.

"The practice of ethnomusicology has been central in the professional lives of ethnomusicologists in Southeast Asia," claims Tan Sooi Beng in her article about activism in Southeast Asian ethnomusicology, pointing to a project of empowerment of youth in Penang, Malaysia, to revitalize traditions and bridge cultural barriers (2008: 69). For her, and for many colleagues elsewhere in Asia, to be an ethnomusicologist means not only involvement in scholarly activities such as teaching, documenting, publishing, and organizing conferences, but also application of the ethnomusicological knowledge toward solving particular cultural problems "so as to bring about change in their respective societies" (ibid.: 70). Terada Yoshitaka provides yet another good example of sensitive work in various formats (e.g., 2005, 2008, 2010, 2011), and so do Weiya Lin, Pamela Onishi, Mayco Santaella and several others. Tan Sooi Beng in this volume and Zhang Boyu in Volume 3 of the *Handbook* present Asian views and approaches from within, while Joshua Pilzer in this volume, Zoe Sherinian in Volume 2, and John Morgan O'Connell in Volume 3 complement them from outside, covering at least some other parts of the world's largest continent.

Practical aspects of ethnomusicology are very much present in Africa, too, from indigenous teaching approaches to music education, preservation of cultural roots, building of musical instruments, to diverse uses of music against xenophobia and prejudices related to HIV/AIDS. The works of Daniel Avorgbedor (1992), Angela Impey (2002), Bernhard Bleibinger (2010), Kathleen Van Burren (2010), along with Andrew Tracey, David Dargie, Diane Thram, and Patricia Opondo, to mention just a few, point to a rich diversity of approaches. In Volume 2, Jeffrey Summitt and Brian Schrag provide their own views and experiences in applied ethnomusicology in Africa.

South America is certainly the site of some of the major ongoing developments in applied ethnomusicology. This is the case thanks to two extraordinary thinkers in the field, Brazilian Samuel Araújo and US-based Anthony Seeger, whose particularly important work and scholarly formation is related to Brazil. Araújo intends "to highlight the political substance and epistemological consequences of new research contexts and roles as one area with potentially ground-breaking contributions toward the emergence of a more balanced social world, i.e. one in which knowledge will hopefully emerge from a truly horizontal, intercultural dialogue and not through top-to-bottom neo-colonial systems of validation" (Araújo, 2008: 14). Seeger's work could justifiably be discussed in any geographic context, as his articles and keynote addresses resound on all continents (2006, 2008). In Volume 2, Holly Wissler demonstrates how applied ethnomusicological projects affect two South American communities, one in the Andes, and the other in the Amazon.

Following Daniel Sheehy (1992) and Anthony Seeger (2006), Maureen Loughran (2008) noted that some leading ethnomusicologists in the North American context, such as Alan P. Merriam (1964), Mantle Hood (1971), and Bruno Nettl (1964, 1983) largely ignored the work of applied ethnomusicologists while presenting the major developments within the discipline.[8] The co-editor of this volume, Jeff Todd Titon, has presented in Section 1 of this Introduction the history of ethnomusicology in North America from his perspective,

as he lived and lives it, adding previously unknown aspects and enriching the general understanding of the discipline. Besides him, several other authors in the *Handbook* refer to
various extents to applied ethnomusicology in North American contexts, including Klisala
Harrison in this volume, Michael Bakan in Volume 2, and Susanne Oehler Herrick, Patricia
Shehan Campbell, Clifford Murphy, and Allan Williams in Volume 3.

My own firsthand experiences are largely linked to Europe, where I was born and
where I live and practice ethnomusicology. This is why the following section will be
about Europe. The authors linked in various ways to Europe in the *Handbook* include
Erica Haskell and Britta Sweers in this volume, Ursula Hemetek in Volume 2, and Lee
Higgins and Dan Lundberg in Volume 3.

SOME EUROPEAN VIEWS: ETHNOMUSICOLOGIES

The fact that there is no single, ultimate definition of ethnomusicology suggests that we
may consider the coexistence of ethnomusicologies, not only in different parts of the
world, but also within a single, no matter how small, location. For instance, while I may
find the definition proposed by my US colleague Jeff Todd Titon ("the study of people
making music") acceptable, my Slovenian colleague, folklorist Marko Terseglav, defines
it very differently, as "a discipline, researching spontaneous folk vocal and instrumental
music, its characteristics and development" (Terseglav, 2004: 124).

In a sharp contrast to Vienna in neighboring Austria, which figures as one of the two
cradles of comparative musicology[9] and is at the same time home to the lasting legacy of
folk music research, ethnomusicology in Slovenia is rooted exclusively in folk music research. Table I.1 points to the major distinctions between the two and relates them to the
current ethnomusicological mainstream.[10]

Table I.1. Comparative Musicology, Folk Music Research, and Ethnomusicology

	Comparative Musicology	Folk Music Research	Ethnomusicology
When?	1885–1950s	From late 18th century	From 1950s
What?	Musics of "primitive peoples" and "high Oriental cultures"	Peasant music	People making music
How?	"Armchair"	Collecting, fieldwork (short-term)	Fieldwork (long-term)
Who?	"Other" people	"Own" people	Any people
Where?	Elsewhere	Within own ethnic/ national realm	Anywhere
Why?	Knowledge	National duty	Understanding

In an article, in which she compares the features of comparative musicology and folk music research in Vienna in the early twentieth century, Ursula Hemetek points to some other important distinctions, for instance, recording with phonograph by the former and notation by ear by the latter; music as text with no context versus music as text with context; interdisciplinarity related mainly to natural sciences versus interdisciplinarity related mainly to humanities; and (particularly important in this context) the association of comparative musicology with the academia-based "ivory tower" versus folk music research's "highly motivated volunteers outside academia" and application of (re-search) results (Hemetek, 2009: 62).

The multitude of languages and nation-state ideologies affected research within the European space differently than in North America and Australia. By far, not all of the European countries came under the umbrella of comparative musicology, but all contributed to the legacy of folk music research. Distinctive developments of the discipline in politically, geographically, historically, demographically, economically, linguistically, religiously, and nevertheless culturally diverse national contexts within Europe inspired studies that testify primarily about the specifics of European ethnomusicologies; put together, they enable comparisons and insights into common features. Interestingly, with a few exceptions (e.g., Clausen, Hemetek, and Saether, 2009; Ling, 1999), Europe was encompassed as a whole primarily by ethnomusicologists from North America (e.g., in Bohlman, 1996, 2004; Rice, Porter, and Goertzen, 2000). Some authors discussed them within the theoretical frame of nationalism (e.g., Bohlman, 2011), some pointed to the shared developmental periods (e.g., Elschek, 1991); yet others inverted the historical trends by placing those seen in Europe a century ago as the inferior Others (Roma and Jews; comp. Wallaschek, 1893) to the forefront of contemporary Europe by naming them "transnational ethnic groups" (Rice, Porter, and Goertzen, 2000).

In the post–Cold War Europe of the 1990s, national ethnomusicologies received considerable attention, including those of Denmark (Koudal et al., 1993), Finland (Moisala et al., 1994), Latvia (Boiko, 1994), Italy (Giuriati, 1995), Spain (Marti, 1997), Croatia (Pettan et al., 1998), and many more. This research trend continued in the 2000s, as reflected in the symposium National Ethnomusicologies: The European Perspective (Cardiff University, 2007) and the plenary roundtable under the same name at the ICTM World Conference (Vienna, 2007), both organized by one of the authors in Volume 3 of this *Handbook*, John Morgan O'Connell, and in subsequent studies.[11]

Let us now take a closer look at the micro-plan of Croatia and Slovenia, since 1992 two neighboring independent European countries, which spent the period of the formation of ethnomusicology first as the parts of the multiethnic Austro-Hungarian Empire (1867–1918), and then as the constituent parts of what later became known as Yugoslavia. As in many other parts of Europe, ethnomusicology in Croatia and Slovenia grew from the national awakening of the nineteenth century and the sense of importance of a nation's "own" folk song for the creation and affirmation of national identity. The characteristic procedure, through the first half of the twentieth century, included extensive fieldwork, notation and analysis of the collected songs, publishing collections, and writing syntheses based on the analysis of collected materials. The aim was to define specific national features, different from those of the neighboring peoples, which would in turn provide the basis for the development of national culture. In Croatia, the key figures, such as Franjo Kuhač (1834–1911) and Božidar Širola (1889–1956), were musicians, to whom the novelties in the field of comparative musicology were known. Kuhač was interested in collecting and writing about folk songs of South Slavs (not exclusively Croats), comparing their features with those of non-Slavs (Germans, Italians, Turks). Širola, himself a composer, even earned a doctorate under the mentorship of comparative musicologist Robert Lach in Vienna, and used comparative methodological procedures in dealing with Croatian folk music. In the Slovenian cultural space, at about the same time, the initiative was taken by two widely trained linguists with Viennese doctorates and an interest in ethnology: Karel Štrekelj (1859–1912) and Matija Murko (1861–1952). Just like their predecessors, as far back as the late eighteenth century, they focused primarily on language in the folk songs. In contrast to Štrekelj's emphasis on Slovenian repertoire, Murko did research (with phonograph), for example, of sung epic poetry in Bosnia, as well.

The next generations of principal researchers included Vinko Žganec (1890–1976) and Jerko Bezić (1929–2010) in Croatia, and France Marolt (1891–1952) and Zmaga Kumer (1924–2008) in Slovenia. Žganec, doctor of law and musician, and Marolt, himself a musician, were typical representatives of folk music research in a cultural historic sense, who institutionalized the discipline in Croatia and Slovenia, respectively. Kumer and Bezić earned their doctorates within the discipline. In contrast to Kumer, who became one of Europe's best and latest representatives of the folk music research domain, Bezić was systematically broadening the scope of ethnomusicology in Croatia by opening the space for research of urban music phenomena and in general of influences from abroad. Thanks to the interaction with his multidisciplinary institutional colleagues in Zagreb, influenced by both American (e.g., Alan Dundes, Dan Ben Amos) and Russian (Kiril Chistov) folklorists, he defined the subject of ethnomusicology as the so-called "folklore music," referring to musical communication in small groups (more in Marošević, 1998). The next (current) generation of ethnomusicologists in both countries is actively involved in what can be called mainstream ethnomusicology.

Within what was Yugoslavia, practically each constituent republic had its own "school of ethnomusicology," with unquestionable commonalities, but also distinctive features. Each of these "schools" was thematically focused primarily on the material from within its own political unit and its own people in the ethnic sense. While the folk music research paradigm was the unquestionable basis, each "school" had a different stance toward the developments of ethnomusicology elsewhere and used the results of the "mainstream" at different paces.

Aware of the discrepancy caused by the lack of comparative musicology at home and even more by the lack of their own interest in studying the Others, Serbian ethnomusicologists decided to translate, with a considerable delay, two books rooted in comparative musicology. The translation of Fritz Bose's *Musikalische Völkerkunde* (1953) was published in 1975, and Curt Sachs's *The Rise of Music in the Ancient World*

East and West (1943) as late as 1980 (Saks, 1980).[12] These books became a window to "folk music from other parts of the world" for generations of students of ethnomusicology in Serbia. The translation of John Blacking's *How Musical Is Man?* (1973) was intended to be a contribution to/from the Sarajevo "school" in Bosnia-Herzegovina (Bleking, 1992).[13] In Slovenia, the translations include Curt Sachs's *Eine Weltgeschichte des Tanzes* (1933) in 1996, Roberto Leydi's *L'altra musica* (1991) in 1995, and Alan P. Merriam's *The Anthropology of Music* (1964) in 2000. The other "schools" felt self-sufficient and did not translate any foreign books with a wider scope of the discipline.

According to Bohlman, "Folk music and folk song as objects have not disappeared from the practices of European musicians and scholars, but have instead provided them with complex ways of connecting tradition to modernity, and of emblematizing the past in the present" (1996: 106). Elschek suggests that in this process, "cooperation with anthropology and ethnology has been more successful than with historical musicology" (1991: 101).

Applied Ethnomusicologies

One could argue whether various colonial expositions and other showcases involving comparative musicologists should be identified as a part of the early history of applied ethnomusicology and to what extent comparative musicology in general contributed to the "public sector" of the discipline.[14] At the same time, it is clear that the other branch of European ethnomusicology—folk music research—was throughout the previous century linked to the applied domain. The principal goal of many folk music researchers, that of protection of their national heritage, implied practical application of their findings. Besides scholarly procedures that usually included field research, transcription, analysis, archiving, and publication, they often actively engaged in the popularization of folk music and dance. Important channels for this were state-sponsored folklore ensembles in Eastern Europe and less formalized revival ensembles in Western Europe. Ethnomusicologists assumed various roles in these processes: providing the ensembles with musics and dances collected in the field, writing musical arrangements and/or choreographies, singing, playing instruments and/or dancing, leading the ensembles, and touring with them.

An increasing influx of immigrants in Western Europe in the second half of the twentieth century gradually raised interest in their musical cultures among ethnomusicologists. In addition to important studies on immigrant musics (e.g., Ronström, 1991) and cultural policies (Baumann, 1991), several ethnomusicologists, particularly in Sweden, became involved in applied projects such as the *Ethno* camp for young musicians in Falun and music-making within the ensembles such as the *Orientexpressen*.[15] In Norway, Kjell Skyllstad initiated the earlier-mentioned three-year project named *The Resonant Community* in several elementary schools in the Oslo area in 1989, bringing together ethnomusicology and music education in paving the way to better appreciation between Norwegians and the immigrants from Africa, Asia, and Latin America through their respective musics (Skyllstad, 1993). Multicultural education, which in the United States "grew out of the ferment of the civil rights movement of the 1960s" (Banks and McGee Banks, 2001: 5), gradually became recognized and also debated in Europe. Krister Malm was actively involved in two relevant events in the 1990s: the European Music Council's conference Aspects on Music and Multiculturalism in Falun in 1995 (Malm et al., 1995)[16] and in the first world conference on music and censorship in Copenhagen in 1998, where the organization Freemuse was established (Korpe and Reitov, 1998). Ursula Hemetek was beginning applied work with various minorities in Austria (Hemetek, 1996), which would later lead to official political recognition of the Romani people in Austria (Hemetek, 2006). My applied work with refugees from Bosnia-Herzegovina in Norway, Croatia, and Slovenia, with the internally displaced victims of the war in Croatia, and with Romani victims of the war in Kosovo has been presented earlier.

In 2003 Italian ethnomusicologists organized the ninth international seminar in ethnomusicology in Venice, titled Applied Ethnomusicology: Perspectives and Problems. While recognizing that "setting up museums, service within administration of colonial empires, organization of concerts, divulgence by means of publication of writings and recordings". . . were part of the professional profile of comparative musicologists at the beginnings of the 20th century, they also noticed recent "significant developments" and pointed to issues such as intercultural education, music in relation to diaspora, immigration, and refugees, "spectacularization" of traditional music, and cultural cooperation projects.[17] One of the curiosities of this seminar is the absence of folk music research.

The further conference-related developments of applied ethnomusicology in Europe are largely linked to the framework of the International Council for Traditional Music (ICTM). They will be systematically presented later in this text.

Let us now, just as in the previous section, turn our attention to the micro-plan of Croatia and Slovenia in order to discuss the stances of the most representative Croatian and Slovenian researchers toward application. Certainly, the publication of national folk song collections was not the final aim of the researchers. Either the early musically trained researchers themselves or other musicians harmonized (e.g., Kuhač) or otherwise "improved" the songs in order to create nationally distinctive art music. Marolt was known for arranging the collected songs for his acclaimed choir and for adjusting the collected dances for the staged performances by his own and other folklore ensembles. Application was somehow seen as a natural extension of research by many of these early ethnomusicologists. In fact, Jerko Bezić in Croatia and Zmaga Kumer in Slovenia were the first ones who restrained from applications, trying "to affirm ethnomusicology as an autonomous discipline based on fieldwork, theorizing, evidence and debate, detaching it from requisite utilitarity" (the original quotation is referring to Bezić only; Ceribašić, 2004: 6).[18] Today's ethnomusicologists in both countries complement their research activities by serving in juries at the reviews of folklore performances at local, regional, and national levels; serving in the organization of festivals, symposia, and other discipline-related events; Croatians are involved in the UNESCO's Intangible Cultural Heritage agendas.

Staff at the research institutes in both Zagreb and Ljubljana comprises specialists in several disciplines, including ethnochoreologists. Inspired by the developments in applied ethnomusicology, at least one researcher, Tvrtko Zebec, theorizes about applied ethnochoreology (Zebec, 2007). Joško Ćaleta, an ethnomusicologist in Zagreb, in whose work research and performing applications are closely intertwined, claims that applied activities are often paying his research activities (interview, July 14, 2014), which is a meaningful point to be taken into consideration.

This section ends with a complementing view from the other side of Europe, from the United Kingdom. In the words of Kathleen Van Buren, "Ethnomusicologists need to think more deeply about how to serve others, not just ourselves, through our work. This means listening to people within communities where we live and work, allowing their perspectives to help guide our choice of our topics and activities, trying to collaborate and respond to their needs when we can, and empowering them rather than ourselves" (2010: 219).

THE INTERNATIONAL COUNCIL FOR TRADITIONAL MUSIC

Perhaps the most efficient access to applied ethnomusicology in the global arena is through the principal international association of ethnomusicologists, which is the International Council for Traditional Music (ICTM), with current representation in more than 120 countries and regions on all continents. The association was established in London in 1947 under the name International Folk Music Council (IFMC). We should keep in mind that the establishment of the IFMC precedes Kunst's book *Musicologica: A Study of the Nature of Ethno-musicology, Its Problems, Methods, and Representative Personalities* (1950) and the wide acceptance of the term *ethnomusicology* that followed.[19] It was an era of comparative musicology and folk music research paradigms, which were affecting each other in various ways and to various extents in various places.

IFMC's roots are clearly in the folk music research paradigm, which is evident from the following description:

> In her capacity as Honourable Secretary of the International (Advisory) Folk Dance Council, Maud Karpeles (1885–1976) organized the International Conference on Folk Song and Folk Dance, held at the Belgian Institute in London, 22–27 September 1947. Delegates from twenty-eight countries participated, mostly appointed by the governments of their respective nations, as well as a UNESCO representative. . . . On the afternoon of Monday, 22 September 1947, the Vice Chairman of the conference, Stuart Wilson (1889–1966), proposed "that an International Folk Music Council be formed."
>
> (www.ictmusic.org; see also Karpeles, 1971)

The article in which Karpeles offered her reflections on the 21 years of existence of the Council says a lot about its intellectual climate, including the sentences "In all parts of the world the traditional practice of folk music is disappearing—gradually in some regions and rapidly in others—and if we are to save our musical heritage for the benefit of our own and future generations, it is necessary to act quickly. Collecting activities are, of course, being carried on, but these must be intensified if precious material is not to be lost. As the saying goes, 'It is later than we think'" (Karpeles, 1971: 29). The attitudes of this kind were later largely discredited in the mainstream of the discipline as "salvage ethnomusicology," pointing to "romanticism, paternalism, and hegemony" (see also Grant, 2014: 80). Cultural relativism and the absence of value judgments became, at different paces in different parts of the world, the *sine qua non* of modern ethnomusicology.[20]

The objectives of IFMC were the following: (1) to assist in the preservation, dissemination, and practice of the folk music of all countries; (2) to further the comparative study of folk music; and (3) to promote understanding and friendship between nations through the common interest of folk music.[21] What matters particularly from the point of view of applied ethnomusicology, besides the applied overtones in the presented objectives, is the envisioned work of the newly established Council. The list of proposals included "the holding of conferences and festivals; the publication of a catalogue of recordings, bibliographies, a manual for collectors, and an international collection of folk songs; the promotion of national and international archives; the institution of a general method of dance notations; and the development of a guide to the classification of folk tunes" (Karpeles, 1971: 17). In the course of 1950s and 1960s, IFMC indeed published several catalogues, bibliographies, dictionaries, manuals, collections, statements, and songbooks. In order to accomplish these aims, the structure of IFMC included not only National Committees, but also the Radio Committee, Folk Dance Committee, and more, the names being subject to change from time to time.

The intention of the IFMC in the post–World War II years was to bring together composers, researchers, and other specialists interested in folk music and dance into a truly international association; even the intention to be related to UNESCO was there from the very inception of the Council. Maud Karpeles's principal source of inspiration was Cecil Sharp, the founding father of the folklore revival in England in the beginning of the twentieth century. Within the newly established Council she became secretary under the presidency of Ralph Vaughan Williams, renowned art music composer and English folk song collector. Members of the first Executive Board likewise included various specialists—by far, not all of them researchers—each from a different country. While referring to legacies of the previous editors, the new editor of the *Yearbook of the IFMC*, Bruno Nettl, noted their determination to "present scholarship of the highest quality and to exhibit samples of what was emanating from research carried on in all parts of the world" and that "[s]cholars from the many nations and cultures of the world do not always think, study, and write in the same style, and the editor of an international publication must tread the thin line between rigid standardization and chaotic diversity" (Nettl, 1974: 7). He intended to broaden the coverage of research to those parts of the world that had not been represented in the *Yearbook* and its predecessor the *Journal of IFMC* thus far.

A particularly important shift was the change of the name of the Council after more than three decades of its existence, strongly argued within a heated discussion by the new Secretary General Dieter Christensen at the 26th World Conference in Seoul, Republic of Korea, in 1981. Erich Stockmann recalls the consequences of this change: "It worked like magic and opened up doors in regions where the word 'folk music' had a somewhat pejorative ring" (Stockmann, 1988: 8).[22] The immediate result was new members in countries on all continents (see also H. M., 1983: 3).

The current official presentation of ICTM ends up with the sentence significant for this Introduction: "By means of its wide international representation and the activities of its Study Groups, the International Council for Traditional Music acts as a bond among peoples of different cultures and thus serves the peace of humankind." The year 1947 marked the start of both the Council and the Cold War period. Until the end of the Cold War in 1991, ICTM was actively involved in crossing the political, administrative, economic, lingual, cultural, and other boundaries set by the two military alliances, while also including in its framework those countries that proclaimed themselves "neutral" and "nonaligned." The Council authorities, including the Presidents, were from any of these politically delineated territories, and the World Conferences, Study Group Symposia, and Colloquia were intentionally taking place in all four of them (NATO, the Warsaw Pact, Neutral, Nonaligned).

Let me document this practice with two extraordinary examples.[23] The first of them takes us to a symposium on Traditional Music in Asian Countries, organized as a joint venture with the International Music Council in 1983. The symposium took place in Pyongyang, DPR Korea, and was attended by scholars from Afghanistan, China, India, Indonesia, Japan, DPR Korea, Mongolia, Pakistan, Papua New Guinea, the Philippines, the USSR, and PR Yemen. The second example refers to the 28th World Conference, hosted jointly by Stockholm (Sweden) and Helsinki (Finland). Its closing ceremony took place on the other side of the Iron Curtain, in Leningrad (USSR; today's St. Petersburg in Russia). The older members of the Council are aware of this legacy and for a good reason proud of it.

Out of the total of 44 World Conferences, 18 took place outside Europe: two in Africa (Ghana, South Africa), seven in Asia (Israel, Republic of Korea, Hong Kong, Japan, twice in China, Kazakhstan), five in North America (three in the US, two in Canada), one in Central America (Jamaica), two in South America (Brazil), and one in Australia. Of those taking place in Europe, four took place in the countries on the Eastern side of the Iron Curtain (Romania, Czechoslovakia, Hungary, German Democratic Republic), one in the nonaligned Yugoslavia, and six in the neutral countries Switzerland, Austria (three times), Finland and Sweden (jointly), and Ireland. The sites of smaller-size IFMC/ICTM gatherings, such as the Colloquia, Symposia of the Study Groups, and from 2015 on also Fora, point to the inclusion of many more countries from the world's political spectrum (e.g., Cuba, Oman, Vietnam). Serving as a communicational channel across any boundaries continues to be the conscious strategy of the Council, which justifies the view that the Council itself is a project in applied ethnomusicology. The ongoing enlargement of the ICTM World Network is a part of the same frame of thought.

THE INTERNATIONAL COUNCIL FOR TRADITIONAL MUSIC AND APPLIED ETHNOMUSICOLOGY

Despite its international aspirations, IFMC was for a long time considered a primarily European association. Europe was the place of its foundation and residence, and Europe was home to most of its members, conferences,[24] and publications[25]—even "folk music" in its name was largely seen as a European marker. As suggested earlier, the name change from "folk" (IFMC) to "traditional" (ICTM) broadened the acceptability of the Council worldwide in the 1980s. The current frame of interests within the ICTM clearly exceeds "traditional" music, but the name of the Council remains the same, for better or worse.[26]

Search for the first mention of applied ethnomusicology in any ICTM context led to the 27th World Conference in 1983 in New York, where Ghanaian ethnomusicologist Daniel Avorgbedor presented a paper titled "The Effects of Rural-Urban Migration on a Village Musical Culture: Some Implications for Applied Ethnomusicology."[27] The next instance took place six years later, at the 30th World Conference in 1989 in Schladming (Austria), where German ethnomusicologist Artur Simon presented his paper "The Borneo Music Documentation Project (Northern Nigeria). Aspects of Documentation, Field Research in Africa, and Applied Ethnomusicology."

The author of the first mention of applied ethnomusicology in the *Bulletin of the ICTM* was John Baily. In his report on the UK National Committee, he included the following, published in April 1988:

> Members of ICTM UK have a particular interest in music in the multi- (or inter-) cultural school curriculum, and we have established a sub-committee to look into the question of teaching resources available in the UK. . . . With the same objectives we are represented on the UK Council for Music Education and Training, which is in the process of setting up a standing committee to look into the place of non-Western music in our education system. . . . Ethnomusicologists, like all other academics in contemporary Britain, have to look to their "performance indicators"; and seek to justify their existence, in part, through this form of applied ethnomusicology.

The next instances were my report on ethnomusicology in Croatia (*Bulletin of the ICTM* #90 from April 1997), in which applied ethnomusicology was related to organization of folklore festivals and amateur musical life; and Cynthia Tse Kimberlin's and Pirkko

Moisala's "In Memoriam" (*Bulletin of the ICTM* #91 from October 1997), where they indicated applied ethnomusicology as one of the areas of interests of Marcia Herndon.

The first article with applied ethnomusicology in its title published in the *Yearbook for Traditional Music* was authored by the Austrian scholar Ursula Hemetek: "Applied Ethnomusicology in the Process of the Political Recognition of a Minority: A Case Study of the Austrian Roma" (*Yearbook for Traditional Music*, vol. 38, 2006). The next major development was the special section, with a group of eight authors, on Music and Poverty, put together by the Finish/Canadian ethnomusicologist Klisala Harrison (*Yearbook for Traditional Music*, vol. 45, 2013). One should of course be aware that the lack of the wording "applied ethnomusicology" does not imply the absence of the articles relevant for the current discussion in the earlier years, with Angela Impey's 2002 essay "Culture, Conservation and Community Reconstruction: Explorations in Advocacy Ethnomusicology and Action Research in Northern KwaZulu" serving as a convincing evidence.

As far as the ICTM scholarly gatherings are concerned, the 15th Colloquium, titled *Discord: Identifying Conflict within Music, Resolving Conflict Through Music*, organized by John Morgan O'Connell in Limerick, Ireland, in 2004 can be interpreted as anticipation of what is to follow. Although music and conflict make a suitable ethnomusicological topic and applied ethnomusicology was not particularly emphasized in the colloquium documents, several presentations pointed to "ethnomusicology as an approach to conflict resolution." The articles developed from this event form the representative ethnomusicological volume on music and conflict (O'Connell and Castelo-Branco, 2010).

The 38th World Conference of the ICTM that took place in Sheffield, England, in 2005 featured applied ethnomusicology and ethnochoreology as one of the themes, pointing to "situations in which scholars put their knowledge and understanding to creative use to stimulate concern and awareness about the people they study."[28] Presenters were invited to consider issues of advocacy, canonicity, musical literacy, cultural property rights, cultural imperialism, majority-minority relations, application of technologies such as the internet and their effects on music and dance. One plenary session explicitly featured applied ethnomusicology,[29] and yet another plenary session considered it among the other subjects.[30]

A symposium titled Ethnomusicology and Ethnochoreology in Education: Issues in Applied Scholarship took place in Ljubljana, Slovenia, in 2006. The members of the ICTM's Executive Board, who came to Ljubljana for their regular annual meeting, and the other invited scholars presented and evaluated their immediate experiences and visions of the efficient transfer of scholarly knowledge into educational domains. Presentations from contexts around the globe discussed modalities of connections between theory and practice, methods of promoting, teaching, and learning of traditional music and dance, and the strategies of preparing textbooks, recordings, and other materials for various stages of educational processes (see the report by Kovačič and Šivic, 2007).

The ICTM's 39th World Conference in Vienna in 2007 featured two important events: a double panel, The Politics of Applied Ethnomusicology: New Perspectives, with six participants, each from a different continent,[31] and a meeting at which 44 members agreed to establish a study group with a focus on applied ethnomusicology.[32] Following the adoption of the definition and mission statement, the Study Group on Applied Ethnomusicology was approved at the Executive Board's meeting in Vienna on July 12, 2007.

The next year, in 2008, Ljubljana hosted the first symposium of the newly established Study Group on Applied Ethnomusicology, which was well attended by scholars from all continents. Anthony Seeger delivered the keynote address. This event featured the history of the idea and understandings of applied ethnomusicology in worldwide contexts; presentation and evaluation of individual projects, with an emphasis on theory and method; and applied ethnomusicology in situations of conflict. It is worth mentioning the use of the Native American "talking circles" as one of the means of communication within this Study Group.

The international intentions of the Study Group continued at the Symposia in Hanoi, Vietnam (2010), Nicosia, Cyprus (2012), East London—Hogsback—Grahamstown, South Africa (2014), Cape Breton, Canada (2016), and Beijing, China (2018).[33]

Thematic frames of the symposia are trustworthy indicators of the dynamics of the Study Group and, to a smaller extent, of the interests of local organizers. In Hanoi, where the joint symposium with the Study Group on Music and Minorities took place, the emphasis was on definitions and approaches to applied work in various geographical contexts; on proactive roles that ethnomusicology can play in contributing to the sustainability of performing arts through archiving, disseminating, contributing to policies, understanding socioeconomic factors, developing audiences and markets, and empowering communities to forge their own futures; and on performing arts in building peace, negotiating power relationships, and strengthening identities through formal and informal education. Note that the use of the term "performing arts" is a manner of paying respect to the perspective, which is widely shared in Southeast Asia.

The symposium in Nicosia featured applied ethnomusicology in the contexts of social activism, censorship, and state control; in relation to various types of disability, pointing to human rights and the making of disability politics and including disability research, special education, and music therapy; and in relation to diverse social configurations of conflict, including interpersonal and intergroup, interethnic, interreligious, and interclass, with emphasis on the divided island of Cyprus.

The symposium on three locations in South Africa opened up the question of institutions, usually associated with formal and informal rules, procedures, and norms, from schools and festivals to large international bodies such as UNESCO, including instituting and institutionalization issues; and the question of media and their social, political, and cultural impacts on applied work.

The symposium in Cape Breton related music to labor and exchange, opening the floor for socio-economic agendas. Intangible cultural heritage was linked to sustainable development and tourism. Pedagogical issues found their place next to research networking at the time of intensified migrations, and methodological agendas with emphasis on collaboration and criticality.

The symposium in Beijing called for the attention to power structures that affect musical practices and their carriers, to formal and informal learning, and to reflections on how we approach cultural sustainability and on the methods we use. This was a joint symposium with the new ICTM Study Group on Music, Education and Social Inclusion.

As far as the publications related to ICTM are concerned, four of them are at disposal to the readers. First, the earlier mentioned double panel that took place at the ICTM World Conference in Vienna in 2007 inspired the creation of the thematic issue of the *Muzikološki zbornik/Musicological Annual*, 46(2), entirely dedicated to applied ethnomusicology (Pettan, 2008).[34] Five ethnomusicologists reflect on their experiences linked to Brazil, Australia, the United States, Malaysia, and former Yugoslavia; the volume also serves as a Festschrift on the 80th birthday of the aforementioned Norwegian scholar Kjell Skyllstad, an important early thinker in applied ethnomusicology.

The second edited volume resulted from the inaugural Study Group's symposium in Ljubljana and is titled *Applied Ethnomusicology: Historical and Contemporary Approaches* (Harrison, Mackinlay, and Pettan, 2010). Its 13 essays, by authors from Africa, Australia, Europe, and North America, are widely used and quoted, in this volume as well, so no additional presentation is needed here.

The third is a special thematic section on Music and Poverty in the *Yearbook for Traditional Music* 45 (Harrison, 2013). Its seven articles address various aspects of this important and largely neglected problem in the diverse contexts of Brazil, Canada, Haiti, India, Nepal, and USA.

The fourth publication is the Finnish journal *COLLeGIUM*. Its volume 21 is entirely dedicated to the theme Applied Ethnomusicology in Institutional Policy and Practice (Harrison, 2016). Based on some of the best presentations from the Study Group Symposia in 2010, 2012, and 2014, the volume features case studies from Australia, China, Germany, the Seychelles, South Africa, United Kingdom, United States, and Zimbabwe.

INDIVIDUAL VIEWS

How else could ICTM contribute to better comprehension of the emerging field? By means of its wide international representation, it can provide us with the perspectives from different geographic and cultural environments. The answers to my five essential questions were provided by five ethnomusicologists, each from a different continent.[35] Some of them are more inclined to applied ethnomusicology than the others, but together, they provide a useful global myriad of perspectives about the field. I asked for anonymous, individual views, therefore they are indicated as "A view from Australia," "A view from Asia," and so on.

1. How would you define applied ethnomusicology, or at least what is its essence in your opinion?

A view from Australia: The application of ethnomusicological method and theory to addressing practical issues.

A **view from Asia:** If we define applied ethnomusicology as research activities with social conscience and political involvement, I think whatever we do as ethnomusicologists should be applied ethnomusicology at least in some ways.

A **view from South America:** I can only see a matter of degree in its definition, acknowledging an aspect, which is inherent to any research, namely its potential to be applied to different purposes. However, in most of what has been termed as such in the humanities one finds embedded ideals of social justice and equity, sometimes of reparation and/or reconciliation, all of which are also subject to different and even contradictory perspectives.

A **view from Africa:** Generally, how our practical work in the field is applied in an academic environment. Music is not taught in an European or abstract way, that is, by explaining music with words, but holistically, by doing—listening, imitating, and playing. Based on that experience we teach African music theory practically on instruments. It is much more appropriate and easier for people to understand musical concepts doing it that way.

A **view from Europe:** I do not subscribe to the term "applied ethnomusicology," although I understand why it is necessary. I think the engagement of scholars with the communities they work with should be/is a given.

2. Have you done any project(s) that would fit into your notion of applied ethnomusicology?

Australia: Preparing indigenous people's land claim is the obvious example, that is, applying knowledge of their musical culture to demonstrate rights over land using an indigenous conceptual system. I was one of three researchers (with an anthropologist and a linguist) who prepared one of the largest such claims. During the hearing of the case (by a Supreme Court judge) songs and dances were performed to demonstrate ownership of the land according to their own system of land ownership.

Asia: Following what I mentioned above, I would like to think all my projects are within the realm of applied ethnomusicology.

South America: They have ranged from short-term documentation projects related to safeguarding and revitalizing traditions perceived to be vanishing to long-term horizontal collaborations with grassroot organizations, forming research groups working on music and social justice among residents of areas affected by patterns of injustice and inequity.

Africa: We also understand applied ethnomusicology as offering of our expertise to people in order to develop a musical environment. This can be in form of workshops, teaching in schools, music projects, community outreach, and curriculum development, which takes the background of people and local needs into consideration. In our current curriculum African music components are compulsory. We just brought new streams and modules to respond to local needs; for instance the course Basic Music Literacy for students from villages who have problems with music theory and music literacy, and the streams Music Technologies and Production and Music and Arts Administration. The two streams aim at providing students with practical skills which make them more employable, and which enable them to start their own business within the music industry. We hope that these two new streams will in the future help to improve the musical infrastructure in the region.

Europe: I was involved in the application of projects to the UNESCO representative list of Intangible Cultural Heritage and served on an advisory committee to the Ministry of Culture on ICH matters. For over 20 years, I also promoted the founding of a national sound archive. Finally, I consider the publication of an encyclopedia—an all-encompassing research project with a wide outreach among musicians, cultural politicians and scholars—as "applied ethnomusicology."

3. Is the distinction between "academic" and "applied" work present in your working environment? If so, how is the "applied" domain valued compared to the "academic" one?

Australia: When I worked at the institute it was required of researchers to demonstrate the benefit of the proposed research to the community. This resulted in a blending of scholarly and applied research. Later, when I was working in the university environment, there was much more emphasis on scholarship for its own sake, and the application of research results was not highly valued.

Asia: There are theorists so to speak who are mainly concerned with the refinement of theoretical explorations. I respect such endeavors as long as they have applicable dimension. The "applied" domain has been treated unfairly as activities conducted by less qualified/serious scholars, partly because of the narrow definition of the "academic" domain, but also due to the inability on the part of "applied" ethnomusicologists to advance a new vision of theory construction.

South America: No.

Africa: A distinction between academic and applied work is still there (for instance when you have to teach different research methodologies or history of ethnomusicology), but the boundaries are quite blurred. A lot of our academic research is based on applied work and—as explained earlier—theory is thought practically (which is the direct application of knowledge obtained in the field).

Europe: I try to avoid making this distinction. But, in my institution we have many projects that can be classified as applied: museum expositions, digitization, community work, projects in schools, etc. I would say 40% applied.

4. Is the "applied" domain present in your teaching curricula?

Australia: I always tried to show the relationship between applied and theoretical ethnomusicology.

Asia: Whenever I teach I emphasize the importance of socially engaged research activities.

South America: Yes, in the obligatory bibliographies of both undergraduate and graduate courses as well as in systematic outreach and research programs.

Africa: We do not offer a degree program or specific modules on applied ethnomusicology. Yet, as already explained, indigenous music is compulsory, theory is taught practically, and articles on applied ethnomusicology are discussed in class. Thus, although not formalized in terms of specific modules, applied ethnomusicology is a reality here.

Europe: In my seminars, I discuss researchers' social responsibilities and the many spheres of ethnomusicological work. But, we do not have a course on "applied ethnomusicology."

5. Do you know of any university offering a course in applied ethnomusicology or applied ethnochoreology?

Australia: No.

Asia: There may be, but not that I know of.

South America: No, but I know several universities that offer opportunities to both graduate and undergraduate students to engage in applied research in the sense I outlined before, as well as portions of their curricular components devoted to applied approaches.

Africa: This is a tricky question. Applied approaches differ from institution to institution, and the motives and conditions are hardly comparable. Unlike other universities in the country, our Music Department had hardly any resources. We had to build up from zero, which means that applied ethnomusicology was a necessity and therefore a reality. At another university, applied ethnomusicology was simply understood as building up an African ensemble. Elsewhere, there was some teaching of indigenous instruments, but not applied ethnomusicology in our understanding. At Kwazulu Natal you find a completely different situation with Patricia Opondo, who is a very focused and an internationally trained academic. Applied ethnomusicology is officially part of the curriculum.

Europe: No.

What can we make of the replies of these five ethnomusicologists? All of them are well established as professionals and work in either university or research institute settings. Their representativeness is balanced in terms of geography and gender, as well, but none of them belongs to a young generation of scholars, which is seeking for more radical solutions, such as active involvement in applied projects as a part of the study curricula. At this point I would like to add that a course in applied ethnomusicology, which counts to the obligatory master level courses, exists since 2012 at the Department of Musicology of the University of Ljubljana.

The International Council for Traditional Music and the Society for Ethnomusicology

In contrast to the eight years younger Society for Ethnomusicology (SEM), which is defined as "a U.S.-based organization with an international membership" (www.ethnomusicology.org), IFMC/ICTM was envisioned in international terms in all respects. Its Secretariat moves its base periodically from one country to another; it has so far been based in the United Kingdom, Denmark, Canada, the United States, Australia, and Slovenia. Both past and current membership figures suggest that SEM, which is the US National Committee of ICTM, is larger than ICTM, but also that the single country with the largest number of members in ICTM is the United States. The two societies have distinctive intellectual histories and the resulting theoretical and methodological paradigms. In words of Dieter Christensen,

> SEM and ICTM are both unique in their roles, and they complement each other; SEM as the regional organization in North America that represents the interests of professional, academic ethnomusicologists in the USA and Canada, and at the same time serves the field of ethnomusicology world-wide through its publications; and the ICTM as the international organization in the domain of traditional music including ethnomusicology that serves scholarship with an emphasis on the mutual recognition and understanding of diverse inquiring minds.
>
> (Christensen, 1988: 17).

IFMC/ICTM cherished various languages in its scholarly publications until 1985, when the last article so far in a language other than English was published in the *Yearbook for Traditional Music*. From 2006 on, the *Yearbook*'s general editor Don Niles reintroduced the practice of adding abstracts in native languages of those people who are the principal subjects of the articles. This practice was originally introduced in the 1980s, following Yoshihiko Tokumaru's proposal.

Jeff Todd Titon has described in Section 1 of this Introduction how the four founders of SEM, led by Alan P. Merriam, rejected Maud Karpeles's invitation to join IFMC and instead decided to keep SEM as an independent society. IFMC reported about the new society in the following manner in its 11th *Bulletin* from 1957: "On November 18th, 1955, at the 54th Annual Meeting of the American Anthropological Association in Boston, the Society for Ethnomusicology was founded for the purpose of establishing communication among persons in primitive, folk, and oriental music, and for furthering research and scholarship in these fields. The Society plans to continue publication of the Ethno-Musicology Newsletter three times yearly, to meet annually in conjunction with societies of anthropologists, folklorists and musicologists, and to engage in other activities of benefit to members" (Anon., 1957: 6).

According to Erich Stockmann, one of the Presidents of the Council, Maud Karpeles was sensitive to occasional criticisms and used to ask him anxiously several times in the course of the 1950s: "Are we really not 'scientific' enough? She knew my answer" (Stockmann, 1988: 5). Dieter Christensen, Secretary General of the Council for 20 years, noted that the "American issue" and the "scientific issue" were clearly related (Christensen, 1988: 14).

There are several important connections between the two societies that should be mentioned here. At the inauguration of IFMC in 1947, seven US "correspondents" were identified, among them Curt Sachs, Percy Grainger, and Alan Lomax. The "Liaison officer" (single national representative) of the United States in the IFMC for 10 years (1952–1962) was Charles Seeger, one of the SEM's founding fathers. Following Seeger's mandate, the United States was uninterruptedly represented in the IFMC/ICTM by the "National Committee" until 1999, starting with Charles Haywood and ending with Ricardo Trimillos. After a five-year break, Timothy Rice, then the SEM President, re-established the connection and SEM became officially recognized as the ICTM's US National Committee.

The first SEM President, Willard Rhodes, later became ICTM's fourth President, while councilor in the first SEM nomenclature Bruno Nettl later served in a variety of roles in both societies, as did (and still do) many other scholars, from the United States and from the other countries.

It is appropriate to complete this section of the Introduction by pointing to a joint Forum, that took place in September 2015 in Limerick, bringing together the two major ethnomusicological associations—ICTM and SEM—around the theme of importance for applied ethnomusicology: Transforming Ethnomusicological Praxis through Activism and Community Engagement. This historical event, the first such collaboration between ICTM and SEM, was co-chaired by the SEM President Beverley Diamond and the ICTM President Salwa El-Shawan Castelo-Branco.

> The Forum will focus on ethnomusicological praxis and collaborative strategies in different international contexts and political situations. While there is now a long history in ethnomusicology of initiatives that have sought to address problems of inequality, disparity and oppression, and a shorter history pertaining to such matters as health and environmental change, the symposium will focus, not on the problems per se, but on the methodologies that could best enable our work to have greater social impact. We are interested in critically assessing and finding strategies and best practices of collaboration, communication and policy formulation.
>
> (from the Call for papers)

This joint event convincingly testifies about the current intellectual climate in both major associations of ethnomusicologists, which is very much in tune with the ideas presented in the *Handbook*.

Notes

1. Controversy over the genre of exploitation documentary, so-called *mondo films* such as this one, suggesting that the genuine documentary footage is sometimes mixed with staged sequences, does not impact the film's symbolic standpoint.

2. The practitioners are scholars whose professional positioning may vary from universities and other schools, research institutes, archives, museums, media, and nongovernmental organizations, to freelance status.

3. Applied ethnomusicology is about how musical practice can inform relevant theory, and about how theory can inform musical practice. Knowledge of data, theories, and methods of ethnomusicology, as much as ethical concerns, are essential.

4. There is a need for increased critical reflection on political agendas, moral philosophies, and ideologies of applied ethnomusicology projects, as well as on the role of personal agency in applied ethnomusicological work.

5. Here she refers to the American Musicological Society.

6. For instance, the Society for Applied Spectroscopy, founded in 1958, has more than 2,000 members worldwide.

7. The aim of the Society for Applied Microbiology is to advance for the benefit of the public the science of microbiology in its application to the environment, human and animal health, agriculture and industry. The aim of the Society for Applied Philosophy is to promote philosophical study and research that has a direct bearing on areas of practical concern, such as law, politics, economics, science, technology, medicine, and education.

8. Timothy Rice's book *Ethnomusicology: A Very Short Introduction*, to the opposite, ends with the chapter titled "Public Service" and points to the fact that "[e]thnomusicologists are increasingly asking themselves the question 'Ethnomusicology for what purpose?'" (2014: 120). It is my hope that this *Handbook* will encourage ethnomusicologists to seek answers to this question, both inside themselves and in the world that surrounds them.

9. The other being Berlin.

10. For some useful current views on comparative musicology, see Schneider (2006), thematic issue of the Polish journal *Muzyka* 1 (2009), and the website http://www.compmus. org.

11. By scholars such as Naila Ceribašić, Marija Dumnić, Adriana Helbig, Ana Hofman, Jelena Jovanović, Ivona Opetčeska-Tatarčevska, Selena Rakočević, Velika Stojkova Serafimovska, Jasmina Talam, Ljerka Vidić Rasmussen and Dave Wilson.

12. In case of Sachs, the German version titled *Die Musik der Alten Welt in Ost und West* (1968) served as the source for translation.

13. The translator Ljerka Vidić Rasmussen used to study there under the mentorship of Blacking's former doctoral student Ankica Petrović. Petrović was widely regarded the first representative of "mainstream ethnomusicology" in what was Yugoslavia. Introduction of new disciplinary paradigms met many obstacles in the intellectual environment rooted in the strong folk music research school established by Cvjetko Rihtman.

14. This section uses parts of one of my earlier articles (Pettan, 2008) and provides updates.

15. For instance, Dan Lundberg, Owe Ronström.

16. The proceedings contain articles by Kristof Tamas, Max Peter Baumann, Mark Slobin, and Krister Malm.

17. This seminar took place just a month prior to the conference *Invested in Community: Ethnomusicology and Musical Advocacy*, which took place at Brown University in Providence, Rhode Island, featuring "applied ethnomusicologists (who)

work as musical and cultural advocates, using skills and knowledge gained within academia to serve the public at large. They help communities identify, document, preserve, develop, present and celebrate the musical traditions they hold dear."

18. This does not count for their institutional colleagues, who continued to supply the arrangements for musicians and choreographies for the dancers in folklore ensembles.

19. The Ukrainian/Soviet folk music researcher Kliment Kvitka (1880–1953) proposed and described the term as early as 1928 (see Lukanyuk, 2006). Interestingly, the second, enlarged edition of Kunst's book was published in 1955 under the auspices of IFMC.

20. See Chapter 2 by Harrison, calling for a reconsideration of this issue.

21. The third objective clearly referred to "recognition of the painful fact that the Second World War had created deep rifts between nations and peoples" (Stockmann, 1988: 2).

22. Paul Rovsing Olsen, the Council's President at that time, provided the following comment: ". . . we hope to have found a name which, much better than the original one, explains what our Council stands for in the world of scholarship—and in the world of ·international organizations. The IFMC has been concerned, from its beginnings, with all kinds of traditional music, not only with 'folk music'. This has not always been understood by outsiders" (Rovsing Olsen, 1981: 2).

23. Don Niles and Krister Malm respectfully shared the details of these events with me.

24. The first IFMC conference took place in Basel, Switzerland, in 1948.

25. The first issue of the *Journal of the International Folk Music Council* (predecessor of the *Yearbook of the International Folk Music Council* from 1969 and of the *Yearbook of the International Council for Traditional Music* from 1981) was published in 1949. The other publication was the *Bulletin of the International Folk Music Council*, starting in 1948.

26. In the forthcoming part of this section I gratefully acknowledge the assistance of ICTM's Executive Assistant Carlos Yoder.

27. A later version was published in 1992 in the journal *African Music*.

28. Applied ethnomusicology (and ethnochoreology) became one of the conference themes 22 years after Avorgbedor first mentioned it in his ICTM conference paper.

29. *Applied Ethnomusicology and Studies on Music and Minorities—The Convergence of Theory and Practice* with Ursula Hemetek, John O'Connell, Adelaida Reyes, and Stephen Wild.

30. Including war and revitalization in Croatia of the 1990s and early 2000s. The session was organized by Naila Ceribašić.

31. Organized by Samuel Araújo (South America) and me (Europe); the other panelists were Maureen Loughran (North America), Jennifer Newsome (Australia), Patricia Opondo (Africa), and Tan Sooi Beng (Asia).

32. I initiated the Study Group and became its first Chair; Klisala Harrison became Vice-Chair, and Eric Martin Usner became Secretary. As I became Secretary General of ICTM in 2011, Klisala Harrison assumed the duties of the Study Group's Chair, Samuel Araújo became Vice-Chair, and Britta Sweers became Secretary. In 2019, Huib Schippers serves as Chair, Adriana Helbig as Vice-Chair, and Weiya Lin as Secretary.

33. The Symposia were hosted by Svanibor Pettan, Le Van Toan, Panicos Giorgoudes, Bernhard Bleibinger, Marcia Ostashewski, and Zhang Boyu, respectively.

34. Scholarly journal, published by the Department of Musicology of the University of Ljubljana. It is available at (http://revije.ff.uni-lj.si/MuzikoloskiZbornik/issue/archive).

35. Section 1 of the Introduction, by co-editor Jeff Todd Titon, covers North America, so I did not include it here.

SECTION 3

··

AN INTRODUCTION TO
THE CHAPTERS

··

JEFF TODD TITON AND SVANIBOR PETTAN

In the Introduction we have identified several activities of contemporary applied ethnomusicologists. The chapters in this volume illustrate a range of these. Cultural policy interventions are discussed by Haskell as she reviews the role of government agencies, NGOs, and the arts in Bosnia-Herzegovina. Her Chapter 6 concerns cultural policies in relation to the arts when communities recover from conflicts and natural disasters. In their wake, cultural aid workers bear much needed resources for music and other expressive cultural activities as they facilitate conflict resolution and cultural development. In addition, two of the authors discuss cultural policy interventions through UNESCO's initiatives in safeguarding intangible cultural heritage; these include Schippers (Chapter 4, Australia), and Titon (Chapter 5, chiefly theoretical). The mixed record of success is leading applied ethnomusicologists to agree that the best outcomes occur in small-scale projects resulting from long-term partnerships and mutual goals. Local and regional cultural differences require that policies adapt to varying conditions. Top-down, bureaucratic solutions are apt to be less successful and more likely to have negative consequences. Such best practices have characterized most, if not all, successful applied ethnomusicology projects, whether cultural policy interventions or not.

Education is a concern of many of the contributors. Sweers, in Chapter 8, points to the importance of intercultural education, and to the efficiency of the didactic teaching aid against right-wing extremism, which raised the attention of local teaching institutions, political institutions, and even the parliament, to her activist project *Polyphonie der Kulturen*. Pilzer (Chapter 7) also recognizes the activist aspect of education. For Schippers (Chapter 4), the educational realm is identified as one of five clusters in his ecosystems of music model. Harrison (Chapter 2) recognizes teaching as one of her four principal ethnomusicological activities. Tan (Chapter 3) realizes the importance of non-formal education in Asia in addressing the issues, such as conflict resolution, peace building, gender sensitization, raising awareness about social inequality, heritage conservation, health campaigns such as AIDS prevention, and more.

Peace, conflict resolution, and cooperation among peoples is another area that appeals to many of the contributors. Haskell's Chapter 6, centered in Bosnia-Herzegovina in the recent postwar period, offers lessons from resilience efforts in the face of conflicts and disasters, where international development prioritizes socioeconomic and political issues while neglecting cultural landscapes. Important aspects of conflict management are imbedded in the studies provided by Harrison (class conflict and conflict of values) and Sweers (conflicts caused by xenophobia and right-wing extremism on the one hand and a marginalization of the victims on the other) in Chapters 2 and 8, respectively.

Medical ethnomusicology, in which ethnomusicologists ally themselves with health-related therapeutic interventions, has a separate *Handbook* in the Oxford series, which readers are advised to consult. The name is a formation derived from the subfield of medical anthropology, considered a branch of applied anthropology. Given its established identity and a growing literature of its own, the editors have not emphasized it in this volume; nevertheless, Pilzer's work with survivors (Chapter 7), which inspires us to go beyond the specific case of Japanese military "comfort women" system in Korea and engage in work with survivors of wars, domestic violence, child abuse, and sexual violence, is an example.

What should be the approaches in applied ethnomusicology to the pertinent issues rooted in colonial history and attitudes? Contributors such as Bendrups (Chapter 1), Harrison (Chapter 2), Tan (Chapter 3), and Pilzer (Chapter 7), remind us in various ways, to various extents, and in various contexts that work under postcolonial circumstances still requires immense sensitivity from the researcher. Pilzer's argumentation refers to the period of Japanese colonialism in Korea (1910–1945), which more than half a century later still leaves some wounds open. Tan points to the consequences of the presence of British rulers in Malaysia in the not so distant past, while Bendrups exercises a critical approach to neocolonial attitudes of Chile toward its "dislocated property" Rapanui. Harrison's work with indigenous peoples also fits in here and forms one of the useful contexts for her proposed model for studying value systems, reconsideration of the value judgments, and an envisioned ethnomusicology of values.

Nationalism is yet another phenomenon that applied ethnomusicologists have to consider. Tan, in Chapter 3, is convincing in her critique of the concept of national culture in Malaysia. The second smallest continent, Europe figures as the second continent according to the number of nation-states, and remains the location of the most devastating wars in human history. Ever increasing migrations from other continents create new challenges to which applied ethnomusicology, as demonstrated by Sweers (Chapter 8), has some efficient replies.

A short-term, temporary form of migration, tourism, has offered a major opportunity and challenge for applied ethnomusicologists. Many have been employed as consultants and culture workers in bringing traditional music to an audience extrinsic to the musical community, as music plays an important role in cultural tourism, which many think can be a driver of local and regional economies while it also sustains older layers of music that are in danger of losing, or have lost, their original cultural contexts. Musical tourism is thought also to constitute a creative economy, but here the applied ethnomusicologist has played the role of critic as well as consultant and advocate (Titon, Chapter 5).

Tourism often has followed UNESCO's safeguarding initiatives, which single out particular musical communities for preservation efforts. But ethnomusicological knowledge is sometimes at odds with the kinds of publicity that attracts tourists, while it may also be incomplete and unreliable, as occurred when the Chinese *guqin* tradition was designated as a masterpiece of intangible cultural heritage (Yung, 2005).

Finally, sustainability is a theme that unites most of the chapters in this volume. Musical, and sometimes also cultural, sustainability is a goal of many arts policy initiatives today (see, e.g., Haskell, Chapter 6). It is often one of the ends of advocacy, and has long been one of the chief reasons for music education. For example, advocacy based on cultural equity and musical rights moves toward sustainability and a kind of musical justice as well as social justice. Schippers's Chapter 4 is far-reaching in this respect, laying out a model for sustainability strategies. Global implications of these strategies were tested within the framework of a mega-project, *Sustainable Futures for Music Cultures: Towards an Ecology of Musical Diversity*, encompassing the range from Australian Aboriginal music to Western classical opera. Titon's Chapter 5 builds on his pioneering work in music and ecology, which he began by asserting that music cultures are ecological systems; that is, as the flow of energy keeps ecosystems functioning, so the flow of music keeps music cultures functioning (Titon, 1984: 9). In Chapter 5 of this volume, Titon discusses sustainability both in terms of its forerunner ideas (preservation, conservation, and safeguarding, with particular attention to their implementation in the US) and by re-examining the uses of sustainability in the two discourse universes where it is most prominent: environmentalist conservation ecology, and economics (Titon, 2009a, 2009b). Pointing out that sustainability is a goal rather than a strategy, he concludes by proposing resilience theory as the appropriate strategy for achieving musical sustainability, and offers two case studies that examine those characteristics which make particular music cultures resilient and therefore sustainable. Sustainability is a recent concept for ethnomusicologists, while resilience is even newer. Their widespread use (and abuse) today requires that applications in various fields of endeavor be undertaken with great care, while values from the humanities provide an appropriate context for thinking about sustainability and resilience in all contexts.

References

Angrosino, Michael V. (1990). *The Essentials of Anthropology*. Piscataway, NJ: Research and Educational Association.

Anon. (1957). "Society for Ethnomusicology." *Bulletin of the IFMC* 11: 6.

Araújo, Samuel. (2008). "From Neutrality to Praxis: The Shifting Politics of Ethnomusicology in the Contemporary World." *Muzikološki Zbornik/Musicological Annual* 44(1): 13–30.

Araújo, Samuel. (2009). "Ethnomusicologists Researching Towns They Live in: Theoretical and Methodological Queries for a Renewed Discipline." *Muzikologija* 9: 33–50.

Araújo, Samuel. (2010). "Sound Praxis: Music, Politics, and Violence in Brazil." In *Music and Conflict*, edited by John Morgan O'Connell and Salwa El-Shawan Castelo Branco, pp. 217–231. Urbana-Champaign: University of Illinois Press.

Araújo, Samuel, and members of the Grupo Musicultura. (2006). "Conflict and Violence as Theoretical Tools in Present-Day Ethnomusicology: Notes on a Dialogic Ethnography of Sound Practices in Rio de Janeiro." *Ethnomusicology* 50(2): 287–313.

Avorgbedor, Daniel. (1992). "The Impact of Rural-Urban Migration on a Village Music Culture: Some Implications for Applied Ethnomusicology." *African Music* 7(2): 45–57.

Banks, James A., and Cherry A. McGee Banks. (2001). *Multicultural Education: Issues & Perspectives*. New York: John Willey & Sons.

Barz, Gregory F., and Timothy J. Cooley, eds. (1996). *Shadows in the Field: New Perspectives for Fieldwork in Ethnomusicology*. New York: Oxford University Press.

Baumann, Max Peter, ed. (1991). *Music in the Dialogue of Cultures. Traditional Music and Cultural Policy*. Wilhelmshaven: Florian Noetzel Verlag.

Berliner, Paul. (1978). *The Soul of Mbira*. Chicago: University of Chicago Press.

Berger, Harris M. (2014). "New Directions for Ethnomusicological Research into the Politics of Music and Culture: Issues, Projects, and Programs." *Ethnomusicology* 58(2): 315–320.

Blacking, John. (1973). *How Musical Is Man?* Seattle: University of Washington Press.

Bleibinger, Bernhard. (2010). "Solving Conflicts: Applied Ethnomusicology at the Music Department of the University of Fort Hare, South Africa, and in the Context of IMOHP." In *Applied Ethnomusicology: Historical and Contemporary Approaches*, edited by Klisala Harrison, Elizabeth Mackinlay, and Svanibor Pettan, pp. 36–50. Newcastle upon Tyne, UK: Cambridge Scholars Publishing.

Bleking, Džon. (1992). *Pojam muzikalnosti*. Beograd: Nolit.

Boas, Franz. (1888). "On Certain Songs and Dances of the Kwakiutl of British Columbia." *Journal of American Folklore* 1(1): 49–64.

Bohlman, Philip V. (1996). *Central European Folk Music*. New York: Garland.

Bohlman, Philip V. (1988). "Traditional Music and Cultural Identity: Persistent Paradigm in the History of Ethnomusicology." *Yearbook for Traditional Music* 20: 26–42.

Bohlman, Philip V. (2004). *The Music of European Nationalism: Cultural Identity and Modern History*. Santa Barbara, CA: ABC-CLIO.

Bohlman, Philip V. (2011). *Focus: Music, Nationalism, and the Making of the New Europe*. New York: Routledge.

Boiko, Martin. (1994). "Latvian Ethnomusicology: Past and Present." *Yearbook for Traditional Music* 26: 47–65.

Bose, Fritz. (1953). *Musikalische Völkerkunde*. Freiburg in Breislau: Atlantis.

Bose, Fritz. (1975). *Etnomuzikologija*. Belgrade: Univerzitet umetnosti u Beogradu.

Brinner, Benjamin. (2009). *Playing across a Divide: Israeli-Palestinian Musical Encounters*. Oxford: Oxford University Press.

Castelo-Branco, Salwa El-Shawan, ed. (2010). *Enciclopédia da Música em Portugal no Século XX*. Lisbon: Círculo de Leitores/Campo das LEtras.

Ceribašić, Naila. (2004). "Double Standards: Negotiating the Place for Ethnomusicologists in Croatia." Conference paper.

Christensen, Dieter. (1988). "The International Folk Music Council and the Americans: On the Effects of Stereotypes on the Institutionalization of Ethnomusicology." *Yearbook for Traditional Music* 20: 11–18.

Clausen, Bernd, Ursula Hemetek, Eva Saether, eds. (2009). *Music in Motion: Diversity and Dialogue in Europe*. New Brunswick, NJ, and London: Transaction Publishers.

Climati, Antonio, and Mario Morra. (1975). *Ultime grida dalla savanna* (film). Rome: Titanus.

Cohen, Ronald D., ed. (2010). *Alan Lomax, Assistant in Charge: The Library of Congress Letters, 1935–1945*. Jackson, MS: University of Mississippi Press.

Diamond, Beverley, and Salwa El Shawan Castelo-Branco, eds. (forthcoming). *Transforming Ethnomusicology*. New York, NY: Oxford University Press.

Dirksen, Rebecca. (2012). "Reconsidering Theory and Practice in Ethnomusicology: Applying, Advocating and Engaging Beyond Academia." *Ethnomusicology Review* 17. http:// ethnomusicologyreview.ucla.edu/journal/volume/17/piece/602 (accessed July 1, 2014).

Ellis, Catherine. (1985). *Aboriginal Music: Education for Living. Cross-cultural Experiences from South Australia*. St. Lucia: University of Queensland Press.

Elschek, Oskar. (1991). "Ideas, Principles, Motivations, and Results in Eastern European Folk-Music Research." In *Comparative Musicology and Anthropology of Music*. edited by Bruno Nettl and Philip V. Bohlman, pp. 91–111. Chicago: University of Chicago Press.

Fenn, John, ed. (2003). *Folklore Forum (Special issue on applied ethnomusicology)* 34(1–2): 119–131.

Fetter, C. V. (2001). *Applied Hydrogeology*. Upper Saddle River, NJ: Prentice Hall.

Fletcher, Alice C., with the assistance of Frances La Flesche. (1994 [1893]). *A Study of Omaha Indian Music*. Lincoln, NE: Bison Books.

Freire, Paulo. (1970). *Pedagogy of the Oppressed*. New York: Herder and Herder.

Grant, Catherine. (2014). *Music Endangerment: How Language Maintenance Can Help*. Oxford: Oxford University Press.

Giuriati, Giovanni. (1995). "Italian Ethnomusicology." *Yearbook for Traditional Music* 27: 104–131.

Gourlay, Kenneth. (1982). "Towards a Humanizing Ethnomusicology." *Ethnomusicology* 26(3): 411–420.

H. M. (Hahn, Man-young). (1983). "Preface." *Yearbook for Traditional Music* 15: 3.

Harrison, Klisala. (2012). "Epistemologies of Applied Ethnomusicology." *Ethnomusicology* 56(3): 505–529.

Harrison, Klisala. ed. (2013a). Music and Poverty (Special Section). *Yearbook for Traditional Music* 45: 1–96.

Harrison, Klisala. (2013b). "Music, Health, and Socio-Economic Status: A Perspective on Urban Poverty in Canada." *Yearbook for Traditional Music* 45: 58–73.

Harrison, Klisala. (2016a). "*Applied Ethnomusicology in Institutional Policy and Practice* (Thematic volume)." COLLeGIUM 21.

Harrison, Klisala. (2016b). "Why Applied Ethnomusicology?" COLLeGIUM 21: 1–17. https:// helda.helsinki.fi/bitstream/handle/10138/167843/Collegium%20Vol%2021%20Introduction. pdf?sequence=1.

Harrison, Klisala, Elizabeth Mackinlay, and Svanibor Pettan, eds. (2010). *Applied Ethnomusicology: Historical and Contemporary Approaches*. Newcastle upon Tyne, UK: Cambridge Scholars Publishing.

Hawes, Bess Lomax. (1995). "Reminiscences and Exhortations: Growing Up in American Folk Music." *Ethnomusicology* 39(2): 179–192.

Haydon, Glen. (1941). *Introduction to Musicology*. New York: Prentice-Hall.

Hemetek, Ursula, ed. (1996). *Echo der Vielfalt/Echoes of Diversity. Traditionelle Musik von Minderheiten—ethnischen Gruppen/Traditional Music of Ethnic Groups—Minorities*. Wien: Böhlau Verlag.

Hemetek, Ursula. (2006). "Applied Ethnomusicology in the Process of the Political Recognition of a Minority: A Case Study of the Austrian Roma." *Yearbook for Traditional Music* 38: 35–57.

Hemetek, Ursula. (2009). "The Past and the Present: Ethnomusicology in Vienna. Some Considerations." *Muzyka* 1(212): 57–68.

Herzog, George. (1936). "Primitive Music." *Bulletin of the American Musicological Society* 1: 2–3.

Hofman, Ana. (2010). "Maintaining the Distance, Othering the Subaltern: Rethinking Ethnomusicologists' Engagement in Advocacy and Social Justice." In *Applied Ethnomusicology: Historical and Contemporary Approaches*, edited by Klisala Harrison, Elizabeth Mackinlay, and Svanibor Pettan, pp. 22–35. Newcastle upon Tyne, UK: Cambridge Scholars Publishing.

Hood, Mantle. (1971). *The Ethnomusicologist*. New York: McGraw-Hill.

Impey, Angela. (2002). "Culture, Conservation and Community Reconstruction: Explorations in Advocacy Ethnomusicology and Action Research in Northern KwaZulu." *Yearbook for Traditional Music* 34: 9–24.

Invested in Community: Ethnomusicology and Musical Advocacy. (2003). Conference on Applied Ethnomusicology, Brown University, March 8–9. Videotapes of presentations by applied ethnomusicologists and community scholars from Europe, the United States, and Native North America may be viewed at http://library.brown.edu/cds/invested_in_community/.

Jordan, Judith V. (2001). "A Relational-Cultural Model: Healing Through Mutual Empathy." *Bulletin of the Menninger Clinic* 65: 92–103.

Juvančič, Katarina. (2010). "Singing from the Dark: Applied Ethnomusicology and the Study of Lullabies." In *Applied Ethnomusicology: Historical and Contemporary Approaches*, edited by Klisala Harrison, Elizabeth Mackinlay, and Svanibor Pettan, pp. 116–132. Newcastle upon Tyne, UK: Cambridge Scholars Publishing.

Karpeles, Maud. (1971). "The International Folk Music Council: Twenty-One Years." *Yearbook of the International Folk Music Council* 1: 14–32.

Keil, Charles. (1979). *Tiv Song*. Chicago: University of Chicago Press.

Keil, Charles. (1982). "Applied Ethnomusicology and a Rebirth of Music from the Spirit of Tragedy." *Ethnomusicology* 26(3): 407–411.

Keil, Charles. (1998). "Applied Sociomusicology and Performance Studies." *Ethnomusicology* 42(2): 303–312.

Kerman, Joseph. (1986). *Contemplating Music: Challenges to Musicology*. Cambridge, MA: Harvard University Press.

Kirshenblatt-Gimblett, Barbara. (1988). "Mistaken Dichotomies." *Journal of American Folklore* 101(400): 140–155.

Koch, Grace. (2013). *We Have the Song, So We Have the Land: Song and Ceremony as Proof of Ownership in Aboriginal and Torres Strait Islander Land Claims*. Canberra: Australian Institute of Aboriginal and Torres Strait Islander Studies, Research Discussion Paper No. 33.

Korpe, Maria, and Ole Reitov, eds. (1998). *1st World Conference on Music and Censorship*. Copenhagen: Freemuse.

Koudal, Jens Henrik, et al. (1993). "[Three articles by different authors (Koudal, Torp and Giurchescu, Hauser) on selected ethnomusicological issues in Denmark]." *Yearbook for Traditional Music* 25: 100–147.

Kovačič, Mojca, and Urša Šivic. (2007). "Ethnomusicology and Ethnochoreology in Education: Issues in Applied Scholarship, Ljubljana, September 21–25, 2006." *Bulletin of the International Council for Traditional Music* 110 (April): 67–69.

Kunst, Jaap. (1950). *Musicologica: A Study of the Nature of Ethno-musicology, Its Problems, Methods, and Representative Personalities*. The Hague: Martinus Nijhoff.

LeGuin, Elisabeth. (2012). "Applied Ethnomusicology and Musicology." *Ethnomusicology Review* 17. http://ethnomusicologyreview.ucla.edu/journal/volume/17/piece/599.

Leydi, Roberto. (1991). *L'altra musica*. Giunti: Ricordi.

Leydi, Roberto. (1995). *Druga godba: Etnomuzikologija*. Ljubljana: Studia Humanitatis.

Ling, Jan. (1999). *A History of European Folk Music*. Rochester, NY: University of Rochester Press.

Lomax, Alan. (1972). "Appeal for Cultural Equity." *the world of music* 14(2): 3–17.

Loughran, Maureen. (2008). "But what if they call the police—Applied Ethnomusicology and Urban Activism in the United States." *Muzikološki Zbornik/Musicological Annual* 44(1): 51–67.

Lukanyuk, Bohdan. (2006). "Do Istorii termina etnomuzikologija" (On the History of the Term Ethnomusicology). *Visnyk Lviv Univ.* 37: 257–275.

Malm, Krister, et al. (1995). *Aspects on Music and Multiculturalism*. Stockholm: The Royal Swedish Academy of Music.

Marošević, Grozdana. (1998). "The Encounter Between Folklore Studies and Anthropology in Croatian Ethnomusicology." *the world of music* 40(3): 51–82.

Marti, Josep. (1997). "Folk Music Studies and Ethnomusicology in Spain." *Yearbook for Traditional Music* 29: 107–140.

Matthews, Washington. (1888). "The Prayer of a Navajo Shaman." *American Anthropologist*, 1(2): 148–171.

McAllester, David. (1989). Unpublished videotape of seminar at Brown University, transcribed by Lisa Lawson. Accessible from the author, and from the American Folklife Center, Archive of Folk Culture, Library of Congress, Washington, DC.

McLean, Mervyn. (2006). *Pioneers of Ethnomusicology*. Mamaroneck, NY: Aeon Books.

Merriam, Alan. (1963a). Review of Henry Weman, "African Music and the Church in Africa." *Ethnomusicology* 7(2): 135.

Merriam, Alan. (1963b). "Purposes of Ethnomusicology: An Anthropological View." *Ethnomusicology* 7(3): 207.

Merriam, Alan. (1964). *The Anthropology of Music*. Evanston, IL: Northwestern University Press.

Merriam, Alan. (1977). "Definitions of 'Comparative Musicology' and 'Ethnomusicology': An Historical-Theoretical Perspective." *Ethnomusicology* 21(2): 189–204.

Merriam, Alan. (2000). *Antropologija glasbe*. Ljubljana: Znanstveno in publicistično središče.

Moisala, Pirkko, ed. (1994). "Ethnomusicology in Finland (eight articles by different authors)." *Ethnomusicology* 38(3): 399–422.

Nettl, Bruno. (1956). *Music in Primitive Culture*. Cambridge, MA: Harvard University Press.

Nettl, Bruno. (1964). *Theory and Method in Ethnomusicology*. Glencoe, IL: Free Press.

Nettl, Bruno. (1974). "Editor's Preface." *Yearbook of the International Folk Music Council* 6: 7–8.

Nettl, Bruno. (1983). *The Study of Ethnomusicology: Twenty-nine Issues and Concepts*. Urbana: University of Illinois Press.

Nettl, Bruno. (1988). "The IFMC/ICTM and the Development of Ethnomusicology in the United States." *Yearbook for Traditional Music* 20: 19–25.

Nettl, Bruno. (2002). *Encounters in Ethnomusicology: A Memoir*. Warren, MI: Harmonie Park Press.

Nettl, Bruno. (2005). *The Study of Ethnomusicology: Thirty-one Issues and Concepts*. New edition. Urbana: University of Illinois Press.

Nettl, Bruno. (2006). "We're on the Map: Reflections on SEM in 1955 and 2005." *Journal of the Society for Ethnomusicology* 50(2): 179–189.

Nettl, Bruno. (2010). *Nettl's Elephant: On the History of Ethnomusicology*. Urbana: University of Illinois Press.

Nettl, Bruno. (2013). *Becoming an Ethnomusicologist: A Miscellany of Influences*. Lanham, MD: Scarecrow Press.

Nettl, Bruno. (2014). "Fifty Years of Changes and Challenges in the Ethnomusicological Field." Interview by Héctor Fouce. *El oído pensante* 2(1): 1–11. http://ppct.caicyt.gov.ar/index.php/oidopensante (accessed March 16, 2014).

Nettl, Bruno, and Philip V. Bohlman, eds. (1991). *Comparative Musicology and Anthropology of Music*. Chicago: University of Chicago Press.

Newsome, Jennifer. (2008). "From Researched to Centrestage: A Case Study." *Muzikološki Zbornik/Musicological Annual* 44(1): 31–49.

Ockelford, Adam. (2013). *Using Zygonic Theory to Inform Music Education, Therapy, and Psychology Research*. New York: Oxford University Press.

O'Connell, John Morgan, and Salwa El-Shawan Castelo-Branco. (2010). *Music and Conflict*. Urbana: University of Illinois Press.

Pettan, Svanibor. (1996). "Making the Refugee Experience Different: *Azra* and the Bosnians in Norway." In *War, Exile, Everyday Life: Cultural Perspectives*, edited by Renata Jambrešić Kirin and Maja Povrzanović, pp. 245–255. Zagreb: Institute of Ethnology and Folklore Research.

Pettan, Svanibor, guest ed. (1998). *The World of Music* 40(3) (*Music and Music Research in Croatia*). Berlin: Verlag für Wissenschaft und Bildung.

Pettan, Svanibor. (2008). "Applied Ethnomusicology and Empowerment Strategies: Views from across the Atlantic." *Muzikološki Zbornik/Musicological Annual* 44(1): 85–99.

Pettan, Svanibor. (2010). "Music in War, Music for Peace: Experiences in Applied Ethnomusicology." In *Music and Conflict*, edited by John Morgan O'Connell and Salwa El-Shawan Castelo-Branco, pp. 177–192. Urbana-Champaign: University of Illinois Press.

Price, Jammie, and Steve Steele. (2004). *Applied Sociology—Terms, Topics, Tools and Tasks*. Boston: Cenage Learning.

Redfield, Robert. (1947). "The Folk Society." *American Journal of Sociology* 52(4): 293–308.

Rice, Timothy. (2014). *Ethnomusicology: A Very Short Introduction*. New York: Oxford University Press.

Rice, Timothy, James Porter, and Chris Goertzen, eds. (2000). *Garland Encyclopaedia of World Music*, Vol. 8: *Europe*. London: Routledge.

Ronström, Owe. (1991). "Folklore: Staged Folk Music and Folk Dance Performances of Yugoslavs in Stockholm." *Yearbook for Traditional Music* 23: 69–77.

Rovsing Olsen, Poul. (1981). "Summing Up the Conference." *Bulletin of the International Council for Traditional Music* 59: 2.

Sachs, Curt. (1933). *Eine Weltgeschichte des Tanzes*. Berlin: Dietrich Reimer/Ernst Vohsen.

Sachs, Curt. (1943). *The Rise of Music in the Ancient World East and West*. New York: Norton.

Sachs, Curt. (1968). *Die Musik der Alten Welt in Ost und West*. Berlin: Akademie-Verlag.

Sachs, Curt. (1997). *Svetovna zgodovina plesa*. Ljubljana: Znanstveno in publicistično središče.

Saks, Kurt. (1980). *Muzika starog sveta*. Belgrade: Univerzitet umetnosti u Beogradu.

Schippers, Huib, and Catherine Grant, eds. (2016). *Sustainable Futures for Music Cultures: An Ecological Perspective*. New York: Oxford University Press.

Schneider, Albrecht. (2006). "Comparative and Systematic Musicology in Relation to Ethnomusicology: A Historical and Methodological Survey." *Ethnomusicology* 50(2): 236–258.

Seeger, Anthony. (1992). "Ethnomusicology and Music Law." *Ethnomusicology*, 36(3): 345–359.

Seeger, Anthony. (2006). "Lost Lineages and Neglected Peers: Ethnomusicologists outside Academia." *Ethnomusicology* 50(2): 215–235.

Seeger, Anthony. (2008). "Theories Forged in the Crucible of Action: The Joys, Dangers, and Potentials of Advocacy and Fieldwork." In *Shadows in the Field: New Perspectives for*

Fieldwork in Ethnomusicology, edited by Gregory Barz and Timothy J. Cooley, pp. 271–288. Oxford: Oxford University Press.

SEM Torture. Society for Ethnomusicology Position Statement on Torture. http://www.ethnomusicology.org/?PS_Torture (accessed July 1, 2014).

Sheehy, Daniel. (1992). "A Few Notions about Philosophy and Strategy in Applied Ethnomusicology." *Ethnomusicology* 36(3): 323–336.

SIL International. SIL International is a US-based, international Christian missionary organization. Formerly the Summer Institute of Linguistics. http://www.sil.org/arts-ethnomusicology (accessed July 1, 2014).

Skyllstad, Kjell. (1993). *The Resonant Community. Fostering Interracial Understanding Through Music.* Oslo: University of Oslo.

Skyllstad, Kjell. (1997). "Music in Conflict Management—A Multicultural Approach." *International Journal of Music Education* 29: 73–80.

Smithsonian: Fletcher. Foreword to "Camping with the Sioux: The Fieldwork Diary of Alice Cunningham Fletcher." Smithsonian Institution, Department of Anthropology. Online exhibit at http://anthropology.si.edu/naa/exhibits/fletcher/foreword.htm (accessed July 1, 2014).

Spradley, James, and David W. McCurdy, eds. (2000). *Conformity and Conflict: Readings in Cultural Anthropology.* Boston: Allyn and Bacon.

Stockmann, Erich. (1988). "The International Folk Music Council/International Council for Traditional Music—Forty Years." *Yearbook for Traditional Music* 20: 1–10.

Tan, Sooi Beng. (2008). "Activism in Southeast Asian Ethnomusicology: Empowering Youths to Revitalize Traditions and Bridge Cultural Barriers." *Muzikološki Zbornik/Musicological Annual* 44(1): 69–83.

Terada, Yoshitaka. (2005). *Drumming out a Message: Eisa and the Okinawan Diaspora in Japan* (film).

Terada, Yoshitaka. (2008). "Angry Drummers and Buraku Identity: The Ikari Taiko Group in Osaka, Japan." In *The Human World and Musical Diversity: Proceedings from the Fourth Meeting of the ICTM Study Group 'Music and Minorities' in Varna, Bulgaria 2006*, edited by Rosemary Statelova, Angela Rodel, Lozanka Peycheva, Ivanka Vlaeva, and Ventsislav Dimov, pp. 309–315, 401. Sofia: Bulgarian Academy of Science, Institute of Art Studies.

Terada, Yoshitaka, (2010). *Angry Drummers: A Taiko Group from Osaka, Japan* (film).

Terada, Yoshitaka, (2011). "Rooted as Banyan Trees: Eisa and the Okinawan Diaspora in Japan." In *Ethnomusicological Encounters with Music and Musicians: Essays in Honor of Robert Garfias*, edited by Timothy Rice, pp. 233–247. Surrey, UK: Ashgate.

Terseglav, Marko. (2004). "Etnomuzikologija." In *Slovenski etnološki leksikon*. Ljubljana: Mladinska knjiga.

Titon, Jeff Todd. (1984). *Worlds of Music: An Introduction to the Music of the World's Peoples.* New York: Schirmer Books.

Titon, Jeff Todd. (1989). "Ethnomusicology as the Study of People Making Music." Paper delivered at the annual conference of the Society for Ethnomusicology, Northeast Chapter, Hartford, CT, April 22.

Titon, Jeff Todd. (1992a). "Music, the Public Interest, and the Practice of Ethnomusicology." *Ethnomusicology* 36(2): 315–322.

Titon, Jeff Todd. (1992b). "Preface." In *Worlds of Music*, general editor Jeff Todd Titon. New York: Schirmer Books.

Titon, Jeff Todd. (2003). "A Conversation with Jeff Todd Titon." Edited and conducted by John Fenn. Special issue on applied ethnomusicology. *Folklore Forum* 34(1–2): 119–131.

Titon, Jeff Todd. (2009a). "Economy, Ecology and Music: An Introduction." *the world of music* 51(1): 5–16.

Titon, Jeff Todd. (2009b). "Music and Sustainability: An Ecological Viewpoint." *the world of music* 51(1): 119–138.

Van Buren, Kathleen J. (2010). "Applied Ethnomusicology and HIV and AIDS: Responsibility, Ability and Action." *Ethnomusicology* 54(2): 202–223.

Van Willigen, John. (2002). *Applied Anthropology* (3rd ed.). New York: Praeger.

Wallaschek, Richard. (1893). *Primitive Musik. An Inquiry Into the Origin and Development of Music, Songs, Instruments, Dances and Pantomimes of Savage Races.* London: Longmans, Green and Co.

Weintraub, Andrew, and Bell Yung, eds. (2009). *Music and Cultural Rights.* Urbana: University of Illinois Press.

Wengle, John. (1988). *Ethnographers in the Field: The Psychology of Research.* Tuscaloosa: University of Alabama Press.

Wong, Deborah. (2014). "Sound, Silence, Music: Power." *Ethnomusicology* 58(2): 347–353.

Yung, Bell. (2009). "UNESCO and China's *Qin* Music in the Twenty-first Century." In *Music and Cultural Rights*, edited by Andrew Weintraub and Bell Yung, pp. 140–168. Urbana: University of Illinois Press.

Zebec, Tvrtko. (2007). "Experiences and Dilemmas of Applied Ethnochoreology." *Narodna umjetnost* 44(1): 7–25.

PART II

THEORETICAL AND METHODOLOGICAL CONSIDERATIONS

CHAPTER 1

....

TRANSCENDING RESEARCHER VULNERABILITY THROUGH APPLIED ETHNOMUSICOLOGY

....

DAN BENDRUPS

> Success in field work depends on the combination of three things: technical know-how, substantive knowledge of subject, and a great sensitivity to the values and feelings of other human beings—these listed in inverse order of importance.
>
> M. Hood (1982 [1971]: 202)

THESE words, buried deep within Mantle Hood's seminal text, *The Ethnomusicologist* (1982 [1971]), articulate an awareness of the intimate, emotional dimensions of fieldwork, reliant as much on subject knowledge as on interpersonal engagement. They appear in the preliminary discussion of Hood's first fieldwork project in West Africa, which had the somewhat applied aim of producing a film documentary about a performance culture that was otherwise largely absent from, or misrepresented in, the Western gaze. As his description of the research process unfolds, Hood's personal interactions with his collaborators are revealed as playing just as important a role as his technical training in achieving his research aims. Indeed, were it not for his resourcefulness in managing relationships with others, one is left with the impression that the fieldwork may have been over before it began. Such impressions are not unique to Hood's experience— they are woven through ethnomusicological discourse from A(ubert) to Z(emp), and they continue to be significant for research in the twenty-first century, where reflexive discussions of interpersonal relationships (whether beneficial or problematic) are now a standard expectation. Nevertheless, Hood's earlier narrative is of particular interest because, in the course of explaining his project's success, he also reflects on its challenges, revealing in the process the extent of his own vulnerability and uncertainty about the direction his work was taking at the time.

I open with this reference to Hood because his experience exemplifies, in my view, an aspect of applied ethnomusicology that is deserving of greater exploration: the potential for applied research outcomes to assist in transcending researcher vulnerabilities and uncertainties in fieldwork. While applied ethnomusicology is frequently framed as being responsive to the needs and vulnerabilities of research collaborators, especially in indigenous and postcolonial contexts, I would argue that it can also serve to provide researchers with a platform for more effective engagement with their research collaborators, and that applied ethnomusicology should therefore be considered not just as a methodological choice, but as an ontological means of enhancing and improving ethnomusicological practice in general. This consideration provides the impetus for this chapter, which is, in turn, concerned with how such processes play out in circumstances of professional and personal vulnerability.

I leave the definition of researcher vulnerability deliberately vague, as different researchers will experience vulnerability in different ways, and always in a manner that is relative to their research context and personal circumstances. As others have observed, researcher vulnerabilities can stem from political interference (Levin, 1996) or natural disaster, to constructs of race (Radano and Bohlman, 2000) and gender (Babiracki, 2008), and even factors such as personality, musicality, physical ability, or ideology. I therefore propose "vulnerability" not as a corollary for weakness or deficit, but as a state of being in which the discursive barriers we erect around our personal and professional selves are revealed and made permeable. This differs from the "confessional" mode of ethnography (see Van Maanen, 1988; also Titon, 2008: 34–35) because the objective is not to indulge in the researcher's experience of vulnerability, but to pragmatically acknowledge that vulnerabilities and uncertainties exist, that this is normal, and that practical measures can be taken to overcome the barriers that these vulnerabilities may produce. I contend that such an approach is required because, despite the excellent reflexive writing already mentioned, fieldwork is still often constructed and communicated in terms of its successes, underscored by the occasional reticence of ethnomusicologists to reveal problematic experiences, lest these be interpreted as resulting from personal inability, deficiency, or unpreparedness.

This focus on researcher vulnerability was inspired by two particular contributions to the second edition of the seminal *Shadows in the Field* (Barz and Cooley, 2008): Deborah Wong's candid approach to revealing her own thought processes when experiencing Asian American performance from an Asian American perspective (2008: 79), and Nicole Beaudry's openness in describing the particular vulnerabilities she faced in her engagements with far north American indigenous communities (2008). However, this chapter is also a direct manifestation of what I and others have described as a typically Antipodean approach to the discipline of ethnomusicology (Bendrups, 2012; Corn, 2009; Wild, 2006), in which applied outcomes are often situated at the forefront of research engagement, especially where marginalized and endangered indigenous music practices and communities are concerned. It begins with a short discussion of applied ethnomusicology that considers the paradigm shift (Kuhn, 2012) that this approach to ethnomusicology has engendered, before providing a targeted overview of influential ethnomusicological works in which various contrasting instances of researcher vulnerability may be observed. It then presents two case studies of applied responses to vulnerability drawn from my own past fieldwork. These examples have been included not because they are particularly important or special, but because they provide an opportunity to be explicit about some of the ways in which researcher vulnerability can be experienced, with a degree of candidness that would not be possible if the discussion were to attempt to deconstruct the work of others. The first of these case studies relates the circumstances surrounding my efforts to establish a digital sound recording archive on the remote Pacific island of Rapanui (Easter Island). The second explains the process surrounding the production of a CD recording containing the intangible cultural heritage of the small community of post–World War II Latvian refugees in Christchurch, New Zealand. These two case studies present many contrasts, yet they both invoke questions of identity and ethnicity, of musical ability and utility, and the blurring of boundaries between professional and personal agency.

The Applied Ethnomusicology Paradigm

Applied ethnomusicology has been enthusiastically embraced by scholars worldwide, and mobilized in diverse research settings, colloquia, and publications. Whether defined as a subdisciplinary field, a research method, a set of principles, or something else entirely, it embodies an epistemic rendering of the reflexive research practices that underpin contemporary ethnomusicology. While it has been correctly pointed out that the component parts of applied ethnomusicology have always been apparent in ethnomusicology, and that applied aims exist as a matter of course in ethnomusicological research, serving to inform the research process (see Merriam, 1964; Seeger, 2008: 286), it is nevertheless significant that scholars have only recently sought to systematize the discourse surrounding this practice by giving it a disciplinary identity.

This process reflects what philosopher Thomas Kuhn has described as a disciplinary "paradigm shift"—a process that he considered crucial to the progress and development of scientific ideas. Kuhn describes a "paradigm" as a set of achievements "sufficiently unprecedented to attract an enduring group of adherents away from competing modes of scientific activity" but, simultaneously "sufficiently open-ended to leave all sorts of problems for the redefined group of practitioners to resolve" (Kuhn, 2012: 10). When conceptualized in this way, there are a series of paradigm shifts that can be perceived in the development of applied ethnomusicology. An enduring example of a paradigm shift in ethnomusicology is the gradual change in research focus from idealized nineteenth-century perceptions of "pure" ethnology toward research practices that respond to an ever-widening array political, social, and economic coercions. Anthropologists Satish Kedia and John van Willigen assert that their own discipline developed on an applied basis, evidenced by the role of English anthropology in training civil servants for colonial posts and in gathering data about colonized and indigenous peoples for the purposes of better governance (2002: 4). Similar principles underpin the training of at least one key Southern Hemisphere ethnomusicologist (Araújo, 2008: 16).

In circumstances where ethnomusicology has been tied more closely to music schools and conservatoria, the trend toward embedding ethnomusicological practice within performance practice, as epitomized by Hood's advocacy for bi-musicality (Hood, 1960) constitutes another paradigm shift, positioning ethnomusicology within the heavily vocational world of the professional performer or composer— a different yet no less influential "applied" research paradigm. This has resulted in ethnomusicologists engaging with musicians from other cultures on an idealized common ground of music making, leading to a research paradigm in which applied objectives, aimed at providing the researchers' collaborators with financial reward, prestige, and/or international exposure, have emerged. This is especially the case in interactions with the commercial music industry and in projects centered on recording and sound reproduction (see especially Feld, 1996; Feld and Crowdy, 2002; Meintjes, 1990; Zemp, 1996).

Kedia and van Willigen signal that an important change in the notion of applied anthropology occurred around the time of World War II, as anthropologists began to respond to the needs and aspirations of the (often disenfranchised and marginalized) people with whom they worked (2002: 8). Similar concerns were voiced in ethnomusicology, and have become ingrained in the discipline's concern for endangered musical practices, as well as the actions of ethnomusicologists as advocates. As Daniel Sheehy poignantly asks, "What ethnomusicologist has never gone out of his or her way to act for the benefit of an informant or community they have studied?" (1992: 323).

In current practice, some ethnomusicologists (and anthropologists, as well as ethnographers in other disciplines) have expanded on this paradigm by using the term "applied" to signify a social activist agenda. Indeed, Kedia and van Willigen define applied anthropology as "the application of anthropological knowledge, methodology, and theoretical approaches to address societal problems and issues" (2002: 1). This may be conceptualized in the ethnomusicological context as an "approach to the approach to the study of music" (Sheehy, 1992: 323), but in actuality, "applied" ethnomusicologists often extend their work into outright and open advocacy for particular musics and peoples, drawing on wide interdisciplinary frames of reference in the process. As Sheehy notes, applied ethnomusicology is a conscious practice that "begins with a sense of purpose [that is] larger than the advancement of knowledge about music" (1992: 323). Thus, the current paradigm of applied ethnomusicology, which incorporates these various preconditions, is sufficiently new and complex to be thought of as a discrete disciplinary entity, even though its parameters and boundaries are yet to be completely defined.

PROFESSIONAL AND PERSONAL
VULNERABILITY

A further understanding of "applied" research concerns the deliberate positioning of the researcher within the description of the field, as reflected in Stacey Holman Jones's attempts at blurring the boundaries between writer and subject (2007), or Ruth Behar's arguments for erasing the line between observed and observer (1996). In both of these examples, the "applied" aspect of the research implicates the researcher herself as an agent or protagonist within the research setting, and in both cases, the researcher is revealed as occupying a somewhat conceptually (if not physically) vulnerable position. Immersive ethnographic fieldwork is a particularly challenging line of work because it necessitates that the (trained) professional undertake her practice in the same space as that in which she is domiciled. It also depends very much on the establishment and maintenance of productive interpersonal relationships, further blurring the boundaries between professional and personal spaces. In these circumstances, seemingly minor misunderstandings can have dramatic consequences, not just for the people and community under the research gaze, but also for the researcher. Nicole Beaudry provides an evocative example of this, in which her polite rejection of a drunk acquaintance's amorous advances inadvertently led to him denouncing her as a "government spy" on local radio, resulting in many of her collaborators temporarily or permanently disengaging from her research (2008: 240).

While much professional attention has rightly been paid to recognizing and minimizing the negative or coercive impact of field research on research participants (especially those who are vulnerable because of histories of marginalization or colonial disenfranchisement), the reflexive critique that underscores this attention has a tendency to position the researcher in a relatively uncritical position of power. Yet, as many reflexive fieldwork narratives emphasize, it is not always the case that researchers feel particularly empowered while in the field, and in many cases, the success of their work depends on the complete surrendering of power. There is, therefore, a contradiction between the potential powerlessness of the fieldwork experience and the empowerment and authority experienced by researchers upon obtaining or resuming their professional places as writers, interlocutors, academics, or performers. While discourses of power and professional or personal vulnerability have engaged quite extensively with gender as a factor of potential significance to fieldwork interactions, they are still far from conclusive. As Carol Babiracki has observed, "those aspects of doing field research that were most closely related to the experience of being female in the field were, and to a large extent still are, discussed not in the official discourse about field research but in a sort of unofficial, underground discourse in which women (and sometimes men) shared experiences and advice about managing sexual miscommunication and harassment..." thus maintaining the illusion of the "ungendered scholar" (2008: 170). I would argue that this underground discourse also extends to researchers who are un-familied, uncompromised by health or well-being concerns, and unburdened by economic hardship. Unfortunately, these invisibilities both deny the vulnerabilities that may be experienced by field researchers and conceal potential opportunities for interpersonal engagement on levels other than those pertaining directly to the object of study. Thus, these important aspects of successful relationship building are also consigned to unofficial discourse.

The personhood of the researcher is, nevertheless, revealed in some contexts as a rich contact zone for interpersonal engagement, especially where accompanying family members are also implicated. This is reflected, for example, in Anthony Seeger's introduction to *Why Suyá Sing* (1987), in which the opening narrative explains the manner in which both he and his wife Judith were taken in by the community, and the particular nuances of their reception as a couple and as individuals. I had a similar experience returning to Rapanui with my wife and infant son some years after my initial fieldwork there. Their presence led to my inclusion in family discussions and domestic contexts (particularly with women) that were previously inaccessible to me as a single, young, male researcher years before. The richness of the domestic space as a site for research is well established. An excellent example of this is provided by Pacific anthropologist Kalissa Alexeyeff, whose study of dance and music in Rarotonga situates the domestic environment as the primary locus of her ethnography (2003). Anthony McCann (2007) takes the domestic frame of reference further, advocating for an approach to ethnography that directly responds to real or constructed notions of family and connectedness, in which interpersonal relationships are not just recognized but foregrounded, in which older collaborators are conceptualized as (cherished) family members, and in which collaborators are valued not just in terms of the knowledge they hold (i.e., as "culture bearers") but also in terms of their life experience:

> [It is] very important for me at the moment to consider this relationship with the people in the communities where I live. . . . [To] consider the ways in which, as an academic, I have been conditioned and trained to write in ways which could often be regarded as very disrespectful if I were to be standing here speaking to them.
>
> (McCann, 2007)

McCann rallies against the eradication of uncertainty from knowledge, reflecting that "[o]ften, it very much involves simply eliminating people from our work. . . keeping people and the richness of their lives away from the heart of our work" (2007).

While they may not always be subject to theorization, these discourses of personhood, family, domestic space, empowerment, and vulnerability have permeated ethnomusicological writing since the 1970s (see especially Berliner, 1978; Kisliuk, 1998; Levin 1996, 2006). For example, Paul Berliner's account of engaging with Shona music and musicians opens with a personified explanation of the pitch structure of the keys of the mbira, with the lowest pitch designated "father," the octave above that "mother," then "child," and so on (1978: 1). His discussion of empowerment in his relationship with master performer Bandambira, meanwhile, is a rather acute example of vulnerability, in which "[Bandambira] decided that I was worthy of being entrusted with the single piece of information that I sought to collect from him only after six years of studying mbira music, three trips to Africa, and many rigorous tests (1978: 7).

Theodore Levin's ethnographic monograph (1996) begins with a depiction of a different kind of vulnerability: brawling and death threats on the train en route to his research site, before his fieldwork had even begun (1996: 2). His recollections of 1970s Tashkent leave the reader in no doubt about the disconcerting starkness of Soviet-era urban planning in Central Asia, which is later contrasted to the richness of the music he encounters. Levin also provides an example of shifting between scholarly and non-scholarly applied engagement with his field, becoming, for a time, a tour and concert promoter as a means of remaining and earning a living in the (former) Soviet Union (1996: 5). These experiences sit among many other anecdotes that evoke the importance of interpersonal engagement and the political, cultural, and geographic complexities faced by the Bukharan Jewish community and others with whom he worked, yet the overall tone of these narratives—and, indeed, the monograph's subtitle, "Musical Travels"—perpetuates a focus on the author as an explorer, vulnerable but resilient in the face of danger and difficulty.

Michelle Kisliuk's various discussions of her engagements with BaAka music and dance (1998, 2008) reveal much more about her own personal vulnerabilities in the field, with extensive segments of writing devoted to instances of confusion, of not knowing what to do during a particular ritual and her inner analysis of what options were available in the moment, or of the challenge of reconciling what she expected of herself with what others expected of her. In one example, she relates her reaction to an unknown woman's request for help tending a cut on her leg during a rare ritual dance:

> I felt squeezed within a paradox. My experience as a researcher of music and dance helped me feel close to the BaAka as performers, while strangers like the woman beside me resisted my efforts to move beyond being stereotyped. She approached me as though I were a nurse-on-demand, undermining, I felt, my developing role as an apprentice [of dance] by insisting instead that I conform to her image of white people with medicine.
>
> (2008: 187)

Kisliuk is, nevertheless, aware of the potential for such reflections to become self-indulgent, and suggests that the way to decide what should be included or excluded from an ethnographic narrative is to "ask ourselves whether an experience changed us in a way that significantly affected how we viewed, reacted to, or interpreted the ethnographic material" (2008: 199).

It is with this advice in mind that I now offer the two case studies of applied research engagement mentioned at the start of this chapter, with the intention of revealing how, in each case, the particular set of vulnerabilities I experienced led me to the pursuit of applied research outcomes, which, in turn, allowed me to transcend the barriers I had faced. Both examples relate to communities that were (and are) marginal and, to some extent, endangered, but in very different ways. The first example, the creation of a digital music archive for Rapanui, pertains to an indigenous people on an island of around 6,000 inhabitants of whom less than 3,000 are active Rapanui language speakers. As Rapanui traditional music is a repository of language, history, and cultural knowledge, traditional songs are very highly valued in Rapanui society, which faces continued neo-colonial pressure from Chile—the South American nation to which Polynesian Rapanui belongs. The second example, the production of a CD of Latvian community music in Christchurch, New Zealand, pertains to a small population of World War II refugees whose numbers have not been replenished through further waves of migration, and whose children and grandchildren have mostly moved away to live and work in larger metropolitan centers such as Auckland or Sydney, consigning the original population to a slow process of disappearance as community members gradually succumb to old age.

CASE STUDY 1: THE CREATION OF A DIGITAL MUSIC ARCHIVE FOR RAPANUI

In January 2002, after six months of precedential study and fieldwork planning, I arrived on Rapanui with the intention of documenting the music culture of this remote and often misrepresented island. The paucity of extant English-language writing on Rapanui music had made me convinced of the intrinsic value of the doctoral research project I had planned—filling an obvious gap in extant knowledge—and I naïvely assumed that my attempt at music-culture documentation would be supported and embraced locally. However, before reaching the point of being able to make any such contribution to knowledge, I went through a process of engagement that many outsiders who work with marginalized, colonized, or otherwise disempowered communities will recognize. This engagement happened gradually over time in dozens of fragmented conversations and encounters, and the following is but one of many that illustrate the interpersonal challenge of conducting community-engaged fieldwork on Rapanui.

In February 2002, the annual Tapati Rapa Nui cultural festival was in full swing, and I undertook to record its musical aspects for reference purposes. On one of my walks to the open-air festival site, I found my path blocked by a six-foot man with a feathered crown that elevated his already grand stature, aggressively wielding an *au* (ceremonial fighting staff, and ancient signifier of authority). A conversation ensued:

> I've seen you around, recording things. Are you a journalist?
>
> No, I'm here to do research. I'm a musicologist.
>
> Who sent you here?
>
> I just decided to come—I am interested in Rapanui . . .
>
> So, what makes you think you can just come here and record things?

Lots of tourists are recording things—all public performances . . .

But you don't have permission.

To record?

No, permission to be on Rapanui.

Whose permission do I need?

The people. Me. You need my permission. You need to give me something back if you are taking things away.

What can I give you?

Right now you can give me your cigarettes, but it's up to you to make up for what you take from here. I'll be watching you. You will need a better answer the next time I stop you, or you'll be off this island.

I was perplexed by this encounter, and retold it to some of the musicians with whom I had begun to collaborate, who were at once amused, embarrassed, and in agreement with the sentiments their compatriot had expressed. While this man's confrontational approach to a "guest" grated with their sense of cultural protocol, the notion that recording equates to "taking" was widely agreed with, as was the invocation of reciprocity, particularly negotiated acts of reciprocity between individuals, as a pathway to permission.

In time, I learned that my confronter was a social agitator and activist known for his quirkiness and assertiveness, publicly tolerated and sometimes encouraged by the wider community, but rarely afforded formal endorsement by Rapanui cultural and political authorities. This man's intense reaction to my mere presence stuck with me for a long time, and I decided that I would not be comfortable with my presence on Rapanui until I could demonstrate reciprocal intentions that even he would consider appropriate. I set out to answer his challenge by taking stock of what I was actually capable of contributing to the community, and to my horror I quickly realized that I didn't really have very much to offer.

Traditional music is important to Rapanui culture because it is a repository of ancient language, of histories, legends, and beliefs, making it a conduit to the ancestors. In the twenty-first century, traditional music also serves political purposes, as a reminder to current political elites that a pre-contact Rapanui once existed. Contemporary music is likewise important as a marker of an independent cultural identity, as a vector of language and performance practices that demark Rapanui culture as being both related to other Polynesian cultures and yet unique. For these reasons, culturally engaged Rapanui music research is complex and demanding, requiring either the ability to materially support the work of musicians, or to make in-kind contributions that add value to the local music scene in ways that serve artistic as well as social and political needs. As a (mere) PhD student, working independently and outside any larger research-funding framework, my capacity to make any significant financial contribution to Rapanui cultural needs was negligible. Rapanui is a lightning rod for boutique cultural tourism because of its unique archaeological heritage, and many of those who work and travel there are either generously funded or independently wealthy. Lacking stores of personal wealth from which to draw, I could only offer my time and skills in return for the investment of time and knowledge that my research collaborators were investing in me.

As a conservatorium-trained trombonist, freelance performer, and school music teacher, I was confident that there may be some outlet for my musical expertise on Rapanui; however, this was not immediately the case. Contemporary performance culture on Rapanui revolves around the guitar, and as a brass specialist, my instrumental skills had no place in the context of local music making. I eventually found opportunities for collaborative performance with local reggae-influenced bands, but within the wider music community, any credibility I might have had as a musician and possible music teacher was countered by the fact that I was useless on guitar. Partly because of these perceived shortcomings as a contemporary musician, I found my research focus gravitating toward more traditional musical forms that were not so guitar-focused. This led to an apprenticeship of sorts with renowned music expert Kiko Pate, of whom I have written elsewhere (Bendrups, 2007), resulting in my acquisition—in memory and on record—of around 130 songs from his repertoire, some of which had been handed down to him directly over generations.

Kiko transmitted this knowledge to me in 2002 and 2003, and I was desperately eager to pass it on to others in the community, but there were two barriers. First, as a non-islander and non-resident, I was incapable of taking up any kind of formal or informal teaching role in Rapanui society, and I could not hope to replicate traditional teaching methods. Second, Kiko was concerned about his repertoire being passed around the community without his direct guidance (I believe he initially consented to teach me because I was an outsider, and therefore unburdened by the intricate internal politics of authority and ownership in Rapanui music). So, having acquired a deep understanding of some rather ancient aspects of traditional Rapanui music, I was not yet authorized to make much of a contribution to the sustainability of this music through further dissemination and transmission. However, having now amassed a substantial collection of field recordings in the course of my daily investigations, my thoughts turned to the field collections of others, and I began to investigate the whereabouts of earlier field recordings taken from Rapanui. If I was ever to answer the question of what I could do for Rapanui culture, then this was surely it: I decided to hunt down every remaining historical recording with a view to securing their digitalization and repatriation to Rapanui.

This plan had quite a few barriers. First, I had no resources from which to seed the beginnings of an archive. Second, I lacked specific training in sound archiving (though many years of performing in commercial music contexts and as an occasional studio musician meant that I had a working understanding of sound recording and production). Third, I had no idea of the actual extent of historical field recordings from Rapanui, or the manner of their preservation in overseas collections. Nevertheless, I suspected that I may have found a moral and ethical justification for my presence on (and "in") Rapanui, and I confirmed this suspicion in multiple conversations with Rapanui musicians and culture bearers including the confronting individual mentioned earlier.

I began to explore the institutions that existed on Rapanui in the hope of finding one with appropriate facilities for hosting a digital music archive. The Father Sebastian Englert Anthropological Museum (MAPSE) was one of two such places (the other being the municipal library), and the museum's capacity to manage archival records had expanded in 2003 with the construction of the William Mulloy Library, funded and built in the famous archaeologist's name, to house his collection of print and media records from his own Rapanui fieldwork in the 1950s, 1960s, and 1970s. The library had new computer terminals, as well as a climate-controlled archive room. State-funded, MAPSE is an incredible resource for such a small island, and I had made occasional research visits there through 2002 and 2003, so I was aware of its value as a repository of cultural heritage. I was also aware of a perception among parts of the Rapanui community of the museum as a neocolonial institution run by Chileans, responding to Chilean government priorities, and therefore "not very Rapanui." I approached MAPSE about the potential of hosting the music archive because of their new facilities, on the one hand, but also because I thought that the music collection might be a way of enticing more local people to frequent the museum, and that this might help to break down some of the barriers between the institution and the community it served. Thus, the choice of the collection's location was not just a matter of facilities, but also an opportunity for improving community engagement with these facilities.

MAPSE was sympathetic to these observations, and offered to house the (future) collection. I proposed that a computer terminal could be loaded with free audio software (*iTunes*, only recently available for PC in 2003), which would serve as a database for the collection, and that a set of high-quality DVD backup disks and a portable hard disk would take up very little space in the archive room. With this agreement in place, I began to look for the field recordings that would complete the collection. I found the first lot closer than expected, in the hands of Rapanui islander Tote Tepano (Figure 1.1).

I considered Tote to be an unconventional individual for Rapanui. Unburdened by family responsibilities, he dedicated much of his time to causes on the periphery of mainstream community interest, such as caring for stray dogs. He was not involved in regular paid employment at that time, but was an adept carver of replicas of traditional artifacts, which he occasionally sold at the artisan market. He was also interested in sound recording—a pursuit facilitated by a cassette tape recorder given to him by a tourist many years before, and supplies of tapes and batteries donated to him on request by the mayor's office. Tote had been my recording companion at the Tapati festivals of 2002 and 2003, and he had made it clear that, while outsiders like me were very welcome, it was also important that these events be captured by a Rapanui person, with a Rapanui perspective. Indeed, Tote had an established reputation on the island as an enthusiastic recorder of events, and he made a small amount of money each year selling duplicates of his cassette recordings to anyone who wanted them. He hoped that this would ultimately develop into a more financially rewarding enterprise over time, as future generations would surely place great value on the intangible cultural heritage he had captured and which he alone possessed.

FIGURE 1.1 Tote Tepano, dressed for Tapati festival participation, carrying tape recorder (photo by the Author).

When I informed Tote of the plan to create a digital archive, he invited me to the small tin-roof shack in which he lived so that I could see the full extent of his past recording efforts. Lined up before me were multiple polystyrene cargo boxes full of cassettes, stretching back to the early 1980s. As far as he was concerned, the archive already existed: boxed up in his comfortable, yet unsealed dirt floor home. Having never received any training in the handling of tape, Tote was unaware of the susceptibility of his tapes to humidity, fungus, and rot, and my initial attempts to convince him of the precariousness of his collection were met with skepticism. This was, after all, his lifelong project and retirement plan. I did what I could to explain how the island humidity and sea air might cause the tapes to corrode, and eventually he began to realize that there were factors beyond his control at play in the preservation of his collection. Tote agreed to allow some of his collection to be digitized and made accessible to the public, in return for permission to store the rest of his collection at the museum, and to be given a space at the museum in which to carry out his recording work.

Digitizing Tote's collection was a far greater task than could be easily achieved on Rapanui. Serendipitously, however, back in Sydney, the Pacific and Regional Archive for Digital Sources in Endangered Cultures (PARADISEC) had been established in 2003 with a mandate to protect recordings of endangered languages. With a native speaker population below 2,000 people at that time, Rapanui was clearly within the "endangered" range, and PARADISEC generously offered to make their facilities available for the digitization of Tote's tapes. With help from MAPSE and from the Rapanui branch of CONADI (the former Corporación Nacional de Desarollo Indígena [National Corporation of Indigenous Development]), we obtained funding from the Chilean government to enable Tote to fly to Sydney with a selection of his recordings, and for six weeks, he shared a one-bedroom suburban Sydney apartment with my wife and I while we went about the digitization process.

The decision to work in this way with Tote was a challenge, not only because of the nature of the work, but also because of how it might be perceived by others on Rapanui. Tote was not someone with whom I had previously shared a close working relationship, and I was concerned that my efforts to work with him instead of some of my closer collaborators and, by this stage, friends, could be a source of confusion or even insult. On my return to Rapanui in late 2004, some musicians expressed concern about my efforts to bring him to Australia, rather than a culture bearer of higher prestige or experience, or someone with established cross-cultural credentials who might be a better ambassador for Rapanui. Indeed, Tote almost didn't make it to Sydney: he had boarded his flight in Chile adorned in traditional regalia, including a crown of feathers and natural fibers that Australian customs officials would not normally permit into the country. At the border inspection, Tote's lack of English and his unusual baggage (consisting a large box of cassettes and a change of clothes) were cause for concern, and it was only by chance that a bilingual Chilean passenger, who was familiar with Rapanui, saw his predicament and stopped to advocate on his behalf with customs and immigration inspectors. Thankfully, both he and the cassettes he carried were cleared, and soon entered into the PARADISEC collection, with copies to be returned to Tote and to the MAPSE library archive for public appreciation.

Digital copies of formal archive collections were much easier to obtain. I had met Archive of Maori and Pacific Music director Richard Moyle through my association with the International Council on Traditional Music (ICTM), and he readily made the Rapanui content of the AMPM available for digital duplication. Two other collections of Rapanui sound recordings belonging to previous ethnographic researchers Jorge Urrutia Blondel and Margot Loyola Palacios were available in university collections in Chile, and thus were easy to access via formal channels. By the end of 2004, I had accumulated a digital collection containing more than 30 hours of historical recordings, much of which had never been heard on Rapanui, and I set about assembling the archive using the free software and computer facilities mentioned above (a more detailed description of this process is provided in Bendrups, 2005). In the hope that future recordings might be added to the collection, I adapted and translated the accession and permission documentation used by PARADISEC for MAPSE purposes, and subsequently set about promoting the digital archive within the Rapanui community.

Outcomes

More than a decade has passed since the Rapanui music archive was first envisioned, and in that time, technological change on Rapanui has resulted in far greater media engagement than could have been imagined in 2003. The island has gone from having sporadic satellite-dependent landline telecommunications access to a widespread pro-liferation of mobile phones and internet cafes, making the fixed-location digital music collection format seem a little outmoded. Nevertheless, certain beneficial outcomes can be observed. For the Rapanui community, the archive provides assurance that (some of) their intangible cultural heritage is protected, as well as providing symbolic affirm-ative resonances of repatriation. Over the last eight years, few of my close research collaborators have actually made use of the archive—they are largely confident enough in their own knowledge of repertoire that they do not seek affirmation from historical sources—but they are glad simply to know that it is there. For Tote Tepano, being in-volved with MAPSE has provided more stability for his recording work, and as his con-tribution is acknowledged directly by name, his role in contributing to the preservation of Rapanui cultural heritage is therefore readily recognized, lending greater prestige to his efforts.[1]

For MAPSE, the music archive is tangible evidence of the museum's commitment to sustaining and preserving Rapanui culture, and has already facilitated further sound recording preservation and repatriation work, such as the Fonck Museum's Felbermayer project in 2012 (see Bendrups, 2013). The music archive's role as a conduit to engagement with the community has, however, been surpassed by a larger digitiza-tion project dealing with historical photographs of Rapanui people and places, which are more numerous, more tangible, and of more immediate and direct relevance to many more individuals in Rapanui society. Nevertheless, the music collection remains prominent in the museum library's organizational structure, and has gone from being a fringe project occupying one computer terminal to an integrated part of the library's collection.

For me, the archive represents a tangible act of reciprocity, and I remain convinced of its value and appropriateness as a response to my inability to contribute meaningfully in other ways to Rapanui music and society. It also provides me with a place to deposit new items as I continue my commitment to returning extant field recordings to the island as and when I find them. As this discussion has revealed, however, the archive was not the original aim of the research, nor was it conceived through any actual expertise or in-terest in archiving. Rather, it came about as a result of my deficiencies and vulnerabilities in other areas. Furthermore, it was achieved through a skill set drawing not from ethno-graphic or archival training but from commercial performance experience, through the exploitation of personal contacts, the goodwill of senior scholars in my region, and the forbearance of my wife and research collaborators in supporting an outcome deemed to be of service to the greater good.

CASE STUDY 2: *UZ TĒVU MĀJĀM* AND
THE CHRISTCHURCH LATVIAN DIASPORA

In 2004, I obtained my first real job in academia, migrating to Dunedin, New Zealand, to take up a position in ethnomusicology and popular music at the University of Otago, where my Rapanui research resonated with the university's strategic goals in Pacific cultural research. A broad requirement of Otago academic staff was (and is) that their research should have some element of local community engagement, and in the process of developing this, I became aware of the community of Latvian migrants in Christchurch, not far from Dunedin. As extant sources assert, music has historically been of enormous significance to the maintenance of Latvian cultural identity (see Boiko, 2001), and this was especially the case for these post–World War II exiles confronted by the political reality of a homeland that had been subsumed into the (former) Soviet Union.

As a descendant of post–World War II Latvian refugees in Australia, I was notionally a cultural "insider" in this community, and my Latvian surname alone is sufficient evidence of this for anyone within the Latvian diaspora. However, as a child of a family that chose to assimilate into Australian society, discarding a homeland language and many other customs that my grandparents perceived as being of little use to a future in Australia, my cultural competency is somewhat lacking. Indeed, I have clear memories as a teenager of being shunned at Latvian community events because of my Latvian language deficiencies. For a child of Latvians to be unable to communicate in Latvian would certainly have been perceived as a tragedy by the more conservative first-generation members of the migrant community. Consequentially, up until the events recounted here, I had little further interaction with the Latvian diaspora community.

My interest in Latvian music had been rekindled on Rapanui. One afternoon in late 2004, having worked together over the course of two years to transcribe, rehearse, and record his songs, Kiko looked at me and said "That's it. That's all my songs. There are others, I guess, but they won't come to me now." I made us some tea, and we sat for a while watching the clouds gather over the Maunga Terevaka volcano. Then with a slightly capricious tone, Kiko said, "So, I've taught you my songs. . . why don't you teach me some of yours?" I initially laughed at the question, as there is no real equivalent of the Rapanui concept of songs as treasured possessions, passed down through families over generations, in Australian settler society. Similar ideas may exist in indigenous Australian music traditions, I replied, but these were outside my experience and capacity to communicate. Otherwise, Australian songs were mostly bastardized Irish ballads or insignificant novelty items referencing typical Australian fauna. That night I continued to reflect on Kiko's question, as I did not feel that I had given him a very good answer, until I realized that perhaps I did possess songs after all: those brought from Latvia and maintained in exile over 60 years, if not by my immediate family, then

FIGURE 1.2 Paulis Puriņš (far left) with Miervaldis Altments (center) at a Christchurch Latvian community celebration in the mid-1980s (photographer unknown).

by my uncle, a choral director, and his many choristers. I resolved to return to Kiko in the near future with a better knowledge of these songs.

It was from this position of vulnerability in my cultural competency that my engagement with the Christchurch Latvian community began, and it was through yet another process of negotiating vulnerabilities that I arrived at the applied research project that is the focus of the following discussion. I ultimately found the Christchurch community to be very welcoming, completely unlike my teenage experiences in Melbourne, but I was initially very nervous about making contact. This nervousness abated with the birth of my son in 2007 (and subsequently, my daughter in 2010), who became the nexus of my interactions with the community, as he, and then she, drew attention away from me at community events. Bearing identifiably Latvian names (Boriss and Maija), my children symbolized the continuity of the Latvian diaspora community in the eyes of some elders, and they were young enough that (unlike me) no level of cultural competency could really be expected of them (and, indeed, still young enough to be taught). As they became a little older, they were able to interact with other Latvian community children, giving me an opportunity to interact with their parents and grandparents without needing (uncomfortable) justifications for this interaction, or for asking questions about musical practices that that I should, if I were culturally competent, already have known. As such, my children became vital collaborators in my research process, helping to compensate for some of my own vulnerabilities.

It was through these interactions that I became aware of a tape recording that had been made in the early 1980s, featuring the guitars and voices of the community's original songmen, Rūdis Krauze (Rudi) and Paulis Puriņš (Paul). Rudi and Paul had been active musicians in Latvia before the war, and after their arrival in Christchurch they became the mainstay of the community's celebrations. That role was subsequently handed over to their protégé Miervaldis "Merv" Altments (in his sixties at the time of writing), who has a particular gift for the more raucous songs in the folk repertoire, and whose presence at each celebration ensures the continuity of live music performance for the community at the time of writing (Figure 1.2).

The recording had been made at the behest of Rudi's son Karl, who arranged for the duo to use up some spare time in a friend's recording studio. The resulting tape contained a number of well-known Latvian folk songs from the 1930s and 1940s, but also an original composition by the duo, *Uz Tēvu Mājām*, "To Father's House." This particular song is a poignant representation of the Latvian diaspora experience, articulating the sense of disjuncture felt by many in the community, exacerbated by the observation that their "fathers' houses" had, by this stage, been collectivized and reallocated to Russian immigrants, as dictated by Soviet policies that sought to erase privilege but also to dilute the ethnic Latvian population to a point where they could no longer lay claim to ethnic difference from Russia:

Uz Tēvu Mājām, "To Father's House"
(Translation by the author)
Uz Tēvu Mājām, sirds man tiecās
To Father's house, my heart will travel
Kur mātes balss man mīļi teic
My mother's loving voice I hear
Tie skaistie meži ezeri un kalni
The beautiful woods, lakes, and mountains
Tie aicinā uz dzimteni
They call to me from my homeland
Tur bērzu birzes tāpat vel zaļos
The birch copses are still green
Un saule druvās zeltu lej
The sun pours gold on the wheat fields
No tālienes es dzirdu zvanu skaņas
From afar, the mellow sound of bells can be heard
Un nopūtas kas skumjas pauž
And the sigh of sadness
Tur meža vidū, tēva mājās
In the middle of the forest, [in] my father's house
Kur mātes soļus atceros
Where I remember mother's footsteps
Tur tagad staigā daudzi sveši ļaudis
There now walk many foreigners
Tas bij kādreiz mans dzimtais nams
In the house where I was born.

The cassette was not commercially released, but was copied and distributed freely throughout the diaspora community, with many copies ending up in Australia, and some possibly reaching the larger Latvian communities in the United Kingdom and Canada. It was also played on New Zealand national radio, with an added verse in English. In this way, *Uz Tēvu Mājām* became known well beyond the rather limited and isolated geography of the Latvian community in Christchurch.

When I inquired as to the whereabouts of a copy of this tape, a worrying realization was made: it appeared that there were no copies left, or that those that did exist were worn out or otherwise unplayable. Once again, it occurred to me that I could play a beneficial role for this community if I could obtain a copy of the tape to digitize. This time, however, I had the full force of my university department's well-appointed recording studio behind me, and funding for the professional production of a CD, including studio mastering and commercial printing. And once again, this initiative would rely on skills in an area of the music practice (studio recording and production) that was not part of my ethnomusicological training, nor encompassed within the usual ethnographic parameters of a small migrant community study.

Karl eventually provided me with a copy of the tape (his last one). Meanwhile, I had approached Merv about recording some of his songs in the recording studio in Dunedin, a project he became quite enthusiastic about. This initiative became the basis for a theoretical exploration of "doing" fieldwork in a recording studio context (see Bendrups, 2011) but also was an opportunity to "give back" to the community by digitally remastering the much-loved recording of Rudi and Paul. The resulting double CD *Lai Atskan Dziesmas* ("Let the Songs Resound," encompassing both the new and the old) was released to coincide with the sixtieth anniversary of the community's arrival in Christchurch.

Outcomes

In this second example of applied ethnomusicology, a typical commercial music production process took the place of other, more traditional approaches to ethnographic fieldwork. The ethnographic engagement happened in the recording studio context, enabling an interpersonal dynamic based less on a dichotomy of researcher-researched, and more on musicians as co-creators of a musical product. While initially unfamiliar with the studio context, Merv had control over the product, and responded well to the opportunity to review and re-record take by take. This process also enabled him to make suggestions about other elements of the recording, such as adding *kokle* (Latvian zither) to certain tracks. I did this myself, as there were no other *kokle* players in Dunedin. The studio production process allowed me to do this in multiple takes, which was necessary because my *kokle* playing skills are very basic, and certainly not sufficient to perform effectively in a live recording context. More importantly, the research process resulted in the remastering and repackaging of the community's sole historical recording, now commemorated and preserved in a more sustainable medium, and presented alongside the contemporary performances of Merv Altments.

CONCLUSION

Both of the case studies presented here reveal researcher vulnerabilities that were either pre-existing or that became apparent during the course of fieldwork, and both demonstrate the potential for practical, applied projects to provide a means of transcending the barriers that these vulnerabilities can create. In both cases, access to a wider network of sound recording production (whether for archival or commercial purposes) proved to be vital, though this reliance on production facilities may simply be a matter of coincidence. Where Tote Tepano was once the only Rapanui islander to be regularly recording performances in his community, legions of Rapanui youth armed with smartphones and other digital recording devices now record local performances, uploading many of them to mass-media internet sites like YouTube, and making recordings of their unique performance culture more readily accessible and widely dispersed than ever before. Where the Latvians are concerned, it is unlikely that the Christchurch community will ever seek to produce another CD, and professional Latvian musicians elsewhere in the diaspora have no trouble procuring recording opportunities when the need arises. So, while I was able to mobilize support for this particular community recording project, this sort of process may be less relevant in the future, as communities around the world have increasing independent access to recording facilities. In the example presented here, commercial-quality record production was never intended as a primary research aim, and was not informed by any particular expertise or skill on my part—it just became the most obvious pathway to achieving objectives that would benefit the community in each case.

As long as ethnomusicology continues to be defined by the centrality of fieldwork to the discipline, there will be interpersonal terrain to negotiate, and researcher vulnerabilities to be acknowledged and confronted. As the case studies presented here demonstrate, the incorporation of applied objectives into the research process can provide an effective way of ensuring that the research is responsive to interpersonal factors and justifiable in its own terms as an act of public or private (interpersonal) good. If anything can be gleaned from the experiences I have recounted here, it is that applied ethnomusicology has a role to play in enabling and embodying fieldwork reciprocity, regardless of whether the research context is in a remote or metropolitan setting, and regardless of the degree to which the research is contributing to broader cultural sustainability.

While the Rapanui example presented a music culture with far greater sustainability needs than that of the Christchurch Latvians (whose music culture is, of course, also sustained in Latvia itself), both communities were receptive to the outputs resulting from the research. I would argue that this is not just because of the cultural value of the digital archive collection or the CD production, but because in each case the outputs were arrived at through a process of negotiation in which both my interests and the interests of my collaborators were considered. Within days of my initial arrival on Rapanui, I realized that my research priorities may not entirely coincide with the interests and priorities of those whose culture I had come to study, and that this was itself a source of substantial vulnerability, as I could be simply asked to leave or desist at any moment. In subsequent research, I have drawn from this experience by trying to establish common ground with research collaborators from the beginning, and it is the epistemic construct of "applied" ethnomusicology, in which mutually beneficial and often tangible outcomes can be foregrounded, that makes such negotiation possible.

NOTE

1. See http://www.museorapanui.cl/Biblioteca/LaColeccion.htm

REFERENCES

Alexeyeff, K. (2003). "Dancing from the Heart: Movement, Gender and Sociality in the Cook Islands." Ph.D. dissertation, Australian National University.

Araújo, S. (2008). "From Neutrality to Praxis: The Shifting Politics of Ethnomusicology in the Contemporary World." *Muzikološki Zbornik/Musicological Annual* 44(1): 13–30.

Babiracki, C. (2008). "What's the Difference? Reflections on Gender and Research in Village India." In *Shadows in the Field: New Perspectives for Fieldwork in Ethnomusicology* (2nd ed.), edited by G. F. Barz and T. J. Cooley, pp. 167–182. Oxford: Oxford University Press.

Barz, G. F., and T. J. Cooley. (2008). *Shadows in the Field: New Perspectives for Fieldwork in Ethnomusicology* (2nd ed.). Oxford: Oxford University Press.

Beaudry, N. (2008). "The Challenges of Human Fieldwork." In *Shadows in the Field: New Perspectives for Fieldwork in Ethnomusicology* (2nd ed.), edited by G. F. Barz and T. J. Cooley, pp. 224–245. Oxford: Oxford University Press.

Behar, R. (1996). *The Vulnerable Observer: Anthropology That Breaks Your Heart.* Boston: Beacon Press.

Bendrups, D. (2005). "Returning Borrowed Goods: The Motive for Establishing a Rapanui Music Archive." In *Refereed Papers from the 1st International Small Island Cultures Conference,* edited by M. Evans, pp. 2–13. Kagoshima; Sydney: SICRI.

Bendrups, D. (2007). "Easter Island Music and the Voice of Kiko Pate: A Biographical History of Sound Recording." *the world of music* 49(1): 112–127.

Bendrups, D. (2011). "Lai Atskan Dziesmas: Latvian Music and Cultural Identity in Twenty-First Century New Zealand." In *Music and Identities: Baltic Sea Region in the 21st Century and New Approaches to Music Analysis.* Mūzikas Akadēmijas Raksti 8, edited by B. Jaunslaviete, pp. 25–33. Riga: Jazeps Vitols Latvian Music Academy.

Bendrups, D. (2012). "Popular Music Studies and Ethnomusicology in Australasia." *IASPM@ Journal* 3(2): 1–15.

Bendrups, D. (2013) "Sound Recordings and Cultural Heritage: The Fonck Museum, the Felbermayer Collection, and Its Relevance to Contemporary Easter Island

Culture." *International Journal of Heritage Studies*, doi: http://dx.doi.org/10.1080/13527258.2013.838983.

Berliner, P. F. (1978). *The Soul of Mbira: Music and Traditions of the Shona People of Zimbabwe.* Berkeley: University of California Press.

Boiko, M. (2001). "The Latvian Folk Movement in the 1980s and 1990s: From 'Authenticity' to 'Postfolklore' and Onwards." *the world of music* 43(2–3): 113–118.

Corn, A. (2009). "Sound Exchanges: An Ethnomusicologist's Approach to Interdisciplinary Teaching and Learning in Collaboration with a Remote Indigenous Community." *the world of music* 51(3): 21–50.

Feld, S. (1996). "Pygmy POP: A Genealogy of Schizophonic Mimesis." *Yearbook for Traditional Music* 28: 1–35.

Feld, S., and D. Crowdy. (2002). "Papua New Guinean Music and the Politics of Sound Recording." *Perfect Beat* 5(4): 78–85.

Holman Jones, S. (2007). *Torch Singing: Performing Resistance and Desire from Billie Holiday to Edith Piaf.* Lanham, MD: AltaMira Press.

Hood, M. (1960). "The Challenge of Bi-musicality." *Ethnomusicology* 4(2): 55–59.

Hood, M. (1982 [1971]). *The Ethnomusicologist* (2nd ed.). Kent, OH: Kent State University Press.

Kedia, S., and J. van Willigen. (2002). "Applied Anthropology: Context for Domains of Application." In *Applied Anthropology: Domains of Application*, edited by S. Kedia and J. van Willigen, pp. 1–32. Westport, CT; London: Praeger.

Kisliuk, M. (1998). *Seize the Dance! BaAka Musical Life and the Ethnography of Performance.* New York: Oxford University Press.

Kisliuk, M. 2008. "(Un)doing Fieldwork: Sharing Songs, Sharing Lives." In *Shadows in the Field: New Perspectives for Fieldwork in Ethnomusicology* (2nd ed.), edited by G. F. Barz and T. J. Cooley, pp. 183–205. Oxford: Oxford University Press.

Kuhn, T. (2012). *The Structure of Scientific Revolutions* (4th ed.). Chicago: University of Chicago Press.

Levin, T. (1996). *The Hundred Thousand Fools of God: Musical Travels in Central Asia (and Queens, New York).* Bloomington: Indiana University Press.

Levin, T. (2006). *Where Rivers and Mountains Sing: Sound, Music and Nomadism in Tuva and Beyond.* Bloomington: Indiana University Press.

McCann, A. (2007). "Crafting Gentleness: The Political Possibilities of Gentleness in Folkloristics and Ethnology." Paper presented at Reflecting on Knowledge Production: The Development of Folkloristics and Ethnology, Estonian Literary Museum and University of Tartu, Tallinn, May 17–19.

Meintjes, L. (1990). "Paul Simon's Graceland, South Africa, and the Mediation of Musical Meaning." *Ethnomusicology* 34(1): 37–73.

Merriam, A. P. (1964). *The Anthropology of Music.* Evanston: Northwestern University Press.

Radano, R. M., and P. V. Bohlman. (2000). *Music and the Racial Imagination.* Chicago: University of Chicago Press.

Seeger A. (1987). *Why Suyá Sing: A Musical Anthropology of an Amazonian People.* Cambridge: Cambridge University Press.

Seeger, A. (2008). "Theories Forged in the Crucible of Action: The Joys, Dangers and Potentials of Advocacy and Fieldwork." In *Shadows in the Field: New Perspectives for Fieldwork in Ethnomusicology* (2nd ed.), edited by G. F. Barz and T. J. Cooley, pp. 271–288. Oxford: Oxford University Press.

Sheehy, D. (1992). "A Few Notions about Philosophy and Strategy in Applied Ethnomusicology." *Ethnomusicology* 36(3): 323–336.

Titon, J. (2008). "Knowing Fieldwork." In *Shadows in the Field: New Perspectives for Fieldwork in Ethnomusicology* (2nd ed.), edited by G. F. Barz and T. J. Cooley, pp. 25–41. Oxford: Oxford University Press.

Van Maanen, J. (1988). *Tales of the Field: On Writing Ethnography.* Chicago: University of Chicago Press.

Wild, S. (2006) "Ethnomusicology Down Under: A Distinctive Voice in the Antipodes?" *Ethnomusicology* 50(2): 345–352.

Wong, D. (2008). "Moving: From Performance to Performative Ethnography and Back Again." In *Shadows in the Field: New Perspectives for Fieldwork in Ethnomusicology* (2nd ed.), edited by G. F. Barz and T. J. Cooley, pp. 76–89. Oxford: Oxford University Press.

Zemp, H. (1996). "The/an Ethnomusicologist and the Record Business." *Yearbook for Traditional Music* 28: 36–56.

CHAPTER 2

....

EVALUATING VALUES IN APPLIED ETHNOMUSICOLOGY

....

KLISALA HARRISON

EVALUATING the purpose and effectiveness of applications of music, music knowledge, and ethnomusicology is currently the focus of much applied ethnomusicology research. Most applied research does not explicate values, even though they are inherent to the work. The term "values" refers here to value judgments that are epistemological in nature or that are experienced ontologically or metaphysically. There is no way that an academic can avoid having values shape what he or she studies and works on, although some social scientists would argue that one should not let values influence the conclusion of research (Weber, 1949: 112). Nevertheless, a growing number of ethnomusicologists assess the success of the interventions they make, sometimes with collaborators, thus promoting the pursuit of what they value. Others assess musical interventions that aim to correct problems such as conflict, poverty, or the erosion of intangible cultural heritage (Harrison, Mackinlay, and Pettan, 2010).

Although a number of scholars have called for further theorization of the nature of evaluation in applied work (Lomax Hawes, 1992; Titon, 1992), such theories remain underdeveloped regarding research practices. In this chapter, I argue that applied ethnomusicology projects should be evaluated in terms of how they navigate the value systems of the people they engage. Applied ethnomusicological work could be much clearer about its values. The study of these value systems—in other words, an ethnomusicology of values—should inform the design and assessment of projects. Such study would contribute to research in applied ethnomusicology and theorize the ethical stances taken in applied work. As the basis for a new model for studying value systems, I propose a return to the idea of value judgments from early ethnomusicology. I illustrate how my model might be used via ethnographic examples from my research, service, teaching, and performance projects on popular music, Indigenous Canadian music, and music theater in the urban poverty context of the Downtown Eastside neighborhood of Vancouver, Canada. I also ask and answer questions about evaluating values in applied ethnomusicology. For example, whose values does applied work support?

APPLIED ETHNOMUSICOLOGY RESEARCH

Ethnomusicologists who research applications of music and musical and ethnomusico-logical knowledge seek to further understand those applications; any increased under-standing ideally informs future applications. Such applied ethnomusicology research is undertaken by ethnomusicologists, and by ethnomusicologists together with non-ethnomusicologists, students, and practitioners engaged in the field (Araújo, 2008).

Evaluation of how applied ethnomusicology projects navigate the value systems of the people they engage can develop in various kinds of social forums. Forums of ap-plied ethnomusicology include all sorts of public presentations (for instance, academic and non-academic publications), social interactions and networks, and the analyses of people's participation in the applications. Needless to say, applied ethnomusicology re-search always includes projects that engage participants.

In academic publications that present research results, many evaluations now com-prise a "planning and testing praxis" that includes reflection on applications as well as relevant descriptions and analyses of cultural patterns (Keil, 1998: 303–304). Recent examples include the edited volume *Music and Conflict* (O'Connell and Castelo-Branco, 2010) and the special half-issue of the *Yearbook for Traditional Music* titled *Music and Poverty*. The former questioned how music has defined conflict differently in different circumstances (e.g., in war or after human displacement); how music can be used to promote peace; and how ethnomusicologists can mediate and resolve conflicts. The latter examined the relationship of music to poverty in Nepal, Brazil, Canada, Haiti, India, and the United States. As editor, I asked contributing authors to begin to theorize music and poverty relationships, with attention to how music may or may not influence aspects of living in poverty (Harrison, 2013a, 2013c).

Non-academic publications evaluating the use of music, music knowledge, and eth-nomusicology in solving concrete problems likewise present results of research, for example, in "gray literature" such as year-end reports of nongovernmental or govern-mental organizations, and in end-project reports for granting agencies. On the other hand, research processes and analyses unfold in social interactions and networks, and in researchers' own analyses. These could be especially influential forums for an eth-nomusicology of values. There, applied ethnomusicologists and practitioners address interventions-in-progress to a greater extent than in academic and gray literatures.

Outside academe, ethnomusicologists interact as volunteers or employees at public, private, or third-sector organizations, where they may evaluate and intervene in music's relationship to an issue or issue area. Such activities inform or shape research. For ex-ample, during the course of my research on music in the Downtown Eastside, I served on the Advisory Committee on Cultural Diversity to the Mayor and Council of the City of Vancouver. Committee members offered input to the council on whether local cul-tural activities, including music, taking place in and funded by the City met the needs of Vancouver's population.

Inside academe, academic institutes, networks, and conferences facilitate applied ethnomusicology research and related analysis. At the symposia of the International Council for Traditional Music (ICTM) Study Group on Applied Ethnomusicology, for example, so-called talking circles discuss applied interests of symposium speakers. These circles are efforts to raise the level of scholarly discourse on topics of applied ethnomusicology research and practice by providing a forum for the cross-fertilization of ideas, finding a common ground of shared meanings and experiences, and formulating pertinent questions and issues for further research.

What ethnomusicology professors identify as applied ethnomusicology for their mentees and students influences the future of the field (O'Connell and Castelo-Branco, 2010: 250). Teaching can be an intervention that stimulates applied research in students. For instance, when I gave, as a Ph.D. student, a guest lecture on Indigenous music in the Downtown Eastside for Jeff Todd Titon's world music class at Brown University, he told me that I was doing "applied ethnomusicology research."

Other examples of applied ethnomusicology research, and their social forums, are not easily classifiable as academic or non-academic, or as research results or processes overall, except in specific cases. The "head work" of applied researchers, which produces critical evaluations and research processes and results, falls into this category. Other examples may include an evaluative part of a musical performance, of a recording (including liner notes as well as the music), of teaching music or about music, or of a museum exhibit—when research lies behind the evaluation.

THE ROLE OF VALUES IN ETHNOMUSICOLOGY AND APPLIED ETHNOMUSICOLOGY

Applied ethnomusicology scholars have claimed that the field is reflexive, including in the field's social forums and in research. Titon stated in 1992 that applied ethnomusicology attempts the

> reflexive theorizing of practice that is aware of the consequences of situating ethnomusicology both inside the academy and outside of it, one that, in the words of Habermas, "investigates the constitutive historical complex of the constellation of self-interests to which the theory still belongs across and beyond its acts of insight," yet one that "studies the historical interconnectedness of action, in which the theory, as action-oriented, can intervene" (1974: 2).

> (Titon, 1992: 319)

Explicating values that are relevant to applied ethnomusicology, which heretofore have been implied, would benefit self-reflection in applied ethnomusicology scholars as well as in other cultural workers making relevant applications.

In the following, I explicate some values of applied ethnomusicological work on musical sustainability. Through this and a second example, I argue for a fuller consideration of values in applied ethnomusicology research. This would include reviving the idea of value judgments from early ethnomusicology.

Efforts and evaluations toward musical sustainability focus mostly on musical sounds, tools, practices, and people (Titon, 2009). Such undertakings include, for example, sound archive projects (e.g., Thram, 2014), museums including musical content and instruments, audiovisual documentation works aimed at preservation (e.g., Simon, 1991), or businesses that make traditional musical instruments (e.g., African Musical Instruments in South Africa; http://www.kalimba.co.za). Some research also theorizes what sustains musical expressions (http://soundfutures.org; http://sustainablemusic. blogspot.com).

Musical sustainability initiatives and evaluations pursue the values—although ethnomusicologists usually do not identify these as such—of sustaining musical genres and instruments and people making music, rather than, for example, respectively censoring, destroying, and discouraging them. These opinions may seem difficult to dis-agree with, but they do not acknowledge the value systems of all people who either cause a need for, or undertake, sustainability activism and scholarship.

A main limitation of the implicit valuation in applied ethnomusicology today is that it sometimes risks shutting out other valued approaches, even though they may be engaged by the project. This critique can be made of much applied work that takes one particular perspective on an issue—for example, of minority rights or conflict—and tries, through applying music, musical knowledge, or ethnomusicology, to work toward resolving the issue.

My second example—which its author does *not* identify as applied—is Steven Feld's project *Jazz Cosmopolitanism in Accra*, which refers to a book (Feld, 2012), and to the recording of 15 DVDs and CDs between 2005 and 2010.[1] Nonetheless, ethnomusicologists often identify the production and dissemination of recordings as actions of applied ethnomusicology (e.g., Seeger, 2006: 223; Sweers, 2010). I use this example to suggest that future work in applied ethnomusicology could theorize values more inclusively as well as more thoroughly.

Jazz Cosmopolitanism in Accra approached recording and values through Feld's notion of acoustemology. Acoustemology refers to the "epistemology of sound" and "sound as a way of knowing and knowledge production" (Feld, 2013). Values locate within epistemologies. I will focus further on one CD, *Bufo Variations*, described in the book. This recording features master drummer and jazz experimentalist Nii Otoo Annan, who improvised—on diverse melodic and percussion instruments, including xylophone, guitar, drums, and bells—12 tracks while he listened on headphones to a looped recording of toads croaking. The CD concept emerged after Feld, when walking in Accra one evening, heard *Bufo regularis* toads singing in the polyrhythm of 3:2:4:6. Feld wondered whether this acoustic environment could have influenced the polyrhythms of Ghanaian music. Before Feld recorded Annan to the track of the toads croaking, he also played to him Bach's *Goldberg Variations* (Annan, 2008; Feld, 2013). Feld stimulated a cosmopolitan music not only inspired by the experience of nature in the world, but also by human experiences of sound and music across culture, place, and time, of immediately known and unfamiliar beings, human and not human. Feld's approach to research and action on acoustemology includes the *possibility* of diverse acoustemologies, and therefore values and value systems, which is what I would like to highlight here.

How can applied ethnomusicologists begin to better understand the different values engaged by their projects? Reviving the idea of value judgments, pioneered by early ethnomusicologists, especially Alan Merriam, provides a basis for addressing the question. In *The Anthropology of Music* (1964), Merriam wrote that early ethnomusicologists made sets of judgments derived from the sound structure studied, unless the culture they were studying already had an elaborated theory of musical sound. In *Enemy Way Music*, for example, David McAllester (1954) had summarized how Navajo music both reflected values across generations and led to value formation. Just after Merriam published his book, Charles Seeger published "Preface to a Critique of Music" (1965). This essay, which elaborates the basic idea found in Merriam (1964), outlined the sorts of human relationships that inform the value-inclinations of the musicologist, as well as the tools that the musicologist used to assert values, which Seeger identified as speech and, less often, music. Seeger also described sources of evidence for value judgments about music—individual taste, collective taste (general and musical), history (general and musical), sciences (non-musical and musical), and law—with the aim of theorizing the criteria and modalities of critiques made about music in musicology.

While Seeger worked with value judgments on a theoretical level, Merriam wrote about methodology. After observing that ethnomusicologists had neglected folk theories about music, Merriam encouraged them to undertake "folk evaluation" as well. Folk evaluation referred to "people who create things and ideas. . . assign[ing] values to their actions" (Merriam, 1964: 31). The idea of value judgments also gave rise to ruminations by future ethnomusicologists about how ethnomusicology methods might approach values. The work tended to identify values as "issues" (Nettl, 1983) within culture, but did not recommend empirical approaches to researching values.

Empirical research, including the possibility of reflexivity, could be especially useful for achieving more comprehensive understandings of values of applied ethnomusicology today. The research, in a larger sense, would also promote better understandings of the processes and effects of applying music, musical knowledge, and ethnomusicology.

Yet such research may seem complicated to do. In applications, different values may be engaged: those of an ethnomusicologist; those of the people applying the music, music knowledge, or ethnomusicology, if different; those of other people possibly participating in applications; those of people affected by applications; and those of institutions financing and otherwise supporting applications. Because applied work can involve so many parties, many possible values can be present. Think also of the huge variety of applied ethnomusicology projects and activities, all variously relating to valued local, societal, national, or global processes (see Seeger, 2006). Thus, research methods need further consideration.

A New Model for Applied Ethnomusicology Research on Values

There are many solutions to what I see as a need to study how applied ethnomusicology engages values explicitly and empirically, and to develop this approach in the field's interrelated research contexts of public presentations and associated feedback, social interactions and networks, and analyses by academics and practitioners. Some approaches might study in depth one topic of valuation by different actors. Others might find ways of defining the multiplicity of values in action among different people putting music, musical knowledge, and ethnomusicology into practice. Value systems may even be studied.

In order to stimulate thinking in the latter direction, I shall present a new model for ethnographic research on value systems: my adaptation of a model proposed by Joel Robbins toward developing the anthropology of the good (Robbins, 2013a). Robbins suggests that empirical and ethnographic research can be used to elaborate the value tendencies that have been identified in political philosophy. Philosophers have identified so-called monists who believe that all values are reducible to one supervalue, such as pleasure, in that each sub-value, for example entertainment, then contributes to the overall supervalue. Pluralists assert that more than one value exists. Sometimes these values conflict with one another, and pursuing one means not pursuing others (Lassman, 2011). Other social formations do not have any hierarchy of values. Robbins, when addressing the practicalities of how to do research, takes inspiration from some of anthropologist Louis Dumont's observations about the nature of values (Dumont, 1980; 1986). Robbins's model maps four key points in what he calls a "continuum of configurations" (Robbins, 2013b) between more monist and more pluralist social worlds in order to argue that all societies include tendencies toward both value monism and value pluralism (ibid.).

I will illustrate Robbins's categories of value systems with examples from Indigenous music programs and multi-ethnic music theater and popular music jams in the Downtown Eastside of Vancouver, where I have spent 15 years studying, performing in and organizing formal music programs offered by organizations, often supported by a combination of funds from the public, private, and third sector. In the three poorest sub-areas of the Downtown Eastside (total population: approximately 6,500), 84%–85% lived below Canada's low-income cut-off dollar amounts in 2001 (Statistics Canada, 2011). Music programs aimed at the poor, especially in music therapy, popular music, and Indigenous music, addressed problems that often accompany urban poverty, such as ill health (including addictions) and crime. Over the years, gentrification has intensified in the neighborhood, bringing in affluent residents and displacing the poor. Related performing arts projects have emerged that aim to develop creative industries, consumed by people who can afford them, including festivals and music theater productions.

My data suggest a slight but possibly significant elaboration of Robbins's model. I will briefly explain one origin of this suggestion before giving my musical examples— another inspiration for my elaboration. Robbins illustrates his model with distinctive cultural groups from different parts of the world with strong traditions of value, referenced below. This highlights, possibly unintentionally, historically continuous and separate value systems.

Music groups in the Downtown Eastside, however, do not have the same degree of continuity or value separation. Formal music programs have emerged as unique local formations in my Indigenous case studies only 10–15 years ago. The popular music programs developed over about 25 years. Different value systems exist side by side in different music groups; individuals can usually participate in the different music groups and their value systems.

Table 2.1 traces the four different value systems that occurred in musical examples from the one neighborhood of the Downtown Eastside, within cultural subgroups. The two columns on the right point out that my examples of multiple values involved more than one time period, or individuals participating in more than one type of musical group. I shall consider Indigenous music groups, popular music jams, and music theater productions. Each type of music group tended to have one dominant value, but individuals participating in numerous group types over time created additional subgroups and value systems.

The first point on Robbins's continuum is *strong monism* in the Dumontian sense. This refers to "a monism that does not fail to recognize values other than its paramount one, nor to assign them levels of their own, but which appears wholly to subordinate all these other values and their levels under a single paramount one" (Robbins, 2013b: 106). Robbins gives the example of Hasidic Jews in Brooklyn who predominantly value the redemption of Jews. Hasidic male activities of worship and studying religious texts support this supervalue.

Even though Robbins's ethnographic examples (2013b) come from relatively bounded cultures, Dumont's work includes value systems and relationships between domains of social action in society as small as the family. In other writings, Robbins states that he does not limit the identification of values and value systems to bounded cultural contexts, but embraces the study of values in all social formations, large and small (Robbins, 2014). The openness of Robbins's model to "dimensional complexity" (Robbins, 2013b: 112) makes it useful for various ethnographic approaches to values, including subgroups like those I discuss. Subgroups are rarely studied ethnographically and explicitly in relation to their values in anthropology (Robbins, personal communication, July 9, 2014) and (applied) ethnomusicology.

Strong monism existed in "cultural healing" programs for Indigenous Canadians that I researched in the Downtown Eastside. Through the singing and drumming of powwow and hand drum music, these programs seek in part to address a Canada-wide situation in which drug and alcohol addictions disproportionately affect Indigenous people compared to non-Indigenous people. Their musical sounds combine musical heritages of a diversity of Indigenous peoples living in Vancouver. Like parallel

Table 2.1. Robbins's Value Continuum Applied to Music

Type of Value	System Definition	Musical Examples: Indigenous, Music Theater and Popular Music Groups in Vancouver's Downtown Eastside	Time Period(s) (#)	Type(s) of Music Groups Participated in by Individuals (#)
Strong Monism	All values support one paramount value or supervalue	Indigenous Canadian "cultural healing" groups using music value well-being re substance misuse	1	1
Monism with Stable Levels	Two values are hierarchically ordered, but each value is sovereign within its confines	One cultural healing group at one organization values different stages of well-being re substance misuse during the music, at different times: people able to abstain from substance misuse, thus being somewhat "healed," in 2003 versus people on drugs or alcohol seeking valued "healing" in 2007. Officiating elders always recognized and valued each stage of recovery, but placed them differently in a value hierarchy.	2	1
Stable Pluralism	More than one value exists and the values are stable[1] or not in conflict	Usually without conflict, different supervalues exist in the cultural healing programs and in the music theater productions involving Indigenous people[2]	1	2
Unsettled Pluralism	Two value systems conflict	Different supervalues exist in popular music jams and music theater productions. The values conflict in a larger class conflict.	1	2

[1] "Relatively stable pluralism" refers to the values being unstable or conflicting only sometimes.

[2] Any occasional, minor conflicts of value resulted in relatively stable pluralism.

pan-Indigenous Canadian and American musics, they insert local styles into types of music disseminated throughout North America. For instance, the powwow music (Browner, 2002) combines local and regional Pacific Northwest Coast First Nations singing timbres and microtonal systems and melodies with dominating musical techniques and repertoires from the Plains.

Elders who supervise music making in the organizations typically have the agency to choose a value system to facilitate. I have documented how elders used powwow and hand drumming to encourage Indigenous people in the Downtown Eastside to replace what some of my interviewees called a "culture" of drugs and alcohol there, with spiritual and cultural norms associated with the music. In prayer circles that always preceded music making, the officiating elder burned sacred plants, and participants took turns speaking about how a hybrid type of spirituality guided "healthy" identifications. The spirituality combined Christianity together with Indigenous spiritual elements indexed by musical sounds, songs, instruments, and ritual paraphernalia (Harrison, 2009). I do not mean to suggest that the idea to replace, via music, one value system with another is not complex, problematic, or even, at times, unfeasible. It can be all of these things. I intend only to point out that as rituals, the cultural healing programs stressed a supervalue of well-being (specifically, experienced absence of addiction). In general, a lot of rituals are monist (Robbins, 2014).

The second point on Robbins's value continuum is *monism with stable levels*. Monism with stable levels refers to a system in which two values are hierarchically ordered in a social group, but each level is comfortably sovereign within its confines. Monism with stable levels can mean that people experience monistic commitments to different values at different times, and that these different values do not conflict in the same individuals (Robbins, 2013b: 107–108).

In my next field example, I show that the valuation of well-being in cultural healing took two forms at two times in recent history, yet occurred in one music group at one organization. In 2003, the officiating elder tended to prevent people who were drunk or on drugs from singing or drumming. This elder highly valued the "healed"—or those well into addictions recovery—over addicts seeking "healing." By 2007, a different elder led the music group. He allowed active addicts to sing and drum together with people who were able to abstain from substance misuse. Healing, not having healed somewhat already (or being able to abstain), became the supervalue.

Some people sang and drummed from 2003 and after 2007. They experienced monism with stable levels in the two contained fields of ethics. These ethics did not conflict because they happened at different times. Robbins cites an example of people experiencing stable monism: Priestless Old Believers in the Russian Urals, who devote the beginning and end of their lives to religious values, but middle life to the worldly pursuit of producing and exchanging material goods.

The third point in Robbins's value continuum is *stable pluralism* (ibid.: 109–110), in which more than one value exists and the values are stable. Robbins's example comes from the Avatip community of Papua New Guinea's East Sepik province. Generally, in pre-contact Sepik societies, a men's initiation cult highly valued a specific ritual hierarchy. Its religious structure valued adult men above women and younger men, who in turn ranked higher than enemy neighbors. A secular sphere of Avatip life, though, involved an equality marked by sensitivity to others and the goal to achieve equivalence through reciprocity. Robbins questions whether this configuration has changed post-contact, but finds no reported evidence of substantial change, hence its relatively stable pluralism.

In the Downtown Eastside, when Indigenous people participated in not only cultural healing but also other sorts of music events in the neighborhood, they experienced relatively stable pluralism. The other events included multicultural music theater productions that aimed at developing creative industries through trying to improve participants' socioeconomic situations and artistic skills. One performing arts company, for example, offered mentorship in acting and singing during rehearsals for theater productions that paid actors and sold tickets. The main value was (professional) showmanship. The music theater contributed to the highly conflicted process of gentrification, as I shall discuss further regarding unsettled pluralism.

Why do I write that Indigenous people participating in both the cultural healing and arts development experienced value pluralism? Indigenous showmanship may not seem the opposite value to healing, but certainly it can be enjoyed in such a way that contradicts some elders' teachings during cultural healing. Gary Oleman, a Salish elder, often talked about the need to "love people not power" (Harrison, 2009). Conversely, gaining training in the arts if it ends in professional or paid artistry means gaining socioeconomic status, which by definition refers to social positions within hierarchies that include music (Harrison, 2013b).

And why relatively stable pluralism? I could see no pressure for cultural healing programs to give up their values for those of arts development or vice-versa. Both types of initiatives, undertaken concurrently by different organizations, welcomed Indigenous people to participate because they were Indigenous. The same individuals could access each type of initiative, and participate for free, or for pay for instance when performing in a music theater production, although arts development performances typically had the gatekeeping process of auditions. Indigenous characters were in high demand; Indigenous people were typically granted onstage roles, even if these possibly amateur actors did not learn lines or attend all rehearsals. I call the situation relatively stable pluralism because if an Indigenous performer auditioned for a music theatre production's band without also auditioning for an acting role, he or she (like a performer of any ethnicity) was rejected, for instance, if life circumstances did not allow for regular attendance of band rehearsals. This tendency did not accommodate, for example, musicians who did not have enough money to buy food, and had to stand in a food line for hours, therefore missing rehearsal, or people who slept on the street and had more pressing concerns, like getting a bed for that night at a local shelter. The musician was forced to choose which was more important to him or her: making music or surviving physically. Producers of music theater, for their part, wished to professionalize as many production values as possible, including musical accompaniment, lighting, staging, and costumes, but working toward professionalizing acting and onstage singing.

The fourth point in Robbins's value continuum is *unsettled pluralism* (Robbins, 2013b: 110–111). Unsettled pluralism refers to when a person or people—Robbins tends to discuss social and cultural configurations more than personal experiences, but he would not preclude the latter (personal communication, July 8, 2014)—experience two different fields of values but these values conflict. Robbins offers an example from his research on Urapmin Christians of Papua New Guinea. Urapmin people define Christian salvation as something that they must attain on their own by avoiding sinful thoughts and behaviors. Robbins defines the primary value of Urapmin Christian experience as one of individualism whose goal is the saved individual. However, individualism played little if any role in traditional Urapmin life, which centered on the production and maintenance of relationships—in other words, relationalism. Urapmin Christians who also have ties to traditional lifeways experience extreme value conflict (ibid.). In my research material, extreme value conflict did not exist in the music options for Indigenous people.

However, unsettled pluralism existed if I shift my view to people of all ethnicities and cultures who participated in popular music jams as well as music theater. The values of these two types of music groups conflict. On the one hand, the music therapy sessions and popular music jams had healing from addictions as their supervalue too. I conducted research in five music therapy practices that prominently encouraged addictions recovery for active addicts using the contestable approach of behavior modification via music. I also investigated, and participated as a violinist, in numerous popular music jams offered at community centers, health centers, and festivals. Most of these events discouraged or prohibited drug and alcohol use. On the other hand, the music theater productions—which include pop operas or theater productions using locally popular songs—have the supervalue of showmanship or professionalization.

Popular musicians who make up the poorest of the poor, but who successfully audition for music theater productions (most successfully for roles as singing actors), experience conflict for one main reason tied to gentrification: the Downtown Eastside increasingly turned into an arts district. As this happened, the popular music jams and music therapy programs closed as their funding dried up. The closures rarely targeted Indigenous programs. At the same time, performing arts projects like music theater aimed at generating creative industries received funding from pro-development private and public sectors. This gave birth to class conflicts between the poor, who valued addictions recovery through popular music, and the proponents of gentrification, who valued professional arts productions supported in part by affluent new residents. Both collaborated in the music theater productions.

At this point, I can suggest an elaboration of Robbins's model to suit applications of music in complex society, of which the Downtown Eastside provides a case study. Even though Dumont, Robbins writes, intended "to capture and help explain what can be seen as the routine existence of both monist and pluralist tendencies in all societies" (ibid.: 103) and Dumont ended up describing "domains of social action" (ibid.: 112), what this all means for taking social action remains unexplored.

When examining the model from the perspective of social action taking place through music or applied ethnomusicology, it can be elaborated as follows. In complex society, individuals have the possibility to access different value systems. In the best case—that is, absent cultural rights violations—individuals can choose to participate in one, or more than one, value system. Individual musicians, then, can choose between different value systems that musical activities and groups support, create, and articulate. Yet groups of individuals can also move between value systems, which can happen at one point in time when groups of individuals participate in different

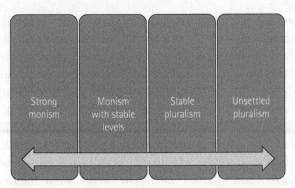

FIGURE 2.1 Musical value systems exist in a continuum in complex society (elaborating Robbins 2013b). The arrow represents the possibility of individual musicians to choose between different value systems, and the possibility of groups of musicians to shift value systems.

music groups that support different value systems. Over time, a musical group also can change the type of value system engaged (see Figure 2.1). Reflecting on such an empirical study of value systems that exist where an application has taken place, or is to take place, can help to make future interventions more precise in terms of intended and actual result.

WHICH VALUE SYSTEM SHOULD AN ETHNOMUSICOLOGIST SUPPORT?

When making an application of music or ethnomusicology, which value system or systems does an ethnomusicologist choose to support? I have faced such decisions when applying music and ethnomusicology in the Downtown Eastside. For example, in the applied ethnomusicology course that I taught at the University of British Columbia in 2009 and 2010, I arranged, with a student, for Gary Oleman to offer an Indigenous Canadian singing workshop that emphasized healing. In our workshop, the elder enacted the supervalue of healing that I described as being present in my example of monism with stable levels. On another occasion, I honored a request from organizers of a music theater showcase to involve my students. The students, all training to be arts professionals, became singers in a choir and musicians in a band of otherwise hired musicians for the DTES (Downtown Eastside) Music Theatre Showcase. Students took on the roles of audio technician and assistant stage director. Several film majors made a documentary that aired on local TV. I felt glad about arranging work experience placements at a time when government funding cuts to the arts made hiring professionals difficult for performance organizers. Yet I despaired that our arrangement still left no places in the band—even minor roles—for instrumental musicians who could not attend rehearsals regularly due to poverty.

After I reflected with the students on the values that we supported, I felt frustrated by my inability to confront value systems that my politics did not support. I had problems with going along with the unsettled pluralism of the music theater showcase.

In addition, my reflection confronted me with unintended consequences of one applied project. It actually changed value systems (my examples of strong monism and monism with stable levels) supported by my politics—mostly because I did not think through the valued consequences and ask the right questions of collaborators beforehand. The value shift resulted from spin-off activities, made possible by Oleman's singing workshop. The idea for the workshop emerged when a Ukrainian choir director, who knew that I researched Indigenous Canadian music, asked me to link her with a local Indigenous singer because she or the community center where her choir was located— I did not ask which one beforehand—wanted to enhance Indigenous collaborations. I connected her with Oleman, but also asked if one of the students could help her— hence our workshop. The workshop, her idea, was for her choir members.

Subsequently, the community center and choir director invited Oleman to offer more workshops, and, with the choir director, to perform in concerts with workshop participants at the community center. These events, though, impacted the overall value system across Oleman's music offerings—which always involved cultural healing values—due to rules for entering the Carnegie Community Centre. The center prevents anyone drunk or on drugs from entering its building, monitoring the building entrance closely with security guards. This institutional context "forced" the supervalue of Oleman's practice to shift from valuing the participation of active addicts to including only people abstaining from drugs and alcohol. Several Indigenous people participated from day to day in music making facilitated by Oleman, at various organizations in the Downtown Eastside that did and did not ban people drunk or on drugs. Their music making toggled between the supervalues of healing and healed detailed earlier (see my paragraphs on monism with stable levels). I worried if these contrasting values ever caused any value conflicts or unsettled value pluralism for participants. I routinely heard about addicts staying sober in order to take part in music at the Carnegie Community Centre, but I also heard that they found that difficult. People undertaking applied work with music must not only limit their analysis to which values they support, but also investigate which values and value systems their efforts change and contest, as well as the consequences.

CONCLUSION

In this chapter, I have called for more work on values in applied ethnomusicology research, which has the possibility of opening up discussions and practices of method and evaluation relevant to applications. Such work would emerge in the current so-cial forums of applied ethnomusicology research—public presentations, social interactions and networks, and analyses of scholars and practitioners. It has the pos-sibility of complementing the previously implicit approaches to values in applied ethnomusicology.

I also have introduced the possibility of an ethnomusicology of values that revives the idea of value judgments from early ethnomusicology. Through empirically investigating values systems of music, such an approach could produce new understandings relevant to applications. Adjusting a model for research on values from the anthropology of the good (Robbins, 2013a), I have emphasized that music groups over time, and individual musicians (forming other subgroups) in complex society, can and do move between value systems that musical practices support, create, and articulate. I have detailed how one can research value systems of music and applied ethnomusicology, and have pro-vided examples.

In closing, I shall ask what further use is empirical research on values and value systems for ethnomusicology and applied ethnomusicology. For instance, an ethno-musicologist can use such research to identify value systems by asking questions like: Which value systems are present in social groups in a given worksite? In complex so-ciety, for instance, where do value systems overlap? How do individuals engage them via music?

When applying music, and musical and ethnomusicological knowledge, it also is important to think critically about the *choice* of a value option of music. It is also im-portant to analyze critically those situations that block value choices. I discussed what was relative about my example of relatively stable pluralism, which involved Indigenous people accessing cultural healing yet also auditioning for music theater roles in arts de-velopment programs. Those who could act and sing generally got onstage roles; if they auditioned as instrumentalists for a back-up band but could not attend rehearsals, they were turned down.

Identifying and evaluating the value systems of a given application and application context can promote critical reflection, for instance, on whether one would choose a similar course of action for a future application. An ethnomusicologist can therefore ask, does an application support, change, or contest what certain social groups (and which ones?) consider good and valued? What are the implications and politics of the applications' value content? Answering such questions can result in future applications that are better informed as to their value content and probable effect.

Acknowledgments

Special thanks to Pirkko Moisala (University of Helsinki) and Joel Robbins (University of Cambridge) for their inspiring, thoughtful, and constructive comments on this chapter.

NOTE

1. When I e-mailed Feld that I wanted to mention his work in this chapter, he reflected that he has not called his work "applied" due to negative connotations of applied anthropology, which serves as a basis for some types of applied ethnomusicology (Harrison, 2012: 506–507). He admitted, though, "all of my recordings are implicit and explicit forms of advocacy, i.e., forms of representation that are made collaboratively, and that principally benefit (financially as well as otherwise) the musicians or communities rather than solely benefit researchers and commercial organizations" (Feld, personal communication, December 26, 2013).

REFERENCES

Annan, Nii Otoo. (2008). *Bufo Variations*. VoxLox. CD produced by Steven Feld.

Araújo, Samuel. (2008). "From Neutrality to Praxis: The Shifting Politics of Ethnomusicology in the Contemporary World." *Muzikološki zbornik/Musicological Annual* 44(1): 13–30.

Browner, Tara. (2002). *Heartbeat of the People: Music and Dance of the Northern Pow-wow*. Urbana: University of Illinois Press.

Dumont, Louis. (1980). *Homo Hierarchicus: The Caste System and its Implications*, translated by Mark Sainsbury, Louis Dumont, and Basia Gulati. Chicago: University of Chicago Press.

Dumont, Louis. (1986). *Essays on Individualism: Modern Ideology in Anthropological Perspective*. Chicago: University of Chicago Press.

Feld, Steven. (2012). *Jazz Cosmopolitanism in Accra: Five Musical Years in Ghana*. Durham, NC: Duke University Press.

Feld, Steven. (2013). "Listening to Histories of Listening: Collaborative Experiments in Acoustemology." Lecture, University of Helsinki, May 5.

Harrison, Klisala. (2009). " 'Singing My Spirit of Identity': Indigenous Music for Well-being in a Canadian Inner City." *MUSICultures* 36: 1–21.

Harrison, Klisala. (2012). "Epistemologies of Applied Ethnomusicology." *Ethnomusicology* 56(3): 505–529.

Harrison, Klisala, ed. (2013a). *Music and Poverty*. Special half-issue of the *Yearbook of Traditional Music*.

Harrison, Klisala. (2013b). "Music, Health and Socio-economic Status: A Perspective on Urban Poverty in Canada." *Yearbook for Traditional Music*: 58–73.

Harrison, Klisala. (2013c). "The Relationship of Poverty to Music." *Yearbook for Traditional Music*: 1–12.

Harrison, Klisala, Elizabeth Mackinlay, and Svanibor Pettan, eds. (2010). *Applied Ethnomusicology: Historical and Contemporary Approaches*. Newcastle upon Tyne, UK: Cambridge Scholars Publishing.

Keil, Charles. (1998). "Call and Response: Applied Sociomusicology and Performance Studies." *Ethnomusicology* 42(2): 303–312.

Lassman, Peter. (2011). *Pluralism*. Cambridge: Polity Press.

Lomax Hawes, Bess. (1992). "Practice Makes Perfect: Lessons in Active Ethnomusicology." *Ethnomusicology* 36(3): 337–343.

McAllester, David. (1954). *Enemy Way Music*. Cambridge, MA: Peabody Museum, Harvard University.

Merriam, Alan. (1964). *The Anthropology of Music*. Evanston, IL: Northwestern University Press.

Nettl, Bruno. (1983). "We Never Heard a Bad Tune." In *The Study of Ethnomusicology: Twenty-nine Issues and Concepts*, by Bruno Nettl, pp. 315–322. Urbana and Chicago: University of Illinois Press.

O'Connell, John Morgan, and Salwa El-Shawan Castelo-Branco. (2010). *Music and Conflict*. Urbana: University of Illinois Press.

Robbins, Joel. (2013a). "Beyond the Suffering Subject: Toward an Anthropology of the Good." *Journal of the Royal Anthropological Institute* 19: 447–462.

Robbins, Joel. (2013b). "Monism, Pluralism, and the Structure of Value Relations: A Dumontian Contribution to the Contemporary Study of Value." *HAU: Journal of Ethnographic Theory* 3(1): 99–115.

Robbins, Joel. 2014. "Pluralismo Religioso E Pluralismo De Valores: Ritual E A Regulação Da Diversidade Intercultural" [Ritual Pluralism and Value Pluralism: Ritual and the Regulation of Intercultural Diversity]. *Debates do NER* 2(26): 15–41.

Seeger, Anthony. (2006). "Lost Lineages and Neglected Peers: Ethnomusicologists Outside Academia." *Ethnomusicology* 50(2): 214–234.

Seeger, Charles. (1965). "Preface to the Critique of Music." *Inter-American Music Bulletin* 49: 2–24.

Simon, Artur. (1991). "The Bornu Music Documentation Project: Applied Ethnomusicology and Cultural Cooperation in Northern Nigeria." In *Music in the Dialogue of Cultures: Traditional Music and Cultural Policy*, Intercultural Music Studies No. 2, edited by Max Peter Baumann, pp. 199–204. Wilhelmshaven: Florian Noetzel Verlag.

Statistics Canada. (2011). *Low IncomeLines, 2009–2010*. Income Research Paper Series. Ottawa: Income Statistics Division. http://www.statcan.gc.ca/pub/75f0002m/75f0002m2011002-eng.pdf (accessed April 11, 2013).

Sweers, Britta. (2010). "Polyphony of Cultures: Conceptualization and Consequences of an Applied Media Project." In *Applied Ethnomusicology: Historical and Contemporary Approaches*, edited by Klisala Harrison, Elizabeth Mackinlay, and Svanibor Pettan, pp. 214–232. Newcastle upon Tyne, UK: Cambridge Scholars Publishing.

Thram, Diane. (2014). "The Legacy of Music Archives in Historical Ethnomusicology: A Model for Engaged Ethnomusicology." In *Theory and Method in Historical Ethnomusicology*, edited by Jonathan McCollum and David G. Hebert, pp. 309–335. Lanham, MD: Lexington Books.

Titon, Jeff Todd. (1992). "Music, the Public Interest, and the Practice of Ethnomusicology." *Ethnomusicology* 36(3): 315–322.

Titon, Jeff Todd, ed. (2009). "Music and Sustainability: An Ecological Viewpoint." Special issue. *the world of music* 51(1): 119–137.

Weber, Max. (1949). *The Methodology of the Social Sciences*, edited and translated by E. A. Shils and H. A. Finch. New York: Free Press.

....

CHAPTER 3

CULTURAL ENGAGEMENT AND OWNERSHIP THROUGH PARTICIPATORY APPROACHES IN APPLIED ETHNOMUSICOLOGY

....

TAN SOOI BENG

INTRODUCTION

....

MANY applied ethnomusicologists engage in action research, a methodology that aims at solving concrete problems rather than hypothetical ones. Besides conserving folk traditions, applied ethnomusicologists have been involved in other areas of action research, such as conflict mediation (O'Connell and Castelo-Branco, 2010; Pettan, 1998, 2008), intellectual property rights (Seeger, 1992), post-disaster reconstructions (Fisher and Flota, 2011), ethics and indigenous rights (Ellis, 1994; Newsome, 2008), representation of minority cultures (Hermetek, 2010; Zebec, 2004), and peace building (Tan, 2008, 2010).

In the developing countries of the Global South, where large sections of the population still live in poverty, ethnomusicologists work with local nongovernmental organizations (NGOs), performing and visual artists, educators, and communities, applying their musical skills and training to challenge social and cultural inequality, monolithic representations of national cultures, and other development-related issues (Dirksen, 2012). The conservation of traditions, including music, in these places often intersects with the struggle for basic rights such as indigenous identity, health, education, housing, land, and other issues. Through social engagement, ethnomusicologists have had to reassess their research methodologies and adapt from other relevant disciplines. Collaboration among the ethnomusicologists, NGOs, and other stakeholders has also resulted in the creation of alternative approaches in research and advocacy that are participatory and that empower communities to make transformations in their own lives.

Nevertheless, ethnomusicological scholarship about these participatory methodologies in action research for addressing development issues that have evolved in the countries of the South remains sparse.[1] One such initiative was a collaborative project conducted by Samuel Araújo and students from the Universidade Federal do Rio de Janeiro Ethnomusicology Lab, together with youths of the Grupo Musicultura, an NGO created by the residents of Mare, a slum area in Rio de Janeiro that has problems of violence, drug trafficking, and unemployment. One of the aims of the project was to document the sounds and music of Mare and their meanings. Participatory strategies motivated by Paolo Freire's "dialogic research" were employed: planning, identifying issues, and devising research themes were carried out by the students together with the residents as co-researchers. As a result of the collaboration, new kinds of information about the various forms of violence and the sounds associated with them were developed. The process of research and the creation of a local music resource center led to increased self-esteem among the youths involved, as well as new knowledge in music and other related performing arts in the area. Conducting research also allowed members of the local research team to move around the neighborhood more freely and to gain respect from the other residents (Araújo and the Grupo Musicultura, 2006, 2008, 2009).

Angela Impey's collaborative documentation project involving the residents of the Dukuduku Forests of the Greater St. Lucia Wetlands Park, South Africa's Northern KwaZulu-Natal province, is another applied ethnomusicology project that uses participatory action research methods for development purposes. The residents were evicted from the park in the 1950s by the white Nationalist government. Having returned to their homeland after apartheid was abolished, the residents are among the most impoverished in the province. Impey worked together with young volunteer researchers of Dukuduku to conduct interviews and to document and conserve the cultures of the residents, which depend on the natural resources of the forests. She adapted the participatory methodologies influenced by Freire's participatory learning and action strategies, which have been applied in development projects, particularly in the areas of health, agriculture, and environment in other developing countries (Chambers, 1997). The process facilitated discussions about the meaning of tradition and identity among the residents and how to represent themselves to visitors. This led to long-standing presentations for tourists, which were organized by the community. Collaborative research fostered sustainability of the traditions, self-representation, and decreased poverty among the Dukuduku. Not only did the project promote cultural tourism, it benefited the residents as well (Impey, 2002: 403).

This chapter contributes to the few written works in engaged ethnomusicology regarding the use of collaborative and participatory action research methodologies to deal with development issues in countries of the South. The chapter first investigates the alternative participatory approaches that have been created in the "theater for development" in Asia, a type of theater that uses various media, such as music, drama, visual arts, photography, or video, to initiate and facilitate discussion and understanding of critical issues affecting the development of communities (Eskamp, 2006). Theater for development has made a long-term impact as a tool used by NGOs for social intervention in Asia. Following this investigation is a discussion of how I have adapted the participatory approaches of theater for development in two main areas of applied ethnomusicology for development work, particularly the organization of the annual Heritage Celebrations and children's music advocacy projects in George Town, Penang, which are aimed at self-representation, recovering of multi-ethnic histories, and peace building.

Learning from the praxis of theater for development, I argue for the promotion of an applied ethnomusicology that is engaged and participatory. For any cultural development project to be sustainable, communities must be empowered and gain confidence to take action in order to make changes in their lives. There is also a need to democratize research and promote collaboration between the researcher and the community so that the latter is engaged and feels a sense of ownership in the entire process for change. For engagement and ownership to occur, participatory approaches for planning, training, research, mapping of issues, analysis, and presentation, drawn from ethnomusicology and other disciplines, such as development studies, cultural and performance studies, applied anthropology, folklore studies, and oral history, need to be developed.

PARTICIPATORY DEVELOPMENT, THEATER, AND ISSUES OF CONCERN

In the 1970s and 1980s, following criticisms of state-directed, top-down development, the World Bank and other agencies of the United Nations began to endorse decentralization and to promote what came to be known as "sustainable development" in the Brundtland Report (WCED, 1987: 43). This resulted in a move toward participatory development, which is seen as the collective responsibility of all the stakeholders, including the government, the corporate sector, and civil society.

A distinction was made between the conventional and participatory approaches to development. NGOs involved in civil society developed participatory ways of working that proved to be more effective than the top-down methods. Primary stakeholders were involved in the planning of their own development and participated in designing, implementing, and evaluating projects in education, health, culture, agriculture, and other sectors. Participatory training and research methods using local knowledge were developed to facilitate stakeholders to identify their own needs. The participatory activities helped the primary stakeholders to become more confident and to overcome the feeling of being powerless. Participation created stakeholder ownership of the activities, which led to pilot projects being transformed into sustainable and long-term initiatives that were taken over by the communities themselves. In development policy, it has been acknowledged that the participation of civil society and ownership of programs are crucial for any project to be sustainable. Critical evaluation is essential to enhance engagement and empowerment (Chambers, 1997; Eskamp, 2006).

Many NGOs involved in civil society development projects in the South have employed the participatory methodologies of theater for development as strategies for bottom-up self-development since the 1970s. Often referred to as participatory theater, process theater, community theater, people's theater, or theater for liberation, the methodologies of theater for development have been successfully adopted by artists and educational groups to encourage learning, discussion, analysis, and understanding of critical issues affecting communities and ways to deal with specific problems. Even though the term "theater" has been used, it is understood that different forms of creative arts and popular media (such as music, dance, drama, visual arts, storytelling, video, or photography) are employed. Local forms of performing and visual arts are encouraged in this kind of theater.

In the last 40 years, the participatory methods of process theater have been adapted in non-formal education in Asia to address issues in relation to conflict resolution, peace building, gender sensitization, raising awareness about social inequality, heritage conservation, and health campaigns such as AIDS prevention, as well as to help children and adults cope with trauma caused by war or natural disasters, such as the 2011 tsunami in Aceh, Indonesia, and improving the lives of the disadvantaged.

Some active theater for development groups include the Manila-based Philippines Educational Theatre Association (PETA), which represents one of the pioneers of process theater in Asia. Politicized by the repression of the Marcos regime, PETA held theater workshops among student groups, labor unions, teachers, farmers, workers, and other communities throughout the Philippines in the 1970s, where they explored a variety of social issues through drama, dance, music, and visual arts.[2] At the turn of the millennium, the Philippines network of theater for development is wide, and there are grassroots groups in all of the islands, which have initiated their own programs and methodologies (Gaspar et al., 1981; Samson et al., 2008). These groups ensure that the network is not centralized in Manila or controlled top-down by a few activist-artists.[3]

In Yogyakarta, Indonesia, Teater Arena (a political theater group) and Studio Puskat (an audiovisual institute sponsored by Jesuit priests) have been making videos advocating grassroots development and social change. Concerned that only a small urban minority is benefiting from top-down development, the two groups came together and ran community theater projects in the rural areas of Indonesia in the 1980s. In the theater project at Tanen, cardboard puppets were used for participatory discussion of the social structure of the community, while the local operatic form *kethoprak* and local dialects were employed for the final presentation. Through the interactive theater activities, the community gained the confidence to express their needs and realized the power of collective action. An important outcome of the workshop was the supply of electricity for all the households and the building of canals for irrigating the rice fields in Tanen. At the leper colony of Lewoleba, the theater practitioners encouraged lepers to perform their experiences about being outcasts in society through storytelling, music, and songs, which they composed themselves. This resulted in greater understanding of the plight of and sympathy for the lepers among the other residents (van Erven, 1992; personal communication, Tri Giovanni, 2008).

Maya and Makhampom are two active process theater groups that grew out of the Thai pro-democracy movement in the early 1980s. They use performances to encourage dialogue and to raise awareness regarding development-related issues among specific target groups. Employing various puppet theater forms, Maya has conducted theater workshops for teachers, students, and communities in the rural areas of Thailand. Interactive and participatory strategies were developed to enable the rural people to gain confidence to speak up, raise issues such as pollution, corruption, malnutrition, and drug abuse, and take action to solve the problems. In the last decade, Maya has developed an Experiential Activities Plan (EAP) through the "Children in the Know" Project, which took place in schools in various parts of Thailand. Participatory activities that included problem identification, individual explanation, group research, and communication through performances and creative arts were created. These activities stimulated the children to learn about maintaining good health, eating the right type of food, living together, not being influenced by social vices and advertisements by the mass media, anti-consumerism, and community spirit (*Children in the Know Curriculum*, n.d.; personal communication, Chitrachinoa, 2008).

Makhampom runs workshops on team building and conflict resolution using process theater at their Living Theatre Centre at Chiengdao. In partnership with the International Rescue Committee (IRC), they have employed participatory theater approaches to explore issues regarding gender-based violence, peace and conflict, and HIV/AIDS at three refugee camps at the Thai-Burma border. For Makhampom, theater and participatory activities are tools to "explore social issues as a group," "build trust and relationships," "begin discussions," "understand different types of conflict," and "make positive changes" (Kellock, n.d.: 7–8; Barber, 2008). As conflict is marked by a lack of trust, team-building activities are important to encourage the participants to participate in dialogue and work together (personal communication, Barber, 2009).

Pedagogy and Participatory Approaches in Theater for Development

As in many participatory strategies for development, including those described by Araújo and the Grupo Musicultura (2008, 2009) and Impey (2002), community process theater has been influenced by the ideas and pedagogy of Brazilian educator Paolo Freire. Freire was critical of the Western pedagogical principle that he called "The Banking Concept of Education," in which knowledge is "a gift bestowed by those who consider themselves knowledgeable upon those whom they consider to know nothing" (Freire, 1972). For Freire, a pedagogy for liberation requires a new kind of teacher who believes in the creativity and knowledge of the oppressed. By analogy, a theater of liberation also requires a new kind of actor who activates the inherent creativity of his or her target group.

Freire emphasized that communication in the form of dialogue between the trainees themselves and their trainers are crucial in empowering communities to be in control of their own development. His concept of "conscientization" is widely used in community theater and participatory development to refer to the process of raising awareness though collective inquiry, dialogue, and action.

Participatory theater has also adapted Augusto Boal's pedagogy of "theater of the oppressed," in which the main objective of theater is to "change the people" from "passive beings" into "subjects, actors, transformers" through dramatic action (Boal, 1979). For Boal, the audience should be involved in the creation and performance of a play. Active participation of the audience will support awareness training and problem-solving at the community level.

Despite differences depending on the issues, sociopolitical contexts, indigenous knowledge, and performing/visual arts of a particular community, theater for development groups in Asia share common participatory activities in the process of creating theater for problem-solving through team building, collaborative research, dialogue, and action:

i. A range of games and theatrical practices promote participation from all members of the target group and help to build self-confidence, trust, and social cohesion, as well as stimulating self-expression and awareness of the possibility of taking action to solve the problems of the community;

ii. Through participatory research, mapping, and analysis, the stakeholders determine the issues that concern them and brainstorm ideas to overcome them collectively;

iii. The participants portray these issues and the possible solutions through a performance/creative work they devise together;

iv. The performance is a community forum where audiences are engaged in the discussion and exchange of ideas with the performers and facilitators. Very often, the final product can be a video, artwork, exhibition, workshop performance, or combinations of different forms of presentations. Indigenous forms of art, dance, music, puppet theater, storytelling, masks, and visual arts known to the community are often employed.

In theater for development, the *process* of creating theater is more important than the *performance*, although local aesthetics are significant. Through the participatory way of working, the stakeholders are empowered to make positive decisions about their lives and turn these decisions into action. In a way, process theater can be seen as a form of action research in which the stakeholders collectively gather data through research, analyze the data, discuss, and take action to improve their conditions. These participatory methods cannot solve the problems of the communities or the inequities of power immediately. Nevertheless, action programs are more likely to continue, even without the presence of the theater facilitators, if the stakeholders or communities have been engaged and have acquired ownership of the entire process of theater making, problem mapping, analysis, and making decisions for change.[4]

ADAPTING THE PARTICIPATORY APPROACHES OF PROCESS THEATER IN APPLIED ETHNOMUSICOLOGY FOR DEVELOPMENT

As an applied ethnomusicologist concerned about development, I have been inspired by the praxis of action research employed by the participatory theater groups in Asia, which involves the collective gathering, interpretation, analysis, and application of knowledge by the community members and seeks to advance their own defined goals. Ethnomusicologists can indeed facilitate to bring about change in the communities they study if they apply the participatory approaches of process theater, which promote dialogue and research for problem-solving, and build confidence and social cohesion.

The following section illustrates how these participatory approaches have been adapted in two cultural projects that I have been involved in to provide spaces for the communities of George Town, Penang, Malaysia, to address their concerns regarding top-down cultural centralization by the federal government and racial tensions in the country. As participatory methods for action research cannot be analyzed in isolation from the sociopolitical context, issues, and cultural roots of a place, let me begin with a short description of the social and cultural concerns of the Penang communities.

Sociocultural Context and Concerns of the Residents of George Town, Penang

Malaysia has a multiethnic and multireligious population of 28.3 million. The citizens consist of 67.4% Bumiputera (translated as "sons of the soil," which comprise Malays and other indigenous groups such as the Orang Asli, Kadazan, Bajau, Bidayuh, Melanau, Penan, etc.), 24.6% Chinese, 7.3% Indians, and 0.7% others (including Arabs, Eurasians, Indonesians, etc.) (Department of Statistics, 2010). Since the colonial days, Malaysia has been characterized as a plural, society where "two or more elements or social orders. . . live side by side, yet without intermingling, in one political unit" (Furnivall, 1948: 446). Ethnicism and racial anxieties have prevailed until recent times.

During the past four decades, the Malaysian state has tried to bring the different ethnic groups together as a nation by centralizing the arts and creating top-down policies pertaining to culture. The National Culture Policy was formulated in 1970 for purposes of national unity following the 1969 racial riots when ethnic relations broke down in Malaysia. In 1971, it was decided at a congress that the national culture should be "based on the cultures of the people indigenous to the region," that "elements from other cultures which are suitable and reasonable may be incorporated," and that "Islam will be an important element" (KKBS, 1973: vii). Consequently, a Ministry of Culture and the infrastructure to implement this national culture were created. Selected Malay forms of music, dance, and theater were streamlined so that they were in keeping with the national culture policy. These streamlined forms were promoted through workshops, competitions, festivals, schools, and universities.[5]

Since the 1990s, there has been a movement toward the creation of a *Bangsa Malaysia* (Malaysian Race) and more recently, *OneMalaysia*, which rests on the cultural identities of the various ethnic communities. The multiethnic extravagant but stereotypical performances organized by the State Culture and Tourism Departments, known to the world as "Malaysia Truly Asia," represent the more recent top-down narratives of multiculturalism in Malaysia. Spectacular cultural shows with representative dances from all the states and ethnic groups have also been created as icons of development, modernity, and harmony. This is exemplified in the annual *Citrawarna* (Colours of Malaysia) street parades organized by the Ministry of Heritage and Tourism, and in the annual *Merdeka* (National Day) celebrations, including performances by the Malaysian People's Drum Symphony, in which over a thousand Malay, Chinese, Indian, Kadazan, Iban, and other traditional drums play together in unity (Tan, 2003).

The creation of the national forms of culture has facilitated the homogenization of selected traditional performing arts genres. Certain forms are chosen as representative of an ethnic group and are decontextualized so that they become part of national culture. While the expression of multiculturalism appears to be promoted by the state, the kinds of cultural differences that can be portrayed are defined by administrators. A kind of stereotypical representation of each ethnic group is promoted, which does not encourage self-expression and exploration at the community level. Indeed, it has become a challenge for community artists to maintain the vitality and creativity of their traditions. At the same time, ethnicism continues to persist in Malaysian society.[6] Unity cannot be imposed through the creation of a national culture based on the culture of one ethnic group or through standardized representations of specific cultural traditions.

The cultural issues presented above predominate on the island of Penang where I live, as the island has been a meeting place for diverse ethnic communities and cultures even before the British colonized the island in 1786. As Penang port developed in the late eighteenth and nineteenth centuries, the trading of spices and the export of tin and rubber attracted settlers from the Malay Archipelago, Thailand, Burma, Hadhramaut, India, China, and Europe. Penang was also an important stopover for pilgrims going to Mecca. The meeting of different peoples in Penang is manifested in the multiple places of worship situated near each other in the inner city, eclectic food and architecture, languages spoken, street names, festivals, and performances. Penang's current population of 1.6 million people remains multiethnic: Chinese of various dialect groups make up 41.5%, Malays originating from different parts of the Malay Archipelago 40.9%, Indians from various parts of India 9.9%, others (including Arabs, Eurasians, Indonesians, Thais, Burmese, and so on) 0.7%, and non-Malaysian citizens 7.0% (Penang Institute, 2015). Cultural borrowing and mixing has occurred as the diverse communities live together in close contact and interaction (Tan, 2011). The monolithic national culture and stereotypical representations of the ethnic groups promoted by the Malaysian state are in contradiction to the lively organic eclectic ethnic cultures on the ground.

Having carried out extensive research on the traditional performing arts of the various ethnic communities in Penang, I am obligated to work with the communities, including musicians and performing artists from whom I have gained information, to address these concerns. Together we have attempted to (1) create spaces for all ethnic communities to represent themselves, recover their multicultural histories, deconstruct stereotypical ethnic representations by the federal government, and show their cultural diversity; and (2) revitalize traditions, bridge cultural gaps, and promote tolerance among ethnic groups, including children, in Penang. We have tried to achieve these objectives through two main projects, namely, the organization of the annual George Town Heritage Celebrations and advocacy heritage programs for children of the city. As illustrated in the following sections, the challenge lies in making these community projects sustainable. Furthermore, the ethnomusicologist not only needs to work in the area of music, but has to include other areas of culture such as theater, dance, crafts, visual arts, rituals, trades, and other cultural assets of the communities.

The George Town Heritage Celebrations

The Heritage Celebrations are held annually on July 7 to celebrate the inscription of George Town, the capital city of Penang, as a UNESCO World Heritage Site.[7] Taking place in and around the historic streets of George Town, the Heritage Celebrations are inclusive and participatory events that aim to provide the multiethnic communities an opportunity to showcase and represent their own heritage to each other, and to Malaysian and international visitors. The community-oriented festivities feature street celebrations of performances, food and crafts, exhibitions, interactive games, open houses, architecture, heritage trails, public talks, and workshops with the participation of all the ethnic communities of George Town.

The two- to three- day festivities and events give a public presence to the histories, cultures, endangered traditions, and art forms of the diverse communities, including those of underrepresented cultural groups that are not projected in national culture projects. Capacity development, knowledge transfer, and the sustainability of the multiethnic cultures and art are the projected outcomes.

The celebrations are coordinated by George Town World Heritage Incorporated (GTWHI), the Penang state agency for heritage, which is responsible for heritage conservation and managing the World Heritage Site of George Town. The core organizing team comprises visual and performing artists and educators who act as program curators; the production team consists of lighting designers, stage managers, technical expertise, and crew. There is also a group of volunteers of young people (mainly from universities, colleges, and high schools) who help to run the celebrations as production crew at performances, information counters, and food and craft stalls. The celebrations are funded by the Penang state government[8] as well as by private corporations.

The local communities are at the heart of the celebrations, as co-organizers, stakeholders, presenters, participants, and carriers of tradition. The organizers envision the celebrations together with the local communities to incorporate indigenous knowledge and perspectives about performance, research, documentation, and presentations. We work with three types of community groups with different levels of participation from each of them:

Group A: Formal religious, cultural, and clan associations that have been established by the different ethnic groups in Penang to take care of the concerns and welfare of their members. They include (1) the Qaryah Masjid Kapitan Keling (community members of the Indian Muslim[9] Kapitan Keling Mosque, the oldest Indian Muslim Mosque in George Town); (2) Gabungan Liga Muslim (The United Muslim League, an association of various Indian Muslim groups, which provides a platform to raise issues of social concern); (3) Penang Chinese Clan Council (comprising the main Chinese clan associations of Penang); (4) Indian Chamber of Commerce, which represents the business operations of the Indians of Penang; (5) Badan Warisan Masjid Melayu, Lebuh Acheh (Heritage Body of the Malay Mosque, Acheh Street, that was set up to preserve the history and heritage of the Malay mosque at Acheh Street); (6) Yayasan Agama Islam Pulau Pinang (Islamic Foundation, Pulau Pinang, whose mission is to promote the Islamic faith); and (7) Persatuan Sejarah dan Warisan Melayu Pulau Pinang (Malay Historical and Heritage Association, Pulau Pinang, which aims at preserving the Malay heritage of Penang). These groups are encouraged to plan and organize their own cultural activities for the Heritage Celebrations.

Group B: Residents of George Town who present and exhibit their family histories, traditional trades, open their houses, and talk to visitors about their lives and work in the heritage enclave; and

Group C: Cultural practitioners and performers of the various ethnic groups who participate in the curated shows and share their knowledge with multiethnic audiences through demonstrations and performance items.

In order to ensure that this community festival is sustainable and that capacity development takes place, the organizing team has employed participatory approaches and action research methods adapted from process theater and participatory development. These methods are aimed at empowering communities to represent themselves so that they are engaged in change and become proactive agents in their own development:

Participatory Planning, Training, and Bottom-Up Organization

Planning, training, and organization are done together with all stakeholders, including the community groups. The workshop is a neutral space for capacity development. We initiate team-building exercises and interactive activities in the locations of the celebrations, and provide tools for research and analysis of the cultural assets of the communities. These activities help the communities to develop the potential to make representations of their own cultural heritage, plan and organize their programs, and stimulate intercultural understanding among all the groups. Training of facilitators from the community takes place.

Participatory Research to Identify Needs, Problems, and Action

We emphasize experiential learning in the heritage zone so that the communities are able to map their own cultures and histories. The formal associations (Group A) take the workshop participants for walks in their own cultural enclaves, identifying the histories, cultures, trades, festivals, food, performances, and crafts that are still being practiced. Participatory mapping and analysis of the cultures and histories from the walk and other secondary sources are carried out.

Cultural mapping and interpretation help to create awareness and appreciation of the cultural assets, histories, and environment of each community. The participants find out about their cultural similarities and differences and discover that cultural mixing has taken place in the food, performing arts, music, and languages of the communities. By creating maps, they reveal their perceptions about their identities and think about how to represent themselves at the Heritage Celebrations.

The main organizers and representatives of the communities are taken on a research trip to Petchaburi, Southern Thailand, to witness, experience, and learn from the community festival held there annually. Petchaburi is known for its traditional crafts such as stucco decorative art, painting, and woodcarving. The George Town representatives get new ideas about the organization, programming, layout, and capacity building of the community festival in Petchaburi, which is inclusive and engages the entire village in the celebrations. Group A community organizers and festival facilitators interact with each other intensively during the visit. The Petchaburi festival organizers (including community members) also make a trip to Penang during the George Town Heritage Celebrations as part of the learning experience and exchange.

For the residents and performers of the city (Groups B and C), such as the owners of recycle shops, lantern makers, hawkers, photographers, or performers, oral interviews are conducted by volunteer researchers to document the histories of their lives, trades, crafts, and performance genres. Photographs and other documents about the family histories, trades, or art forms are collected. The interviewers set up connections with the wider community through relatives, neighbors, and friends.

Participatory Presentations

At the end of the workshop, the different stakeholders of Group A come together to share their experiences and projected programs for the heritage celebrations. The content is related to the living environment, history, and experiences of the target communities and is of direct relevance to them.

Participatory and Interactive Activities during the Celebrations

Group A: "Community Celebrations"

During the heritage celebrations, the communities present their research findings and cultural activities in various forms, which engage the audiences interactively. For example, in 2013,[10] the Penang Chinese Clan Council held its celebrations in the vicinity of Meng Eng Soo (translated as Memorial Hall of Heaven) at Rope Walk, which was the ancestral hall of the Ghee Hin Chinese Secret Society[11] built in 1890. The building has been restored and is managed by the Penang Chinese Clan Council today. Street interactive activities were organized by clan members to invite audience participation. The community members compiled the history of the Chinese clans in Penang, which was exhibited on posters and has recently been published as a book. They set up pavilions where visitors could search for the origins of their family names. Audiences could also visit the Meng Eng Soo building, where there were ancestral worshipping demonstrations. They could taste traditional Chinese food and tea (prepared by the community members), purchase artworks, or take part in street cultural performances.

In 2013, the Indian Muslim community of the Kapitan Kling Mosque exhibited old photographs and descriptions about the historical development of the community around the mosque and the early development of Arabic and Tamil education among the community since the nineteenth century. Built in 1801, the mosque is named after Kapitan Kling, the first superintendent of the mosque, which used to serve the Muslim section of the Indian troops brought by the colonial British government. During the heritage celebrations, the members of the community also demonstrated the cooking of Indian Muslim traditional cuisine, which could be tasted by visitors. Visitors could also try out the traditional way of grinding (*giling*) spices and beans using grinding stones, make tea called *teh tarik* (translated as "pulling the tea"), play traditional games, watch performances of *qawwalli* (a form of Sufi devotional music), and participate in the longest *roti canai* (a type of bread which originated in Malaysia) competition.

At Queen Street, one of the streets of the Indian enclave known as Little India, a *nasi kandar* (type of Indian Muslim food) festival was organized by the United Muslim League together with all the *nasi kandar* restaurants in town. The history of *nasi kandar* and the meaning of the term were made known to visitors through announcements. In the past, hawkers balanced a pole on their shoulders (*kandar*) as they carried the plain rice (*nasi*) with spicy curry dishes (meat, seafood, vegetables, boiled eggs) and sold them in the streets of Penang.[12] During the Heritage Celebrations, visitors could choose from the best *nasi kandar* stalls, which lined the entire street.

The historic Malay community around the Acheen Street mosque presented traditional arts and crafts, cakes (*kuih*), Malay games like playing with tops, *nasyid* (cantillations in praise of Allah and the Prophet Muhammad), *qasidah* (classical songs based on poetry), and talks about the Islamic faith. Acheen Street was the site of the earliest Arab urban community in Penang and the center of the spice trade. It was also known as the Second Jeddah, as pilgrims from different parts of Southeast Asia waited for their boats to Jeddah and Mecca in the nineteenth and early twentieth centuries. Built in 1808, the Acheen Street mosque was the center for prayer and Islamic teachings preparing pilgrims for their journey to Mecca. Islamic literature was printed by the printing presses that emerged in the area around the mosque. The streets near the mosque were alive with shops, hotels, and shipping ticket counters to cater to the pilgrims.

Kollatam stick dance, horse and peacock dances, and Indian martial arts were presented by the Hindu Indian community at the Mahamariamman Temple, the temple of the goddess Mahamariamman. Built in 1833, the temple is known for its festivities, which include dances and music, when the goddess is taken around the neighboring streets of Little India during the Navarathri festival. Additionally, the 2013 heritage celebrations were enhanced by the Indian classical Bharata Natyam and Gujarati folk dance, and music performances organized by the Indian Chamber of Commerce at a nearby space in Little India.

Group B: Residents of George Town: "Up Close and Personal"

To encourage community participation in constructing the local history of George Town, GTWHI conducted a pilot oral history documentation project, entitled *Cherita Lebuh Chulia* (1945–1970) (Story of Chulia Street), with the residents of the street in 2013. Chulia Street was one of the first streets constructed in George Town by Francis Light, a British trader who founded Penang in 1786. Home to many ethnic communities, this street was the main commercial and residential street, and the core road for local transport since the nineteenth century. As such, it was the principal route for festivals and cultural processions such as the Maulidur Rasul (birthday of Prophet Muhammad), Thaipusam (festival during which Hindus take a vow to offer the *kavadi*, a physical structure balanced on the shoulders of the devotee, to implore for help from, or in thanksgiving to, Lord Murugan, the Hindu God of War and Victory), and festivities of Chinese Gods such as Toa Peh Kong and the Nine Emperor Gods, when decorated floats line the streets.

Activities were organized along Chulia Street during the heritage celebrations, including an interactive exhibition featuring three-dimensional maps, videos, printed panels, and a printed comic book. Big board cutouts of the main personalities and events led audiences to the actual sites. Video screenings of the documentation were held at selected coffeeshops (*kopitiam*), where residents could share their memories and experiences in a relaxed manner. The video recordings also acted as tools for getting feedback from the community and for giving voices to the old people who have lived in the city for many decades. Special walking tours to visit the local residents in Chulia Street, such as the key maker, hair dresser, soy milk maker, photographer, and watchman, were held. Audiences were invited to share their impressions at a chit-chat corner.

Elsewhere, visitors from and outside Penang were taken on walks to visit traditional traders such as the lantern maker, printing press owner, religious bookseller, signboard maker, tombstone engraver, and many more, who demonstrated and told the stories of their lives to the visitors.

Group C: Curated Shows: "Stories under the Stars"

In the evening, free outdoor multicultural folk performances by local artists of all ethnic backgrounds were curated at two main open-air sites at the heritage enclave, where the communities and residents of the city as well as outsiders came to watch and celebrate together. Some of the performances included the Malay *boria* (skits, dance and music), Thai *menora* (musical dance theater, see Figure 3.1), Peranakan Hokkien rhymes, Malay/Thai *wayang gedek* (shadow play), and Teochew rod puppet theater.[13] All the groups interacted with the audience through demonstrations and explanations of the historical development of the forms, which were all documented on video. For instance, the Peranakan (local-born Chinese who have adapted to Malay customs and culture) taught the audience how to sing Peranakan rhymes as part of their presentation. The performers were encouraged to make representations of their own cultures without having to adhere to any cultural policy. The show ended with the audience participating in dance together with all the performing groups. In 2013, a Taiwanese glove puppet troupe, the Taiyuan Puppet theater, known for its innovative movements, was invited to

FIGURE 3.1 Community performance *Opera Pasar*; children performing the clog dance at the market, 2008.

join in the celebrations. This was to inspire local practitioners with new ideas. Following the celebrations, a workshop was held for the local practitioners of the glove puppet theater and the Taiwanese troupe to foster exchange and learning.

Participatory Evaluations

Evaluations using questionnaires and focused interviews were carried out to get feedback from the communities and volunteers about the organization of the celebrations, use of space, problems faced, and ideas about how to improve future heritage celebrations.

Social Impact and Outcomes

Through the participatory processes involving research, members of the communities are engaged in the heritage celebrations and are empowered to represent and revitalize their own cultures. Even though the problems of cultural representation cannot be completely resolved through the celebrations, the communities are able to showcase their own cultures, which offer variations to the stereotypical ethnic representations by the federal government. The communities become aware of the possibilities of contesting state representations through the performances and events they organize.

The communities acquire ownership of the festival as they take part actively in its planning, research, and implementation, and they are inspired to continue to organize and participate dynamically in it annually. Cultural gaps are bridged as the different ethnic communities are exposed to each other's cultural resources and come together for discussion at workshop meetings. The organizers of the workshop and celebrations (including the ethnomusicologist) act as facilitators in the participatory processes in order to have a shared understanding of community needs and to provide the tools for research and presentations. As part of the process, they also train younger volunteers, who are included and engaged in the planning, organization, management, and running of the celebrations. Capacity building and skills development take place through cultural documentation, mapping, and presentations.

These projects have also helped to bring performances, visual arts, food, and crafts out of buildings and back to the streets and public spaces where they were traditionally enjoyed by the communities at large. Multiethnic audiences are also able to access the presentations in a relaxed manner, and yet learn about, and experience how traditions can be used in new ways.

Advocacy Projects with Young People

In addition to working with adult communities, it is also important to educate young people to reclaim their multiethnic histories and traditions, promote diversity, deconstruct cultural stereotypes, and enhance tolerance, as they represent the future members of civil society. To this end, I have worked long-term on musical-theater projects with children and youths of mixed ages, gender, and ethnicity, to provide a venue for them to address issues of identity and heritage, and to acquire skills in the traditional performing arts. The target group comprises young people (aged 10–19) from different schools inside and outside the city of George Town. The facilitators include multiethnic musicians, dancers, dramatists, visual artists, lecturers, and students of the university (Tan, 2008).

The young people also explore other issues important to the communities in George Town through these musical theater projects. Recent performance projects include *Kisah Pulau Pinang* (The Penang Story, 2006), *Ronggeng Merdeka* (Independence Ronggeng, 2007), *Opera Pasar* (Market Opera, 2008; see Figure 3.2), *Ko-Tai Penang* (Penang Ko-Tai, 2009/2010), *Ceritera Lebuh Carnavon* (Carnavon Street Story) (2011), and *George Town Heboh—Streets Alive* (2012). These musical theater projects have investigated the alternative people's histories of Penang, which are not found in school history textbooks, such as the gentrification of heritage buildings, saving the wet market, and environmental issues, as well as stimulating other community interventions.

Adapting and localizing theater for development, the performance-oriented projects use participatory approaches that focus on local needs and interests, are performed in public community spaces, and engage the multiethnic communities in the processes of doing art. These approaches include the following:

FIGURE 3.2 Siamese in Penang performing the Menora at the Heritage Celebrations, 2013.

Participatory Planning

We collaborate with different stakeholders and involve community participation in the children's advocacy projects. While funding is mainly from the Penang state government and other private firms, interested parties involved in the initial planning include university lecturers, students, historians, teachers, craftsmen, traditional artists and performers, conservationists, and clan associations. They provide information, skills, knowledge, workshop space, or musical instruments.

Participatory Training

The process theater workshop provides the site for participatory training and learning activities. The training design involves team building, skill building, and capacity building. During all the stages of training, a variety of drama games and exercises are used for ice breaking. Warm-up sessions help the participants and facilitators to get to know one another and establish a sense of ensemble and trust through games and group dynamic activities. These activities also help to instill confidence for self-expression.

Participants undergo skill training in selected traditional and contemporary art forms with artists. They are also given tools for research, such as methods of conducting oral interviews and participant observation. This is to enable them to collect their own data regarding specific cultural assets of the community (such as music, movements, festivals, craft, architecture, food) and to connect them to present-day cultural, religious, and social contexts.

Participatory Research, Learning, and Mapping

The city and its people provide the actual environment for experiential learning. Besides talks and watching audiovisual resources about the history and context of a particular location to be studied (such as the market or a street), the youths are taken for guided walks where they observe, listen, and record sounds using MP3 players and video cameras, movements, and conversations. They interview specific people, including their own grandparents, uncles, and aunts, about the topics they are studying. In *Opera Pasar* (a story about conserving the heritage market at Campbell Street), the young people talked to the traders of the market such as the vegetable seller, fishmonger, chicken seller, and butcher about their trades and the history of the market. Participatory mapping of the locations of the stalls and the conflicts and issues that occurred in the space over time were then carried out. Cultural mapping and participatory analysis of the oral histories, photographs, and audiovisual recordings helped to create awareness of the issues and appreciation of the wet market. Once they got over the smell of fresh fish and wet floors, the young participants (many of whom are accustomed to shopping at supermarkets) became crusaders to preserve this old market with its beautiful façade.

Participatory Creation and Performance

The participants then collectively put together what they observed and collected from their fieldwork with the musical skills they learned in the form of a dramatic musical dance composition. The stories, issues, and maps were used by the children in the story-telling, song lyrics, and movements of their musical theater.

In the *Opera Pasar* project, communicating what they learned to the community at the market itself added to the excitement of the young participants. The site-specific performance juxtaposed local folklore with festivals, the past with the present, animals with humans. It mixed the different local languages of Penang with the eclectic musical traditions from Malay *dikir barat* (folk-singing genre), Hokkien rhymes, Chinese opera, and jazz. There was improvisation of the music, which combined the use of everyday objects and junk materials with more traditional instruments such as the *gamelan*, and various types of storytelling. The young dancers used their bodies to convey their impressions of the market, ranging from chickens being slaughtered, fish being caught in the sea, mutton being hung, or buying and selling in the market.

The participants were involved in different forms of border crossings in the learning and production process, which helped in integration. The story, music, and movements employed were based on experiences of real-life people of various ethnic backgrounds in the inner city of Penang. The characters mixed Hokkien, Malay, English, Tamil, and Mandarin phrases, embodying typical conversations at the Malaysian marketplace, coffeeshop, homes, and schools.

Participatory Evaluations

Critical evaluations regarding the workshop process and content are carried out based on focused interviews and questionnaire evaluations. This is to find out what the young people and communities think about the project, the problems faced, and what they have learned. This allows for improvements in future projects.

Social Impact and Outcomes

Besides the investigation of local cultures and concerns, the entire participatory process of the musical theater (as exemplified by *Opera Pasar*) has promoted the spirit of goodwill and building bridges among young people of various ethnic origins. It has encouraged cross-cultural understanding and interaction by incorporating participants, artists, and facilitators from different ethnicity and class backgrounds. The young participants have been given a safe space to relate intensively with others outside their own racial group. Through participatory research, the young people learn about each other's history, religion, and culture. Through intensive interaction during the workshop and performances, they learn to appreciate and mix with children of different backgrounds. This contributes to peace building. By crossing stylistic and ethnic boundaries, that is, by representing themselves in ambiguous ways (shown by blending languages, singing, and dance styles, which occurs in their daily lives), the young people subvert the essentialist ethnic representations of the state. They begin to appreciate cultural differences and develop perspectives that are more inclusive.

The practice of "making theater" is also extended to the community, focusing on issues relevant to the community. The participants not only "give back" to the communities (from whom they obtained their research materials) but create new knowledge by bringing their energy, creativity, and insights through performance. The experience is empowering, both for the performers and the community. In the midst of the *Opera Pasar* project, the young people found out that several tenants in the vicinity of the market were being moved out, as they could not pay the high rents. They discovered that George Town's living cultural heritage faces a threat as traditional communities who have been living in the inner city since World War II are being forced to vacate their premises to make way for upmarket businesses like boutique hotels, pubs, and restaurants. This not only gave the young performers extra motivation to tell their story but a channel for the tenants to make known their plight. The Campbell Street heritage market still stands, and the traders have been able to continue selling their goods today. However, many of those renting houses in the vicinity have been moved out to make way for new restaurants and coffee houses.

Nonetheless, an exciting outcome is that in having contributed to the research, making of the compositions and performance itself, the young people develop a sense of affinity to the predicaments of the traders and the wet market. They gain ownership of the reconstructed musical traditions, and begin to internalize traditional music through new and engaging channels. Empowerment and ownership ensure that musical traditions will be conserved in their traditional sociocultural contexts of performance, and not just in the archives.

TOWARD A PARTICIPATORY APPLIED ETHNOMUSICOLOGY FOR SOCIAL INTERVENTION

This chapter sees applied ethnomusicology as a type of social intervention in which the researcher mediates problem-solving and cultural or social conflict among the disadvantaged or marginalized (Harrison, Mackinlay, and Pettan, 2010). As ethnomusicologists take on new roles in the field, their research methodologies and approaches need to be evaluated and changed. I have tried to show in this chapter that conventional ethnomusicological undertakings, such as fieldwork and research through interviews, participant observation, audiovisual recordings, analysis, skill training in performing traditional instruments, and other forms of local theater and dance, remain important tools for cultural conservation. Nevertheless, for social intervention to take place, participatory approaches that can strengthen the self-esteem and confidence of the target groups by self-expression, interaction, and involvement need to be incorporated. These approaches are often interdisciplinary and are drawn from other fields such as development studies, performance studies, pedagogy, anthropology, and oral history. In order to bring about change in society, it is necessary to develop an alternative participatory applied ethnomusicology that is inclusive, plural, and interdisciplinary in approach, and that incorporates the diverse voices of the people with whom we work.

Learning from the practice of process theater for development, this chapter advocates a shift from the neutral objective collection and analysis of ethnographic data[14] toward action research, which is participatory where the researcher collaborates with the community in all aspects of the research that aims at improving the quality of life of the community. The community then becomes an active participant in the dialogue, investigation, decision-making, and action taken, rather than remaining "the Other." The multiplicity of voices reduces the power of any dominant voice and breaks down hierarchies.

Through the examples of the Heritage Celebrations and children's music advocacy programs in Penang, I have shown that the participatory methods of process theater, such as participatory planning, training, mapping, learning, analysis, and presentation, are practical instruments of participatory action research and applied ethnomusicology. Participatory methods are tools for promoting dialogue and building self-confidence and community.

The participatory approach of working is based on the following:

1. Participation of all stakeholders, which includes contributing ideas, reflecting, and taking initiatives for action collectively;
2. Research and mapping of issues and locations as a group;
3. Dialogue and exchange of ideas together through the process of creating and presenting theater or creative work;
4. Stakeholder ownership of the process and content of the research;
5. Decisions for action to be made by all stakeholders whose lives will be affected by the action;
6. Adaptability and creativity in methodologies, as there is no single rule for problem-solving;
7. Facilitator training among the community for follow-up work; and
8. Networking with other groups with similar interests and strategies as part of the exchange and experiential learning.

The overall effect of these creative participatory processes is "empowerment"; communities and young people gain the capacity to make positive choices about their future and transform these decisions into action. They gain access to knowledge through research so that they can take part in the democratic process. The stakeholders gain confidence to enter into dialogue with others, and take practical action as individuals or as a group. They are able to generate new knowledge and to challenge conventional history and cultural representations by the more powerful.

As soon as action research becomes participatory in nature, the researcher's position becomes equal to that of the other participants. The stakeholders collectively conduct research, mapping, analysis, and interpretation of social problems within the community, which ultimately aim at the improvement of the quality of their own lives. Once engaged in the entire process of planning, research, analysis, decision-making, problem-solving, and the creation of artworks, the stakeholders make the activities their own, feel committed to the objectives, and can carry on even without the presence of the ethnomusicologist outsider. The collaboration and project are then likely to succeed.

In participatory action research, there is a delicate relationship between empowerment of the community and the role of the ethnomusicologist researcher. The applied ethnomusicologist needs to find a balance between his or her own needs and the needs of the community. Ethnomusicologists act as facilitators or catalysts, providing the tools for participatory research, spaces and forums for dialogue, methods for capacity building, and the training of other facilitators. They must respect and acknowledge the resources, experiences, and skills of the participants. As facilitators, they need to cross disciplines and move between music, dance, theater, crafts, other creative arts, politics, history, and other fields, depending on the cultural assets and concerns of the community. They must be compliant and creative in adjusting their topics and methods depending on the social and cultural factors at play.

In the context of community development, as I have highlighted earlier, creative participatory processes are vehicles for participation and a forum for raising and analyzing local problems. A major outcome is the empowering of community members who, prior to participating in these projects, had little or no say in decision-making. Nevertheless, there is a need to emphasize that participatory methods can only act as tools for intervention in communities striving for self-reliance and change. These methods do not resolve problems such as the inequalities, racial tensions, or problematic representations totally, but they help to illustrate and expose the issues. Group discussions and evaluations serve as interventions or problem-posing strategies, which can lead to further action.

The case studies of Penang also illustrate that research and documentation are essential tools for social intervention. As Arjun Appadurai (2006: 175, 176, 177) has written in his article "The Right to Research," it is important for the "bottom thirty percent of the world's population in poor countries who might not get past secondary schools" to "make independent inquiries about their own lives and worlds. Developing the capacity to document, inquire, analyze, and communicate results has a powerful effect on their capacity to speak up as active citizens on matters that are shaping their city and their world." Writing, photography, drawing, creating videos, singing, and acting are ways to communicate research findings and analysis to the public. He cites the Mumbai-based Partners for Urban Action and Research (PUKAR) as an example, where young people are taught certain forms of research and analysis to enable them to study their own lives and the cities where they live, and to disseminate their results through various types of media such as photography or writing.[15]

Finally, the processual and participatory way of working toward the organization and running of the Heritage Celebrations and children's advocacy musical-theater projects may be viewed as a step toward the democratization of cultural research and learning. Acquiring the ability to conduct research, investigate, analyze, and communicate findings in creative ways can help communities and young people to voice their opinions regarding issues that are affecting them and their communities.

NOTES

1. It should be noted that participatory action research has been established in applied anthropology and public folklore much earlier than in ethnomusicology. As an example, theater, music, and film have been used by activists in the southern Appalachian Mountain region of the United States as participatory action research with community leadership since the 1970s. For further information, see the website of Appalshop, a media, arts, and education center in Whitesburg, Kentucky, http://appalshop.org (accessed January 13, 2014). In the field of ethnomusicology, Jeff Todd Titon has written about participatory action research with Old Regular Baptists of Southeastern Kentucky, in the United States. In collaboration with the Indian Bottom Association of Old Regular Baptists, he has co-produced two Smithsonian Folkways albums of their music. For more information, see Titon (1999), Fenn and Titon (2003), and the website http://www.folklife.si.edu/resources/festival1997/baptists.htm (accessed January 13, 2014).

2. See van Erven's (1992) seminal study on the Philippine, Korean, Indian, Indonesian, Thai, and Japanese theater for liberation networks in the 1970s and 1980s. Based on research in these countries, he has written about the practitioners, methodologies, and content of the theater for liberation workshops and the scripts of plays performed by the prominent groups in these countries. According to van Erven, the impact of these theater programs has been so powerful that theater practitioners in some countries have been threatened with guns and even imprisonment.

3. This section about the programs and approaches of the theater for development groups in Asia is based on personal research and interviews with established groups and practitioners in the Philippines, Indonesia, Thailand, and Japan. The research was funded by the Asian Public Intellectuals (API) Fellowship, Nippon Foundation, Japan in 2008–2009.

4. See Tan (2009) for a report of how various groups in Japan, Thailand, Philippines, and Indonesia have used the arts and other forms of popular media to empower young people to understand and deal with issues, concerns, and changes in their lives. The API project report discusses the role of communication media in democratic expression, team building, participatory processes, and engagement of the stakeholders and youths of the communities in the projects.

5. See Tan (1990) for a discussion of the Malaysian government's efforts to create a national culture in the 1970s and 1980s and the responses from the various ethnic and social groups involved in the arts.

6. I analyze the processes of cultural centralization, effects of the national policy on the traditional performing arts, and the re-creation of tradition by arts administrators from the 1970s until the turn of the millennium in Tan (2003).

7. The state government of Penang has sponsored an annual month-long festival of arts and culture known as the George Town Festival since 2010 to celebrate the inscription of George Town as a world heritage site (together with Melaka). The community-oriented Heritage Celebrations are among the core events of the month-long festival.

8. It should be mentioned that Penang is one of the few states of Malaysia governed by the opposition party, the Democratic Action Party (DAP), and the chief minister is a Chinese from DAP. Consequently, the people of Penang are given more opportunities to challenge federal cultural and other policies that are perceived to be discriminatory.

9. The Indian Muslim community has emerged as a result of the marriage of Malays and Indians.
10. For more information about all the programs of the heritage celebrations, see www.heritagecelebrations.info or www.facebook.com/GeorgeTownCelebrations.
11. Secret societies are triads or brotherhoods of sworn association, that engage in activities outside the law and share a common system of signs and initiation rites. Secret societies were banned by the British colonial government in Malaysia in the early twentieth century.
12. See Tan (2011) for more detailed descriptions and video recordings of the multicultural performing arts, crafts, festivals, and food of Penang.
13. See Tan (2011) for more information about the diverse performing arts of Penang.
14. Araújo (2008) is critical of colonial narratives that inform the traditional methods of ethnomusicological research based on "conventional ethnography," that is, based on "participant observation," "analyzed and presented in a neutral way." This type of research fails "to produce real engagement with the researched." For him, the discourse of academia reduces the power of people in defining, preserving, and presenting their cultures.
15. Appadurai (2006: 167) states that it is the right of the poor to "claim the right to research." He argues for the need to "de-parochialize the idea of research," which should not be seen as an activity of those with certain training and class background. Rather, research should be made available to ordinary people, as it is a way to increase their knowledge in relation to some goal or task.

REFERENCES

Appadurai, Arjun. (2006). "The Right to Research." *Globalisation, Societies and Education* 4(2): 167–177.

Appalshop. http://appalshop.org (accessed January 13, 2014).

Araújo, Samuel. (2006). "Conflict and Violence as Theoretical Tools in Present-Day Ethnomusicology: Notes on a Dialogic Ethnography of Sound Practices in Rio de Janeiro." *Ethnomusicology* 50(2): 287–313.

Araújo, Samuel. (2008). "From Neutrality to Praxis: The Shifting Politics of Ethnomusicology in the Contemporary World." *Muzikološki zbornik/Musicological Annual*, Ljubljana XLIV(1): 13–30.

Araújo, Samuel. (2009). "Ethnomusicologists Researching Towns They Live In: Theoretical and Methodological Queries for a Renewed Discipline." *Muzikologija/Musicology* 9: 33–50.

Barber, Richard. (2008). *The Art of Peace: A Toolkit of Theatre Art for Conflict Resolution.* Bangkok: Makhampom Foundation.

Boal, Augusto. (1979). *Theater of the Oppressed.* New York: Urizen Books.

Chambers, Robert. (1997). *Whose Reality Counts? Putting the First Last.* London: Intermediate Technological Publications.

Department of Statistics, Malaysia. (2010). http://www.statistics.gov.my/portal/index.php?option=com_content&id=1215 (accessed September 17, 2013).

Dirksen, Rebecca. (2012). "Reconsidering Theory and Practice in Ethnomusicology: Applying, Advocating, and Engaging Beyond Academia." *Ethnomusicology Review* 17, http://ethnomusicologyreview.ucla.edu/journal/volume/17/piece/602 (accessed September 17, 2013).

Ellis, Catherine. (1994). "Powerful Songs: Their Placement in Aboriginal Thought." *the world of music* 36(1): 3–20.

van Erven, Eugene. (1992). *The Playful Revolution, Theatre and Liberation in Asia*. Bloomington and Indianapolis: Indiana University Press.

Eskamp, Kees. (2006). *Theatre for Development: An Introduction to Context, Applications and Training*. London: Zed Press.

Fenn, John, and Titon, Jeff Todd. (2003). "A Conversation with Jeff Todd Titon: Interviewed by John Fenn via e-mail, January 2003." *Folklore Forum* 34: 112.

Fisher, Joseph P., and Brian Flota, eds. (2011). *The Politics of Post-9/11 Music: Sound, Trauma, and the Music Industry in the Time of Terror*. Burlington, VT: Ashgate.

Freire, Paolo. (1972). *Pedagogy of the Oppressed*. London: Penguin.

Furnivall, J. S. (1948). *Colonial Policy and Practice: A Comparative Study of Burma and Netherlands India*. New York: New York University Press.

Gaspar, Carlos, et al. (1981). *Creative Dramatics Trainors' Manual*. Hong Kong: Plough Publications.

Harrison, Klisala, Elizabeth, Mackinlay and Svanibor, Pettan, eds. (2010). *Applied Ethnomusicology: Historical and Contemporary Approaches*. Cambridge: Cambridge Scholars.

Hermetek, Ursula. (2010). "Applied Ethnomusicology as an Intercultural Tool: Some Experiences from the First 25 years of Minority Research in Austria." Proceedings of CAIR10, the first Conference on Applied Interculturality Research, Graz, Austria, April 7–10, 2010.

Impey, Angela. (2002). "Culture, Conservation and Community Reconstruction; Explorations in Advocacy Ethnomusicology and Action Research in Northern KwaZulu." *Yearbook for Traditional Music* 34: 9–24.

Kellock, Willow. (n.d.). *Understanding Theatre as a Tool for Peace: An Introduction for Community Workers on the Thai Burma Border*. Chiengmai: Makhampom.

KKBS (Kementerian Kebudayaan, Belia dan Sukan Malaysia or Ministry of Culture, Youth and Sports Malaysia). (1973). *Asas Kebudayaan Kebangsaan [Basis of National Culture]*, Kuala Lumpur.

Newsome, Jennifer. (2008). "From Researched to Centrestage: A Case Study." *Muzikološki zbornik/Musicological Annual*, Ljubljana, XLIV(I): 31–50.

O'Connell, John Morgan, and Salwa El-Shawan Castelo-Branco, eds. (2010). *Music and Conflict*. Urbana: University of Illinois Press.

Penang Institute. (2015). *Quarterly Penang Statistics, Population*. http://penanginstitute.org/v3/resources/data-centre/122-population (accessed February 12, 2015).

Pettan, Svanibor, ed. (1998). *Music, Politics, and War: Views from Croatia*. Zagreb: Institute of Ethnology and Folklore Research.

Pettan, Svanibor. (2008). "Applied Ethnomusicology and Empowerment Strategies: Views from Across the Atlantic." *Muzikološki zbornik/Musicological Annual* XLIV(1): 85–99.

Pettan, Svanibor. (2010). "Applied Ethnomusicology: Bridging Research and Action." *Music and Arts in Action* 2(2): 90–93.

Samson, Laura L., et al. (2008). *A Continuing Narrative on Philippine Theatre: The Story of PETA (Philippine Educational Theater Association)*. Quezon City: PETA.

Seeger, Anthony. (1992). "A Few Notions about Philosophy and Strategy in Applied Ethnomusicology." *Ethnomusicology* 36(3): 323–336, Special Issue: Music and the Public Interest.

Tan, Sooi Beng. (1990). "The Performing Arts in Malaysia: State and Society." *Asian Music* 21(1): 137–171.

Tan, Sooi Beng. (2003). "Multi-Culturalism or One National Culture: Cultural Centralization and the Recreation of the Traditional Performing Arts in Malaysia." *Journal of Chinese Ritual, Theatre and Folklore* 141: 237–260.

Tan, Sooi Beng. (2008). "Activism in Southeast Asian Ethnomusicology: Empowering Youths to Revitalize Traditions and Bridge Cultural Barriers." *Muzikološki zbornik/Musicological Annual*, Ljubljana, XLIV (I): 69–84.

Tan, Sooi Beng. (2009). "Participatory Arts and Creative Media in Asia: Engaging Communities and Empowering Youths For Change." In *Confluences and Challenges in Building the Asian Community in the Early 21st Century, The Work of the 2008/2009 API Fellows*, edited by Patricio N. Abinales, pp. 162–172. Bangkok: The Nippon Foundation Fellowships for Asian Public Intellectuals.

Tan, Sooi Beng. (2010). "Crossing Stylistic Boundaries and Transcending Ethnicity through the Performing Arts." In *Building Bridges, Crossing Boundaries: Everyday Forms of Inter-Ethnic Peace Building in Malaysia*, edited by Francis Loh Kok Wah, pp. 223–236. Selangor: The Ford Foundation, Jakarta, and the Malaysian Social Science Association.

Tan, Sooi Beng. (2011). *The Multicultural Performing Arts, Crafts, Festivals and Food of Penang* (DVD set and book). Pulau Pinang: School of the Arts, Universiti Sains Malaysia.

Titon, Jeff Todd. (1997). "Articles from the 1997 Festival of American Folklife Program Book." http://www.folklife.si.edu/resources/festival1997/baptists.htm (accessed January 15, 2014).

Titon, Jeff Todd. (1999). "'The Real Thing': Tourism, Authenticity, and Pilgrimage among the Old Regular Baptists at the 1997 Smithsonian Folklife Festival." *the world of music* 41(3): 115–139.

World Commission on Environment and Development (WCED). (1987). *Our Common Future*. Oxford: Oxford University Press.

Zebec, Tvrtko. 2004. "The Challenges of Applied Ethnology in Croatia." *The Anthropology of East Europe Review* 22(1): 85–92.

Interviews

Barber, Richard, May 30, 2009, Makhampom Living Theatre Centre, Chiengdao, Thailand.

Chitrachinoa, Santi, October 29, 2008, Maya, The Art and Cultural Institute for Development, Bangkok, Thailand.

Tri Giovanni, August 13, 2008, Yayasan Puskat, Yogyakarta, Indonesia.

CHAPTER 4

. . . .

APPLIED ETHNOMUSICOLOGY AND INTANGIBLE CULTURAL HERITAGE

Understanding "Ecosystems of Music" as a Tool for Sustainability

. . . .

HUIB SCHIPPERS

IN 1964, William Kay Archer published "On the Ecology of Music," a five-page essay in *Ethnomusicology* (8[1]: 28–33), in which he argues:

> In a time when the total pattern of musical dissemination, consumption and response is undergoing extraordinary changes, it may be as fruitful to consider sources of raw materials for instruments, patterns of leisure, technological developments, musical "listening-spaces" and the like, as to consider the music itself.
>
> (Archer, 1964: 28–29)

Although he does not develop this idea in any great detail (Archer primarily focuses on social and aesthetic considerations in the following pages), it does help trace back the "wellsprings" of explicit ecological thinking on music over half a century.

In the five decades since, a number of authors have invoked ecology as an approach or metaphor for thinking about music cultures. Most notable among these is Jeff Titon, who developed this view over a period of 25 years through his writings, his lectures, his blog (http://sustainablemusic.blogspot.com/), and a themed edition of *the world of music* on ecology and sustainability that he edited in 2009. In that volume, he strongly links ecological understanding to sustainability and, outlining the contents of the volume, provides a much more comprehensive list of factors in the ecosystem of music, including the following:

Cultural and musical rights and ownership, the circulation and conservation of music, the internal vitality of music cultures and the social organization of their music-making, music education and transmission, the roles of community scholars and practitioners, intangible cultural heritage, tourism, and the creative economy, preservation versus revitalization, partnerships among cultural workers and community leaders, and good stewardship of musical resources.

(Titon, 2009a: 5)

Critiquing cultural heritage management initiatives that approach preservation statically, he argues that stewardship in relation to musical ecosystems "offers the most promising path toward sustainability in musical cultures today" (ibid.: 11) as "living heritage 'masterpieces' are best maintained by managing the cultural soil surrounding them" (2009b: 124). That is a leading thought throughout this chapter.

Other authors have explicitly or implicitly invoked the ecology metaphor to elucidate the network of forces that impact the sustainability of specific music genres. Daniel Neuman (1980) was probably the first, by dedicating a full chapter to "The Ecology of Hindustani Music Culture," covering "the producers of music, the consumers of music, the contexts of music events, and the technology of music production and reproduction" (1980: 203). Others include Slobin (1996) for Eastern and Central European music, Ramnarine (2003) for Finnish folk music, Sheehy (2006) for Mexican Mariachi music, and Howard (2006a, 2006b) for Korean music, to name just a few.

In that way, factors that influence musical vibrancy have been identified in specific cultures for several decades. However, they have hardly been explored systematically across genres and cultures. In one way, this can be explained from the fact that each music genre is best approached in its own right, as well as an aversion to comparative approaches in our discipline—which have been passionately discredited since the 1950s. This was arguably due more to conceptual and ideological weakness than to structural flaws (cf. Nettl, 2010: 71, 82), although Lomax's *Cantometrics* probably failed to gain broad support from the 1960s due to the latter, overclaiming correlations between musical characteristics and societal structures (Lomax, 1976). In the current debate concerning sustainability, however, I would argue there is a compelling reason to revisit comparative approaches without a strong Eurocentric bias, which can assist in exploring links between music sustainability and ecology from a contemporary, holistic, and global perspective.

ECOSYSTEMS OF MUSIC

There is a 65-year gap between the time that Haeckel introduced the concept of *ecology* in 1870 as "the study of all those complex interrelations referred to by Darwin as the conditions of the struggle for existence" (quoted in Stauffer, 1957: 140), creating a fertile, practical, philosophical, and metaphorical framework to explore sustainability, and the launch of the term *ecosystem*, which I would argue invites more concrete reflections on the forces that affect a phenomenon. While the latter developed in biology as well, the term *ecosystem* is both derived from and applicable to a wider intellectual space. A. G. Tansley borrowed from the sciences when he first used it, arguing to consider

> the whole system (in the sense of physics), including not only the organism complex, but also the whole complex of physical factors forming what we call the environment of the biome, the habitat factors in the widest sense. Though the organism may claim our primary interest, when we are trying to think fundamentally we cannot separate them from their special environment, with which they form one physical system.
>
> (1935: 299)

Ecosystems have since been used to describe animal habitats, resources, cities, and increasingly other environments, which can "include humans and their artifacts" to the point "that it is applicable to any case where organisms and physical processes interact in some spatial area" (Pickett and Cadenasso, 2002: 2). That provides fruitful ground for looking at music cultures.

Arguably, ethnomusicology—and to some extent historical musicology—has already used this approach: primarily in regard to localized genres, with a wealth of focused ethnographic studies from the 1960s, and regarding individual music cultures and genres more in their diasporic and global contexts since the 1980s. Individual musicians, instrument makers, communities, educators, the music industry, opinion leaders, and public authorities are among the direct actors, while not only the physical environment and climate, but also war, discrimination, and disease are among the indirect forces in such ecosystems.

Undeniably, it is both easy and tempting to appeal "to natural imagery to justify critiques of the detrimental impact of transnational industry practices on sub-dominant music cultures and styles" (Keogh, 2013: 11), and to make facile links between music ecosystems and sustainability efforts, imbibing them with a sense of moral justness, perhaps much like the word *authentic* is used in music performance contexts (cf. Cook, 1998: 11–13; Schippers, 2010: pp. 47–50; Taylor, 2007: p. 21). Similarly, it is easy to succumb to a historically and intellectually unsound tendency to impose a static, preservationist approach on music genres as objects. While many archiving efforts, recording projects, festivals, and even the highly visible *Masterpieces of Intangible Cultural Heritage* initiatives of UNESCO still seem to approach music genres as artifacts rather than organisms, there is increasing consensus that a dynamic approach to processes of music sustainability and change is imperative. It is broadly acknowledged that instruments, styles, and genres have been emerging and disappearing throughout history and across cultures as a largely "organic" process.

In fact, the concept of ecosystem fits current thinking on how music sits within its environment remarkably well, almost to the point that it can be considered literal rather than metaphorical. We don't have to stray far from Tansley's (1935) description to define a *music ecosystem* as

> the whole system, including not only a specific music genre, but also the complex of factors defining the genesis, development and sustainability of the surrounding music culture in the widest sense, including (but not limited to) the role of individuals, communities, values and attitudes, learning processes, contexts for making music, infrastructure and organisations, rights and regulations, diaspora and travel, media and the music industry.
>
> (Schippers after Tansley, 1935: 298)

It is easy to argue in parallel with Tansley that, though historically *music genres* may have claimed our primary interest, when we are trying to think fundamentally, we cannot separate them from their special environment, with which they form one physical system.

That in turn invites a brief discussion of the terminology and rhetoric of sustainability. In music, as in many other disciplines, *ecosystem* associates with *sustainability* in the context of other widely used terms such as *preservation, safeguarding, salvaging,* and *maintaining.* The first three of these run the risk of coming across as defensive and patronizing. They imply risks of stasis, ossification, and even strangulation of living traditions, as well as disempowerment and other risks of government interventions or institutionalization. The term *maintaining* (commonly used in the context of preserving languages internationally) is much less harsh, and perhaps the strongest competition for *sustaining. Maintaining* does suggest aiming for a status quo, however. Etymologically, *maintaining* means holding *in* the hand, (Fr., *maintenir*), while *sustaining* implies holding a hand *under* something for support (Fr., *soustenir*). Therefore, I would argue that the term *sustaining* has the best chance at transcending any "tradition under siege" associations, suggesting a gentler process, and leaving room for taking into account multiple forces working on a phenomenon—while it is still allowed to breathe.

If *sustainability* is the preferred terminology, three key questions need to be answered: whether (any—or all) music needs to be sustained; what is to be sustained; and finally, how this can be operationalized. This will be the focus of much of the rest of this chapter.

While some may believe that *all* music should be preserved, it is clear that over the course of history thousands of music genres have emerged and disappeared due to "natural" causes. Not all of us are up in arms about this at every single occurrence. For instance, the rise and decline of crooning (McCracken, 1999) was a process that did not cause indignation from a sustainability perspective. In addition, it is useful to keep in mind that much music does not need additional support. Most music cultures adapt successfully to changing environments, and often benefit from them. Music genres once constrained to a single locale are now available across the planet. The issues of markets, power, and perceptions of prestige that underlie this reality have created shifts in musical dynamics that benefit many, but threaten the futures of other forms of musical expression. Arguably, this occurs well beyond the evolutionary processes that have predominantly governed musical diversity in earlier periods. Anthony Seeger expresses his concern about global risks to certain categories of intangible cultural heritage succinctly:

> The problem is it's not really an even playing field: it's not as though these are just disappearing, they're "being disappeared"; there's an active process in the disappearance of many traditions around the world. Some of them are being disappeared by majority groups that want to eliminate the differences of their minority groups within their nations, others are being disappeared by missionaries or religious groups of various kinds who find music offensive and want to eliminate it.
>
> (QCRC, 2008)

Other factors that can be beneficial or detrimental—often without a particular aim or focus on music—include technological developments, copyright legislation, infrastructural challenges, socioeconomic change, wars, disease, and educational systems, as well as developments in travel, migration, business, and communication (cf. Letts, 2006; Malm, 1993; Taylor, 2007; Titon, 2009a). Considering all these factors, the focus of sustainability in this context is not necessarily the preservation of all forms of musical expression, but a future for those that musicians, communities, and other stakeholders feel are worth preserving and developing, and which are at risk due to a range of circumstances beyond their control. Some of these circumstances can be influenced to some extent (like funding or education); others are largely outside human control, including conflict, disease, or natural phenomena such as the slow sinking below rising sea levels of the Takū Atoll (Moyle, 2007). These may impact music practices on many levels, necessitating more creative lines of action to keep music vibrant in a changing environment.

Next is the question of *what* is to be sustained. Is it the musical sound, the performance tradition, the transmission processes, the audience, the commercial value, the social, cultural, or spiritual context, or the musical practice at large, including its underlying values and attitudes? The balance between these differs from tradition to tradition and stakeholder to stakeholder, and they are often interrelated. While it is perfectly possible to "freeze" a specific musical expression on video or audio recording, for a practice to be sustainable it tends to need a combination of at least some of the following components: a robust transmission processes, strong links in the community, prestige, appropriate settings and infrastructure for practicing the music, supportive media, an engaged music industry, and laws and regulations that do not impede negatively on the genre, much in line with the Titon quote earlier in this chapter.

For most genres and traditions, these do not form a neat and static set of characteristics, but a diverse and not always coherent one. This lack of coherence is not necessarily a weakness: it potentially creates the resilience to deal with inevitable changes due to social and cultural change, globalization, commodification, and recontextualization. Efforts aimed at preserving music as an object or artifact risk creating a false sense of security: well-preserved recordings, carefully crafted slick presentations for broad audiences, and institutionalized education or performance practices can lead to ossi-fication by not allowing change, or an artificial "new life" supported financially and or-ganizationally, but devoid of links with community or a creative lifeline to new ideas. "Hold still, let me preserve you" may be convenient from a logistical perspective, but it is an altogether inappropriate approach to sustaining a living tradition, and may lead to a "slow puncture" demise of the music over one or two generations (Schippers, 2009: 202). Howard (2012), among many others, argues that "cultural conservation needs to be dy-namic" (p. 5), and conceived "as a way to organise 'the profusion of public and private efforts' that deal with 'traditional community cultural life' (Loomis, 1983, iv)" and which "we together with our constituents, share in the act of making" (p. 6).

Related to this are the concepts of tradition, authenticity, and context. As I have argued elsewhere (Schippers, 2010: 41–60), static approaches to each of those concepts may have done more harm than good to the thinking on, education in, and practice of music outside the Western classical canon: "The nature of tradition is not to preserve intact a heritage from the past, but to enrich it according to present circumstances and transmit the result to future generations" (Aubert, 2007: 10). Similarly, as discussed above, au-thenticity is highly contentious and laden. Paradoxically, it had opposite meanings in the emergence of early music practice in the 1960s and 1970s ("Authentic is as close to the original as we can get") and in rock music of the same period ("Authentic is as far from copying existing models as possible"). Moreover, the reference for authenticity, the "moment of authenticness," may well be rather randomly or even self-servingly chosen by a self-proclaimed authority. In that sense, it is similar to the idea of "the right con-text": virtually all music traditions reinvent, redefine, and recontextualize themselves as a matter of course. Hybridization and transculturalization are not exceptions, but the norm in virtually all music that we know, even though few realize as they enjoy a sym-phony that if one were to exclude all influences from the Western orchestra that can be traced back to the world of Islam—which includes, strings, reeds, percussion, and brass—there would be little left on stage.

All of this presents a potent case for regarding the past, present, and future of musical practices as part of a complex and often delicate ecosystem. The final key issue in the discussion of "What is to be preserved?" is defining the scope of ecosystems of music for the purpose of this discussion. The literature on ecosystems at large (e.g., Pickett and Cadenasso, 2002) allows room for both very narrowly prescribed boundaries as well as working on a vast scale. In some cases it makes sense to draw a narrow circle around a valley in the Swiss Alps or a Pacific island that harbors the community, is the birth-place of its composers, teachers, and performers, has provided the raw materials for instruments, and is the site of transmission processes, performance, and other aspects of what Small calls "musicking": "to take part, in any capacity, in a musical performance, whether by performing, by listening, by rehearsing or practising, by providing material for performance (what is called composing), or by dancing" (Small, 1998: 9).

In such a scenario, influences from beyond the circle are seen as intruders into the ecosystem, like an oil spill threatening a coral reef. However, as myriad external influences increasingly form an integral part of virtually all music practices, it may be more accurate and fruitful to regard *all* forces that impact upon the music as part of the ecosystem, including technology, commercialization, legislature, globalization, and media. As Wong (QCRC, 2008) reminds us, we are working in "environments which are going to be commodified, and mediatized, and globalized." This allows for a much more comprehensive picture of both potential and challenges for sustainability.

It also assists in addressing one of the concerns of Keogh (2013: 6) and others: that the applied ethnomusicologist who works toward preservation or sustainability interferes with the ecosystem.

I would argue that this is not the case in the approach proposed here: ethnomusicologists who strive to preserve—aspects of or certain approaches to—a particular genre or tradition are *part* of the ecosystem. As Pickett and Cadenasso point out, the concept of ecosystems "now supports studies that incorporate humans not only as externally located, negative drivers, but also as integral agents that affect and are reciprocally affected by the other components of ecosystems" (2002: 7). The core in this approach lies in not excluding *any* factors from the ecosystem.

Mapping key clusters of forces working on any music genre within a wider music culture generates a simplified graphic representation of a music ecosystem, with the genre at the center, surrounded by factors impacting it, positively or negatively, single or multidirectional.

Figure 4.1 represents five clusters of possible factors influencing the sustainability of a music practice or genre, starting with community-related ones on top, then those relating to education, those involving infrastructure and regulations, media and the music industry, and finally contexts, values, and attitudes. For any specific tradition, the importance of each of those (the size of the balloon, if you will) will vary: paying audiences and formal curricula may be irrelevant to many forms of religious music, and country music survives excellently without grants and legislation. Often, the forces within a cluster will interact (music programs in schools invite formal curricula and the development of pedagogical materials), and forces between clusters may interrelate: the high prestige of opera leads to interest by broadcasters and recording companies, with the exposure triggering grants and subsidies for performances and buildings, extensive learning opportunities, and high social status of opera singers.

Absent from this diagram is explicit mention of well-recognized forces on music sustainability, such as globalization and conflict. In this model, these are best regarded not as single influences, but as ones that may have effects across the clusters: globalization influences industry, institutions, values, and attitudes; while conflict may affect ethnic and gender issues, sites for performance and creativity, and

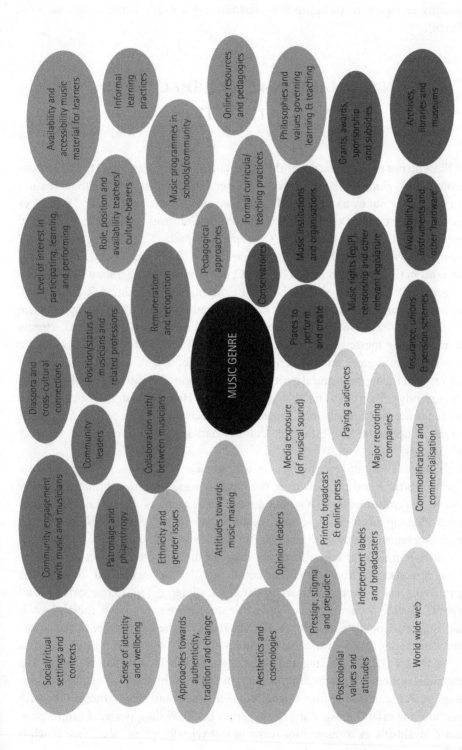

FIGURE 4.1 Ecosystem of Music.

Availability and accessibility music material for learners

Informal learning practices

Online resources and pedagogies

Philosophies and values governing learning & teaching

Grants, awards, sponsorship and subsidies

Archives, libraries and museums

Level of interest in participating, learning and performing

Role, position and availability teachers/culture-bearers

Music programmes in schools/community

Formal curricular/teaching practices

Music institutions and organisations

Availability of instruments and other 'hardware'

Diaspora and cross-cultural connections

Position/status of musicians and related professions

Remuneration and recognition

Pedagogical approaches

Conservatoires

Music rights (egiP), censorship and other relevant legislature

Community engagement with music and musicians

Community leaders

Collaboration with/ between musicians

MUSIC GENRE

Places to perform and create

Insurance, unions & pension schemes

Patronage and philanthropy

Ethnicity and gender issues

Attitudes towards music making

Media exposure (of musical sound)

Paying audiences

Major recording companies

Social/ritual settings and contexts

Sense of identity and wellbeing

Approaches towards authenticity, tradition and change

Aesthetics and cosmologies

Opinion leaders

Prestige, stigma and prejudice

Printed, broadcast & online press

Independent labels and broadcasters

Commodification and commercialisation

Postcolonial values and attitudes

World wide web

community engagement (ranging from abandoning a music genre to finding new resilience).

INTERNATIONAL PERSPECTIVES
AND INITIATIVES

These ideas do not exist in a vacuum. The importance of sustaining—and the challenges to maintaining—global musical diversity have been widely recognized with increasing urgency, as borne out by a suite of UNESCO conventions, declarations, and initiatives put in place over the past 14 years, flowing from its *Universal Declaration on Cultural Diversity* (UNESCO, 2001): the UNESCO's *Convention for the Safeguarding of Intangible Cultural Heritage* (UNESCO, 2003), the *Convention on the Protection and Promotion of the Diversity of Cultural Expressions* (UNESCO, 2005), and the *Declaration on the Rights of Indigenous Peoples* (United Nations High Commission for Human Rights, 2007). While building on initiatives going back many decades in countries like Japan (since 1950) and Korea (since 1982; see Howard, 2012), and not unchallenged in all aspects (such as reducing music genres to artifacts), the UNESCO initiatives have caused a groundswell of awareness, interest, activities, and policies to stimulate the maintenance and diversity of intangible cultural heritage since the beginning of the third millennium. This is currently perhaps most notable in China, where Helen Rees signals "an avalanche of policies, procedures, regulations, projects, and concepts that have poured forth since China dived head-first into intangible cultural heritage protection around the year 2000" (2012: 35).

While the intensity of recent efforts in this arena across Asia is striking, they are not limited in time and place. During the past decades, numerous initiatives (many sponsored by governments, NGOs, and development agencies) throughout the world have provided support for specific music cultures over defined periods of time, ranging from single events or festivals to projects running for a number of years. They constitute positive impulses for the cultures targeted, but their long-term effect is often difficult to demonstrate. Another way to counteract decline in musical diversity has been to document traditions that are in danger of disappearing. Across cultures and continents, this has occurred on a considerable scale for over 100 years, mostly by colleague ethnomusicologists (cf. Nettl, 2010). The results of these efforts are stored in various formats and locations, from local and regional repositories to archival networks like DELAMAN (Digital Endangered Languages and Musics Archives Network) and international centers such as the Smithsonian. In this way, the sound of many traditions is being preserved, allowing future generations to access and reconstruct if they wish (at least to some extent) musical styles and genres that have disappeared. In some cases these are invaluable as communities seek out lost repertoire, but often their reach is limited.

Timothy Rice criticizes methods that are exclusively "aimed at their accurate preservation as sound, film, or video recordings." He argues, "A corollary of this theory-
and-method combination is that a practice has been preserved when converted into a
recording, that is, into a fixed text or monument—perhaps analogous to the way jam
preserves fresh fruit" (1997: 102). A further reservation is that archival recordings often
implicitly suggest authenticity, purity, justness, and even "museumness" (cf. Cook,
1998: 30) for a particular recording of a particular repertoire, and in that way may stifle
the "natural" development of repertoire or interpretation.

Similar arguments can be made for the creation of national troupes or orchestras
mixing the music of different cultural backgrounds, for revivals, and for the institutionalization of training professional musicians. The first tends to objectify music, ignore cultural context, and harmonize divergent styles and even tonal systems. As Titon
points out, the second embodies "a paradox: what is presented there as authentic cannot
possibly be so, because it is staged" (2009b: 121). Feintuch firmly critiques revivalists
who "assert that they're bolstering a declining musical tradition. But rather than encourage continuity, musical revivals recast the music—and culture—they are referring
to" (1993: 184). Finally, higher music education runs the risk of canonizing and ossifying
music through fixing repertoire and curricula, and highlighting measurable aspects of
music learning over more ineffable ones (Schippers, 2010: 61–75). Indeed, valuable as
they are, such efforts do not always provide sufficient basis for the actual survival of musical styles as part of an unbroken, living tradition, which many will argue is a key condition for maintaining the essence (explicit and tacit, tangible and intangible) of specific
styles and genres.

FIVE DOMAINS

This brings the discussion to the question of *how*? Given the situation described above,
it seems there is scope for an angle complementary to existing, more narrowly focused
preservation initiatives: for approaching music as governed by ecosystems, for exploring
the sustainability of music cultures in closer collaboration with communities. This
would be in line with the third of Dan Sheehy's four proposed strategies of applied ethnomusicology: "providing community members access to strategic models and conservation techniques" (1992: 331). It also resonates with Titon's idea of stewardship, which
"repositions culture workers collaboratively, both as students of community scholars
and music practitioners, and simultaneously as teachers who share their skills and networking abilities to help the musical community maintain and improve the conditions
under which their expressive culture may flourish" (2009b: 120).

Such an enterprise requires a framework to map not only a community's histories and
"authentic" practices, but also their dynamics and potential for recontextualization in
their contemporary environment. This includes considering new musical and technological realities, changing values and attitudes, as well as social, political, and market

forces. The ethnomusicological literature of the past 50 years already presents a wealth of information on the nature and present state of many specific music cultures, based primarily on wide consultation with musicians and their communities. More recently, we find increasing attention for other stakeholders, such as public authorities, educational institutions, and the music industry, complemented by documentaries, press, policies, and data gathered from government sources, NGOs, educational authorities, cultural organizations, media, and business. An excellent example of this is the volume on *East Asian Music as Intangible Cultural Heritage* (Howard, ed., 2012), which includes essays dealing with tourism, top-down preservation policies, the role of the media, and political issues.

With such a vast body of information, the key challenge is choosing ways of organizing and analyzing data and insights and their impact on music cultures. I propose that an attractive and insightful way of doing so is a framework of five domains that contain the crucial elements of most "ecosystems of music," as represented in Figure 4.1 in this chapter: systems of learning music; musicians and communities; contexts and constructs; regulations and infrastructure; media and the music industry. Table 4.1 summarizes the key aspects of each of these domains in prose.

These domains cover most key aspects relevant to the sustainability of almost any musical practice, irrespective of specific musical forms or content, and as free as possible from Eurocentric bias. Most of them are well documented. For instance, "musicians and communities" and "contexts and constructs" have been at the center of much ethnomusicological research for five decades. "Systems of learning music" and "media and the music industry" have gained increased attention since the 1980s. "Regulations and infrastructure" have attracted sporadic attention in the discipline, but have been the realm of public authorities and NGOs. For example, the International Music Council report on musical diversity instigated by UNESCO (Letts, 2006) provides a wealth of information on a number of important non-musical factors that affect the viability of specific music cultures, such as copyright, politics, and regulations.

Television and radio broadcasting policies, like those that attempt to encourage or protect local music through laws that require they are allocated a percentage of airplay, have a wide and deep influence on sustainability. Several countries have employed legal provisions to protect folklore through copyright (e.g., Bolivia in 1968, Senegal in 1973, and Ghana in 1985), and some have a system whereby royalties are payable upon use of folklore for economic gains, which in turn are "sometimes earmarked for the preservation of traditional culture and/or the promotion of cultural creation" (Blaukopf, 1992: 33). These policies are of course dependent on politics, lobbying, and the ideologies of those in power, and consequently vacillate from country to country, and from governmental era to era.

In order to understand the influence of these domains on sustainability, it is important to regard not only each individual domain, but rather the whole as the ecosystem. Each of the domains above overlaps and interrelates in how it affects music cultures.

Table 4.1. "Ecosystems of Music": A Framework for Understanding Aspects of Sustainability

1. Systems of learning music	This domain assesses the transmission processes that are central to the sustainability of most music cultures. It investigates balances between informal and formal education and training, notation-based and aural learning, holistic and atomistic approaches, and emphasis on tangible and less tangible aspects of "musicking." It explores contemporary developments in learning and teaching (from master-disciple relationships to systems that are technology/web-based), and how non-musical activities, philosophies, and approaches intersect with learning and teaching. These processes are examined from the level of community initiatives through music education to the level of institutionalized professional training.
2. Musicians and communities	This domain examines the positions, roles, and interactions of musicians within their communities, and the social basis of their traditions in that context. It scrutinizes everyday realities in the existence of creative musicians, including issues of remuneration through performances, teaching, portfolio careers, community support, tenured employment, patronage, freelancing, and non-musical activities, and the role of technology, media, and travel in these. Cross-cultural influences and the role of the diaspora are also examined.
3. Contexts and constructs	This domain assesses the social and cultural contexts of musical traditions. It examines both the setting of music practices and the underlying values and attitudes (constructs). These include musical tastes, aesthetics, cosmologies, socially and individually constructed identities, gender issues, as well as (perceived) prestige, which is often underestimated as a key factor in musical survival. It also looks at the realities of and the attitudes to recontextualization, authenticity, and context, and explicit and implicit approaches to cultural diversity resulting from travel, migration, or media, as well as obstacles such as prejudice, racism, stigma, restrictive religious attitudes, and issues of appropriation.
4. Regulations and infrastructure	This domain primarily relates to the "hardware" of music: places to create, perform, practice, and learn, all of which are essential for music to survive, as well as virtual spaces for creation, collaboration, learning, archiving, and dissemination. Other aspects included in this domain are the availability and/or manufacturing of instruments and other tangible resources. It also examines the extent to which regulations are conducive or obstructive to a blossoming musical heritage, including grants, artists' rights, copyright laws, sound restrictions, laws limiting artistic expression, and adverse circumstances, such as obstacles that can arise from totalitarian regimes, persecution, civil unrest, war, or the displacement of music or communities.
5. Media and the music industry	This domain addresses large-scale dissemination and commercial aspects of music. In one way or another, most musicians and musical styles depend for their survival on the music industry in its widest sense. Over the past 100 years, the distribution of music has increasingly involved recordings, radio, television, and more recently, internet (e.g., downloads, Podcasts, iTunes, YouTube). At the same time, many acoustic and live forms of delivery have changed under the influence of internal and external factors, leading to a wealth of new performance formats. This domain examines the ever-changing modes of distributing, publicizing, and supporting music, considering the role of audiences (including consumers of recorded product), patrons, sponsors, funding bodies, and governments who "buy" or "buy into" artistic product.

First published in Schippers (2010: 180–181).

For example, change can be driven by a combination of changing values and attitudes, technological developments, and/or audience behavior. The manner of music transmission is often strongly determined by its institutional environment, and media attention, markets, and audiences can often be linked to issues of public perception and prestige.

For example, Western classical opera may be argued to be one of the least likely genres to survive by virtue of its almost insurmountable requirements in terms of infrastructure (a theater with excellent acoustics, a large stage, and a flight tower), high-level training of the participants (soloists, chorus, orchestra, conductor, director), and audience (sufficiently refined to appreciate the event, sufficiently affluent to afford tickets). However, the art form has survived for over 400 years, currently on carefully constructed prestige that inspires an elite community and associated markets (including governments, corporate sponsors, and philanthropists) to support it. Vulnerability due to high demands in Domains 1, 2, and 4 is counteracted primarily by maintaining high prestige (Domain 3).

Other traditions without such demands, such as traditional Aboriginal music, are in peril, while others flourish in spite of a history of colonialism and drastic changes of context, such as North Indian classical music, having successfully survived centuries of colonialism and major recontextualizations from Hindu places of worship to Muslim courts, from the houses of courtesans to respectable middle-class audiences, and on to new listeners through broadcasting, recordings, and the diaspora, fed by a strong sense of nationalism (Bhakle, 2005).

Over the past few years, several senior ethnomusicologists have commented on the desirability of a systematic study of sustainability across musical traditions to avoid "re-inventing the wheel every time we face a community that's trying to preserve its own traditions" (Seeger, QCRC, 2008). Trimillos expressed interest in a "deductive approach" based on five predetermined categories of data "as opposed to so much of ethnomusicological study which goes to a culture and does it inductively" (QCRC, 2008). Speaking of globalization, commodification, and media, Wong argued what is needed is a "very practical and visionary approach to these matters" (QCRC, 2008). Meanwhile, Moyle reminded us that "our job as sympathetic and supportive outsiders is properly that of an on-request caretaker and facilitator, but not as an arbiter of what should be preserved and what should not be" (QCRC, 2008).

Taking an approach informed by the considerations outlined above, detailed and realistic pictures can be conjured of threats and opportunities in relation to contemporary contexts, traditional and potential new audiences, approaches to transmission to next generations, as well as the presence or absence of community, media, commercial, institutional, and public support. Findings across these domains can be analyzed and turned into accessible online resources that are not only of value to ethnomusicologists, but specifically geared to assist communities in performing and developing the music they value in the way they value it.

SUSTAINABLE FUTURES

From 2009 to 2014, an international research consortium was enabled by a large Australian Research Council Linkage Grant to extensively test this approach on nine diverse case studies: Mexican Mariachi, Ghanaian Ewe music, Amami Shima Uta, Korean SamulNori, Hindustani music from North India, Vietnamese *ca tru*, Indigenous Yawulyu songs from Central Australia, Balinese gamelan, and Western opera. The project made a deliberate choice to focus not only on "endangered" music cultures (as has largely been the practice), but equally on "successful" ones. The rationale for this was that while the former may provide profound insight into the main obstacles encountered by living music cultures in need of safeguarding, the latter can reveal possible pathways to removing such obstacles. So while Aboriginal music from Central Australia and Vietnamese *ca tru* would be "in urgent need of safeguarding" in UNESCO terms, Ghanaian Ewe music, Amami Shima Uta, and Korean SamulNori face much less fatal challenges, and notwithstanding issues in some areas, Hindustani music, Mexican Mariachi music, Balinese gamelan, and Western opera are largely thriving, according to most observers and stakeholders.

Sustainable Futures for Music Cultures: Toward an Ecology of Musical Diversity summarizes the aims of the five-year, $5 million project in its website (soundfutures. org), as follows (cf. Schippers and Grant, 2016):

> Sustainable Futures for Music Cultures celebrates the cultural diversity of our planet. It acknowledges that there are serious challenges to many music cultures that are the result of recent changes in "musical ecosystems." It aims to identify ways to promote cultural diversity and ensure vibrant musical futures in line with those called for by organisations like UNESCO. Sustainable Futures seeks to counteract the loss of music cultures by identifying the key factors in musical sustainability, and making this knowledge available to communities across the world. In this way it aims to empower communities to forge musical futures on their own terms.

In order to structure the project across nine very diverse case studies, guidelines for the research teams were developed, featuring some 200 questions and subquestions across the five domains. These were carefully formulated by Research Fellow Catherine Grant, in collaboration with the teams, to ensure optimally compatible data. For example, the following questions structure the section on Domain 4 (Infrastructure and regulations):

4.1. **What formal structures are in place to help musicians in your culture,** with regard to creating; performing; learning; teaching; collaborating; touring; preserving or promoting the music culture? For example, which of the following exist: musicians' unions; teachers' associations or bodies; performers' agencies; formal networks or societies; virtual spaces for collaborating / performing; cultural organizations or institutions; provisions for amateur / community music-making; awards and prizes?

4.2. **How do musicians source instruments?** Are they expensive / difficult to source? Are there physical or intangible restrictions on instrument-making? Who makes musical instruments? How are they trained, and by whom? Are there enough instrument-makers? Do they earn a living from their craft? How does this differ from five / twenty years ago? How is it changing now? Have there been significant recent changes in materials or design of instruments?

4.3. **Apart from musical instruments, what other tangible resources,** equipment, or paraphernalia are required for performing, creating, or transmitting your music culture? Are they expensive / difficult to source? How does this differ from five / twenty years ago? How is it changing now?

4.4. **Where are musicians in your culture located** when they perform rehearse / practise; teach / learn / create; record; publish; broadcast?

4.5. **What other conditions are needed for performing, creating, or transmitting your music** culture? Are they difficult to access / expensive? How does this differ from five / twenty years ago? How is it changing now?

4.6. **Are there festivals and competitions for your music?** What is their focus with regard to tradition versus innovation? What are the benefits or drawbacks with regard to their effect on performance practices? How are judges appointed? What are the criteria for excellence? Who decides? What is the role of the media in the festivals/competitions?

4.7. **Which non-musical factors impact directly or indirectly on your music culture?** Do any of the following play a role: level of poverty; government regimes; civil situation; health issues; land reform / land rights; displacement or population drift; environmental changes; climate; geographical distance

4.8. **Which traditional authorities impact on your music culture?** Are they local / state / federal or national / international / church or religious?

4.9. **Are there issues of censorship or repression that impact on your music culture?** Are these political, religious, gender-based, or other? Are artists / musicians given special "allowance" to dissent, as their role, or even duty? Do musicians self-censor? If so, why?

How would you describe the regulation of freedom of expression for your music culture, along the continuum from totally repressed to totally free?

4.10. **What are the copyright laws, if any, that affect your music culture?** Are they enforced? If your music is "traditional," is it considered free of copyright? If not, who owns it?

4.11. **Which other government or government-induced laws and regulations exist** that directly or indirectly affect musicians and music-making, either positively or negatively? Do you (have to) deal with artists' rights; taxation laws; free trade policies; sound restrictions; work permits; censorship laws; education regulations (curriculum / other); royalty collection and distribution; broadcast regulations (quota of locally produced music / other); and/or venue restrictions (hours of operation / smoking / drinking / other)?

What has been the general trend with regard to amendments or revisions to law and regulations affecting your music culture in the last, say, twenty years? Do they reflect a general tightening or relaxing of rules? How do you envisage the next five years in this regard?

4.12.   **What forms of assistance does the government provide** to economically develop the music sector? If any, are they provided through state-owned entities; through subsidies; through tax concessions; through public/private partnerships; and/or through financial instruments (e.g. access to loan funds)?

4.13.   **Where are these forms of support directed?** To live performance (including venues, cultural centers, festivals); record production and distribution; music video production; music publishing; broadcasting; internet and multimedia; improving business practices; building music exports; statistics collection; training; and/or other?

4.14.   **What is the position / status of your music culture, internationally?** Are there formal recognitions of its value, such as UNESCO Oral Masterpiece / Intangible Cultural Property? What are the procedures that lead to such recognition?

4.15.   **How, if at all, do governments at any level seek to protect or promote:** your music genre; other music genres within your country; music genres of immigrant communities?

Does the government have a cultural plan in place that may impact your music genre? Are there publically available government documents or reports relating to your music genre? Are they widely known? What function do they serve?

4.16.   **What is the impact of the government's attitude to cultural diversity** and multiculturalism (or national cohesion/cultural purity) on your music culture?

4.17.   **What external support (if any) is required to be a successful musician?** Is it government backing; sponsorship / grants / funding; institutional and community support (performance venues; resources); public support (audiences; purchase of recordings; radio airplay)

(QCRC, 2010: 15–17)

Researchers were asked to seek answers to *all* questions across the five domains, and emphatically indicate those that were not applicable, as they might indicate areas unexplored in the ecosystem. They did so by applying insights from (mostly many decades) of engagement with the specific culture, targeted fieldwork, and an average of twenty interviews per tradition across the domains. As became apparent in November 2013, when nine advanced draft reports were tabled before a gathering of 30 international scholars and musicians at a final working conference chaired by Anthony Seeger in the context of the *5th IMC World Forum on Music*, this led to both obvious and unexpected early insights through and across the five domains, some of which include the following.

Systems of Learning Music

As could be expected, systems of learning music play a key role in every music culture, whether they are formal or informal, aural or notation-based, live or online, real-time or based on recordings, self-driven, community organized, or institutionally based. Striking findings were that in some cultures, such as Balinese gamelan and Ewe percussion, the learning process is so embedded in the lives of young people that they are likely to say they never "learned music." Another notable insight across the case studies was that there is not necessarily a one-to-one relationship between highly formalized and highly structured. At a deeper level, there are similarities in terms of structured progression only when the learner is ready between learning opera at a conservatorium and community-based transmission processes such as those in Central Australia, although the nature of the "exams" may differ. Finally, there is an inkling that formal education is not necessarily always the ideal: while it has advantages in terms of stability and prestige, in some cases it could even be seen as a last resort if transmission within the community no longer meets the needs of the genre.

Musicians and Communities

Community engagement in the widest sense is at the heart of sustainability in many music cultures, from village squares to opera first night crowds. The drivers for this engagement range from entertainment to necessity, from shared beliefs to prestige. Recognition by the community (in money or otherwise) is of great importance for sustainability. There is a broad spectrum of levels of engagement between musicians and with the "inner circles" of the tradition, often containing important quality control mechanisms. In issues relating to sustainability, a single inspired individual or a small motivated group often plays a remarkable role in reinvigorating a tradition.

Contexts and Constructs

The contexts of some music cultures are stable, but most change over time, often drastically: many music cultures demonstrate remarkable adaptability. In that sense, recontextualization is an asset rather than a weakness. In terms of values and attitudes, a wide range of belief systems, from aesthetic to religious to political, can be either conducive or an obstacle to any music. Prestige in its various incarnations is possibly a central driver for sustainability, and resonates across the Domains.

Regulations and Infrastructure

Most cultures have access to some support for music in terms of infrastructure, media exposure, or funding. However, the correlation between funding and sustainability does not seem to be strong; not unlike formal education, dependence on grants is a potential weakness from a sustainability point of view. Specific legislation regarding music is most notable in the area of intellectual property, copyright, and performing rights. While these do not generally generate a substantial income stream for the vast majority of musicians, they do constitute an important moral recognition of their contribution. Other rules and regulations may affect music inadvertently, such as laws governing sound and public spaces. The need for dedicated infrastructure is low for most music genres: they often use spaces that have multiple functions: village squares, pubs, big houses. Only in rare cases—like Western opera—do the needs become so high that they can easily become a major liability to sustainability.

Media and the Music Industry
Since their first rise to prominence on the back of technological developments some hundred years ago, media and the music industry have played a significant supporting role in the dissemination of music and building the reputations of musicians. In spite of much talk about commodification, even at the peak of the record industry few world music genres generated a substantial income for many individual musicians or groups. However, there has always been a close, two-way relationship between media exposure and prestige, which in turn can open avenues to financial sustainability. After the collapse of the recording industry, online environments have created massive exposure, with an impressive scope for niche markets and online communities that may benefit "small musics" in decades to come.

(QCRC, 2013)

While each of the domains can be regarded to some extent as an ecosystem in its own right, the full picture emerges only when examining a music culture across the domains, following Pickett and Cadanasso's suggested line of questions: "Exactly what components and entities are linked to one another? Which ones are only indirectly connected? What parts of a system are tightly coupled and which only weakly coupled?" (2002: 4). In examining music ecosystems, there are obvious and surprising connections. High-level practices tend to have a solid system of transmission, but not all do, and certainly not all have institutionalized transmission. Opera is strongly dependent on government support throughout Europe and Asia, but Hindustani classical music is barely supported by the Indian government. Probably the strongest correlation across domains is prestige, as mentioned before, which may inspire learners to seek skills in a music, communities to engage with it, contexts of music to be celebrated, infrastructure to be provided, and people to buy tickets or recordings.

ENGAGING WITH COMMUNITIES

A framework that provides such practical insights into the workings of the sustainability of music may help address one of the great challenges of (especially applied) ethnomusicology: building meaningful and mutually beneficial relationships with communities (cf. Harrison, 2012; Harrison, Mackinlay, and Pettan, 2010; Pettan, 2008; Sheehy, 1992). As practical, intellectual, and moral approaches to ethnography are becoming increasingly sophisticated (Barz and Cooley, 2008), most contemporary ethnomusicologists have moved far away from going into the field and considering their recordings and data their property to the point of commercializing them for their own profit. Attributing rights and making material available to individuals and communities are common practice now. But the range of this "giving back" is quite substantial and deserves scrutiny

in this context: providing CDs of field recordings and musicological analyses of repertoire may not be the most meaningful—or even ethically sound—way of giving back to
communities, especially if they do not possess the equipment, inclination, education, or
frame of mind to make such artifacts useful to them. Many ethnomusicologists working
with a single genre over a long period of time are addressing this by seeking appropriate
ways of giving back by ongoing negotiation and progressing insight, in close consultation with communities.

The ambition of the *Sustainable Futures* project was to make available the insights into
ecosystems of music to communities in two ways: through targeted, community-driven
initiatives, and through an interactive web resource. For *ca tru*, an example of the former
and one of the triggers for *Sustainable Futures*, four years of contact back and forth has
helped to inspire a project to create a viable performance format and income source for
musicians by linking the chamber music tradition to the high-volume international cultural tourism to Vietnam:

> Building on its 2009 recognition by UNESCO as Intangible Cultural Heritage
> in urgent need of safeguarding, *Ca Tru Vietnam* aims to create a context which
> reestablishes the refined urban expression of this genre in a sustainable environ-
> ment. Combining the interest of refined Vietnamese and international audiences,
> this enterprise will open a ca tru house in Hanoi (once the home to many such
> establishments) on a commercially viable basis, using the high-end of cultural
> tourism to Vietnam as its primary market. This will reconnect the genre to its former
> basis of support, private patrons, providing a basic but stable income for up to ten ca
> tru musicians, technicians and cultural workers. Linked to this will be performances
> and lessons for Vietnamese audiences and young people, ensuring the intergenera-
> tional transmission of the genre without continuing dependence on external funding
> or state support.
>
> (Ca tru Vietnam project plan, 2010)

Such approaches can be developed tailor-made for many traditions, emphatically using
an understanding of the entire ecosystem to forge new pathways in specific areas to
make a genre stronger or survive.

This process becomes much more challenging when making available resources that
are not targeted at a single group, but at users from cultures around the world. As part of
the *Sustainable Futures* project, an online resource has been developed for making available strategies and examples to communities across the world who are passionate about
preserving music they value, aiming to assist in understanding, planning, executing, and
evaluating specific interventions in musical ecosystems to increase sustainability (cf.
Grant, 2014). At the heart of this tool is an online diagnosis tool that brings back the core
of any music ecosystem to ten questions with up to five subquestions each, generating a
tentative report that may inspire individuals and communities in the steps they choose
to take and alliances they choose to form to ensure a vibrant future for their music (see
Figure 4.2). While there are inevitable shortcomings to such an approach, it is a start. At

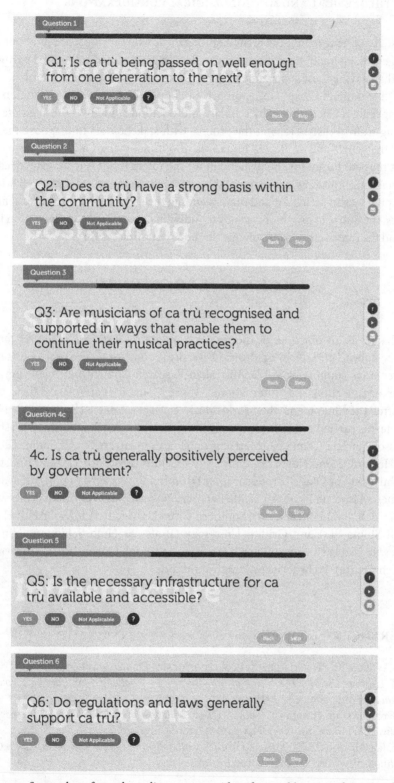

FIGURE 4.2 Screenshots from the online survey to identify possible areas of concern for sustainability on soundfutures.org.

the least, it can serve to build awareness among those who care most deeply about specific music genres, giving them more agency in deciding courses of action and partnerships rather than having these superimposed by scholars, NGOs, or public authorities.

The "five-domain ecosystem" approach can hopefully serve as an instrument to describe specific music cultures by scholars and doctoral students, with the potential of initiating fruitful discussions in the process with stakeholders to diagnose the condition of the genre, and strategize initiatives to optimally align all forces for a diverse, vibrant musical future for the planet. For all the reservations one may have regarding understanding music as ecosystems, the approach seems to resonate well with current approaches to caring for and understanding the sustainability of music genres and cultures, the desire to give more agency to individuals and communities within the culture, and the role of ethnomusicologists in the twenty-first century.

ACKNOWLEDGMENTS

This chapter is an outcome of the research program: *Sustainable Futures for Music Cultures: Toward an Ecology of Musical Diversity* (2009–2014). The project was realized with generous support from the Australian Research Council Linkage Program and partner organizations the International Music Council (Paris), the Music Council of Australia (Sydney), and the World Music & Dance Centre (Rotterdam). Nine research teams carried out the research, led by scholars at the University of Washington (Professor Patricia Campbell, Mariachi music), the University of London (Professor Keith Howard, SamulNori), the University of Lund (Professor Hakan Lundstron, ca tru), University of Otago (Professor John Drummond, Western opera), the University of Sydney (Associate Professor Linda Barwick, Yawulyu; and Associate Professor Peter Dunbar-Hall, Balinese gamelan), Southern Cross University (Professor Phil Hayward, Amami Shima uta) and Griffith University (Professor Huib Schippers, Hindustani music, who also led and coordinated the project through Queensland Conservatorium Research Centre). Website: www.soundfutures.org.

REFERENCES

Archer, William Kay. (1964). "On the Ecology of Music." *Ethnomusicology* 8(1): 28–33.

Aubert, Laurent. (2007). *The Music of the Other: New Challenges for Ethnomusicology in a Global Age*. Aldershot, UK: Ashgate.

Barz, Gregory, and Timothy J. Cooley. (2008). *Shadows in the Field: New Perspectives for Fieldwork in Ethnomusicology*. New York: Oxford University Press.

Bhakle, Janaki. (2005). *Two Men and Music: Nationalism in the Making of an Indian Classical Tradition*. New York: Oxford University Press.

Blaukopf, K. (1992). "Mediamorphosis and Secondary Orality: A Challenge to Cultural Policy." In *World Music, Musics of the World: Aspects of Documentation, Mass Media and Acculturation*, edited by M. P. Bauman, pp. 19–36. Wilhelmshaven, Germany: Florian Noetzel Verlag.

Cook, Nicholas. (1998). *Music: A Very Short Introduction*. New York: Oxford University Press.

Feintuch, B. (1993). "Musical Revival as Musical Transformation." In *Transforming Tradition: Folk Music Revivals Examined*, edited by N. V. Rosenberg, pp. 183–193. Urbana: University of Illinois Press.

Grant, Catherine. (2014). *Music Endangerment: How Language Maintenance Can Help*. New York: Oxford University Press.

Harrison, Klisala., E. Mackinlay, and S. Pettan, eds. (2010). *Historical and Emerging Approaches to Applied Ethnomusicology*. Newcastle upon Tyne, UK: Cambridge Scholars Publishing.

Harrison, Klisala. (2012). "Epistemologies of Applied Ethnomusicology." *Ethnomusicology* 56(3): 505–529.

Hayward, Philip. (2005). "Culturally Engaged Research and Facilitation: Active Development Projects with Small Island Cultures." In *Proceedings of the First International Small Island Cultures Conference*, edited by M. Evans, pp. 55–60. Sydney: Small Islands Cultures Research Initiative.

Howard, Keith. (2006a). *Preserving Korean Music: Intangible Cultural Properties as Icons of Identity*. Aldershot, UK: Ashgate.

Howard, Keith. (2006b). *Creating Korean Music: Tradition, Innovation and the Discourse of Identity*. Aldershot, UK: Ashgate.

Howard, Keith. (2012). "Introduction: East Asian Music as Intangible Cultural Heritage." In *Music as Intangible Cultural Heritage: Policy, Ideology and Practice in the Preservation of East-Asian Traditions*, edited by Keith Howard, pp. 1–21. Farnham, UK: Ashgate.

Keogh, Brent. (2013). "On the Limitations of Music Ecology." *International Journal for Music Research Online*, April 2013. http://www.jmro.org.au/index.php/mca2/article/view/83 (accessed December 16, 2013).

Letts, Richard. (2006). *The Protection and Promotion of Musical Diversity*. http://www.unesco.org/imc/ (accessed March 1, 2008).

Lomax, Alan. (1976). *Cantometrics: An Approach to the Anthropology of Music*. Berkeley: University of California Extension Media Center.

Loomis, Ormond H., ed. (1983). *Cultural Conservation: The Preservation of Cultural Heritage in the United States*. Washington DC: Library of Congress.

Malm, Krister. (1993). "Music on the Move: Traditions and Mass Media." *Ethnomusicology* 37(3): 339–352.

McCracken, Allison. (1999). "'God's Gift to Us Girls': Crooning, Gender, and the Re-Creation of American Popular Song, 1928–1933." *American Music* 17(4): 365–395.

Moyle, Richard. (2007). *Songs from the Second Float: A Musical Ethnography of Takū Atoll, Papua New Guinea*. Honolulu: University of Hawai'i Press.

Nettl, Bruno. (2010). *Nettl's Elephant: On the History of Ethnomusicology*. Urbana: University of Illinois Press.

Pettan, Svanibor. (2008). "Applied Ethnomusicology and Empowerment Strategies: Views from Across the Atlantic." *Muzikološki zbornik/Musicological Annual* 44(1): 85–99, special issue on applied ethnomusicology.

Pickett, S. T. A., and M. L. Cadenasso. (2002). "The Ecosystem as a Multidimensional Concept: Meaning, Model and Metaphor." *Ecosystems* 5: 1–10.

QCRC (Queensland Conservatorium Research Centre). (2008). *Twelve Voices on Sustainable Futures*. Video. Brisbane: QCRC.

QCRC (Queensland Conservatorium Research Centre). (2010). *Sustainable Futures for Music Cultures: Towards an Ecology of Musical Diversity—Case Study Guidelines*. Brisbane: QCRC.

QCRC (Queensland Conservatorium Research Centre). (2013). Report on the Final Working Conference on "Sustainable Futures for Music Cultures." Brisbane: QCRC.

Ramnarine, Tina K. (2003). *Ilmater's Inspiration: Nationalism, Globalization, and the Changing Soundscapes of Finnish Folk Music*. Chicago: University of Chicago Press.

Rees, Helen. (2012). "Intangible Cultural Heritage in China Today: Policy and Practice in the Early Twenty-First Century." In *Music as Intangible Cultural Heritage: Policy, Ideology and Practice in the Preservation of East-Asian Traditions*, edited by Keith Howard, pp. 23–54. Farnham, UK: Ashgate.

Rice, Timothy. (1997). "Towards a Mediation of Field Methods and Field Experience in Ethnomusicology." In *Shadows in the Field: New Perspectives for Fieldwork in Ethnomusicology*, edited by Gregory F. Barz and Timothy J. Cooley, pp. 101–120. New York: Oxford University Press.

Schippers, H. (2009). "From Ca Tru to the World: Understanding and Facilitating Musical Sustainability." In *Musical Autoethnographies*, edited by B. Barlett and C. Ellis, pp. 197–207. Brisbane: Australian Academic Press.

Schippers, Huib. (2010). *Facing the Music: Global Perspectives on Learning and Teaching Music*. New York: Oxford University Press.

Schippers, H., and Grant, C., eds. (2016). *Sustainable Futures for Music Cultures: An Ecological Approach*. New York: Oxford University Press.

Sheehy, Dan. (1992). "A Few Notions about Philosophy and Strategy in Applied Ethnomusicology." *Ethnomusicology* 36(3): 3–7.

Sheehy, Dan. (2006). *Mariachi Music in America: Experiencing Music, Expressing Culture*. New York: Oxford University Press.

Slobin, M., ed. (1996). *Returning Culture: Musical Changes in Central and Eastern Europe*. Durham, NC: Duke University Press.

Small, Christopher. (1998). *Musicking: The Meanings of Performing and Listening*. Middletown, CT: Wesleyan University Press.

Stauffer, Robert C. (1957). "Haeckel, Darwin and Ecology." *The Quarterly Review of Biology* 32(2): 138–144.

Tansley, A. G. (1935). "The Use and Abuse of Vegetational Concepts and Terms." *Ecology* 16(3): 284–307.

Taylor, Timothy D. (2007). *Beyond Exoticism: Western Music and the World*. Durham, NC: Duke University Press.

Titon, Jeff Todd. (1992). "Music, the Public Interest, and the Practice of Ethnomusicology." *Ethnomusicology* 36(3): 315–322, special issue on music, the public interest, and the practice of ethnomusicology.

Titon, Jeff Todd. (2009a). "Economy, Ecology and Music: An Introduction." *the world of music* 51(1): 7–13.

Titon, Jeff Todd. (2009b). "Music and Sustainability: An Ecological Viewpoint." *the world of music* 51(1): 119–138.

UNESCO. (2001). *Declaration on the Promotion of Cultural Diversity*. http://portal.unesco.org/ en/ev.php-URL_ID=13179&URL_DO=DO_TOPIC&URL_SECTION=201.html (accessed March 31, 2015).

UNESCO. (2003). *Convention for the safeguarding of the Intangible Cultural Heritage*. http://portal.unesco.org/en/ev.php-URL_ID=17716&URL_DO=DO_TOPIC&URL_ SECTION=201.html (accessed March 31, 2015).

UNESCO. (2005). *Convention on the Protection and Promotion of the Diversity of Cultural Expressions*. http://portal.unesco.org/en/ev.php-URL_ID=31038&URL_DO=DO_ TOPIC&URL_ SECTION=201.html (accessed March 31, 2015).

United Nations High Commission for Human Rights. (2007). *Declaration on the Rights of Indigenous Peoples*. http://www.un.org/esa/socdev/unpfii/documents/DRIPS_en.pdf (accessed March 31, 2015).

CHAPTER 5

SUSTAINABILITY, RESILIENCE, AND ADAPTIVE MANAGEMENT FOR APPLIED ETHNOMUSICOLOGY

JEFF TODD TITON

INTRODUCTION

SUSTAINABILITY is a hard concept to avoid these days, and resilience is not far behind. We are urged to conserve energy, carpool, turn down the thermostat, use renewables, recycle our waste, lower our carbon footprint, and live sustainable lives to maintain a sustainable planet. Conservation ecologists and environmentalists manage ecosystems to prevent species extinction and maintain biodiversity. Developmental economists promote modernization and sustainable development, while ecological economists remind us about environmental constraints on trade, markets, corporations, and governments. Some business economists have argued that corporations will better be able to profit and sustain themselves if they think of their activities as taking place within an ecosystem consisting not only of predators and prey but also allies and competitors.

In applied ethnomusicology, sustainability does not directly reference green energy or developmental economics, although it may involve them. Rather, it refers to a music culture's capacity to maintain and develop its music now and in the foreseeable future. Applied ethnomusicologists today, as in the past, often try to aid musicians and their communities in sustaining their musical activities. Many of us have considered it an ethical imperative to do so, a giving back to individuals and communities we consider to be our colleagues, friends, and teachers in exchange for what they have given us—information, music, friendship and social life, pleasure, and in many cases the basis for the research that not only advances knowledge but also helps us advance our careers.

Sustainability is a relatively new term for ethnomusicologists, but many ideas related to sustainability have been with us for decades: documentation, archiving, and preservation; conservation, safeguarding, revitalization, and renewal. *Resilience* is an even newer term, not yet in common use among us; but it has many advantages and, I believe, deserves to enter the discussion surrounding applied ethnomusicology. One of the difficulties with sustainability and its related ideas is that they are ends, not means; they are goals, not strategies. Resilience, on the other hand, offers a strategy, a means toward the goal of sustainability. Resilience refers to a system's capacity to recover and maintain its integrity, identity, and continuity when subjected to forces of disturbance and change. Insofar as music cultures are systems, they too exhibit resilience to a greater or lesser degree. Resilient systems share certain characteristics. Identifying what makes a music culture vulnerable, what makes it resilient, and ameliorating the former while strengthening the latter becomes, therefore, a practical strategy for enhancing a music culture's sustainability. Resilience does not simply mean "learning to live with it," as people new to the term mistakenly think. Nor does it mean hunkering down in a defensive stance. Rather, resilience implies a way to manage disturbance and change and guide the outcome toward a desirable end.

This chapter is written to begin theorizing resilience as a sustainability strategy for applied ethnomusicologists. Just as conservation biologists intervene in the environment to restore, maintain, and develop ecosystems, so applied ethnomusicologists intervene in music cultures. Like it or not, we are committed to putting ethnomusicological knowledge and insight to practical use in order to improve musical life. We are guided by values. We are meddlers. We are experimenters, we live with uncertainty, we expect sometimes to fail, and we hope to learn from our failures. The strategy I am theorizing here for applied ethnomusicology has been called *adaptive management* by those who have been working with resilience strategies for a variety of systems, not just environmental ecosystems. Adaptive management is succeeding in strengthening resilience and decreasing vulnerability in social groups facing undesirable change, and in individuals facing stress and trauma. Applied to organizations, adaptive management not only enhances resilience but remodels behavior based on a new understanding: that organizations are not merely competitors, but rather exist interdependently with allies and competitors within larger ecosystems—think of the complex relations among Apple, Google, and Microsoft, for example.

Sustainability is current, while resilience and adaptive management point toward the future of applied ethnomusicology. Much of it represents new thinking, while drawing lessons from applied ethnomusicology's prior interventions, the decades-old ideas that have animated them, and the relationships between applied work in ethnomusicology and that of two of our sister, fieldwork-based disciplines, applied anthropology and public folklore. (I might also have considered applied sociology, but this sprawling chapter is already broad enough in scope.) Therefore, I treat the historical background of the ideas—preservation, conservation, and safeguarding—that both preceded and contribute to sustainability and resilience. As these ideas originated elsewhere—the conservation of natural resources, for example, and the historic preservation of material objects—I discuss them in their original contexts in addition to their later adoption in applied ethnomusicology and public folklore. Finally, I turn to sustainability and then to resilience, again with reference to their origins elsewhere, in this case economics (sustainable development) as well as environmentalism, before moving to their applications in applied ethnomusicology. I concentrate on the United States because I am most knowledgeable about these policy concepts, strategies, and their histories in my homeland. Nevertheless, these ideas and their applications flow globally, and they move in different directions and at different rates outside the United States. The most prominent contemporary music sustainability project is based not in the United States but in Australia (see Schippers, Chapter 4 of this volume). UNESCO is the major player in the international arena, but their conservation rhetoric remains wedded to older concepts involving preservation and safeguarding heritage, while for them sustainability operates in the realm of economic development, not musical and cultural continuity.

CONSERVATION: NATURAL, CULTURAL, AND MUSICAL

Ethnomusicologists are conservationists, whether preserving and transmitting knowledge of music or, in the case of applied ethnomusicologists, conserving musical practice itself. In addition to documenting and preserving the music of the world's peoples for research purposes, applied ethnomusicologists have sometimes intervened on behalf of music cultures to help them conserve music thought to be threatened and endangered, usually by modernization and development. In many ways, these musical and cultural conservation efforts have been modeled on those that preceded them in nature conservation, or the conservation of natural resources.

Ever since the early Enlightenment, preservation and conservation have been closely related. Taken as near synonyms, their meaning is to maintain an object or system insofar as possible in its present state, to protect it from change, usually for contemplation, research, display, and perhaps for use. Conservationists who distinguish their activities from preservation emphasize conservation's restorative aspects—restoring a historical musical instrument, for example, or a painting, or a dinosaur, or an ecosystem. Conservationists acknowledge change but try to manage it in order to prolong a desired state. Preservationists (who may nonetheless call themselves conservationists) think of themselves more as protectors. They sometimes criticize conservationists for setting an additional priority on yield or harvest or use, rather than interfering as minimally as possible in order to preserve the original object or system, as they would do. Preservationists would, for example, prefer to keep a historical musical instrument "as found" in a deteriorated state, for study, rather than to restore or repair it for display or use (Barclay, 2004). Although the debate between preservationists and conservationists is most prominent in the environmental movement (deep ecologists versus "wise use" conservationists), in this chapter I use *conservation* as the cover term for both preservation and conservation, distinguishing the two when desirable.

Nature conservation, or conservation of natural resources (they are not the same thing, for nature need not be regarded as a resource), is surely as old as the earliest hunters who realized they must not slaughter the entire herd, or the first growers who saved seeds. There is evidence of Italian violin-makers during the time of Stradivarius and afterward conserving the forest trees producing violin-tone wood, and of a plea from the Englishman John Evelyn before the Royal Society in 1662, advocating that trees be replanted to preserve the forests, which were being harvested at an alarming rate (Allen, 2012; Evelyn, 1664). German, French, and British conservationists during the eighteenth and nineteenth centuries similarly worked for forest preservation based on scientific principles, and much was accomplished, particularly in British India throughout the nineteenth century (Barton, 2002). The origins of the US conservation movement may be found in the writings of naturalists such as John (1699–1777) and William (1739–1823) Bartram, and Henry David Thoreau (1817–1862), while novelists such as James Fenimore Cooper (1789–1851) expressed a preservationist philosophy through characters such as Natty Bumppo, who, like the Native Americans, used only enough natural resources to provide for basic needs (Cooper, 1823). In the later nineteenth and early twentieth centuries, the writings of John Burroughs (1837–1921) and John Muir (1838–1914) were especially influential. Muir not only founded the Sierra Club, which became an important nature advocacy group, but also successfully lobbied the US Congress for the establishment of the first National Park, Yosemite, in 1890, the first in a succession of national parks, which came to embody the US conservation movement, and led to the establishment in 1905 of the US Forest Service, the state fish and game conservation departments, and so on.

However, the split between preservationists and conservationists was already underway, as Muir (the preservationist) spoke out against the national Forest Service's efforts to manage the US-owned parks and forests for timber harvesting. Gifford Pinchot, the Forest Service director, termed his scientifically guided conservation policies "wise use," a phrase that has endured. A pragmatist, Pinchot's idea of wise use was based in government management for the public good, which meant protecting the forests as a renewable resource so that the public would continually enjoy its benefits, including tree harvesting and mining as well as recreation (Miller, 2001). His successor, William Greeley, transformed the Forest Service into an agency whose principal function was to prevent forest fires, while enabling the timber companies to make enormous profits by clear-cutting huge tracts. The Sierra Club and other preservationists were outraged, but so was Pinchot. As the twentieth century wore on, the preservationist wing of the conservation movement was criticized on the grounds that purchasing natural areas in the Eastern states, or seizing them through eminent domain, forced removal of populations living on those lands, while their recreational use was limited chiefly to those wealthy enough to travel and vacation there. Today, when conservation heritage trusts buy up and set aside farmland and seashore, critics charge that this is accomplished at the expense of economic development and jobs.

Conservation of cultural resources may be traced, among Europeans, to those Renaissance aristocrats of an antiquarian bent who traveled to observe ruins and kept objects in private *kunstkammer*, wonder rooms or "cabinets of curiosity." These little theaters were the precursors of museums and contained cultural relics of all kinds, as well as natural history specimens from the plant and animal world. Museums followed, and eventually a historic preservation movement (to use US terminology) arose to safeguard historically important buildings and monuments on their original sites. An example is Stonehenge in the United Kingdom, where such activities are termed "heritage preservation." Artifacts of music cultures (e.g., ancient musical instruments) have been preserved over the years in cabinets of curiosity, museums, libraries, or repositories dedicated to instruments and, since the early twentieth century, to recordings and other media. Most ethnomusicologists maintain personal archives for research purposes, gradually passing them along to archival institutions. Museum collections may be found at the Musée de l'Homme, the Smithsonian Institution, and elsewhere. Examples of dedicated sound archives include the Berlin Phonogramm-Archiv (begun in 1900), the Archive of American Folk Song (1928) at the Library of Congress, and the British Library Sound Archive (1955). Repatriation, or returning recordings and other musical artifacts to the indigenous peoples from whom they were collected and taken, has underlined a third purpose: safeguarding (Newell, 2003). "Digital preservation" is yet another contemporary preservation activity, saving space and converting the printed or recorded artifact to a more easily maintained, perhaps more permanent, medium. However, digital preservation transforms the original medium; it does not protect it.

Conservation, of course, has a strong preservation component, sometimes with additional elements such as restoration. Archives and museums practice conservation when they restore deteriorating artifacts closer to a presumably original state, as they do with dinosaur bones, paintings, and musical instruments. Conservation places less emphasis on protection and setting aside, and more emphasis on continuing utility, than does preservation. Demonstrating and exhibiting collections may also inspire conservation in music cultures. The director of the Smithsonian Institution, S. Dillon Ripley, conceived of performances at the museum in which the artifacts would be demonstrated in use, for the public. "Take the objects out of their cases and make them sing," he wrote (http://www.folklife.si.edu/center/legacy/ripley.aspx). Although some of these demonstrations involved crafts and the application of traditional cultural knowledge, music was the most common kind of performance. The Smithsonian Festival of American Folklife, which began in 1967, is an example. Until then, most folk festivals exhibited marginal, dying, remnant traditions. But the Smithsonian festivals underlined a conservation element that encouraged the participants to maintain those traditions within their own cultural groups.

"Cultural conservation" entered the US public folklore discourse in the late 1970s, partly in response to a change in the idea of American identity, from a "melting pot" in which immigrant cultures and ethnicities would forge a single new type of American, to a "mosaic" that recognized, honored, and thereby meant to conserve elements of American ethnic diversity and cultural pluralism. In that same decade, three federal folklore agencies were established that greatly influenced traditional arts policy, including music. Their mandate was to support the folk and traditional arts, which were viewed as the expression of a culturally, ethnically, religiously, racially, occupationally, and regionally diverse set of communities that, taken together, made up the mosaic society of the United States. Music was an important community folk art, perhaps the most evident, along with foodways, dress, religious practice, language, and so forth. The three federal agencies were the Office of Folklife Studies at the Smithsonian Institution (the national museum for American history), the Folk Arts Division of the National Endowment for the Arts (NEA), and the American Folklife Center of the Library of Congress. Each played a crucial role in developing cultural conservation, an early version of sustainability for the traditional arts.

The Smithsonian's involvement was the earliest of the three, and remained the most visible. The Smithsonian's folk festival (1967–present) led to the establishment of a separate folklife division in 1980, now called the Center for Folklife and Cultural Heritage. Held in the nation's capital, at first the Smithsonian's festival followed the model of the Newport (Rhode Island) Folk Festival, which since 1959 had presented a majority of professional folksingers, making careers from their music in the folk revival, with other, lesser-known musicians who came to be known as tradition-bearers or source musicians. The former were later termed "revivalists," which meant that they had not been born and raised within the musical communities that carried the music they performed now, from a stage for an audience. They had learned it from recordings, from other revivalists, or in some cases directly from source musicians. These latter, on the other hand, had known the music they performed from childhood, when it prevailed in their communities, and although they may have had professional careers at one time, most were not earning their living as performers at present. Many of these were from American minority groups, or from regions where modernization came late and the older folk traditions had lingered. Among the professional folksingers were Joan Baez, Oscar Brand, Peter, Paul, and Mary, and Bob Dylan; among the tradition-bearers were African American musicians such as Mississippi John Hurt, Cajun musicians such as the Balfa Brothers, and those from the Appalachian Mountain region of the American South, such as Clarence Ashley. In the early 1970s the Smithsonian festival stopped presenting the revivalists and in so doing unintentionally ghettoized authenticity in the folk arts by means of ethnic, class, and regional criteria. Those who produced the folk festivals began to hope that the national attention gained from the festival might enhance the prestige of these source musicians in their home communities, and help to preserve the musical traditions they represented.

This notion of conservation differed, of course, from archival preservation, as interventions could be targeted to aid particular traditions. This goal was realized by the Folk Arts Division of the NEA, which was (and is) a funds-granting agency. Monies were (and still are) granted to folk artists in the form of fellowships, and to organizations involved in preserving and conserving the folk arts in various regional and ethnic communities throughout the United States. The Folk Arts Division guidelines articulated the program's goal: to help folk artists and their communities value their traditional expressive culture and move into their futures, steadied by continuity with the past. In other words, the guidelines were meant to help folk artists and communities conserve their traditional cultural beliefs and practices while becoming more modern. When I served on the Folk Arts Division's grant decision-making panel in the early 1980s, for example, I realized that recent immigrants from Southeast Asia were a targeted group. Folk Arts staff told us that their abrupt removals to the United States following the war in that region had caused cultural trauma, and that in this crisis their folk traditions were liable to disappear within a single generation if nothing was done to help them.

The American Folklife Center, established in 1976, was neither a festival-producing agency nor a granting organization. It combined the Library of Congress's folk music archive, which had been established in the 1920s, with a series of public initiatives that involved partnerships with cultural organizations in various regions of the United States and that served to identify, document, and present the results back to the region, in an effort to strengthen regional and occupational folklife. Typically these initiatives began with surveys and culminated in a series of recommendations, along with a traveling exhibit. Today the Center defines its mission as to "preserve and present American folklife through programs of research, documentation, archival preservation, reference service, live performance, exhibitions, publications, and training" (http://www.loc.gov/folklife/aboutafc.html). Surveys characterized their efforts in the 1970s and 1980s, while in the 1990s partnerships with other agencies, including the National Park Service, were undertaken for cultural conservation.

In the 1980s the Folk Arts Division of the National Endowment for the Arts built an infrastructure of folklorists, employed chiefly in the state arts agencies. By the end of the decade almost every state of the union had at least one. They undertook state-based surveys to identify and document folk artists, and mounted exhibits and festivals to present them to the general public. The state folklorists' functions also included grant-giving to local folk and traditional arts organizations. They hired contract fieldworkers to carry out some of the documentation and presentation activities. Where possible, they used the same authenticity criteria as the Smithsonian festival, seeking out tradition-bearing folk artists who had been born and raised with their community's traditions, rather than revivalists who had come to them later in life. The result was a folk artist inventory that also served the Smithsonian's folklife office, which had decided to give over one section of the festival to a different state of the union each year. Fieldworkers who had documented state folklife often were involved in presenting it in the nation's capital. They also were available to the American Folklife Center for its various regional initiatives.

As these efforts bore fruit, and not coincidentally employed hundreds of folklorists and some ethnomusicologists with graduate degrees, the leaders in this burgeoning field of public folklore began to reflect on what it was they were doing. Each agency articulated its goals with increasing precision, whether in terms of cultural equity, cultural pluralism, or—in what came to be the term most everyone eventually settled on—cultural conservation. In so doing, they increasingly defined cultural conservation in terms of heritage.

In 1982 the American Folklife Center produced a book, coordinated by Ormond Loomis, entitled *Cultural Conservation*. They had been tasked with compiling a report for the US Secretary of the Interior "on preserving and conserving the intangible elements of our cultural heritage such as arts, skills, folklife, and folkways" (Loomis, 1982: 1). The Department of the Interior was the appropriate government agency because they were responsible for conservation of public resources. For the distinction between tangible and intangible cultural elements, the document drew on the practice of Asian societies, particularly Japan, which identified "intangible properties" as resources to be under government protection, folk artists among them (ibid.: 13). This identification of exceptional traditional artists as "national treasures" had already been the impetus behind Bess Lomax Hawes's successful 1980 proposal to the National Endowment for the Arts to establish and permit the Folk Arts Division to select the National Heritage Fellows, identifying a dozen outstanding American folk artists each year and offering them a cash honorarium of $5,000 and a ceremonial recognition in Washington, DC. This tangible/intangible distinction became much better known in its UNESCO incarnations. US folklorists ultimately came to critique it on the grounds that in the practice of folklife, tangible and intangible were inseparable (Hufford, 1994: 2). The Loomis document identified two components of cultural conservation: preservation and what it called "encouragement." By preservation was meant activities involving planning, documentation, and maintenance; by encouragement was meant publication, public events, and education, in order that a healthy traditional expressive folklife culture would enable a community's sense of integrity and enhanced identity to flourish. In this way, cultural conservation was to be more than simply preservation and maintenance. Encouragement looked to a cultural future in which folklife played an important role. Cultural conservation was more effective than preservation, for "preservation plans can divert undertakings that would disrupt normal cultural development" (Loomis, 1982: 10), and "to endure a group must pass on its distinguishing attributes from one generation to the next. Such attributes are the essence of cultural heritage" (ibid.: 3), and "it is possible, however, to temper change so that it proceeds in accordance with the will of the people, and not in response to the pressures of faddish trends or insensitive public or private projects. Conservation denotes efforts which. . . ensure natural cultural growth" (ibid.: 29). Leaving aside for the moment what "natural" cultural growth might be, this rhetoric reflects an anti-modernist agenda, opposed to materialism and consumer society and the cultural homogenization allegedly resulting from mass media and national brands. The Loomis document criticized identifying heritage items on a list, as UNESCO later was to do in compiling an inventory of world masterpieces of intangible cultural heritage (hereafter ICH) (ibid.: 16). Finally, cultural conservation drew the analogy between biological diversity and cultural diversity—if the one was good, so was the other (ibid.: 11). Thus many, if not most, of the arguments that would later surface in the cultural sustainability discourse in the new millennium had already been anticipated in this document. It became a working document for public folklore agencies in the 1980s.

In the 1980s and 1990s the National Endowment for the Arts' Folk Arts Division continued to support organizations, projects, and artists, and to grow the network of state folklorists, who in turn initiated projects within their states and regions. These projects were aimed primarily at increasing opportunities for traditional folk artists to continue practicing their art. One of the most successful of these was the apprenticeship program, in which tradition-bearers were paid to teach younger members of their families, communities (and, in some instances, revivalists) their music, crafts, and so forth, in an effort to transmit the folk arts to the next generations. Its only problem was that it was chronically underfunded, which diminished its overall impact. Concerts and festivals not only showcased traditional music but also gave the tradition-bearers and source musicians recognition, acknowledgment, and prestige within their communities. The Smithsonian's was the largest of these festivals. Another was the National Folk Festival, a Washington, DC–based festival since 1969, which also came to be advised chiefly by folklorists, and which in the late 1980s embarked on a new strategy of moving its venue to a new city every three years, in the hope that the city would continue supporting the festival after they moved on to the next site. A few cities did: Lowell, Massachusetts, has sponsored its festival for more than 20 years, while Bangor, Maine, has kept its festival going for more than 10. In the 1990s, the Smithsonian festivals took on an increasing international flavor, when one section of the festival was devoted to presenting the folklife of a nation other than the United States, resulting also in international cooperation among folklorists.

In 1990, the American Folklife Center held a conference on "Cultural Conservation: Rethinking the Cultural Mission." From that conference emerged the book *Conserving Culture: A New Discourse on Heritage* (Hufford, 1994). New was the emphasis on heritage, along with the realization that cultural conservation worked best when folklorists, applied ethnomusicologists, and other cultural specialists partnered with community leaders and organizations to work toward mutually approved and understood goals. In her Introduction, Hufford acknowledged that the cultural conservation movement places a value on both tangible and intangible culture marked for conservation, terming it *heritage*, something from the past which is both "ours" and worth preserving. Yet when folklife specialists began working with various constituencies to conserve heritage, it became clear that the separation of tangible and intangible heritage was misleading, particularly in those areas where the two were intimately bound up, such as intangible folk knowledge derived from interactions with the tangible environment. A second problem arose when folklife specialists attempted to "impose external standards on local communities" (ibid.: 2). A top-down approach could easily overlook or even discredit local knowledge, while outside experts imposed policies that proved unhelpful. A third problem arose in the "tendency of heritage planning to authenticate past cultures and environments [which] effectively reduced the power of present-day communities to manage the environments on which their dynamic cultures depend" (ibid.: 3). On the other hand, Hufford affirmed the term "conservation," writing that it acknowledged the dynamic aspects of culture, whereas "preservation" implied constancy. In other words, heritage need not be a thing of the past. Hufford argued forcefully for cultural partnerships between folklife specialists and community members whose local knowledge was essential, so that the goals were mutual and the policies reflected broad agreement among all stakeholders.

Yet cultural conservation had its critics. Most prominent among these was folklorist Nicholas Spitzer, whose background included cultural conservation work for the Smithsonian Institution and a term as Louisiana state folklorist. Best known as the host of the public radio program *American Routes*, and now also a professor at Tulane University, Spitzer argued in a series of presentations beginning in 1987 that conservation bound public folklore to an "ethically problematic" organic metaphor in which cultures follow a natural cycle of birth, growth, and decay. At its worst, this analogy smacked of Spencerian cultural evolutionism. Rather than work as conservationists to rescue cultures from threat and endangerment, Sptizer wrote, it would be better to think in terms of conversations with cultures to further "continuity, equity and diversity" (Spitzer, 2007 [1992]: 95–96). Had Spitzer looked more closely at the environmental movement, he might have mentioned that nature conservationists were aiming to further continuity, equity, and diversity within ecosystems; and he must have known that public folklorists engaged in cultural conservation work had those ends in view as well. Nonetheless, Spitzer reminded folklorists to consider the limitations of the ecological trope: that culture does not necessarily behave like nature. Nor does nature necessarily behave like culture (Titon, 2008–, 2013). Cultural conservation was critiqued also, by several, on the grounds that it proceeded from a romantic and nostalgic bias toward the past, one which was ill-equipped to analyze correctly the contemporary forces propelling cultures forward. Nevertheless, for nearly 30 years cultural conservation remained the dominant paradigm within public folklore, while it also guided applied ethnomusicologists in their work on behalf of music cultures. If cultural conservation has given way in the new millennium to cultural sustainability, the two paradigms nonetheless have much in common. Applied ethnomusicologists and public folklorists today are beholden to the history of cultural conservation, whether they know it or not.

SAFEGUARDING

UNESCO is the major international force on behalf of cultural conservation today; but the word UNESCO chose for it is "safeguarding." In the English language, safeguarding connotes preservation, not conservation. UNESCO had early in its history enacted Conventions (treaties that are binding only on nations that sign them) protecting historic sites, monuments, and architecture throughout the world, particularly against the ravages of war; but in the 1970s and 1980s their discussion turned to protecting traditional culture itself, usually termed *folkways, folklife,* and *folklore.* Eventually, in 1989, after years of international consultation, debate, and discussion, UNESCO issued a "Recommendation on the Safeguarding of Traditional Culture and Folklore" (http://portal.unesco.org/en/ev.php-URL_ID=13141&URL_DO=DO_TOPIC&URL_SECTION=201.html). Many of the safeguarding ideas embodied in that cultural conservation document, and in its later implementation through two Conventions (in 2003 and 2005), could also be found in cultural conservation discourse that was occurring in the United States (see http://www.unesco.org/culture/ich/index. php?pg=00006 and http://www.unesco.org/new/en/culture/themes/cultural-diversity/cultural-expressions/). Indeed, the word "safeguard" had appeared in the American Folklife Center's 1982 report on *Cultural Conservation*: "The ultimate aim of documentation and of the other strategies that combine in cultural conservation must be to *safeguard* and promote the community life and values of ethnic, occupational, religious, and regional groups by recognizing and protecting the treasured patterns that arise from their ways of life" (Loomis, 1982: 17–19; italics mine).

Significantly, however, in its 1989 Recommendation, UNESCO defined *preservation* and *conservation* exactly opposite to the common US understanding of the two terms. For UNESCO in 1989, conservation was what those in the United States understand as archival preservation. It was "concerned with documentation regarding folk traditions and its object is, in the event of the non-utilization or evolution of such traditions, to give researchers and tradition-bearers access to data enabling them to understand the process through which traditions change" (http://portal.unesco.org/en/ev.php-URL_ID=13141&URL_DO=DO_TOPIC&URL_SECTION=201.html)   Meanwhile,   for UNESCO preservation involved what we in the United States think of as conservation of living traditions. It was "concerned with protection of folk traditions and those who are the transmitters, having regard to the fact that each people has a right to its own culture and that [its culture] is often eroded by... the industrialized culture purveyed by the mass media. Measures must be taken to guarantee the status of and economic support for folk traditions both in the communities that produce them and beyond" (ibid.).

The 1989 UNESCO Recommendation fell on deaf international ears, as only a half-dozen nations responded (Aikawa, 2001: 13–14). As a result, throughout the 1990s UNESCO discussed ways of galvanizing international support, culminating in a 1999 conference sponsored by UNESCO and the Smithsonian Institution and leading to the 2003 Convention for the Safeguarding of the Intangible Cultural Heritage, which generated a mechanism for identifying outstanding examples of ICH ("world masterpieces"). In this document, the term *folklore* was replaced by *intangible cultural heritage*, and *conservation* was dropped while *preservation* and a host of other activities were subsumed under the cover term *safeguarding*, defined as a combination of "identification, documentation, research, preservation, protection, promotion, enhancement, transmission... and revitalization" of ICH (http://portal.unesco.org/en/ev.php-URL_ID=17716&URL_DO=DO_TOPIC&URL_SECTION=201.html). UN members were asked to sign the treaty and then to begin nominating outstanding examples of their ICH for inclusion on a list of "world masterpieces." If UNESCO approved the nomination, then the nation was obligated to undertake various actions to safeguard the ICH masterpiece, which they had promised in their nominating application. These usually included further documentation and interpretation, stimulus and promotion, and dissemination, which often resulted in cultural heritage tourism. Despite UNESCO's good intentions, in the United States safeguarding carried the unfortunate additional

purifying connotation of cleansing and deodorizing, derived from the name of a popular soap sold in the United States and marketed under the brand name "Safeguard." For
political reasons the United States has not signed either of the 2003 or 2005 UNESCO
ICH Conventions. US folklorists and ethnomusicologists have, of course, discussed the
UNESCO ICH initiatives, but in general they have been critical of the results (Weintraub
and Yung, 2009).

SUSTAINABILITY

In Theory

Sustainability, as I have noted, has much in common with preservation, conservation,
and safeguarding. Some advocates of sustainability emphasize that their attitude toward
development is progressive. Conservationists, they say, would prefer to manage things
to maintain present conditions or restore earlier ones; sustainability advocates recognize that change is both natural and inevitable, and seek to manage change in order to
guarantee continuity, integrity, and resource availability for the future. The predominant sustainability discourses take place in economics, ecology, and environmental
studies. Sustainability in economics means *sustainable development*; in ecology it refers
to the stability of ecosystems; in environmental studies it centers on energy conservation and carbon emission reduction. Although the idea long preceded the use of the
term, *sustainable development* appears to have entered public discourse first in the *World
Conservation Strategy* of the International Union for the Conservation of Nature and
Natural Resources (IUCN, 1980). *Sustainable development* also occupied a prominent
place in *Gaia: An Atlas of Planet Management* (Myers, 1992 [1984]). But it was with *Our
Common Future* (World Commission on Environment and Development, 1987), usually
referred to as the Brundtland Report, for the UN, where the term *sustainability*, coupled
with *development*, captured the imagination of the public policymakers. Particularly
in the arena of developmental economics, where the chief problems were identified as
third-world population growth, poverty, outmoded and inefficient agriculture, lack of
industry, poor infrastructure, and so forth, sustainable development was viewed as a
reasonable solution, famously defined in the Brundtland Report as "development that
meets the needs of the present, without compromising the ability of future generations
to meet their own needs." Environmentalists interpreted the sustainability mandate as
confirming their agenda: limits to growth, conservation of resources, safeguarding biodiversity, transitioning energy from fossil fuels to renewable sources, and so forth. Most
economists, on the other hand, thought that sustainable development confirmed their
belief that advances in science and technology would increase efficiency and solve third-
world problems. The environmentalists placed their emphasis on sustainable, while the
economists took comfort in development. In retrospect, of course, it can be seen that for
economics, sustainable development is not a new concept, but rather a reinterpretation

of the conservation concept of wise use and sustainable yield, which I have already traced to Renaissance Europe. For environmentalists, sustainability evoked the old idea of the "balance of nature" or, as it was expressed by natural historians including Gilbert White, Henry David Thoreau, and even by Charles Darwin, "Nature's economy"—the idea that, left to its own devices, nature tended toward efficiency as its parts worked together for the benefit of the whole (Worster, 1994). For ecologists, sustainability evoked the scientific version of natural balance, expressed in the idea that an ecosystem tended "naturally" to move toward a state of stability, or dynamic equilibrium, except when disturbed.

Among applied ethnomusicologists and public folklorists, the ecologists' understanding of sustainability has been the most influential. As pointed out earlier, in the new millennium cultural conservation has become cultural sustainability while musical conservation has become musical sustainability, in both cases continuing the eco-trope. However, developmental economics is not without influence. For example, UNESCO views safeguarding ICH as a part of the UN's economic development mandate. Culture must be safeguarded not merely because it is part of our human heritage, but because culture is "the mainspring of sustainable development" (http://www.unesco.org/new/en/culture/themes/cultural-diversity/diversity-of-cultural-expressions/the-convention/what-is-the-convention/). In addition, in the contemporary field of arts advocacy, one of the most powerful arguments advanced is that the arts are an economic engine (Throsby, 2010). In this vein, applied ethnomusicologists and public folklorists sometimes advocate heritage tourism (festivals, living history museums, historic tours, etc.) to fuel local and regional economies, believing that this will also give a boost to traditional music cultures and other arts.

Sustainability carries with it the notion of finite resources that are in danger of exhaustion. Given infinite abundance, there would be no need to think in terms of using resources in a sustainable way. If it is acceptable to speak of music as a human resource, then plainly it is a renewable one. As long as people can sing, they are not in danger of using up the resources required to make music. But just as language itself is not endangered whereas individual languages have gone extinct and others are going extinct, certain musics—that is, music cultures—and genres and instruments are endangered. Of course, those engaged in salvage folklore and ethnomusicology were well aware of these threats; indeed, it could be said that the impulse to preserve music arises at least partly from sadness over impending loss. Among US folklorists, as we have seen, conservation moved out of the museums and into living (or, rather, supposedly dying) cultures with the object of renewal and revitalization. As I wrote above, only a small number of US ethnomusicologists took part in the cultural conservation movement led by US public folklorists. Most US ethnomusicologists continued to do their research outside North America, where their experiences with musical and cultural conservation were various and diffuse.

Although sustainability did not make an impact in ethnomusicology or folklore until the new millennium, it is helpful to see how the concept was implemented in late twentieth-century developmental economics and the environmental movement, the two areas where it remains most deeply embedded today. Sustainability comes to ethnomusicologists with baggage from economics and environmentalism. Critics pointed out that sustainable development that reduced overall short-term resource yield would only exacerbate third-world poverty in the face of population growth, but proponents argued that a combination of smart market regulation, wise political policies, and advances in technology would greatly increase efficiency, productivity, and ultimate yield, and that the rising tide would lift all boats. The results of sustainable development initiatives are mixed. Economic successes have occurred in some areas, failures in others. Cultural anthropologists working in indigenous societies critique sustainable development on the grounds that it is a new form of Western colonialism that destroys traditional knowledge, lifeways, and cultural integrity. Meanwhile, resource exploitation and environmental degradation continue, though perhaps at a lesser rate, while living standards rise in some nations and stagnate elsewhere, and while income inequality also is on the rise. Nonetheless, sustainability brought environmental considerations into economics as never before.

The work of ecological economist Herman E. Daly has been notable within sustainable development. Daly was important not only as a theorist but also as an actor on this stage, for from 1988 to 1994 he was the senior economist at the World Bank. Daly began his career in the 1970s by opposing the possibility of continuous economic growth. He maintained that in their models economists ignored the environment at their peril. Constrained by the environment, the world economy was better viewed as a steady-state, dynamic equilibrium (Daly, 1991 [1977]). After the Brundtland Report, Daly endorsed sustainable development. He defined it in terms borrowed from "wise use" conservation practice, that is, as sustainable yield, in which the renewed resource is able to exceed the amount harvested or lost to disasters such as disease or fire. Alarmed at the way *sustainable development* was being used synonymously with *sustainable growth*, Daly argued that development need not imply growth. "When something grows it gets bigger. When something develops it gets different," he wrote. "The earth ecosystem develops but it does not grow. Its subsystem, the economy must eventually stop growing but continue to develop. The term 'sustainable development' therefore makes sense for the economy but only if it is understood as 'development without growth'" (Daly, 1993: 267–268). Unfortunately, Daly's sensible distinction failed to influence most developmental economists. Not surprisingly, the business world also adopted the idea of sustainable development, but in their hands it became a synonym for sustainable growth. To corporations intent on global competition, growth seemed necessary for survival. Many corporations adopted "green" practices, such as recycling waste, at the same time that they continued using up finite resources while researching technology for more efficient productivity and wiser use.

Daly was not the only economist to make use of ecology when discussing economy. In the 1990s, around the same time that Daly was proclaiming sustainable growth an oxymoron, James F. Moore argued that corporate leaders should understand their firms to be actors within ecosystems where they must not only compete but also cooperate in order to ensure the sustainability of the entire system and themselves within it. Just as predators and prey are interdependent in a natural ecosystem, so are corporations interdependent in a business ecosystem, even when they are rivals. His classic case in point was the cooperation and competition between Apple and Microsoft (Moore, 1993). Whereas Daly's distinction between development and growth was ignored by those economists, business leaders, and government policymakers who maintained a bias toward growth, Moore's idea of business ecosystems caught on, augmented by Paul Hawken's popular writing on the subject (Hawken, 1994). Today it is a commonplace to speak of the Apple ecosystem or the Google ecosystem. Daly and Moore believed that ecosystems were self-regulating and moved toward a stable, though dynamic, equilibrium.

Ecological thought had little impact on folklore and ethnomusicology until the new millennium, but its effect on cultural anthropology in the past century was significant. In fact, the sub-discipline of cultural ecology gathered momentum in the 1950s and was well established a decade later (Netting, 1977). It treated human groups and their behavior from an ecological perspective (Rappaport, 1979). Modernization and progress in so-called underdeveloped nations in the post–World War II era had been a concern of developmental anthropologists all along, with some applied anthropologists working to further it, others critiquing it, yet others undermining it through action anthropology and by privileging local knowledge over a modern worldview. Sustainable development, as defined in the Brundtland Report, was useful to economic anthropologists concerned with the impact of modernization and progress on the environment. Cultural anthropologists used the sustainable development concept to probe the interface between the environment and economic equity as well as political ecology. John Van Willigen concluded in *Applied Anthropology* (3rd ed.) that "[s]ustainability has come to be expressed in a wide range of [anthropological] themes in addition to economic development. These include biodiversity, climate change, soil and water conservation, efficient and renewable energy use, air quality, solid waste, population planning, forestation, and alternative agriculture" (Van Willigen, 2002: 74). Yet, as I mentioned earlier, applied anthropology is the target of a stinging contemporary critique coming from anthropologists specializing in indigenous studies, because of its historical alliance with developmental economics. The bad odor attached to it might threaten applied ethnomusicology, but it must be noted that applied ethnomusicology arose well after applied anthropology, during the period of postcolonial critique; and that applied ethnomusicology's ideological stance is anti-colonialism.

Concerns with sustainability and the environment were also, of course, central in the environmental movement, represented within the science of ecology by a growing sustainability discourse in conservation biology, which also came to be known as *conservation ecology*. Michael Soulé, the founder of conservation biology, defined its "proper objective" as the "protection and continuity of entire communities and ecosystems." Conservation biologists are concerned less with "maximum yields, and profitability, and more [with] the long-range viability of whole systems and species. . . . Long-term viability of natural communities usually implies the persistence of diversity" and, because of human-made disturbances to these communities, requires redress through active management (Soulé, 1985: 728–729.) In emphasizing continuity and viability, Soulé is speaking of sustainability, but not of sustainable development. His de-emphasis on yields underlines the major difference between sustainable development, which has an economic end, and conservation biology's idea of sustainability, which concerns long-term endurance of ecosystems and maximizes biodiversity over yield. As conservation biology grew into an applied "crisis discipline," some wished to adapt it for sustainable development; yet Soulé's original vision of biodiversity remained central, while it impacted environmental activists and ecologists alike. Already in 1993, ecohistorian Donald Worster could write, "There is a widespread implication. . . that sustainability at bottom is an ecological concept: the goal of environmentalism should be to achieve 'ecological sustainability'" (Worster, 1993: 148). Worster worried that sustainability carried economic yield connotations of conservation's "wise use" back into the discussion, albeit under a new name. Furthermore, he pointed out the problems with the idea of ecosystem sustainability in the face of the changed ecological paradigm, which had abandoned ideas of stability and a balance of nature (ibid.: 149–150). Nonetheless, the contemporary environmental movement embraces sustainability, to the point that it has become a vogue word for various eco-conscious activities.

In Applied Ethnomusicology

As I mentioned at the outset of this chapter, US ethnomusicologists and other culture workers helped to sustain musicians, musical traditions, and music cultures long before the term *sustainability* became operative in the late 1980s, and before it entered ethnomusicological discourse in the 2000s. In the 1890s a privileged, anti-modernist wing within the Progressive movement established settlement schools for the poor in New York and Chicago, as well as remote rural areas such as the southern Appalachian Mountains, where immigrant and native traditions were collected from elders and taught to youngsters. The well-known Appalachian singer Jean Ritchie (1922–2015) grew up near the Hindman Settlement School in southeastern Kentucky, where many of her sisters attended; after she left Kentucky for New York, she took a job at a settlement school, where her singing came to the attention of Alan Lomax and others in the folk revival scene, and her career as a tradition-bearer was soon launched (Ritchie, 1955). While it suffered from *noblesse oblige*, the Progressives' uplift agenda for the poor favored the conservation of folk traditions, both rural and immigrant. Music and dance were prominent among those singled out for preservation and revival. Generations of American children learned them in school. This was not archival preservation, but sustainability within living cultural groups, in an effort to restore and maintain personal and cultural identity and integrity under the psychologically dislocating pressures of modernization.

Other twentieth-century efforts at sustainability before the term gained currency were directed at individual musicians rather than cultural groups. Although most folklorists and ethnomusicologists believed that folk traditions were endangered and would diminish and eventually disappear, it might be possible to help outstanding musicians revive and maintain their careers, even if it meant bringing their music to a different audience, the urban middle class, whose ethnic and regional traditions had vanished into the melting pot. Alan and John Lomax's work in this vein with the African American folksinger Huddie Ledbetter (Lead Belly) is a case in point (Porterfield, 2001). In certain parts of the United States, folk festivals became occasions to reintroduce traditional musicians to their own cultures and bring them to the attention of a wider public, thereby stimulating them to maintain their musical skills and repertoires. Festivals such as the one started in Asheville, North Carolina (1928–present) by Bascom Lamar Lunsford are examples. In the 1950s and 1960s, rediscovered traditional blues singers and old-time string band musicians, as well as tradition-bearing folksingers, were promoted on the newly reinvigorated folk music revival circuit. Musicians such as the aforementioned Jean Ritchie, Son House, Clarence "Tom" Ashley, Bill Monroe, and Almeda Riddle—regarded as authentic representatives of their regions and musical traditions because they had grown up learning them—mingled with folk music revivalists in widely promoted folk music concerts, as well as festivals that drew many thousands of spectators.

Many of the those who promoted the sustainability of musical genres such as blues and bluegrass in the 1960s were themselves young, folk revival musicians, and some later became folklorists and ethnomusicologists. These included William Ferris, whose efforts to sustain blues in Mississippi included cultural tourism (especially for Europeans), a boost to the career of B. B. King, and promotion of the career of country blues singer Son Thomas. Ferris brought King to be an artist-in-residence at Yale, where Ferris taught as a professor of American Studies for a few years before returning to his native Mississippi to found the University of Mississippi's Center for the Study of Southern Culture. From 1997 to 2001 Ferris was director of the National Endowment for the Humanities, the first and only time that a folklorist has held this position, the most powerful cultural post in the United States. Kenneth Goldstein and Roger Abrahams both collected, recorded, and promoted folk musicians in the 1950s and 1960s folk music revival; they became professors of folklore at the University of Pennsylvania. My own trajectory was similar. While a graduate student, I joined Lazy Bill Lucas's blues band in Minneapolis in the late 1960s out of a desire to learn more about a music I had already been playing for several years. Soon, wanting to give something back, I saw that I could promote my new friend's solo career, by publishing my interviews with him in fan magazines devoted to African American blues music, which led to a recording contract for him as well as an appearance at the 1970 Ann Arbor Blues Festival. David Evans's path was similar to mine. He researched blues while in graduate degree programs in folklore, promoted some of the blues singers' careers, and eventually became a professor of ethnomusicology, at the University of Memphis.

The most significant relationship for what would become sustainability was that which developed in the 1960s between folklorist and bluegrass musician Ralph Rinzler (1934–1994) and Cajun fiddler Dewey Balfa (1927–1992). Their partnership ushered in a revitalization and revival of Cajun music beginning in the late 1960s within French

Louisiana and elsewhere. Although the sustainability concept was not available to describe it then, it remains one of the most effective instances of a US vernacular musical and cultural sustainability intervention. I have written about this elsewhere, so a summary here will suffice (Titon, 2009c: 130–131). One of the promoters of the Newport Folk Festival, Rinzler had invited Balfa, among others, to perform at the festival. Balfa's local newspaper had questioned whether that old-fashioned, "chanky-chank" music ought to represent the region at such an important festival. Surely Balfa and the others would be laughed off the stage, the paper had editorialized. But instead, the Newport audience would not let them leave the stage, calling for encores. Balfa returned to Cajun country so energized that he became a cultural ambassador and took his family band on tour throughout the world. But more than that, he led a cultural revival movement within his Cajun community that eventually extended even to a renewal of the Cajun French language. Whether or not Rinzler was responsible for doing anything more than galvanizing Balfa's latent sustainability talents, he understood what could be accomplished by a partnership between culture workers like himself and community leaders like Balfa. When, a few years later, Rinzler founded the Smithsonian Festival of American Folklife, he spread this idea among the festival workers and the group of folklorists and ethnomusicologists who came to join him in Washington, DC, in the 1970s, one that included Bess Lomax Hawes (1921–2009) and her brother Alan Lomax (1915–2002), as well as ethnomusicologists Daniel Sheehy and Thomas Vennum, along with folklorist Alan Jabbour, all of whom were to become deeply involved with the formation and early years of the National Endowment for the Arts' Folk Arts Division, the American Folklife Center at the Library of Congress, and the Smithsonian's Center for Folklife and Cultural Heritage. To a greater or lesser degree, all of this work was animated by this vision of the possibilities of cultural renewal and sustainability as a result of various interventions: grants from the National Endowment for the Arts, the Smithsonian's festivals, and the American Folklife Center's surveys and exhibitions. However, *sustainability* was not the operative term at the time, and as I discussed earlier, when in the early 1980s they began to theorize about what they had done and were doing and wanted to do better, they called it *cultural conservation*. But in defining it as "encouragement" along with preservation, they were thinking about sustainability.

The founding generation of the Society for Ethnomusicology was interested primarily in basic research and scholarship, not applied work. However, David McAllester and Mantle Hood undertook some interventions that could be considered applied, even though they never discussed them in those terms. McAllester was active in the field of pre-college music education, working with the Music Educators National Conference to include world music in the curriculum for youngsters aged 6–18. His own research was with the Navajo, and although he was adopted by a Navajo family, he did not actively seek to influence the future of Navajo music, preferring to leave that to the Navajo themselves. Hood, on the other hand, intervened in Bali, both as a patron of the arts and in encouraging the revival of gamelan gong-making and performance. A section near the conclusion of his book, *The Ethnomusicologist*, is entitled "The Impact of the Ethnomusicologist" and concludes by reporting on the way his work and appreciation of their artistry raised the status of traditional musicians, and music and dance in their community, and gave them impetus to continue (Hood, 1971: 358–371).

Only a few US ethnomusicologists were involved in these musical and cultural conservation efforts, as noted earlier. At the Smithsonian Institution and associated in one way or another with the folklife office were Thomas Vennum and, in the late 1980s, Charlotte Heth, who had become director of their Native American museum initiative. A few ethnomusicologists worked as presenters at the Smithsonian's folklife festival—I had done so in 1976, for example—and in 1988 ethnomusicologist Anthony Seeger became the director of the Smithsonian's newly acquired operation, Folkways Records. Judith Gray, who had studied ethnomusicology at Wesleyan University, was hired as an archivist by the American Folklife Center. The Folk Arts Division of the National Endowment for the Arts involved the most ethnomusicologists. Daniel Sheehy, who received his Ph.D. in ethnomusicology from UCLA, was the assistant director throughout the decade, while the Folk Arts panelists who met four times per year to advise the agency and recommend grant and heritage awards included ethnomusicologists Charlotte Heth (serving 1981–1982, 1987), myself (1981–1983), Robert Garfias (1982–1983), Jacqueline DjeDje (1983–1985), Ralph Samuelson (1984–1985), Hector Vega (1984–1986), Lorraine Sakata (1986–1989), Ric Trimillos (1987–1988), Adelaide Schramm (1988–1989), and Thomas Vennum (1989). A few more worked in state agencies such as arts councils, either doing contract fieldwork and festival and exhibit production, or as arts administrators. Each of us had a commitment to applied ethnomusicology and to musical and cultural conservation in our own academic and public work, but altogether we were only about 5% of the ethnomusicologists working in the United States at that time. The fact that most US ethnomusicologists researched music cultures outside the United States severely limited the percentage that might have participated, however. In short, while in the 1980s public (sector) folklore developed a strong US infrastructure, employing folklorists at the national and state government levels, there was nothing comparable in scope for US ethnomusicologists. The vast majority remained scholars aiming their research at colleagues while teaching students in the academic world. Some, however, were developing a commitment to applied ethnomusicology (see Murphy, Chapter 5 of Volume 3).

Ethnomusicology's involvement in sustainability during the 1980s came chiefly from commitments to musical individuals and communities that were resulting from fieldwork, not from alliances with public folklore. While it was true even then that almost all fieldwork conducted by US academic ethnomusicologists was accomplished for the purposes of scholarship and contributions to knowledge about the music of the world's peoples, many ethnomusicologists were forming friendships with their principal informants (some of which led to marriage) and began asking how "giving back" might also be extended to communities. This was the same generation that had begun reciprocity of this kind in the 1960s as graduate students. Also, at this time, the "crisis" in US cultural anthropology was leading to a new reflexivity among North American ethnomusicologists who, in questioning their own subject positions and their rights to claim knowledge and authority, of necessity were considering the impact of their research on the communities studied, in addition to the impact of their studies on themselves. Notable in terms of their movement in the direction of applied ethnomusicology and sustainability were second-generation US ethnomusicologists Paul Berliner, Steven Feld, and Anthony Seeger. Berliner's work with Shona *mbira* music and musicians was unusually reflexive for its time, concerned as it was with the ethnomusicologist's subject position vis-à-vis the people whose music he was learning (Berliner, 1978). Feld and Seeger undertook ethnographic fieldwork among tropical rain forest peoples, with scientific research as their principal goal; but each scholar gradually developed a sense of responsibility to help their subjects maintain their music and culture in the face of modernization. Feld's efforts with the Kaluli in Papua New Guinea included a reflexive postscript to the second edition of *Sound and Sentiment* (Feld, 1990). Seeger began to investigate legal means of protecting Suya culture, including copyright for their music (Seeger, 1991). Some ethnomusicologists undertaking graduate study in the 1980s were strongly affected by the currents of experimental ethnography and applied ethnomusicology; among them, Michelle Kisliuk wrote a reflexive ethnography of another tropical rain forest people, the BaAka (Kisliuk, 1998). Alan Lomax should also be considered in this light. Although Lomax meant cantometrics to be scientific, aimed it at anthropologists and folklorists, and seldom was reflexive, his work on behalf of musical and cultural equity was implicit in this research, and explicit in his strongly-felt influence on the cultural conservation movement in US folklore (Lomax, 1972).

It was conservation ecology's notion of diversity, coupled with equity and ecojustice, that provided the basis for sustainability thinking in folklore (cultural sustainability) and ethnomusicology (music culture sustainability and the persistence of musical traditions) in the twenty-first century. Within ethnomusicology, "Music and Sustainability" was the title of a panel presentation for the 2006 annual conference of the Society for Ethnomusicology. A special journal issue on music and sustainability published three years later included the papers from that panel plus two others (Titon, 2009a). The essay introducing the special issue proposed that music is

> a biocultural resource, a sound-producing activity natural to humans that comes into being as music through sociocultural processes. . . . Efforts to sustain music are best directed at, and regarded as, sustaining selected sociocultural activities that encourage music's production and maintenance. In short, sustaining music means sustaining people making music. Then if one grants that sustaining music is a legitimate public policy pursuit, a number of further questions arise: what are the wisest policies, how may they be achieved, and what role might ethnomusicologists play in defining them?
>
> (Titon, 2009b: 6)

The essays in that issue addressed music and sustainability from different vantage points, but all were concerned with music cultures in a state of revitalization. In the United States, these music cultures, particularly when regarded as expressions of ethnic identity, are cultural policy targets. Applied ethnomusicologists ask how healthy these musical cultures are, and what can be done to help them survive and flourish, while at the same time honoring their traditional practices. Repatriation of archival recordings has been an enormous help to a number of them. In her essay for the special journal issue on music and sustainability, Janet Topp Fargion mentioned the Passamaquoddy recordings made more than 100 years ago by Jesse Walter Fewkes (Topp Fargion, 2009: 78). Wayne Newell, an educator and Passamaquoddy community scholar helping his nation to revitalize traditional music and language, uses these recordings and finds them invaluable (Newell, 2003). This way of thinking about preservation is critical to Topp Fargion's holistic redefinition of field recordings. Recordings have always held a central place in ethnomusicological research. Yet among ethnomusicologists today, field recording itself may be becoming endangered. For one thing, it is increasingly difficult to keep pace with changing technological developments. For another, as social texts become more central to ethnomusicology, documentary field recordings recede in importance, along with musical transcription and analysis. Topp Fargion's essay showed how a more inclusive approach to research, particularly for sustainability purposes, enables the field recorded document (ibid.).

In that same special journal issue on music and sustainability, Mark DeWitt and Tom Faux both presented case studies of particular musical cultures in a state of revitalization. DeWitt portrayed a Creole music and dance scene in northern California that is largely self-supporting, based not only on a core of Creole (and to a lesser extent Cajun) out-migrants from Louisiana, but also on a group of folk music and dance revivalists who, although not growing up in Creole or Cajun culture, have joined it. Although some of the Bay Area musicians have received recognition and support from arts councils and other agencies, most have received little or none. The health of this scene does not depend on stimuli from external agencies. But as it is competing with an ever-compelling musical marketplace, its vitality can be lost in a generation (DeWitt, 2009).

For that reason, "passing it on" is a major concern of arts policy. Apprenticeship, funded by arts agencies, in which younger members of an arts community learn from respected elders, is one of the most widely praised forms of intervention. And in those instances where the master artists are, or become, community scholar-practitioners, "passing it on" becomes an important internal consideration. The experiences of Don Roy as discussed by Tom Faux are a case in point. Unlike the Creole music and dance in northern California, Franco-American music in New England has received support from cultural agencies, particularly for festivals and tours; but, as Faux pointed out, Roy understood that these tourist-oriented expressions usually failed to foster the long-term, community social capital that sustains a music and dance scene. And so Roy teaches group lessons, and the teaching not only facilitates music but also encourages community-building. One of the reasons, perhaps, that Don Roy is uneasy at cultural agencies labeling him a Franco-American musician is that he understands that this music transcends ethnic boundaries and attracts contemporary contradance musicians in New England who are identified with "Yankee" (traditional British) rather than French culture (Faux, 2009).

The ecosystem analogy that enabled the application of these principles to cultural management on behalf of musical sustainability has recently been subjected to a critique by Brent Keogh. In a wide-ranging review of the ecological trope in ethnomusicological theory, Keogh concludes that in considering musical cultures as ecosystems, and in following the principles of natural management (that is, by "following nature" in privileging diversity, interdependence, and so on), we would be mistakenly attributing good intentions to nature, whereas "Nature does not care whether a particular species thrives or perishes and no one species is more important that any other. . . . Nature does not care about diversity, it does not manage its economy because Nature [sic] is not an agent" (Keogh, 2013: 6). Keogh confuses agency (action) with intention, because common language does in fact assign agency to nature, as in statements such as "canals carved by the agency of the river." Granted, the Christian worldview that gave rise to the widespread Enlightenment idea of nature as the Great Economist saw a divine hand behind nature. And, indeed, certain conservation ecologists do attribute good outcomes to natural processes; for example, two of Soulé's value statements for conservation biology are that "diversity of organisms is good" and that "evolution is good" (Soulé, 1985: 730–731).

But there is a difference between good outcomes and intentions. Wetlands, for example, provide flood control, wildlife habitat, and so forth. One can say without violating scientific principles that flood control is the result of the agency of wetlands. Those of us working with the ecosystem analogy in applied ethnomusicology are not attributing good intentions to nature, pleasant as it is to entertain the fancy that nature "cares" when good outcomes occur. Of course, nature also acts destructively. Nor is nature indifferent. In the tradition of scientific realism, nature simply "is," as an external reality. Where sustainability is a desired outcome, it does not require belief in agency within nature. It is neither necessary nor desirable for conservation ecologists to anthropomorphize nature when harmonizing human interventions in the natural world with ecological principles in order to maximize desired outcomes. Nor is it necessary for applied ethnomusicologists to attribute agency to nature when working with that ecological analogy in cultural policy. It would be difficult to conclude that applied ethnomusicologists who base management of musical cultures on an ecosystem resilience paradigm attribute agency to nature or, for that matter, to culture. Keogh's critique of the eco-trope, like Spitzer's critique of conservation, points to the limitations they believe arise from employing analogies between culture and nature. The relationship between the two is, however, complex, as is the history of that relationship (Titon, 2013).

When back in the late 1970s I began exploring music cultures as ecological systems, the analogy I had in mind was between music and energy; that is, as energy flowed in a natural ecosystem in a feedback loop among so-called producer organisms and consumers, so in a music culture music flowed in a feedback loop among producers and consumers (Titon, 1984: 9). The analogy I have borne in mind is thus not merely at the system attribute level, but a more basic analogy between the driving forces in these two systems, namely energy and music. Indeed, ecological principles are derived from human constructions of the natural world to begin with. As we shall see in the next section, ecologists who favor the resilience paradigm not only deny agency to nature but also are skeptical of equilibratory constructions of nature.

RESILIENCE

Within the larger discourse of sustainability among ecologists, a related term, *resilience*, has provided a different and, many think, more promising direction for ecosystem management. Advocates of resilience emphasize that whereas sustainability is a goal, resilience is a strategy. Like sustainability, resilience thinking has been taken up by economists, including business economists, and by psychologists and social workers, who recommend resilience to their clients as a response to disruptive change in their lives. To date, resilience has not had much, if any, impact in ethnomusicology, applied or otherwise. In this chapter I begin exploring how applied ethnomusicologists might employ resilience as a strategy. Nonetheless, resilience has already entered public discourse, where its use is becoming more frequent.

Like sustainability, resilience has been used to mean two different, but related, ideas. In popular usage, resilience sometimes means resistance; but more precisely, resilience means the ability to bounce back. Consider a system such as a forest, a pond, a music culture, a computer, or a human being. To use a homely example, imagine a person on the verge of catching a cold. Persons may increase their resistance by boosting their immune system with echinacea, vitamin C, and so on. Resilience, on the other hand, refers to a person's ability to recover after catching a cold. Going from not having a cold to having one represents a change in state or, as ecologists call it, a regime shift from one state to another—in this case from a more desirable equilibrium (health) to a less desirable one (having a cold). The more resilient a system, the more quickly it recovers, and the more fully it returns toward its previous state. Ecologists stress that a resilient system need not bounce back entirely to its previous state; in the face of disturbance it may—indeed probably will—change; but a resilient system recovers to the point where it is able to retain sufficient integrity to keep performing its core functions (Gunderson, Allen, and Holling, 2009: xiv–xvi). Summarizing ecological thought about resilience, Philip S. Lake writes, "The capacity to weather a disturbance without loss is defined as resistance, whereas resilience is the capacity to recover from a disturbance after incurring losses, which many be considerable" (Lake, 2013: 20).

Resilience strategies are meant to exhibit resilience themselves; that is, managing for resilience means living with a degree of uncertainty (although trying to minimize it). It means to experiment, sometimes to fail, and to adapt management techniques so as to learn from successes and failures. In the current phraseology, resilience thinking requires adaptive management. Adaptive management anticipates, and reacts to, changing circumstances, changes in values, and changes in knowledge. Resilience is meant to be pragmatic and realistic (Norton, 2005). Environmental studies professor Lance Gunderson explains that "Adaptive management is an approach to natural resource management that was developed from theories of resilience. Adaptive management acknowledges the deep uncertainties of resource management and attempts to winnow those uncertainties over time by using management actions as experiments to test policy. Management must confront various sources of complexity in systems, including the ecological, economic, social, political, and organizational components of these systems as well as the interactions among system components. . . . Adaptive management attempts to bring together disciplinary approaches for analysis and assessment and then integrate those ideas with policy and government in the social arenas in a framework some describe as adaptive governance. . . [which is] a framework for managing complex environmental issues. . . the social and human context" (Gunderson, Allen, and Holling, 2009: xx). Resilience thinking is implemented through adaptive management. Restoration ecology is one area of application. Here, adaptive management attempts to increase an ecosystem's resilience and tip it back to a more desirable state.

Interestingly, many resilience advocates contrast resilience with sustainability not only by regarding the former as a strategy and the latter as merely a goal, but also by linking sustainability to the old "balance of nature" equilibrium paradigm, which has been abandoned by most ecologists, even though many conservationists, cultural and otherwise, still believe in it. In other words, the majority of contemporary ecologists no longer believe that ecosystems exhibit periods of prolonged stability as well as an overall tendency to move toward a single, balanced equilibrium, a climax state. Rather, they accept that in complex systems disturbances and changes are the norm, and that there is no natural balance at a climax equilibrium point, but rather any number of tipping points that, when passed, bring about regime shifts to different states of temporary equilibria, some more desirable than others (Pickett and White, 1985: 155–156). Resilience strategies are meant to achieve and maintain the most desirable states whenever possible.

For some resilience advocates, abandoning the idea of stability in ecosystems also means abandoning a cornerstone of "wise use" conservation and sustainability thinking: that endangered renewable resources would "naturally" recover when harvest rates were reduced to a more sustainable level, as in a forest or fishery. Such recovery was predictable under the balance of nature paradigm, but it could not be anticipated after a regime shift to a less desirable state. The abrupt collapse of fisheries, without any real prospect of return, lends credence to the newer paradigm involving regime shifts, and indicates a need for a change in strategy and policy (Gunderson, Allen, and Holling, 2009: xiii–xiv). Gunderson continues: "A resilience approach opposes the preoccupation with increased production/yields/returns through increased efficiency. . . and control of natural variation. In contrast resilience thinking captures, and in fact embraces, the dynamic nature of the world. It recognizes the perils of optimizing for particular products. . . . It leads to an understanding of the critical thresholds in the systems we depend upon, and, once a system has crossed such a threshold into an undesirable regime, resilience thinking explains why it can be so difficult to move out of that condition, and what might be done about it" (Walker and Salt, 2006: 140).

Resilience strategies also are employed in current economic practice, and they are not new. Diversification, a common resilience strategy for sustainability, is proverbial; most languages contain wise old sayings such as "Don't keep all your eggs in one basket." Farmers understand that monoculture is vulnerable to predators, disease, and erratic weather. Organic farmers work to improve the soil, which boosts resilience in the face of disturbance. Investors are urged to allocate funds to more than a single type of asset. Business corporations employ similar resilience strategies, diversifying products, sources, and distribution channels. If they consider themselves part of larger ecosystems, they understand that alliances, even with competitors, build resilience. Insofar as applied ethnomusicologists follow business models, particularly when advocating for heritage tourism and the creative economy, they may choose to adopt resilience strategies similar to these. Diversification is an adaptive risk management technique.

In putting ethnomusicology to practical use, then, applied ethnomusicologists would be wise to consider resilience strategies and adaptive management when partnering with cultural organizations where sustainability is a policy goal. Whether working directly with music cultures in participatory action research, sometimes as members of those music cultures ourselves, or whether working for, or with, government agencies, arts councils, museums, historical societies, and other nonprofit organizations with an agenda that includes sustaining, or restoring, particular music cultures, we would do well to recognize regime changes and implement resilience strategies. As usual in such cases, questions arise over what is to be sustained or restored in a music culture— repertoire, style, performance practice, function and context, feelings and experiences, careers, and so forth—and how best to sustain what is to be sustained. Many of these are questions of value as well as management strategy, and they involve trade-offs.

Moreover, it is crucial to consider a sustainable music culture not as a stable, climaxed ecosystem but as a desired regime. In other words, strategies should not be aimed chiefly at removing supposedly "unnatural" distortions, as outlined in *Cultural Conservation* and quoted earlier in this essay (". . . it is possible, however, to temper change so that it proceeds in accordance with the will of the people, and not in response to the pressures of faddish trends or insensitive public or private projects. Conservation denotes efforts which. . . ensure natural cultural growth" [Loomis, 1982: 29]). "Natural cultural growth" is a fiction; there is no reason to believe it any more than to believe in the balance of nature. Instead, resilience strategies of adaptive management respond to forces of disturbance and change, some good and some not so good, in an attempt to establish or restore, and then maintain, desired regimes.

As directed at traditional music within ethnic communities, the cultural conservation and safeguarding movements discussed earlier usually claimed that their interventions were being done on behalf of music cultures that were threatened and were headed toward a regime change. "Safeguarding" assumes that the regime change has not yet taken place, that the heritage remains to be preserved. Sustainability, while more flexible in concept, also assumes that the tipping point has not yet been reached, and therefore that major aspects of the current regime are worth sustaining. In reality, many traditional musics had already undergone regime change to an undesirable state. The traditional aspects were at best a remnant, and therefore the desired end was restoration to a former state, rather than conservation or safeguarding of a present one, even if this could not be articulated or admitted as such. In other words, culture workers, particularly those dealing with heritage, are sometimes trapped in a preservation discourse that magnifies the presence, and importance, of a threatened tradition. If the tradition already has largely succumbed, for political reasons the discourse may have to emphasize sustainability; but the strategies ought to be aimed at restoration and resilience.

I turn now to ask what general characteristics of complex systems make certain ones resilient in the face of disturbance, and what make others vulnerable? After identifying some, I consider resilience in two contrasting amateur music cultures and see what kinds of strategies are likely to work and what may fail.

Andrew Zolli and Ann Marie Healy point out five characteristics of resilient systems. These overlap to some degree. They are (1) feedback mechanisms to alert a system to an impending change; (2) built-in mechanisms for dynamic reorganization in the face of disturbance; (3) a structure consisting of modular components that can be repaired or replaced individually, thus preventing the necessity to repair or replace the system as a whole; (4) an ability to detach parts and diversify, thus localizing operations and reducing dependencies without undermining the whole; and (5) clustering, or the ability to aggregate under favorable conditions and grow. We may add (6) social capital, when the resilient system is a cohesive social group. "Resilient communities frequently [rely on] informal networks, rooted in deep trust, to contend with and heal disruption. Efforts undertaken to impose resilience from above often fail, but when those same efforts are embedded authentically in the relationships that mediate people's everyday lives, resilience can flourish" (Zolli and Healy, 2012: 9–13). Other characteristics of resilient systems are (7) diversity, and (8) innovation (Walker and Salt, 2006: 145–148).

Consider resilience and adaptive management in two contrasting music cultures, the Old Regular Baptists in the coal-mining country of the US southern Appalachian Mountains, and the old-time string band revival, dispersed in communities throughout the United States with some smaller groups elsewhere, such as Ireland. In more than 200 years, the music of the Old Regulars has not undergone a significant regime change. Old-time string band music has done so, although most revivalists persist in believing otherwise. Conditions within the two music cultures are significantly different, particularly in terms of geographical distribution, economic dependence, and social organization. Resilience strategies will reflect these differences and others.

The Old Regular Baptists are a regional music culture, living in an area that includes the mountainous, coal-mining portions of a few contiguous southeastern states, chiefly in southeastern Kentucky, southern West Virginia, and southwestern Virginia. Although a small number of out-migrated Old Regular Baptists have established churches in Ohio and Florida, 95% exist within this mountainous, coal-mining region (Figure 5.1). They are organized into 17 Associations. Each Association consists of anywhere from about 5 to 30 churches, each church with its own congregation and ministers. Altogether they number about 10,000 people. They possess the oldest English-language singing tradition in the United States, lined-out hymnody. This music

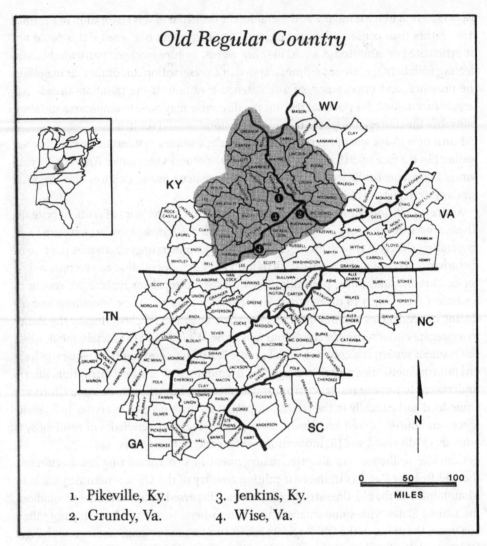

Old Regular Country

1. Pikeville, Ky.   3. Jenkins, Ky.
2. Grundy, Va.   4. Wise, Va.

FIG. 5.1 Location of Old Regular Baptist Churches in the Southern Appalachian region. Source: Howard Dorgan, *The Old Regular Baptists of Central Appalachia* (Knoxville: University of Tennessee Press, 1989), p. 3.

proceeds without congregational song books and without musical notation. The tunes are in oral tradition. One of the men with the ability to lead songs sings out the words one line at a time, singing them to a special lining tune for each hymn. The congregation joins the leader to sing back the words one line at a time, to a tune that is related to but more elaborate than the lining tune. The hymnody is unaccompanied and in free rhythm, and is characterized by melismatic melodic elaboration, each singer being free to "curve" the basic melody with more or fewer passing tones. The result is a thrilling heterophonic unison for the singers, in step but out of phase. To non-participants it may sound mournful and disorganized. This music has been described in more detail elsewhere, while field recordings also are available. It descends from the practice of the sixteenth-century English parish church, and was the "old way of singing" characteristic of the Massachusetts Puritans and their descendants until it was eclipsed by the reform efforts of music educators in the eighteenth century. Scholars of American hymnody thought it had gone extinct, but it was discovered in the middle of the twentieth century to have survived among groups of old-fashioned Baptists in the southern Appalachian Mountains, where it persists most strongly among the Old Regular Baptist denomination (Dorgan, 1989; Titon, Cornett, and Wallhausser, 1997; Titon, 1999).

For resilience, the Old Regulars have great strengths in many of the characteristics identified by Zolli and Healy. Feedback is one. They are self-consciously old-fashioned and safeguard their religious beliefs and practices closely. For at least 150 years they have carefully monitored possible intrusions from other religions, including such things as foreign missions, Sunday school, and the use of musical instruments in worship. They have resisted newer musical styles and repertories, most notably gospel songs and harmony singing. These remain tempting for some, but in fact the church leaders do not permit the congregations to sing gospel songs or to sing in parts. Modular structure is another resilience characteristic of this group. Their feedback mechanisms are reinforced by a hierarchically organized, modular structure in which each church functions as a single module. Their number rises and falls as some join the Association and others occasionally fall away, or go "out of correspondence," as they say—usually over disputes in doctrine. The Indian Bottom Association, in southeastern Kentucky, has in fact gained churches and members during the 25 years that I have known them. Informal networks in a community of deep respect is another resilience characteristic of this group. Communication and trust among the Old Regular Baptists is facilitated by the habit of visiting: each church holds its worship service and a business meeting only one weekend per month. This means that Old Regular Baptists attend their home churches but once a month while visiting other churches three or four times each month. Ministers do the same, as do persons with the knowledge and ability to lead the songs. All of these aspects of church governance and organization, coupled with a close and caring social life, make the Old Regular Baptists resilient, and have kept them so for more than 150 years.

However, in some ways the Old Regular Baptist music culture is vulnerable. Their total population is relatively small, and new church members must reside within a narrow geographic region. This region sees little in-migration and is gradually losing population. One does not join the music culture easily, by volunteering to do so; one must join a church, and the churches have membership requirements based on religious belief and how one lives one's life. The songs are difficult to learn and sing until one has been immersed in the music for a while. Other church denominations in the region, with different, easier, and more modern-sounding ways of singing, compete with Old Regular Baptists for members. But their greatest vulnerability, I believe, is economic dependence. They are concentrated in a region dominated by a single industry: coal mining. Since the 1930s, automation in the mines has gradually diminished the overall number of workers, but in the past few decades, strip mining and then mountaintop removal, which require many fewer laborers, have greatly accelerated this trend, increasing unemployment and poverty in the region. Low-paying jobs in fast-food restaurants and shopping centers are available, but they provide only supplemental income and cannot support a family, whereas coal mining, although dangerous, does not require much formal education and pays a living wage. The future of coal mining itself also is uncertain, given increasing environmental regulation, and the decreasing proportion of coal in the US energy mix. Meanwhile, strip mining and mountaintop removal greatly disturb the mountain ecosystems, increasing flooding, earthquakes, and pollution in the land and water, causing illness and death. Black-lung disease from coal dust had been an ever-present threat, but with mountaintop removal the environment itself is endangered, along with all life in the region. How long the population can remain viable in that area is an open question; and if they had to disperse, it is not known whether Old Regular Baptists would out-migrate to areas in sufficient numbers to re-establish their churches and Associations.

Resilience strategy for adaptive management would suggest addressing the economic and environmental problems of coal-mining dependence first and foremost. To help alleviate poverty and modernize the region, the federal government has undertaken economic projects ever since the War on Poverty in the 1960s. These efforts have improved roads, consolidated schools, and built hospitals; but the economic problems remain. In 2014 the federal government announced a fresh initiative, and couched it in the rhetoric of sustainability and resilience. In January of that year, President Obama announced that southeastern Kentucky had been targeted as one of the first "promise zones" for economic development. Details remain sketchy as I am writing this, but among the goals are job creation, growing small businesses, job training and retraining, all to implement a "sustainable economic effort across eight counties. . . focused on diversifying southeastern Kentucky's economy to make it more resilient" (White House Fact Sheet, 2014). The outcome of this initiative will not be known for some years.

Tourism, including eco-tourism, may be one industry targeted for expansion; the region has many lovely natural sites, but it also suffers from a reputation for poverty and violence that is unattractive to tourists. Heritage tourism, based on the region's rich heritage of crafts and music (ballads, old-time and bluegrass string band music, the roots of country music, and so forth) would also be a possibility, but despite some efforts in that direction, it has not proved an economic panacea. And even if it did, Old Regular Baptists would not wish to participate as the regular objects of heritage tourism. As the moderator (elected head) of the Indian Bottom Association told me many years ago, "We're not anxious to be studied." Over the years, he said, a number of visitors had "flown in, taken a shallow look, and flown out," and their impressions had been predictably shallow as well (Cornett, 1990). I believe that performing their music and worship (for to them, music is worship) regularly at heritage sites within the region could transform their worship experience and degrade it into something other than worship: an object for a tourist gaze that would be unacceptable to them. And, of course, the idea of turning it into an economic engine for profit is contrary to their religious beliefs.

Ironically, the feedback mechanisms within the Old Regular Baptist communities are very sensitive to musical and cultural threats; but the threat of changing economic conditions is not within the domain of church governance. Outsiders who advocate today for economic alternatives tend to be dismissed as untrustworthy environmentalists who would eliminate coal mining entirely, thereby bringing the economy to an abrupt and disastrous halt.

Applied ethnomusicologists seeking to apply adaptive management strategies to help Old Regular Baptists sustain their music—which, by the way, they are eager to maintain—would not serve them well, then, by attempting to make them the objects of heritage tourism and the creative economy, even though that is the predominant strategy for cultural sustainability in the US traditional arts today, and an important strategy elsewhere in the world, particularly in Europe (Throsby, 2010). It might also occur to an applied ethnomusicologist to consider whether Old Regular Baptist music might be sustained in a revival mode, similar to the way a related traditional American music, Sacred Harp (or shape-note) singing, is currently being enjoyed and propagated. Old Regular Baptist music has, in fact, undergone a kind of revitalization and renewal within the Old Regular Baptist communities, partly as a result of attention from scholars and cultural specialists. But their music is not in a revival stage, in the sense that people from outside their communities are joining in and spreading and developing the music elsewhere. There are no folk music revivalists gathering to sing Old Regular Baptist songs, nor are there likely to be. A full comparison with the Sacred Harp revival is beyond my scope, but it may be useful to draw certain contrasts here.

Sacred Harp, or shape-note, singing developed as part of a musical reform movement involving written notation in shaped notes (diamonds, triangles, squares, and circles) that made it easier for people to learn to read and sing from staff notation. In fact, this music literacy movement was meant to overcome the perceived problems in the "old way of singing," which is to say the heterophonic, lined-out hymnody of the Puritans and their descendants (such as Old Regular Baptists) who, according to the reformers, were making an awful noise, not a joyful one. Although this movement to sing from notation gradually succeeded in New England beginning in the late eighteenth century, where it was put to use for part singing in standard Western choral harmonies, a grass-roots shape-note movement arose in the South during the mid-nineteenth century, and soon local amateur musicians were harmonizing traditional melodies (including many in the Old Regular Baptist repertory) for part singing in shape-notes, but in unconventional harmonies (employing parallel fifths, for example) and voicings. This way of singing and the songbooks associated with it, such as *The Sacred Harp*, became very popular among Baptist and Methodist denominations in the South, and eventually among gospel hymnodists, whose books later in the nineteenth century also were printed in shape-notation. Although this music was sung in churches, it also became popular among community singing groups, and in particular Sacred Harp singing groups arose, chiefly associated with Baptists but not as a formal part of worship or church activities.

Eventually Sacred Harp singing became a community activity, with singing conventions of its own; partisans traveled considerable distances to participate in regional and state Sacred Harp singing conventions. Although these Sacred Harp sings gradually diminished in the first half of the twentieth century, during the waves of folk music revival that have occurred in the United States since the 1950s, Sacred Harp singing became a popular choral activity, to the point that there now are Sacred Harp singing gatherings in every state of the union, and most of them are not associated in any formal way with religious practice, although the repertory is based in the Sacred Harp song book and the revivalists mingle with traditional singing groups that remain in the South (Bealle, 1997; Miller, 2008).

Could Old Regular Baptist music undergo such an exogamous revival? To me, it seems highly unlikely. Although the music is attractive to a small number of outsiders, including some Sacred Harp singers, it does not exist in community sings outside church worship, in any formal sense. Old Regular Baptist families sing when they get together, but it is quite informal and different from a community singing event. Such "sings," in other words, and singing conventions that became normal for Sacred Harp singers and provided a ready-made structure for revivalists, are absent in Old Regular Baptist practice. Of course, that could change. But whereas beginners rely on Sacred Harp songbooks for lyrics and music notation, they would be unable to use their music-reading skills to sing Old Regular Baptist music, because Old Regular Baptist song books lack music notation. Recordings could provide a model, but very few recordings are available. The melodies, particularly the lining tunes, would have to be learned by imitation and memorized. Unlike Sacred Harp music, which has a leader who swings arms to mark a steady meter, Old Regular Baptist songs do not have a conductor or exhibit a pulse beat. Nor is there a single melody; and although a skeletal tune does exist, a proper realization involves individual elaboration. Indeed, one learns to "curve" the melody appropriately only through long experience in singing it within an Old Regular Baptist community. An anecdote from my personal experience will illustrate. After spending much time with them and my recordings of their music, I had learned to sing along with them; I could follow the melodies and also sing some on my own, however tentatively. I invited two friends to come with me to an Old Regular Baptist worship service. Although they both were skilled musically, they told me they could not find the melodies in the sea of sound that the group made. Of course, after several visits they would have been able to distinguish them; but their experience reveals how inaccessible the music is for a beginner.

The other music culture that here provides an example for resilience and adaptive management is the old-time string band music revival. The repertoire consists primarily of tunes played in the rural American South for dancing during the period from the Civil War to the period between the World Wars. Folklorists began recording this music in the 1930s, but the collecting accelerated in the urban folk revival movement that began in the 1950s. Now not only folklorists, but also musicians who wanted to learn this music, were recording it from the older musicians, most born before 1900, who remembered the repertoire. Some of this same repertoire had also been recorded on commercial 78 rpm discs in the 1920s and 1930s aimed at a Southern audience. In its heyday, this old-time string band music was performed, and the repertoire shared, by both white Southerners and African Americans. It developed primarily as an oral tradition over the course of 150 years, as more and more tunes were brought into the repertoire, others underwent modification, and all circulated locally and regionally. Starting around World War I, the music fell into decline with the older square and round dances it had accompanied, replaced by ballroom dancing and the music that was appropriate for that style. During the same post-1950 folk music revival that strengthened Sacred Harp singing, old-time string band music also staged a comeback, as the older tradition-bearing musicians performed at festivals and college campuses and other venues and attracted a cadre of young musicians who had not heard this music before but who soon made it their own. Some of them moved south to live and work in the areas where remnants of the musical tradition remained, and beginning in the late 1950s they gathered in various old-time string band "festivals" at places such as Galax, Virginia, Union Grove and Mt. Airy, North Carolina, and more recently, Clifftop, West Virginia. Although the musicians call these gatherings "festivals," they are unlike the folk festivals, where music is performed from a stage and for an audience. Instead, at an old-time string band festival, thousands of musicians gather chiefly to mingle and participate in hundreds of small, spontaneous jam sessions throughout the festival grounds. Sometimes, as at Galax, bluegrass jams are also part of the festival. It is a participatory, not a presentational music (see music example 5.1). Summer instructional camps also arose beginning in the 1980s, and as the revival has grown, their number has increased. At the beginning, they employed some of the older, tradition-bearing musicians as teachers, who showed how they played by demonstrating the music, sometimes slowly. As they passed away, some of the most skilled revivalist musicians took their places, leading jams and workshops and teaching classes.

Although the string bands of the nineteenth and twentieth centuries had included various non-stringed instruments, such as harmonicas, organs, and whatever else was popular or handy, the revival string band musicians settled on fiddle, banjo, and guitar as the primary instruments, to which sometimes a string bass and/or a mandolin was added. Indeed, by the time the music began to be recorded in the 1920s, fiddles, banjos, and guitars were the most popular; however, the guitar was relatively new to the music, having entered late in the nineteenth century, long after fiddle and banjo had delineated it. In addition to this concentration of instruments, other changes resulted from the revival. Banjo players have narrowed the variety of picking styles that were prevalent before the revival to one dominant style, the so-called clawhammer (a down-picking) style, while the rhythms of the tunes have taken on a more modern syncopation and drive, sometimes referred to as "festival style." Tunes played at festivals, aided by a combination of conviviality and stimulants, can put musicians into a quasi-trance during performance, as the tune may repeat 20 or 30 times and continue for as long as a half an hour, the groove shared by all players. And whereas the music's primary function until the end of World War II was for accompanying the dance, today the occasion for the music is the jams. The word "jam," borrowed from jazz, connotes the informal and fluid membership in any old-time string band session. The music is not improvisational in the way that jazz is; the melody is prominent at all times, with slight though meaningful variations introduced primarily by fiddlers. Jams have an informal, laissez-faire atmosphere, though an implicit etiquette prevails. Although the fiddle is the lead instrument, no single leader decides which tunes will be played; instead, different musicians, usually fiddlers, start tunes and when others recognize them, they join in—or if they don't recognize them, they learn them as they play them. The jam as I have described it, particularly as it occurs at festivals and in people's homes (often with pot-luck meals) or, increasingly, in public venues where it may be overheard by non-musicians, is an informal gathering of whichever musicians are invited (or not) and show up. It is a musician's music, done for the pleasure of the musical experience and the sociability of the occasion.

The old-time string band revival exhibits resilience in certain areas but not others. New members are joining the music culture every year, coming from all US regions and walks of life. The number involved with old-time music fluctuates and is probably uncountable, but anecdotal evidence would place it around 15,000, not much larger than the total of Old Regular Baptists. The group is welcoming and there are few if any requirements, other than an interest in playing this music. By contrast, to join the Old Regular Baptist music culture one must live within a small region and profess and practice particular religious beliefs. In terms of accessibility, then, the old-time string band revival is much more resilient. Its structure is very different also. The music culture centers on a "scene," or subculture, not a membership organization (Pfadenhauer, 2005). Unlike Old Regular Baptists, the old-time string band music revival has little formal organization and no hierarchical structure. It is an affinity scene, a loose collection of small, informal groups anywhere in size from two to about a dozen persons who gather to socialize and play music together. At the festivals, of course, people from many of the smaller groups travel to take part and roam from one group to another, looking for old friends and acquaintances, and for peak musical experiences in jams. The informal aspects of the music, and the high value placed on spontaneity and serendipity, make hierarchical social organization even more difficult. Such egalitarianism extends even to the food supplied at these gatherings, which inevitably results in a pot-luck in which everyone brings some food and all share. To be sure, organizations produce the festivals and the instructional camps, but insofar as the festivals are chiefly spaces set aside for informal gatherings and a great many spontaneous jam sessions throughout the festival grounds, the production does not extend much beyond planning activities, keeping order, and running contests, which many feel are peripheral and do not participate in. For the vast majority, the participatory jam sessions and the socializing are the reasons for festival attendance. The instructional camps exhibit a good deal more organization, with reservations, accommodations, wages for instructors and staff, food catering, lessons, and workshops, along with evening jams. Participants pay money to attend and expect to improve their musical skills.

Although old-time string band revivalists are conscious of changes in the music culture, and some are concerned that these are not for the better, the scene has no hierarchy, no leaders to counter threats to its sustainability, no way in which individuals can manage more than a small part of the scene. In this voluntary association, leading by example is the principal means of influence. Any musician who fears that the music scene may be changing in ways not to his or her liking seeks out other musicians who share his or her preferences, and usually finds them, rather than attempting to influence the course of the music's development. The musicians are dispersed across the United States and may be found almost anywhere—old-time string band jams are popular in Ireland, for example. For that reason, the jams exhibit an almost perfect modularity, except that aside from sharing repertoire, instruments, playing techniques, and to some degree musical style and social rules, there is no whole system, only a scene with various parts. The parts are not like cells integrated into an organism, as Old Regular Baptist churches are integrated into Associations. Those parts—the social structures that come together for the jams, in home neighborhoods and at distant festivals—are by nature able to detach themselves, dissolve, re-form or not, and also to cluster, a feature of resilient systems. Such a system, without a hierarchically organized whole, exhibits a certain kind of resilience. It almost automatically self-reorganizes in response to change and disturbance. However, this flexibility also means that it can more easily change state, as it did when it entered the revival stage, significantly in those aspects mentioned earlier. The musicians themselves do not think of this as a regime change, because the repertoire, instruments, and playing styles exhibit continuity. The participants believe they are continuing a tradition, and many think that by playing the old tunes and keeping them alive they are preserving it. But at the same time, in the past 50 years they have modified the social aspects of the scene considerably. Jam sessions as well as festivals are the most important of these, but they are inventions of the revival, and without them the scene would not exist. Prior to the revival, the music was played principally for dances and in contests. Another, more recent innovation is the instructional camps.

An applied ethnomusicologist seeking to help the music culture sustain itself through adaptive management would not encounter the main problem facing Old Regular Baptists, namely, dependence on a single, regional industry that is itself under threat and in turn threatens the environment sustaining the population in the region as a whole. But in attempting to aid the scene, applied ethnomusicologists would encounter difficulties not present among Old Regular Baptists. For example, an applied ethnomusicologist might conceive of the revival as a regime change and imagine that the participants would prefer to return to the older social forms; but most would not. The applied worker would need to bear in mind that the revival has its own way of carrying on a musical tradition but with newer social formations. Furthermore, whereas adaptive management could operate among Old Regular Baptists through their organizational hierarchy, there is in fact no way to "manage" the old-time string band music revival because it lacks the institutional structures and leaders to carry out such management. The self-organizing aspects of the revival are so strong that an applied ethnomusicologist might wonder whether aid and advice is desirable, let alone whether it is administratively possible.

On the other hand, an applied ethnomusicologist might, in partnership with certain musicians, come to realize that threats to the ethos of spontaneity and serendipity do exist, particularly in the instructional camps. In the 1950s and 1960s, the early decades of the old-time string band revival, learning the music took place chiefly by informal imitation, whether of other musicians or of recordings, as it had done before the revival stage. Although a more experienced musician might demonstrate a technique to a learner, teaching in the form of lessons did not exist. This began to change in the 1970s, first through class lessons held at musical instrument shops, and not long after that in classes held at the instructional camps. These teachers usually instructed by ear, going over a tune phrase by phrase, demonstrating techniques, without any musical notation to guide the students. Nonetheless, because the students pay money for this instruction, an atmosphere of middle-class expectation increasingly surrounds these camp activities, which now can include evaluation and critique and resemble art music pedagogy in certain aspects that exert pressure toward formalization. Under these conditions, the remaining old-timers who grew up in the pre-revival music culture usually do not make the most effective teachers, even though their playing exhibits the characteristics thought to be most authentic to the tradition and, for advanced musicians who can learn by imitation, they are the most desired teachers. Private lessons are becoming increasingly available, almost always taught by revivalists. Music camps now offer instruction in several different musical traditions more formal than old-time string band music. Some of these, like Scottish fiddling, have depended on tune books and music notation for more than a century. In others, such as contradance music, notation has always existed alongside oral tradition, but for instruction notation has become standard. Some in the old-time music community resist notation as they would resist an infection, thinking it works against the spontaneity they prize. Given that the instructional camps exhibit more structure than the jams or festivals, and given that the musical instruction influences the scene's future, adaptive management to maintain the spontaneity and serendipity of the old-time string band revival scene might be appropriate.

Ironically, public folklorists and applied ethnomusicologists' efforts to manage and sustain old-time music, including string band music, have by and large confused and upset the revivalists. The culture workers did so in the 1970s by dividing the folk revival scene into tradition-bearers and revivalists, and the division persists. In making that distinction, they ascribe authenticity to the tradition-bearers and grant them funding support, while they deny both to revivalists. Revivalists seldom are hired to perform at the folk festivals or are funded in other ways. Given the cultural conservationists' views that equate authentic traditional music cultures with ethnic minorities and working-class communities, it seems unlikely that the revival movement will be targeted for funding. Nor does it need such interventions, because among other things it is not endangered. Nonetheless, some of the revivalist musicians would like the honor of being selected to perform at these festivals. When they bother to consider it, they resent being categorized as inauthentic. They argue that because the tradition-bearing source musicians have adopted them into their communities, they have already been authenticated by those whose authentication matters most. In contrast, Old Regular Baptist communities, which fit the cultural conservationists' criteria as tradition-bearers perfectly well, have gained much from partnerships with applied ethnomusicologists and public folklorists. They have become stewards of their music, and they understand that it is not only valuable to them for worship but also valuable to others who prize outstanding musical traditions as part of the cultural matrix of the nation. Yet the greatest threat to their musical and cultural future is economic and environmental, and here the role, if any, for applied ethnomusicologists and other culture workers is not yet well defined.

CONCLUSION

Resilience refers to a system's capacity to recover its integrity, identity, and continuity when subjected to forces of disturbance. Insofar as music cultures are systems, they too exhibit resilience to a greater or lesser degree. Resilience and adaptive management have had a life within ecological thought and the environmental movement, psychology (not treated here), and economics. They offer promising sustainability and restoration strategies for applied ethnomusicologists, as for public folklorists. However, they must be understood with reference to the baggage they bring. "Yield" and "development" are not appealing concepts to many culture workers. And while "management" is an appropriate strategy for conservation biologists, it is not without its problems when human beings are subjected to it. Among those is the negative connotation that management has acquired when applied to ways in which entities such as nation-states or corporations attempt to control their citizens or workers. I have already alluded to the critique leveled at modernization and developmental applied anthropology as a new form of colonial management, from radical anthropologists working in indigenous studies. However, indigenous knowledge forms the basis for a bottom-up applied anthropology, just as in applied ethnomusicology (Sillitoe, 1998).

Foucault coined the term *biopower* to describe the way in which modern nation-states regulate their citizenry, particularly in reference to controls over excesses of the body (and body politic). Their disciplinary power is even more effective because the regulations become internalized as culture. Foucault is working in a tradition pioneered by Karl Marx, who wrote about the Protestant religion's emphasis on bodily discipline (drunkenness, for example, as a sin), effectively providing efficient, submissive factory workers for the capitalists. George Orwell's prophetic *1984* portrayed such a society as a police state. These, of course, are forms of management; and a quick response to this apparent problem is to say that the kind of cultural management I've been advocating (and practicing) for nearly five decades is not and never has been top-down, but rather grows out of a partnership between the culture worker and the community leaders and tradition-bearers. In an ideal case, the culture worker learns the music culture's sustainability goals and helps its people plan and then implement a sustainability strategy in which they self-manage, relying on the culture worker as a collaborator and consultant, perhaps more in the role of coach than manager. In American baseball we call them managers, but in football and basketball they are called coaches. Of course, both manage the games, employing short- and long-term strategies, and by putting the players in positions where they have the best chance to succeed. Both coach their players, teaching them better techniques. Interestingly, coaches appear in contemporary Euro-American cultures in "the game of life": people hire coaches for public speaking, for dress and appearance, for health, for social relationships, for business negotiations, and so forth. Many do not seem to mind being coached. Some want it, thinking it will advantage them. Why, then, the resistance to being managed, when one is willing to be coached? Perhaps the manager is thought to be impartial, whereas the coach is empathetic.

Marx, Orwell, and Foucault shared that resistance to management. It impinged on autonomy and freedom; it abrogated natural rights. Being managed meant being told what to do, what to say, even what to think, when one didn't want to be told—and then being coerced to do it. The difference, with coaching, is the willing partnership: presumably we want to be coached, even if we don't want to be managed, because we conceive of the goal as our own. Adaptive managing may be regarded as coaching, then, when applied ethnomusicologists partner for sustainability.

Resilience and adaptive management abandon the questionable assumption that music exhibits "natural cultural growth" that proceeds to desired ends when freed from the fashionable and faddish trends that distort its true direction. Instead, resilience recognizes that perturbation, disturbance, and flux are constant characteristics of any complex system. Resilience theory and adaptive management practice therefore attempt to identify what makes a music culture vulnerable to regime shift, and what makes one resilient, and to ameliorate the former and strengthen the latter. Resilience theory and adaptive management offer promising directions for applied ethnomusicologists working toward sustainability in music cultures.

REFERENCES

Aikawa, Noriko. (2001). "The 1989 Recommendation on the Safeguarding of Traditional Culture and Folklore: Actions Undertaken by UNESCO for Its Implementation." In *Safeguarding Traditional Cultures: Global Assessment*, edited by Paul Seitel, pp. 13–19. Washington, DC: Smithsonian Office of Folklife and Cultural Heritage.

Allen, Aaron S. (2012). "'Fatto Di Fiemme': Stradivari's Violins and the Musical Trees of the Paneveggio." In *Invaluable Trees: Cultures of Nature, 1660–1830*, edited by Laura Auricchio, Elizabeth Heckendorn Cook, and Giulia Pacini, pp. 301–315. Oxford: Voltaire Foundation.

Barclay, Robert. (2004). *The Preservation and Use of Historic Musical Instruments*. London: Earthscan.

Barton, Gregory. (2002). *Empire Forestry and the Origins of Environmentalism*. Cambridge: Cambridge University Press.

Bealle, John. (1997). *Public Worship, Private Faith: Sacred Harp and American Folksong*. Athens: University of Georgia Press.

Berliner, Paul. (1978). *The Soul of Mbira*. Berkeley: University of California Press.

Cooper, James Fenimore. (1823). *The Pioneers*. New York: Charles Wiley.

Cornett, Elwood. (1990). Elwood Cornett, interviewed by Jeff Todd Titon, Blackey, KY. Recording and transcript in possession of the author.

Daly, Herman E. (1991 [1977]). *Steady-State Economics*. Washington, DC: Island Press.

Daly, Herman E. (1993). "Sustainable Growth: An Impossibility Theorem." In *Valuing the Earth*, edited by Herman E. Daly and Kenneth N. Townsend, pp. 267–274. Cambridge, MA: MIT Press.

DeWitt, Mark F. (2009). "Louisiana Creole Bals de maison in California and the Accumulation of Social Capital." *the world of music* 51(1): 17–34.

Dorgan, Howard. (1989). *The Old Regular Baptists of Central Appalachia: Brothers and Sisters in Hope*. Knoxville: University of Tennessee Press.

Evelyn, John. (1664). *Silva: A Discourse of Forest Trees and the Propagation of Timber in His Majesty's Dominions*. London: John Martyn for the Royal Society.

Faux, Tom. (2009). "Don Roy, Fiddle Music and Social Sustenance in Northern New England." *the world of music* 51(1): 36–54.

Feld, Steven. (1990). *Sound and Sentiment*. 2nd ed. Philadelphia: University of Pennsylvania Press.

Gunderson, Lance H., Craig R. Allen, and C. S. Holling. (2009). *Foundations of Ecological Resilience*. Washington, DC: Island Press.

Hawken, Paul. (1994). *The Ecology of Commerce: A Declaration of Sustainability*. New York: HarperBusiness.

Hood, Mantle. (1971). *The Ethnomusicologist*. New York: McGraw-Hill.

Hufford, Mary, ed. (1994). *Conserving Culture: A New Discourse on Heritage*. Urbana: University of Illinois Press.

IUCN. (1980). *World Conservation Strategy: Living Resource Conservation for Sustainable Development*. International Union for the Conservation of Nature and Natural Resources, Gland, Schweiz. A pdf of this book is available on the Internet. https://portals.iucn.org/library/efiles/documents/WCS-004.pdf.

Keogh, Brent. (2013). "On the Limitations of Music Ecology." *Journal of Music Research Online* 4: 1–10.

Kisliuk, Michelle. (1998). *Seize the Dance*. New York: Oxford University Press.

Lake, Philip S. (2013). "Resistance, Resilience and Restoration." *Ecological Management and Restoration* 14(1): 20–24.

Lomax, Alan. (1972). "Appeal for Cultural Equity." *the world of music* 14(2): 3–17.

Loomis, Oromond, coordinator. (1982). *Cultural Conservation*. Washington, DC: Library of Congress, American Folklife Center.

Miller, Char. (2001). *Gifford Pinchot and the Making of a Modern Environmentalism*. Washington, DC: Island Press.

Miller, Kiri. (2008). *Traveling Home: Sacred Harp Singing and American Pluralism*. Urbana: University of Illinois Press.

Moore, James F. (1993). "Predators and Prey." *Harvard Business Review*, May–June, 75–86.

Myers, Norman. (1992 [1984]). *Gaia: An Atlas of Planet Management*. New York: Anchor.

Netting, Robert McC. (1977). *Cultural Ecology*. Menlo Park, CA: Cummings.

Newell, Wayne. (2003). "Returning Sounds to Communities." Panel discussion among Wayne Newell, Blanche Sockabasin, and Jeff Todd Titon. Invested in Community: Ethnomusicology and Advocacy Conference, Brown University, March 8–9. A video of this presentation is accessible at http://library.brown.edu/cds/invested_in_community/030803_session3.html.

Norton, Barley. (2005). *Sustainability: A Philosophy of Adaptive Ecosystem Management.* Chicago: University of Chicago Press.

Rappaport, Roy. (1979). *Ecology, Meaning and Religion.* Berkeley, CA: North Atlantic.

Ritchie, Jean. (1955). *Singing Family of the Cumberlands.* New York: Oak.

Pfadenhauer, Michaela. (2005). "Ethnography of Scenes." *Forum: Qualitative Social Research* 6(3): n.p. http://www.qualitative-research.net/index.php/fqs/article/view/23/49.

Pickett, Steward T. A., and P. S. White. (1985). *The Ecology of Natural Disturbance and Patch Dynamics.* Orlando, FL: Academic Press.

Porterfield, Nolan. (2001). *Last Cavalier: The Life and Times of John Lomax.* Urbana: University of Illinois Press.

Seeger, Anthony. (1991). "Singing Other People's Songs." *Cultural Survival Quarterly* 15(3): 36–39.

Sillitoe, Paul. (1998). "The Development of Indigenous Knowledge: a New Applied Anthropology." *Current Anthropology* 39(2): 223–252.

Soulé, Michael. (1985). "What Is Conservation Biology?" *Bioscience* 35(11): 727–734.

Spitzer, Nick. (2007 [1992]). "Cultural Conversation." In *Public Folklore*, edited by Robert Baron and Nick Spitzer, pp. 78–103. Jackson: University Press of Mississippi.

Throsby, David. (2010). *The Economics of Cultural Policy.* Cambridge: Cambridge University Press.

Titon, Jeff Todd, Elwood Cornett, and John Wallhausser. (1997). *Songs of the Old Regular Baptists: Lined-Out Hymnody from Southeastern Kentucky.* Washington, DC: Smithsonian Folkways CD SFW 40106.

Titon, Jeff Todd, gen. ed. (1984). *Worlds of Music.* New York: Schirmer Books.

Titon, Jeff Todd. (1999). "'The Real Thing': Tourism, Authenticity and Pilgrimage among Old Regular Baptists at the 1997 Smithsonian Folklife Festival." *the world of music* 41(3): 115–139.

Titon, Jeff Todd. (2008–). Sustainable Music (blog). http://www.sustainablemusic.blogspot.com.

Titon, Jeff Todd. (2009a). Music and Sustainability (special issue). *the world of music,* 51(1).

Titon, Jeff Todd. (2009b). "Economy, Ecology and Music: Introduction." *the world of music* 51(1): 5–16.

Titon, Jeff Todd. (2009c). "Music and Sustainability: An Ecological Viewpoint." *the world of music* 51(1): 119–138.

Titon, Jeff Todd. (2013). "The Nature of Ecomusicology." *Musica E Cultura* 8: 8–18.

Topp Fargion, Janet. (2009). "'For My Own Research Purposes: Examining Ethnomusicological Field Methods for a Sustainable Music." *the world of music* 51(1): 75–93.

Van Willigen, John. (2002). *Applied Anthropology: An Introduction* (3rd ed.). Westport, CT: Greenwood.

Walker, Brian, and David Salt. (2006). *Resilience Thinking: Sustaining Ecosystems and People in a Changing World.* Washington, DC: Island Press.

Weintraub, Andrew, and Bell Yung. (2009). *Music and Cultural Rights.* Urbana: University of Illinois Press.

White House Fact Sheet. (2014). *President Obama's Promise Zones Initiatives.* http://www.whitehouse.gov/the-press-office/2014/01/08/fact-sheet-president-obama-s-promise-zones-initiative.

World Commission on Environment and Development. (1987). *Our Common Future.* Oxford: Oxford University Press. Also available at http://www.un-documents.net/ocf-12.htm#I.

Worster, Donald. (1993). *The Wealth of Nature.* New York: Oxford University Press.

Worster, Donald. (1994). *Nature's Economy* (2nd ed.). Cambridge: Cambridge University Press.

Zolli, Andrew, and Anne Marie Healy. (2012). *Resilience.* New York: Free Press.

PART III

CONFLICTS

CHAPTER 6

....

THE ROLE OF APPLIED
ETHNOMUSICOLOGY IN
POST-CONFLICT AND
POST-CATASTROPHE
COMMUNITIES

....

ERICA HASKELL

APPLIED ethnomusicologists and cultural advocates have contributed to facilitating conflict resolution and cultural development in postwar and post-catastrophe environments. In the wake of both conflicts and natural disasters, cultural aid workers bear needed resources and are often welcomed with open arms to host countries. This chapter outlines the multiple roles that applied ethnomusicologists, and cultural projects in general, can have in post-conflict and post-catastrophe situations. In both kinds of catastrophes, practitioners have applied their skills to ease social upheaval, create economic opportunities for musicians, and strengthen existing cultural venues and institutions, as well as establish new ones. In other cases, musical and cultural projects are developed and run by actors with relatively little expertise in cultural issues. This chapter also addresses some fundamental challenges that applied ethnomusicologists face in navigating the diverse field of international development in which social, economic, and political concerns often sideline equally important cultural ones. I focus on some of the similarities and differences between post-conflict and post-disaster cultural communities through the lens of applied ethnomusicology. While the main case studies are drawn from the author's long-term fieldwork in Bosnia-Herzegovina on the postwar cultural environment there, more general findings are informed by visits to other post-catastrophe environments.

I have chosen to link two kinds of catastrophes, war and natural disaster, not to blur their differences but rather because many international aid agencies react to their results in similar ways. Nongovernmental organizations (NGOs), which are often sources for cultural-re-development funds, use "humanitarian aid" as a blanket term for any kind of human assistance. In this way, the "need" that humanitarian organizations seek to ameliorate can vary from basic sustenance and housing to civil society building and educational reforms. Based upon my own research in post-conflict Bosnia-Herzegovina, I share several findings about the ways in which musicians can be impacted by disasters as venues and employment are in shorter supply, distribution channels are shut down, performance contexts shift, and large institutions are threatened. In the field of ethnomusicology, my research is grounded in the research of scholars of Southeast European music (Helbig, 2005, 2008; Laušević, 1996, 1998, 2000; Maners, 2000; Pettan, 1998a, 1998b, 1999, 2001, 2008; Ramet, 1994, 1996; Sugarman, 1999a, 1999b; Urbain, 2008), ethnomusicologists who write about the broader transition from socialism to democracy in Eastern Europe (Buchanan, 1995; Rice, 1994; Silverman, 1996, 1989; Slobin, 1996), and writings about the application of ethnomusicological knowledge for the public good.

Humanitarian situations offer special opportunities and challenges to ethnomusicologists focused on aiding and advocating for musical communities at risk. In settings where outsiders' involvement is widespread, a common characteristic of post-catastrophe situations, applied ethnomusicologists may be allowed added access to tangible and intangible resources,[1] although they may also face daunting logistical problems.

I begin here with a short case study about one postwar project in a village in Bosnia-Herzegovina, followed by a discussion of some general findings on cultural aid in post-catastrophe settings. I then discuss the impact that catastrophes can have on music venues. Through the lens of a postwar project in Central Asia, I address some of the ways in which the disruption of travel and forced migration affect musicians and their communities. The Pavarotti Center in Mostar serves as an example of how funds raised through concert advocacy have been employed by one NGO. In the final section of this chapter, I share a case study of a small record label's partnership with a foreign NGO, meant to address shifts in the musical marketplace, that resulted from the Bosnian conflict.

THE MOZAIK COMMUNITY DEVELOPMENT FUND AND GUČA GORA

In 2002, seven years after the end of the conflict in Bosnia-Herzegovina the Non-Governmental Organization Development Foundation, now renamed Mozaik Community Development Foundation, began research to select a region in the country for a "living heritage network" funded by the King Baudouin Foundation based in Belgium, as well as the Open Society Fund, Soros. At the time, some of the King Baudouin Foundation's projects supported "living heritage" in Macedonia, Bosnia-Herzegovina, Romania, and Bulgaria, while others aimed to elevate social and economic ills that resulted from the war. By funding local heritage, the organization hoped to make a "lasting contribution towards greater justice, democracy and respect for diversity" (see http://www.kbs-frb.be/content.aspx?id=290655&langtype=1033)[2] as well as stimulate "local communities in the creative use of their cultural resources," which they believed could act as an engine for local development (www.kbs-frb.be). Through their contributions, Bosnian Living Heritage Network sought to facilitate the sharing of values and ideas about community development through cultural resources (www.mozaik.ba/english/html/livingheritage.html).[3] To recognize and emphasize the important role of living heritage in alleviating poverty, social tensions, and regional instability, the foundation staff chose specific projects not primarily for their cultural authenticity or value, but rather for their ability to build civil society.[4] The foundation argued that emphasizing living heritage was a "unique approach to community development because it places people first, and intercultural relations at the heart of sustainable development" (ibid.). After a year-long research period, in which an advisory board made up of local experts traveled throughout the country, they chose central Bosnia-Herzegovina as a regional focus because of its rich mix of ethnic groups, brutal experience during the war, and the perception that there was much progress to be made in the area of cultural identity, which had been used by political, military, and religious leaders to fuel the conflict.

Unlike many international NGO projects introduced by international organizations after the war throughout Bosnia-Herzegovina, which primarily focused their funding activities on the largest cities, Mozaik chose the *selo*, or village, as the stage on which the most progress toward community development could be made. Experts on the advisory board chose specific villages, and members of the communities were invited to apply for small living heritage grants. Guča Gora was one of the villages selected. This small, rural, primarily Catholic village, in the central region of Bosnia-Herzegovina, was founded by Franciscan monks more than 800 years ago, and the cathedral they built was the largest structure in Europe for the following 30 years. The Franciscans in Guča Gora, with their emphasis on education, also founded the first high school in Bosnia-Herzegovina. To locate an existing community group or create a new one to fund, Mozaik Foundation staff facilitated a gathering of 10 community leaders from Guča Gora, whom they asked to brainstorm about the needs of the village. In this session, Gučogorci were educated about the work of the foundation and were taught how to present themselves within the guidelines of the grant requirements. Members decided that a cultural center, in which the folkloric dance and music group "Sloga" could rehearse and other local groups could meet, was the best compromise between the village's needs and Mozaik's granting requirements. By this time the leaders in the village were experienced at fitting their local community's needs into the narrow and often confusing categories established by funders.

Officially recognized in 1922, in the 1930s Guča Gora's Sloga was defined as a Seljačka sloga (village harmony), similar to many other rural groups in the region. In the early 1950s, with the formation of Socialist Yugoslavia, the politically driven transformation of the existing peasantry and its folklore groups to official status brought new folkloric group categories. The organizational framework of folklore groups meant that the Guča Gora group gained official *izvorna* (or "spring," meaning authentic) group status and became simply "Sloga." By calling themselves "Sloga," they were voicing a conscious but silent resistance to the new Yugoslavian organizational structure (Ceribašić, personal communication, 2005). Its categorization as an *izvorna* folkloric group meant that, unlike the concept of stylized folklore performed by *kulturno-umjetnička društva* (cultural-artistic associations, KUDs), the group performed only local Guča Gora songs and dances in its repertoire, without major changes to the original music or lyrics.[5] Because of the homogeneous ethno-religious character of the village, most of the songs the group sang were drawn from traditions they characterized as Croatian Catholic, in direct comparison to neighboring Muslim villages. Sloga primarily performs *svatovske pjesme* (wedding songs) and other songs connected to customs, rituals, and everyday life. Their singing techniques involve alternating solos with *potresanje* (shaking) as well as singing with exclamation at the end of the phrase "oj," called *ojkanje*. In the former Yugoslavian KUD system, *izvorna* KUDs were excluded from the KUD system, a system in which KUDs had the opportunity to perform outside the domestic realm. Stylized KUDs performed folk music and dance suites that incorporated examples and sometimes costumes from each of the former Yugoslav republics. The importance of such KUDs as a tool and vessel for ideological messages, such as "brotherhood and unity," has been well documented by ethnomusicologists and anthropologists (Buchanan, 1995; Kurkela, 1995; Maners, 2000).

Throughout the group's existence, Franciscan monks, and more recently Yugoslav ethnomusicologists,[6] have gathered and transcribed some 70 distinct folk songs from Guča Gora. Of particular local interest are those songs that Gučogorci believe are inspired by the sound of their church bells. Although the songs themselves are not sacred, the tones they reference are of central importance to the Catholic faith in the villagers' lives, their everyday soundscape, and thus their sense of identity. Other KUDs that performed and competed in countrywide and international folk festivals often selected songs from Guča Gora to fulfill the Croatian element of their folkloric suites. The village was, and is still, surrounded by several small Muslim villages.

During the most recent war in Bosnia-Herzegovina, as with many villages in the region, a majority of its inhabitants were forced to flee to safer locations both in and outside the country. Guča Gora was targeted by a force of mujahideen fighters who left the village flattened and burned. As described by one villager, "a group of approximately thirty Arab guerrillas rampaged through the church with their weapons held in the air, shouting *Allah Akhbar!* They knocked over pews and other sacred symbols of the ancient church, vandalized the historic and irreplaceable mural above the main altar, and finally scraped off the faces of Jesus and the Virgin Mary on another painting near the altar" (Kohlmann, 2004). This account mirrors the ethno-religious nature of the conflict in which Bosnian Croats (Roman Catholics), Bosniaks (Sunni Muslims), and Bosnian Serbs (Serbian Orthodox) participated in violence against each other during different periods of the war.[7] In 2002 a third of the surviving villagers made the difficult decision to return to Guča Gora to rebuild their lives. In the intervening years, most Gučogorci had settled in other countries, and some had even begun their own folklore groups abroad. When they were asked by the Mozaik Foundation to list the village's needs, understandably those who had returned to Guča Gora prioritized rebuilding the village, on a material level, from the damage of the war, above all other goals.

We can categorize humanitarian efforts in postwar environments into phases, as early assistance was aimed at solving basic needs for water, food, and shelter. Following the Dayton Accord,[8] a number of international organizations flowed into the country with a host of new and less tangible diplomatic, social, economic, political, and cultural goals. These efforts have been categorized by international actors within the larger context of "nation building" and have often been largely unregulated, mostly because the domestic government was and continues to be highly divided. International organizations and politicians working in Bosnia-Herzegovina maintain a level of governing and financial power, augmented only by the promise of future EU membership. The plethora of NGOs now in Bosnia-Herzegovina, seen together, constitute a new funding structure, complete with its own language, categories, and procedures. When inhabitants of Guča Gora returned to their village in 2002, organizations disbursed applications for grants targeted at rebuilding. In the first year of their return to Guča Gora, the organization United Methodists Committee on Relief was the only one to finally offer funds for rebuilding the village.

The Mozaik Foundation's emphasis on civil society building was not originally a primary concern for this postwar village, but community leaders had learned in the years after the war that if they were strategic, their needs could sometimes be molded to fit NGOs' mission statements. After meeting with the Gučogorci, Mozaik Foundation responded to the village's letter of intention with suggestions and extensive editing. At the time, this process was one of the most cooperative and intensive cultural granting procedures being used in the region. In the final ranking of applications, Sloga was lauded primarily for their intention to involve a large number of Gučogorci in volunteer activities, their good financial intentions, and their plans for the long-term sustainability of the folkloric group. To fulfill the self-sustainability aspect of the application, the group noted their future intention to procure costume materials for 22 members, to make the costumes themselves, and to record an album for local distribution.

When I questioned Mozaik about their choice of Sloga, the staff members were careful to make clear their disinterest in the musical merits or authenticity of the group and to highlight the group's importance for creating harmony in the community. From my review of Sloga's letter of intention, it is clear that members presented those qualities as valuable not to themselves but to their funder. Such tailoring of intentions is, of course, common in grant applications. However, the application and training process asked community leaders to define the group and its value within the context of civil society and left other aspects of musical performance up to the musicians and dancers. Because the merits of the application did not hinge on authenticity or specific performances, members of Sloga embraced their history and heritage as their own, rather than something bestowed upon them by an outside force. In conversation with me, they also openly stated that they saw Sloga as a symbol of survival against the attacks their village had experienced during the war. It is significant that throughout this process Mozaik maintained its financial power to include and exclude groups based upon the ways in which they presented themselves. Although I am not aware of any overtly political material included in Sloga's repertoire, when I asked how the organization would respond to the group performing songs that were nationalistic in nature or disparaging to neighboring Muslim villages, Mozaik employees informed me that the folklore group would be asked to change their program. Evidence of such censorship, or at least the power to censor, in the name of interethnic and inter-religious cooperation, metaphorically referred to as "harmony," is evident in other postwar projects (Haskell, 2011) and also in socialist-era KUD performances. In my discussions with Sloga, members demonstrated their understanding of the organization's power. Singers and dancers felt honored to receive international support, and saw their three-year relationship with the Mozaik Foundation as a stamp of approval for their preservation of heritage and non-political activities.

The revival of Sloga from the rubble in Guča Gora illustrates the strength of music and dance to draw a community together toward a common goal. In the Bosnian context, Sloga's story also reminds one of the possibly divisive nature of music that represents one ethno-religious group. This is especially true when seen within the larger region. Mozaik's efforts to convey democratic models and community-building processes may be of most use to Sloga on a local level, as they forge some kind of self-sustainable future, which may require them to navigate various NGO applications in the years to come, as the present government does not maintain the Yugoslav-era funding structure for KUDs. The merits of Mozaik's living heritage network await a more involved study, but it is undeniable that through their assistance this small central Bosnian village is now able to offer visitors much more than the now-popular war tourism. It is clear that the present postwar cultural funding environment in Bosnia-Herzegovina poses multiple challenges for historic folklore groups such as Sloga, as they reinvent an identity that is in keeping with and sometimes dependent upon their understanding of the concept of "civil society."

POST-CATASTROPHE AID ENVIRONMENTS

In my work in post-conflict Bosnia-Herzegovina, the impetus to help, advocate, and support artists within the context of this discipline was strong. The case of Sloga in Guča Gora serves to show some of the complexity that funders and musicians face in post-catastrophe environments. Musicians in communities that have experienced seismic shifts, of the natural or manmade kind, are often painfully aware of their pressing needs and are willing to share ideas about solutions. As expressed in the above narrative, political, economic, and social shifts and transitions can impact musicians and the communities of which they are a part. Catastrophe-ravaged environments can present stark possibilities for improving musicians' lives and, sometimes, even generate new funding sources. Applied ethnomusicologists in post-conflict and post-catastrophe situations may find themselves in multiple roles, from grant-writer to concert-promoter, as they endeavor to help people. In both situations, practitioners have applied their skills to ease social upheaval, create economic opportunities for musicians, and strengthen existing cultural venues and institutions, as well as establish new ones. Actors have sought to fill post-conflict and post-catastrophe cultural and institutional voids by creating new performance venues, media outlets, music schools, museums, and sustainable businesses. In the case of the Guča Gora, community leaders had learned how to navigate funders' goals over the years, but in newer disaster areas applied ethnomusicologists may find that their understanding of the aid environments may be helpful to musical communities.

Applied ethnomusicologists, development workers, and humanitarians have played a variety of roles in their efforts to repair the havoc wreaked by catastrophes, be they human or nature made. While the physical outcome of disasters is often visible in crumbling building facades, impassable bridges, and uninhabitable homes, it can be more difficult to assess the impact such calamities have upon musical communities and the institutions that buoy them.[9] Indeed, warring parties have targeted cultural institutions, such as libraries, as they attempt to obliterate or even just confuse historical accounts. "Libricide" has been committed in several regions, including Tibet, Cambodia, Kuwait, China, and many parts of Europe. In their article titled "Culture and the New Iraq," Julie Edwards and Stephan Edwards write that "Obscuring history, obliterating cultural memory, erasing identities, and intimidating local populations are all wartime strategies achieved by targeting libraries . . . " (Edwards and Edwards, 2008). On the heels of catastrophe, aid agencies may assume that cultural production has been impacted, without assessing how or to what degree. I encountered this phenomenon in Bosnia-Herzegovina, when international humanitarian organizations and embassies assumed that, along with food, citizens needed "culture aid" in the form of visiting musicians or international forms of music (Haskell, 2011). Artistic and traditional expression was thought to have been damaged, just as mortar rounds had penetrated city buildings. Ethnomusicologists have valuable skills that can help in assessing how musical communities and cultural institutions have or have not been impacted by catastrophes through their detailed and localized research approaches. Scholars may also find that they can aid NGOs in locating local cultural experts and practitioners to advise on the applicability of their new projects. Even aid agencies' misconceived ideas about how music communities have been impacted by disasters may free up valuable resources that applied ethnomusicologists and their partners may find useful.

Here I argue for a multifaceted view of these environments—not only as communities in need of assistance, but as places in which creativity can flourish. As this is a handbook for applied ethnomusicologists, I also address some of the practical aspects of working in disaster-impacted realms. While post-disaster environments present risks to researchers, they also offer opportunities in the area of helping people and communities and gaining access to financial resources.

I approach this topic having spent almost a decade living in the postwar city of Sarajevo. Although "postwar" is only one of many characteristics of that city, much of my fieldwork there revolved around understanding the impact that violent conflict had had upon musicians and musical institutions.[10] In my travels to other postwar and post-catastrophe cities, such as Phnom Penh and New Orleans, I noticed cultural-re-development projects that were similar to those I had studied in Bosnia-Herzegovina. This chapter is an attempt to generalize about these fields to better understand the similar characteristics that post-conflict and post-disaster communities have as aid environments. Examples of post-conflict projects are drawn from Bosnia-Herzegovina, Cambodia, and Afghanistan; post-catastrophe phenomena are illustrated by cases in post-Katrina New Orleans and post-earthquake Haiti. Numerous projects exist in each of these locales, and thus I do not seek to present a complete assessment but rather to use specific projects to highlight the following shared issues: musical venues, disruption of travel and forces migration, concert advocacy, commemorations, shifts in markets, and closures or changes to cultural institutions.

MUSICAL VENUES

Just as a storm may decimate a swath of land or a community, conflicts often leave behind post-disaster areas, such as no-man's-lands between front lines, as well as strategic damage to essential facilities that can impact all levels of people's lives. Wars and natural disasters, of course, greatly vary in the destruction they leave behind. Musicians experience upheaval just as do others in their communities, finding it difficult to fill their basic human needs. As I have, many ethnomusicologists working in such areas help friends, collaborators, and informants they meet in the field. Indeed, some scholars feel that reciprocity is a central element of their scholarly work. While internal or civil conflicts often leave behind protracted divisions mirrored in divided communities, wars of occupation sometimes result in political and/or social power shifts that impact alliances that artists had prior to the conflict. Any number of lasting ailments can follow a disaster. Often some form of economic hardship follows, and it is common for trade routes to be impacted, currencies to be devalued, and other forms of economic distress to exist. In addition to the logistical and practical concerns that musicians and their institutions share with others in their communities, they face special issues.

Post-disaster environments present challenges and opportunities as musicians seek old and new contexts for performance. Catastrophes may destroy established performance venues, forcing musicians to not only find places to perform but also, at times, new audiences. During the siege of Sarajevo (1992–1996[11]), many large and small professional and amateur ensembles continued to perform and draw large audiences, despite the significant dangers they faced in doing so. One young concert organizer explained, "Hundreds of new bands have sprung up since the war started. It's a paradoxical situation. In these depressive times, everyone wants to expend energy doing something creative" (Kalendar, 1996). Musicians sought out performance venues that met their needs for a level of security and secrecy to avoid attack, but that could also accommodate their musical genre. In the face of great adversity, new venues, and thus contexts, for performance emerged. As the siege continued, musicians found that they had to be inventive in repairing equipment, as most normal trade with the outside world had ceased. In the postwar context in Sarajevo, some young musicians recast wrecked and rubble-filled buildings as outdoor festival venues.[12] These spaces signified not only the recent history of the region but also highlighted the enormous political and social journey young people felt they had begun toward a lasting peace. By performing in unorthodox and unsanctioned spaces, artists and musicians also contested the long-established cultural bureaucracy in the city. In this way musical sound took over parts of the city that had, before the war, had other uses.

Many aid responses to musicians' practical needs after natural disasters have, rightly so, sought to solve practical and logistical problems. After the catastrophic flooding that resulted from Hurricane Katrina, the New Orleans Area Habitat for Humanity gathered donations to build a "Musicians' Village" in the Upper Ninth Ward where, before the catastrophe, there had been a large concentration of musicians. The organizers of this high-profile project argued for the importance of reconstructing a stable neighborhood where a musical community had existed before the flooding. Musicians' proximity to each other was central to their livelihood and the creative relationships forged over generations. The project builders sought to transport pre-catastrophe musical communities back to their original soil.

The project originally sought to rebuild more than 70 single-family homes for local musicians in an effort to preserve the cultural presence that had existed before the flooding. Well-known jazz musicians, as well as several celebrities, drew attention to the project, which now also includes the Ellis Marsalis Center for Music.[13] As is true in the case of Hurricane Katrina, domestic and international media attention about a disaster can draw a large amount of money for re-development campaigns such as this. The New Orleans Habitat Musician's Village continues to organize benefit concerts in order to support the community and its cultural activities. The project did not delve into the historic reasons for some musicians being relegated to the particularly poor neighborhood most impacted by the flooding, nor did Habitat for Humanity attempt to confront such difficult questions. The long-term positive or negative effects of this particular project have yet to be analyzed.

DISRUPTION OF TRAVEL AND FORCED MIGRATION

For musicians who rely on travel to reach their audiences, catastrophes can cause a (sometimes massive) loss of income.[14] Many ensembles are unable to overcome the significant logistical hurdles and physical distance from their audiences and fellow musicians that they face after a catastrophe. Both conflicts and natural disasters may make it impossible for musicians to travel across political or natural borders. In these situations, they may also find that their musical products cannot be distributed as they once were. In these cases, efforts like that of the Aga Khan Foundation in Central Asia to fund musicians' travel, concerts, and distribution can be central to a musician's career and may even spur interest in the musical form among audiences for whom they perform.

In 2000 the Aga Khan Development Network began a multipronged project in Central Asia to promote the region's cultural resources to the rest of the world, document local traditions, and aid in the transmission of traditional skills from generation to generation through a funding arm called the Aga Khan Trust for Culture (http://www. akdn.org/AKTC).[15] In the case of Afghanistan, the Trust created a Music Initiative to attempt to reinvigorate musical traditions that had been quieted by harsh Taliban measures to ban music. During the Rabbani Period (1992–1996) and after the Taliban took Kabul, a music ban forbade all live and recorded music (Baily, 2001). Like others in communities impacted by human or natural catastrophe, many Afghan musicians left the country to live in refugee communities away from their homes. Musicians in diaspora communities in Pakistan and around the world exhibited resilience in the face of social, economic, and physical upheaval by continuing to play and to pass on their musical traditions.[16] Although they had fled their homeland, or had been forced to leave, many musicians continued to play in new settings, instrument makers continued to make instruments, even though it was sometimes difficult to find materials, and soon diaspora communities became the main source for Afghan music recordings (Broughton, 2002). By 2000 the Aga Khan Music Initiative had begun a focused project to revive fundamental cultural institutions and ancient oral traditions by founding music schools in which master musicians share their skills with students through traditional vernacular pedagogical methods. Creating spaces and institutions for "master-apprenticeship" (*ustad-shagird*) meetings and relationships is a way of preserving the way in which students learn. Although this focus may seem like an effort to enshrine traditional ways of transmitting culture, in other areas of the project artistic collaboration, and even change, were valued. In this way, the architects of the project saw musical traditions not as stagnant but rather constantly shifting. The project seeks to revitalize musical communities by creating incentives for refugee musicians to return to their homeland to teach young Afghan musicians in master-apprentice training centers in Kabul and Herat. It also includes music research and archiving in Herat and Badakhshan, as well as outreach to schools, instrument-making workshops, and public performances.

Indeed, many Afghan musicians have faced several political and social shifts in their lifetimes so that the performance contexts, audiences, and even the meaning of their music have changed. The Music Initiative is funded consistently, and it continues to exist partially by redirecting profits from album sales back into on-the-ground projects. The final and most high-profile element of the Fund for Culture involves promoting music through concerts outside the region, as well as recording and disseminating music from Central Asia around the world through a partnership with Smithsonian Folkways Records (http://www.folkways.si.edu/find_recordings/CentralAsia.aspx).[17] What began as a project focused in Central Asia has now expanded to communities in the Middle East, North Africa, and South Asia. This multipronged project exemplifies the sizable impact that applied projects can have on a population during turmoil when a project is informed about a musical community's needs.

There are other cases in which refugee and other diaspora communities have offered valuable transnational partnerships to aid post-disaster communities in documenting, performing, and teaching their music to new generations. Diaspora groups offer economic and organizational help, as well as reintroducing cultural traditions to their homeland (Hamera, 2002).[18] In response to the 2010 earthquake in Haiti, the diaspora funded Haitian Arts Alliance, based in Miami, spearheaded a project to repatriate recordings made by Alan Lomax in the 1930s. In addition to repatriating the recordings in an attempt to heighten local interest in the music, this project represents an effort to draw media attention to the importance of music in people's lives.

Members of the Cambodian diaspora, many of whom left the country during the Khmer Rouge occupation, have played an active role in the creating, recording, and international distribution opportunities for local musicians as cultural institutions were closed or destroyed during the conflict. Based in Massachusetts and heavily supported by the Cambodian diaspora on the West Coast of the United States, the Cambodian Living Arts organization supports "revival of traditional Khmer performing arts to inspire contemporary artistic expression" (http://www.cambodianlivingarts.org/). According to their mission statement, this organization recognizes the shared ownership of Khmer traditional arts and highlights the importance of the arts in processes of reconciliation and healing after war. Like the Aga Khan Music Initiative in Central Asia and the Middle East, Cambodian Living Arts offers networking, educational, and mentorship opportunities, as well as career development and "income generating projects for master performing artists" (https://www.facebook.com/Cambodianlivingarts/info).[19] Groups such as the Los Angeles–based psychedelic nostalgic rock band Dengue Fever have traveled extensively through Cambodia to raise awareness about Cambodian Living Arts and then have donated their earnings to the organization. Part of diaspora strength, as is true in both the Cambodian and Haitian cases, is their ability to offer more funding than local communities have access to after a disaster.

CONCERT ADVOCACY

In addition to the many disadvantages that musicians confront during social, economic, political, and physical upheaval, international press coverage of catastrophes can draw abundant donations from distant audiences. For each of the disasters mentioned, numerous concerts have been planned, broadcast, and recorded by an array of organizations around the world to raise awareness and money.[20] Concert advocacy is an effective way to raise money, although, for musicians on the ground, where and how the money is spent may be more important than the particular celebrity musicians who perform. Nongovernmental organizations that have access to funds raised through concert advocacy would certainly do well to work with local and international cultural experts in deciding how, where, and over what period to allocate funds. Post-catastrophe environments tend to be flush with short-term ideas and projects but have a dearth of long-term sustainable solutions, especially in the area of culture.[21] The following is a description of a cultural center funded by humanitarian concerts held outside Bosnia-Herzegovina before and after the conflict.

WAR CHILD AND THE PAVAROTTI CENTER

One of the most publicized cultural centers in Bosnia-Herzegovina, the Pavarotti Center, was originally funded by millions of euros donated through an international organization called War Child. The organization was founded in Britain in 1993 by two filmmakers, Bill Leeson and David Wilson, who had just returned from the former Yugoslavia, where they had made a film about the role of artists in war. In their travels and work they had both been shocked by the plight of children in the conflict region and consequently decided to use their film and entertainment industry connections to raise money for aid agencies operating in the region. Later both realized that, rather than donating money to other organizations, they should create their own. War Child's first project, to set up mobile bakeries to feed refugees and war victims during the conflict, was conducted in cooperation with the British Government and the United Nations High Commission for Refugees (UNHCR). This project was based in Medjugorje,[22] where it fed Croatian refugees throughout Western Bosnia-Herzegovina.

Upon War Child's discovery that diabetic children in Bosnia-Herzegovina were receiving little or no insulin, because clinics had been closed or were inaccessible due to war, the organization began to ferry insulin into besieged Sarajevo on Red Cross flights and to distribute the medicine directly to the children. Today, War Child is still one of the main suppliers of diabetic medicines throughout Bosnia-Herzegovina; it now receives additional funding from the US Office of Development Assistance, the UNHCR, and the European Union. But by far the largest and most involved project for War Child was the Pavarotti Music Centre in Mostar (see Haskell, 2003).

Brian Eno, the well-known British popular musician with recordings *Music for Airports* and *Thursday Afternoon* and producer of multiple U2 releases and other albums, and Tom Stoppard, screenplay writer of such acclaimed films as *Brazil* and *Empire of the Sun*, were among many high-profile patrons of War Child. In fact, it was with Eno's encouragement that War Child started "delivering music aid into Bosnia" (War Child brochure, 2000). On September 4, 1995, some of the best-known bands and musicians in Europe entered studios with the intention of recording tracks and then producing an album to raise money for the children caught up in the war. The album was released in September 9, 1995, titled *Help*,[23] selling more than 71,000 copies on the first day and raising millions of pounds.

With the success of the *Help*[24] album and the support of their newest patron at the time, Luciano Pavarotti, War Child began to implement and fund almost 20 humanitarian projects in Bosnia-Herzegovina. The projects were varied, focusing on assistance with medical care, food provision, and educational and social welfare programs. In 1996, shortly after a fragile peace had been brokered in the region, War Child purchased a bombed-out building in Mostar, a city in the center of the Herzegovinian region in which some of the most intense fighting had taken place during the war. War Child, with its slogan "Helping the innocent victims of war," planned to rebuild the structure as a music center. The center was built on the south side of the old city of Mostar, which, before the war, had been the Luka Primary School. The brochure for the center stated that it was "created from the shell of a bombed-out building, and will now be a peaceful environment where music can be taught, played and enjoyed" (PMC brochure, 2000).

The opening of the center was announced on December 21, 1997, in local as well as international media, like this:

> Italian tenor Luciano Pavarotti and famous friends from the entertainment industry attended the opening of the Pavarotti Music Center on Sunday December 21st, in the divided town of Mostar to reunite children from Bosnia's three ethnic groups. In driving rain the helicopters arrived, carrying the celebrities from Split, Croatia. . . .
>
> (PMC brochure, 2000)

From its inception, the mission of the project was meant to heal a national divide between the three ethnic groups. The goal is consistent with the way in which the international media portrayed the conflict in Bosnia-Herzegovina, but did not reflect the local demographic of Mostar at the time. Unfortunately, after the conflict few Bosnian-Serbs returned to the city. Although before the war the population of Mostar was mixed, it is now predominantly Bosniak (about 51 percent) and Croat (about 45%). Most people in these communities live separately in different areas of the city.

The center was planned to be a place in which children from the region would have the opportunity to benefit from music therapy. In their promotional material, War Child defined the center as a

> forward-looking and open-ended facility, where every kind of music making can take place. All four main functions—music tuition, music therapy / workshops, recording studios and performance areas—are allowed and encouraged to overlap so each space is designed to be multi-functional, within a clear overall framework.
>
> (War Child bulletin, 2000)

The organizers of the center referenced the Joint Declaration of the 1982 International Symposium of Music Therapists in defining music therapy; the following statement is included in their literature:

> Music Therapy facilitates the creative process of moving toward wholeness in the physical, emotional, mental, and spiritual self in areas such as: independence, freedom to change, adaptability, balance and integration. The implementation of Music Therapy involves interactions of the therapist, client and music. These interactions initiate and sustain musical and non-musical change processes which may or may not be observable. As the musical elements of rhythm, melody and harmony are elaborated across time, the therapist and client can develop relationships which optimize the quality of life. We believe Music Therapy makes a unique contribution to wellness, because man's responsiveness to music is unique.
>
> (ibid.)

The relationship defined in this statement between therapist and client is clearly hierarchical, as the European expert (in the early years of the center, all therapists were British and Dutch) applies therapy to Bosnian children. Wound into the practice of music therapy is the theory that music, on its own, removed from cultural or political context, heals. The curriculum at the center includes an African Drum Workshop, which organizers say appeals to children who are beginners, as well as advanced players between the ages of 4 and 17. In recent years the workshops have also been extended to a local hospital for children with disabilities and a school for the blind. Workshops in which children from different ethnic groups play music together and then proudly perform can certainly result in positive experiences.

In contrast, ethnomusicologist Svanibor Pettan founded, with Norwegian musicologist Kjell Skyllstad, a project titled *Azra* in Oslo, which sought much the same kind of cultural exchange as War Child seeks in Mostar. The two scholars saw the possibilities of musical exchange between the majority community of Norwegians and a Bosnian refugee minority seeking asylum from the conflict in their homeland. The project was rooted in the three activities of research, education, and music-making:

> At its center was the ensemble *Azra* consisting of Norwegian music and Bosnian musicians, some of them refugees. The goals of *Azra* were to strengthen the Bosnian cultural identity among the refugees from Bosnia-Herzegovina in Norway and to stimulate mutually beneficial cross-cultural communications between the Bosnians and the Norwegians.
>
> (Pettan, 1999: 289)

The *Azra* project emphasized music as the central mode of exchange. It was through sharing musical differences and similarities that musicians, as well as audience members, were introduced to each other and came to know each other. Indeed, music must have

had healing effects upon those who participated in the *Azra* activities, as it was primarily based upon person-to-person, and then community-to-community, exchange of
music. The involvement of two music scholars from both communities allowed music
to be the focal point, and included a grounded discussion and description of the music's
place in each environment. In comparison, the War Child project focused on healing
war wounds rather than on music. In this way, music was distributed by professionals
and received by war-traumatized individuals.

Much of War Child's emphasis on medical aid to traumatized children is due to
the organization's history as first a granter of humanitarian aid and only second a cultural facilitator. In its publicity the center equates humanitarian aid with music aid, as
Bosnian-Herzegovinian children wounded by the war[25] are referred to the center by
medical, social, and educational authorities. Indeed, after the war, music therapy was
a largely foreign concept in Bosnia-Herzegovina. In the years since the founding of the
center, War Child has added an outreach program to refugees through the local psy-
chiatric hospital. The model of providing music therapy to conflict-stricken children
requires that trauma be diagnosed, a cure be administered, and final results be tested.
The following description of music therapy makes it clear that the style, origin, and history of the music are not central to its efficacy:

> Children were brought together in shelters and cellars, in bombed ruins and, when
> safe, in open spaces, to make and listen to music, to sing, to beat drums, to strum
> guitars, to act and react together through music. These workshops began to take a
> structured form with War Child's association with Professor Nigel Osborne, who
> had organized a children's opera in Sarajevo at the height of the war.
>
> (www.pavarottimusiccentre.com)

These medically derived components are, on a whole, unidirectional. International
experts are responsible for diagnosing the ailment, administering a cure, and deter-
mining the success of the treatment.

In addition to music therapists, the center also has recording studios. Access to a recording studio is advantageous to musicians who are already established and has, over
the years, proved to be a useful tool for young musicians. Throughout its years of work
in the region, War Child has received sizable support from the Croatian government,
an important detail since Mostar was so heavily fought over between Bosniaks and
Bosnian-Croats:

> War Child has lobbied extensively inside the political/ social structures of The
> Republic of Croatia and has won support from all political parties in Zagreb, in-
> cluding the ruling HDZ. In addition major music personalities in Croatia have
> agreed to be associated with the Center and work with their colleagues from Mostar
> and Sarajevo to ensure that its success is not only local but regional.
>
> (War Child Bulletin, 2000)

Although practitioners of music therapy aim to choose music that is apolitical, for the local community, funding is an important marker of political agenda. That the project was funded by the Croatian government signals to Bosniaks living in the city that an outside power is involved. It is exactly such external political and economic support (from Serbia and Croatia) that allowed the war in Bosnia-Herzegovina to continue for such a long time and for nationalistic stereotypes to succeed. Had the center been founded by local members of the Mostar community, it may not have had such lavish recording studios and important visits from European celebrities, but it might have been grounded in the community. Several years after War Child opened the Pavarotti Center, the OKC Abrašević Youth Center was founded by the local community in the center of Mostar (http://www.okcabrasevic.org/index.php?option=com_content&view=article&id=176&Itemid=58). Drawing its name from a Yugoslav-era cultural center, the center is a vibrant venue for concerts, art exhibitions, and film screening.

In the past years, War Child has continued to use the enormous support it receives from the media and music and entertainment industries to raise funds for its projects and also to "advance public awareness of the daily struggle facing children in war zones" (War Child brochure, 2000). Although War Child began its work in the former Yugoslavia, it has expanded its field of operations to include some of the other wars that are currently affecting millions of children around the planet. By the time War Child began work in Mostar, the organization had already piloted several projects in postwar regions throughout the world. During the 2003 war in Iraq,

> ... eighteen top pop stars, including Paul McCartney and George Michael, released an album to raise money for child war victims in Iraq. Former Beatle McCartney, who made a live recording of his song "Calico Skies," said: "Whatever the politics, whatever the rights and wrongs of war, children are always the innocent victims. So I am delighted to make this small contribution." The charity said the "Hope" album, whose contributors also include David Bowie and Avril Lavigne, was not a political album. "The plight of children transcends politics. These songs are a plea for hope without which the children of Iraq have nothing at all."
>
> (Reuters, London, April 22, 2003)

With its growth, War Child has sought to create projects that will be applicable to different cultural settings. Indeed, to a certain extent, international donations are dependent upon the breadth of involvement the organization can have across the world.

Unfortunately, in the last decade large portions of the original sum donated through album and concert ticket sales were lost or stolen. The center's loss of such a large-scale investment remains a stain on Bosnia's donor history and tarnishes future foreign investment in the cultural realm. That said, concert advocacy remains one of the most vibrant mechanisms for gathering global humanitarian support from diverse audiences.

COMMEMORATIONS

Among local communities, political parties as well as cultural institutions may seek out traditional musicians to perform in commemorative events. Musicians can offer particularly symbolic and metaphorical weight to events as communities commemorate loss, survival, or even attempt to heighten memories of the past through nostalgia. Just as during other social or political upheavals, such as revolution, during postwar and post-catastrophe situations musicians and music can be powerful political and social symbols.

Given the socio-religious divide between communities in post-conflict Bosnia-Herzegovina, several urban projects have emphasized reconciliation through the metaphor of "sharing the stage," while rural projects highlight strengthening civil society institutions (Haskell, 2011).

Indeed, in the Bosnian general election of 2000, several years after the conflict, the Organization for Security and Co-operation in Europe (OSCE) launched a get-out-the-vote campaign targeted at young voters. OSCE officials commissioned an "election song" titled "Zgrabi svoju sreću" ("Grab Your Chance"), which was performed by three musicians (Irina Kapetanović, Marija Šestić, and Sanja Volić), each representatives of one of the three main ethnic groups in Bosnia (Bosniak, Bosnian-Serb, Bosnian-Croat). Their Western-style punk rock anthem was followed by an OSCE-sponsored music video featuring the song, and both were broadcast throughout the country in the days leading up to the election. OSCE's entrance into the politics of culture in Bosnia received mixed reviews from its target audience. When Bosnian youth expressed their distaste for the song, saying that it was condescending and imperialistic, international officials were puzzled. While, at the time, the OSCE was a new player in the politics of culture in Bosnia, the public was accustomed to attempts by the Yugoslav regime to sponsor music as a symbol of political and social unity. Perhaps their dissatisfaction was due to the OSCE's exclusion of any Bosnian musical features so wildly popular among the country's youth. This campaign's mixed reception illustrates some of the complexities facing international cultural sponsors who seek to effect political and social change through music. Such projects use music as a tool for impacting primary social and political problems by "performing" reconciliation and modeling harmony on the stage.

On a practical level, commemorations may offer musicians a chance to concertize, although some may find the post-disaster concert to be a minefield of special interests and, in the case of post-conflict areas, politically divisive parties. Ensembles, especially those that draw from local traditions, perform commemorative events meant to mourn a community's disaster as well as celebrate survival. This tie to a period in time evokes powerful emotions but can also have lasting political implications. Such situations can result in dynamic and sometimes contentious relationships between indigenous (or local) and foreign actors. As musicians in politically and socially volatile communities may be concerned that their musical practices and traditions are threatened, this chapter contends that such situations may be the most opportune times for applied ethnomusicologists to engage and find support for their work. While tracking the opportunities for cultural development created after humanitarian disasters, it is essential that applied projects that be sustainable as well as locally derived and authored.

SHIFTS IN MARKETS

In Bosnia-Herzegovina the conflict and the postwar security and political situation significantly impacted the flow of music, in all forms, across borders. State institutions, such as radio and television stations, which had facilitated a shared sense of nationhood through cultural understanding and government policies, largely collapsed or became arms of one of the national factions. Record producers and musicians, hoping to sell their recordings across post-Dayton borders to the regional audience that spoke Bosnian/Serbian/Croatian, found travel and shipment difficult, costly, and time-consuming. Musicians in Sarajevo during the siege paid dearly for instruments, amplifiers, and cassettes passed hand-to-hand under the airport, in the tunnel leading to Dobrinja.[26] Some musicians who, before the conflict, had toured with ease between Sarajevo, Belgrade, and Zagreb, as well as throughout Europe, encountered visa limitations that greatly restricted their ability to perform across the region. Just as the conflict tore apart some mixed marriages, as husbands and wives found themselves and their families on different sides of the conflict, so were several bands forced to break up because of their mixed membership. In the postwar period, after many borders had been opened, musicians still faced a nationalization of the markets, in which some labels were only interested in promoting music consistent with their political and/or national interests. In my travels around Bosnia, I met several entrepreneurs who expressed to me their aspirations to use the internet or radio to unite groups of fans across borders. Indeed, young musicians and audiences in Sarajevo often found it easier to go online to find music from bands in the region than take a train or bus to attend a live concert.

Since the conflict, the process of opening borders for travel in the region and greater Europe has been slow, just like any tangible or intangible reconstruction. In November 2010, the European Union interior ministers lifted visa requirements for citizens of Bosnia and Albania. Visa requirements for Serbia, Macedonia, and Montenegro were lifted a year earlier than those of Bosnia and Albania, in December 2009. Prior to this agreement, anyone who wanted to travel outside the country was forced to wait in long lines outside European embassies, fill out lengthy forms, and await the visa verdict, which would sometimes take weeks to arrive. Now, for the first time in almost 15 years, Bosnians can freely travel to European countries.

An experience common among many musicians around the world has been the implosion of local music markets because of the steady advancement of digital music sources into audiences' lives. Changes in the structure of the music market may exacerbate already limited distribution possibilities for musicians in post-disaster environments. Dependent upon the genre of music, applied ethnomusicologists may find that introducing musicians to record labels and other music outlets outside the disaster area can open up new opportunities for musicians. The following is a description of a donor/ record label partnership that sought to address the issue of the shifting music market in Bosnia after the war.

A PROFITABLE PARTNERSHIP

Gramofon Records is an example of a Sarajevo-based postwar record label that sought to help musicians navigate shifts in the market that resulted from the conflict and economic recession in Bosnia-Herzegovina. The small but prolific Gramofon Records was established in 2003, founded by Edin Zubčević, who also runs the Sarajevo Jazz Festival. On their website, the staff explains that they "prefer artistic projects which are innovative, urban, authentic or important in some other way." They also note that they are "trying to preserve and document [the] music heritage of Bosnia-Herzegovina" (http://www.gramofon.ba/discography_about.php?lang=en). Gramofon Records' discography has three separate editions: "*novi* gramofon" (new gramofon), which is described by the record staff on their website as "different styles and types of music, actual production (new music, electronic, improvised music, jazz. . . .)" (ibid.); "*etno* gramofon" (ethno gramofon), described as "traditional and sacred music"; and "gramofon classic," which they hesitantly describe as "so-called classical music." Connected to these editions, the label also has a category called *gramofon video*, on which documentary films, music videos, and artistic video works are released. The label's success is due in large part to a long-term partnership with a Swiss NGO.

In 2004, the Swiss Cultural Program (a shared program of the Swiss Arts Council, Pro Helvetia, and the Swiss Development Cooperation, SDC) agreed to support the label through Aida Cengić, who was the Head of the Pro Helvetia office at the time of research. Before receiving support from Pro Helvetia, Zubčević's small staff at Gramofon were already running the two-week annual Sarajevo Jazz Festival, as well as acting as booking agents for musicians wanting to perform in Bosnia-Herzegovina. As a company, they boasted an impressive list of clients, booking the majority of large-scale events in Sarajevo. I learned from Cengić that Pro Helvetia was particularly interested in Gramofon's viability as an already existent business and a local creation run by a small local staff. In addition to these reasons, Zubčević was an attractive candidate because he was and continues to be a part of the new generation of cultural organizers who have their eyes on the goal of future EU accession and are actively engaged in making money in their new free market economy. Zubčević explained the opportunity he saw on the musical horizon following the war to boost the alternative music scene.

> We can talk about the limits of good taste when we talk about it, but not go any further. So, it's not about [supporting] a sophisticated culture, for that of course there is no cultural policy. Even in such a mess it creates the perfect ambience to what happens to us, what happens [over] the last five or ten years. And that is that we have a situation where in fact what would be... at best a kind of subculture, a kind of parallel world, in fact our reality and our entire culture.
>
> (Zubčević, 2006)[27]

Zubčević's excitement about creating "a parallel world" where alternative political and social opinions, as well as musical styles, may flourish is evident.

Although, like most nationally funded arts councils, Pro Helvetia's main focus is to promote Swiss artists within Switzerland, they also take up the task of international cultural diplomacy and regional development. In my conversations with cultural figures in Sarajevo about international/foreign funding for musicians, artists, and other performers, Pro Helvetia always came up as the most progressive and well-respected of the funders. This success was often described to me in comparison to heavy-handed efforts or cultural projects that were out of touch with local interests. The organization's historic sensitivity to local expression within the domestic Swiss context is also illustrative of their approach to supporting international projects.

In 1939, Pro Helvetia became Switzerland's Arts Council, as laid out in the Pro Helvetia Act of that year. At present, the Swiss parliament allocates support for the organization every four years "to promote artistic creation, support cultural exchange both within Switzerland and with foreign countries, disseminate culture and campaign for folk culture" (http://www.prohelvetia.ch/APPLICATIONS.7.0.html?&L=4). These tasks are understood "as a mandate to promote public awareness of the arts, to encourage reflection and debate on cultural needs and cultural policy, to promote Swiss arts abroad, and to foster encounters with the cultures both of Switzerland's various regions and of other countries" (http://www.prohelvetia.ch/Mission-Statement.67.0.html?&L=4). Pro Helvetia began working in Sarajevo in 1999 and had Swiss representatives based in seven different countries in the region of Southeastern Europe.

Pro Helvetia's mission statement comprises five sections: mandate, targets, values, tools, and position. "Pro Helvetia contributes to the development and opening up of society. It fosters diversity of cultural expression. It promotes Switzerland's image abroad and encourages a multi-faceted self-perception at home." Consistent with their approach to Gramofon, Pro Helvetia makes the following statements about how they understand the value of art:

(1) Art is an experiment; the Arts Council supports fresh and courageous projects.
(2) Art is about difference; the Arts Council highlights both differences and common

ground. (3) Art is controversy; the Arts Council encourages critical debate. (4) Art is about respect; the Arts Council advances cultural learning.

(Ibid.)

Pro Helvetia's mandate of fostering creativity, engagement, and cooperation has been exhibited in the organization's support of Gramofon. Those who seek to instill ethno-religious divisions in Bosnia-Herzegovina might charge Pro Helvetia with fomenting revolution among these alternative groups and their audiences. Several of the bands originally signed to Gramofon employ musical styles that are not indigenous to Bosnia-Herzegovina, such as reggae, rap, dub,[28] and jazz to draw young listeners to concerts, while the political topics of their songs include critiques of the domestic political situation, individual politicians, democracy, corruption, and the Dayton Agreement.

Unlike other postwar cultural projects in which funds were dispersed by international organizations in an ad hoc and thus inconsistent manner, Pro Helvetia employed the use of scheduled micro-grants. In the field of development, such small grants are also called mini-grants. Micro-grants have been used in development projects around the world to help engage citizens in their communities through market activity without the weight of crippling debt. In the American context, micro-grants have been a particularly popular way of supporting artists and musicians.[29]

Just as the mechanisms and methods for delivering funds were central to the sustainability of the projects, Pro Helvetia's procedure for choosing cultural projects was novel at the time. When the Pro Helvetia office was originally set up in January 2003, Cengić organized a meeting of local experts, from different fields of art, and one representative from the headquarters in Zurich. In the gathering, locals greatly outnumbered the Pro Helvetia staff. Independently, the group also met with 15 additional experts in the field of culture to put together a countrywide analysis. The experts were scholars and cultural organizers chosen to represent various cultural sectors. In her interview with me, Cengić explained:

Based on that analysis and based on their inputs during those two days, we developed a country concept in which we said [that] we are interested in young people, we are interested in [the] formation [of] professional development. Also, based on my knowledge of the situation, we came up with five ideas. One of those five ideas was Gramofon. So then I knew about Edo's [Edin's] aspirations to do some publishing. And then we sat to discuss about it. "Are you still in?" and he said, "Yes, yes, very much so." So this is the initial conversation that took place.

(Cengić, 2006)

There was also a steering group, based in Zurich, which was in charge of approving or rejecting proposed projects. After approval, Cengić was given an additional three months to develop the project. Her goals during that period with Zubčević were "to develop all [of] the activities, to develop [an] action plan, to develop [the] budget into tiny little detail, to develop strategy for the second and third years" (Zubčević,

2006). After the process of analysis and development, the project was finally signed in January 2003. According to Ćengić, funding levels by Pro Helvetia are based more on the strength of the individual projects than on some sort of pre-allocation to specific countries.

Of the original projects proposed by Ćengić, only two were approved. In response to my questions about whether she was disappointed by the fact that all of the proposals were not accepted, Ćengić calmly responded, "You can't get everything. My experience says it's a good rule not to do more than three cooperation projects at the same time" (Ćengić, 2006). In the postwar years in which Pro Helvetia was more active in the region, the organization also spent 100,000 Swiss francs a year (approximately $102,650) on "small action" projects in each country within the region. Unlike larger and more engaged projects based on long relationships, such as that with Gramofon, small action grants are meant to provide limited one-time funding. In Bosnia-Herzegovina, Pro Helvetia has used these for a wide range of activities, including exhibitions, concerts, musicians' tours, and theater performances. Small action grants may also be dispersed in cooperation with larger projects. In the case of Gramofon, individual musicians may receive such grants to assist them in activities ancillary to the label's budget.

I have noted the imbalanced sponsor-recipient relationship that developed, or was built, into many other cultural projects I researched in Bosnia-Herzegovina. Unlike the organizers of those projects, both Zubčević and Ćengić were adamant about defining their relationship as a balanced and cooperative one. When I asked Zubčević to explain how he dealt with the issue of sponsorship, he was careful to underline Gramofon's independence.

> It's not, it's not sponsorship. It's not. . . . We're doing. . . . Cause we used to be NGO, and we established the company, which is actually part of cultural industry. And, actually, my idea is that we have from NGO work, cause we, as I said, we got know how, we got to learn how to do certain things and we know how to make money. And we learn how to. . . how to. . . be active in the culture industry. . . because there is no culture industry here.
>
> (Zubčević, 2006)

One of the reasons for his obstinate response is that over the life of the project, Pro Helvetia has provided low-level but consistent operational funds to Gramofon in the form of small yearly matching grants. Explained by Pro Helvetia as a partnership, the relationship is based upon financial support that is contingent on the release of a certain number of CDs and continued financial earnings by the label. The aim of this small-level institutional granting initiative by the Swiss is to guide the label to future self-sustainability. The project represents a specific approach to funding in that it does not focus on a one-time event but on long-term sustainability in the area of culture. Zubčević explained to me his understanding of the partnership and Gramofon's responsibilities to Pro Helvetia.

And after one year they said: "Let's sign the contract for three years and let's see [if] will we do in [the] next year." And every three months we're writing reports. Financial reports, narrative reports, whatever. And step by step so we established a relationship. Actually, we consider the office from Pro Helvetia as a partner, as a member of the staff but it also has authority. "You know, you should release CD, that CD." So, they remind us sometimes, you know. Because they say, "You said that you're gonna release six CDs, you released five, why does that happen?" We say: "Because of that," "OK then do that again, we'll pay you money." Because we propose [a] certain program, and if we don't fulfill what we're supposed [to do] it's not OK, [but] it's not serious.

(Zubčević, 2006)

For Zubčević, the most significant gain the label has made, due to Pro Helvetia's support, has been their ability to build a well-produced and packaged body of Bosnian-Herzegovinian music that is accessible to local and international markets. Part of making Gramofon releases available to international markets involved inviting a consultant from Switzerland who had been running a successful label called Intakt Records (http://www.intaktrec.ch/), a major Swiss jazz label, for more than 20 years. Talking about the consultant, Patrick Landolt, Čengić stressed his personality, knowledge, and willingness to help. "The industry. . . he knows it inside out. And he is [the] kind of person who wants to help. He was the best consultant for this job" (Čengić, 2006). Packaging was also a major issue for Gramofon before they received support from Pro Helvetia. Now Gramofon CDs are all packaged in high-quality cardboard digipacks, often accompanied with liner notes.

By funding Gramofon, Pro Helvetia hoped to contribute to diversifying and developing the local music market, as well as create an identifiable Bosnian product for international markets. The donor actively supported this goal by inviting an experienced recording entrepreneur and record label director to Sarajevo to advise Gramofon about global markets, recording techniques, and packaging. Packaging, at least at the time of release, helped Gramofon to stand out in the international market.

In their mission statement, Pro Helvetia's policy explains their support for a "diversified, lively and innovative cultural scene" and equates musicians and artists in the scene as aiding in democratic expression. Gramofon's role as one of the only alternative or engaged record labels in the country is central to its support by Pro Helvetia and also to the difficulty it faces in competing with popular music labels in the country. The partnership between Gramofon and Pro Helvetia represents an exception in the world of cultural funding in Sarajevo, as the organizers of the project have emphasized slow growth created with minimal support over a long period of time. Yearly microgrants made it possible for Zubčević to rely on Pro Helvetia's support without limiting his freedom. The choice by both organizers to work with musicians and bands willing to criticize present social and political situations helped to support a struggling scene in an impossible post-conflict period marred by rampant piracy, strong borders, and an economically depressed population. Because of Pro Helvetia's support, many of the bands on the Gramofon label have found a safe place to contest difference, to voice differing and often political opinions, and to incorporate new genres into the Bosnian soundscape.

CLOSURE OR CHANGES IN CULTURAL INSTITUTIONS

Many large cultural institutions founded during the socialist period in Yugoslavia in Bosnia-Herzegovina, such as museums, concert venues, festivals, and music schools, have not fared as well as new ones such as Gramofon Records. This is partly because of their inability to fit within a new and highly factionalized political context. The best cultural and historical example of this is the Zemaljski Muzej (the National Museum), which was closed in October 2012. Because of a lack of governmental funding, the museum is no longer able to accept visitors (Hooper, 2012). The divisive political situation that emerged after the signing of the Dayton Peace Accord in 1995 left formerly Yugoslav institutions in a political void, as in this case the history the museum had told through its exhibitions and holdings no longer resonated with some highly politicized audiences. Activist ethnomusicologists navigating post-conflict environments may require extensive local networks on all sides in order to achieve any level of success in helping already existent institutions. Sadly, but perhaps realistically, the Bosnian case highlights the reality that many post-conflict cultural institutions may be forced to choose sides, and that this act may impact the kinds of cultural material they present to the public. Applied ethnomusicologist may find, in situations such as this, that their ability to navigate aid agencies by writing grants can be invaluable to the musicians for whom they advocate. Sources for assistance may range from foreign embassies to regional funds. In many cases, such grant writers will find that their arguments for cultural funding must be linked directly to other overarching social and political goals tied to the grantors' interests, as was true in the Guča Gora example.

CONCLUSION

Applied ethnomusicologists and cultural advocates have contributed greatly to facilitating conflict resolution and cultural development in postwar and postcatastrophe environments. In the wake of both conflicts and natural disasters, cultural aid workers bear much needed resources and are often welcomed with open arms to host countries. In other cases, musical and cultural projects are developed and run by actors with relatively little expertise in cultural issues. In situations in which NGOs and institutions are trying to fill basic needs for the communities they serve, cultural products can have ancillary value: drawing a crowd, including people, raising money, selling a product, and explaining new concepts. Musicians are also used by politicians and communities alike to symbolize how innocent citizens have been impacted by natural or man-made disasters.

This chapter has addressed some fundamental issues that applied ethnomusicologists face in navigating the diverse field of international development in which social, economic, and political concerns often sideline equally important cultural ones. I have painted with broad strokes in an attempt to illustrate phenomena I recognize across many post-disaster realms. Each of these projects responds to struggles that musicians and their communities face in times of crises by attempting to advocate for musicians. I have also attempted to share some lessons for how applied ethnomusicologists can assist musical communities in the aftermath of social, political, and natural catastrophes. I have sought to identify lessons learned in the past and to suggest how some of the pitfalls to cultural assistance might be avoided in the future by applied ethnomusicologists working in post-conflict and post-catastrophe communities. I have also noted the opportunities, particularly financial, that post-disaster conditions provide to creative advocates who can capitalize on new funding resources for the good of musical communities.

NOTES

1. The Mostar bridge and the city around it has been the site of the single largest international effort to restore Bosnia-Herzegovina's cultural heritage since the war. The "Old Bridge Area of the Old City of Mostar" project was overseen by UNESCO and the Aga Khan Foundation. It is a UNESCO World Heritage site.
2. See the foundation's mission statement, which also includes a commitment to creating a better society, as well as encouraging new projects in the regions in which they work. http://www.kbs-frb.be/content.aspx?id=290655&langtype=1033 (accessed October 2013).
3. www.mozaik.ba/english/html/livingheritage.html (accessed September 2003).
4. In their article Foley and Edwards (1996) define civil society as "the realm of private voluntary association, from neighborhood committees to interest groups to philanthropic enterprises of all sorts, has come to be seen as an essential ingredient in both democratization and the health of established democracies."
5. These groups were organized in all parts of Yugoslavia, in rural as well as urban settings. According to anthropologist Lynn Maners, KUDs were originally "modeled on Soviet institutions and formally sponsored by state institutions such as universities and workers organizations" (Maners, 2000: 303). This undertaking was made in an effort to "create a Yugoslav national identity, composed of [state] approved diverse identities" (ibid.).
6. Although the Gučogorci I met remembered other ethnomusicologists who had visited the village over the previous decades, I only found recordings collected by Ankica Petrović. They are currently housed in the Ethnomusicology Archive at the University of California Los Angeles.
7. For a more in-depth discussion of the mosaic of religious belief in Sarajevo and throughout Bosnia, see the writings of the following three anthropologists: Sorabji (1989), Lockwood (1978), and Bringa (1995).

8. The 1995 agreement brought the three and one-half year armed conflict to an end, as well as formalizing and legitimizing ethno-religious borders won during the conflict.

9. Examples of major projects to rebuild and preserve tangible culture include Bamiyan (Afghanistan), Mostar bridge (Bosnia-Herzegovina), The Iraqi National Museum, and the Ninth Ward in New Orleans.

10. Portions of this chapter previously appeared in Haskell (2011).

11. Among journalists, the siege of Sarajevo is often referred to as the longest in the history of modern warfare. See Connelly (2005).

12. The Rock Under Siege (1996) concerts are a good example of the kinds of "underground" performances that took place during the conflict. They were held in a club in the center of the city, and the organizer Aida Kalendar explained to me that some audience members had to travel long distances to attend. The Futura Festivals (1998–2002) took place in unconventional spaces like factories and damaged buildings. See Haskell (2011).

13. The Musician's Village consists of 72 single-family homes as well as five elder-friendly duplexes and the "Center," which is a 17,000 square-foot performance venue equipped with recording facilities, a computer center, and listening library, a dance studio, classrooms, and teaching facilities. http:///www.nolamusiciansvillage.org/ (accessed September 18, 2013).

14. During the siege of Sarajevo and even after the conflict had ended, musicians found that their music distribution outlets were greatly narrowed. Those who had toured before the war now found themselves hesitant to perform for audiences with whom they might have been at war just a few years before. See Haskell (2011).

15. http://www.akdn.org/AKTC (accessed May 2014).

16. Adelaida Reyes (1999) has written extensively about refugee musicians in her book.

17. http://www.folkways.si.edu/find_recordings/CentralAsia.aspx (accessed June 2014).

18. In her article, Judith Hamera chronicles a refugee Khmer family's statements about the importance of Cambodian classical dance in their efforts to both heal from the genocide in that country and also instill cultural values of the homeland in their children.

19. https://www.facebook.com/Cambodianlivingarts/info (accessed September 24, 2013).

20. To name a few, Hope for Haiti Now, A Concert for Hurricane Relief, and the Concert for American Bosnian Relief Fund.

21. See "Aiding Harmony? International Humanitarian Aid and the Role of Applied Ethnomusicologists," in *Shared Musics and Minority Identities* (Ceribašić and Haskell, eds. (2004), as well as Haskell (2003).

22. Medjugorje, which means "between the hills," a small town in Herzegovina, has become well known in Bosnia-Herzegovina, and the world, because of the apparitions of six young people who claim to have seen visions of the Madonna. It is claimed that beginning on June 24, 1981, the Blessed Mother appeared to them, and later told the visionaries that God had sent her to our world to help followers convert their hearts and lives back to Him. The town and its cathedral have become a meeting point for Christians and an ending point for many religious pilgrimages. The religious nature of the town made it central to much conflict during the war.

23. The Help project was the brainchild of Tony Crean and Andy McDonald of Go! Discs.

24. War Child has produced a number of so-called "peace albums and events," including the album 1 Love, the Feast for Peace program, a documentary titled *Musicians in the War Zone* (Iraq, Sierra Leone, Thai-Burmese), two War Child Concerts in Canada, and many more. These events and projects are organized primarily to heighten awareness

internationally about the plight of children of war and also to raise money for humanitarian projects in postwar countries.

25. In their literature, War Child organizers quote a UNICEF report that found the level of trauma among the children of Mostar was the highest recorded anywhere in the former Yugoslavia.

26. Dobrinja is a residential neighborhood where much of the front-line activity took place.

27. Zubčević (2006).

28. In the 1960s, the dub genre of music developed out of reggae. Dub musicians rely heavily on instrumental remixes of recordings that they manipulate to create songs. Generally, the drum and bass parts are emphasized. For a more detailed description, see Scaruffi (2003).

29. We might also refer to these grants as micro-patronage, as they are termed in the following website: http://blog.alrdesign.com/2009/05/micro-grants-for-artists.html.

REFERENCES

Baily, John. (2001). *Afghanistan: "Can you stop the birds singing": The Censorship of Music in Afghanistan.* Copenhagen: Freemuse.

Bringa, Tone. (1995). *Being Muslim the Bosnian Way: Identity and Community in a Central Bosnian Village.* Princeton: Princeton University Press.

Broughton, Simon. (2002). *Breaking the Silence: Music in Afghanistan.* Afghanistan/UK. Simon Broughton. 60 min. film in color. In English.

Buchanan, Donna A. (1995). "Metaphors of Power, Metaphors of Truth: The Politics of Music Professionalism in Bulgarian Folk Orchestras." *Ethnomusicology* 39(3): 381–416.

Čengić. (2006). Interview with author.

Ceribašić, Naila. (1998). "Folklore Festivals in Croatia: Contemporary Controversies." *the world of music* 40(3): 25–50.

Ceribašić, Naila, and Erica Haskell, eds. (2004). *Shared Musics and Minority Identities. Papers from the Third Meeting of the "Music and Minorities," Study Group of the International Council for Traditional Music (ICTM)*, Roč, Croatia.

Cohen, Cynthia. (2008). "Chapter 2: Music: A Universal Language?" In *Urbain 2008, 26–39. Music and Conflict Transformation: Harmonies and Dissonances in Geopolitics.* Tokyo: The Toda Institute for Global Peace and Policy Research.

Connelly, Charlie. (October 8, 2005). "The New Siege of Sarajevo." *The Times (UK).* Accessed September 10, 2013.

Edwards, Julie, and Stephan P. Edwards. (2008). "Culture and the New Iraq: The Iraq National Library and Archive, 'Imagined Community', and the Future of the Iraqi Nation." *Libraries & the Cultural Record* 43(3): 327–342.

Foley, Michael, and Bob Edwards. (1996). "The Paradox of Civil Society." *Journal of Democracy* 7(3): 38–52.

Hamera, Judith. (2002). "An Answerability of Memory: 'Saving' Khmer Classical Dance." *TDR* 46(4): 65–85.

Haskell, Erica. (2003). "Music Aid to Bosnia-Herzegovina: International Cultural Funding of Post-war Events." Master's thesis, Brown University.

Haskell, Erica. (2011). "Aiding Harmony? Culture as a Tool in Post-conflict Sarajevo." Ph.D. dissertation, Brown University.

Helbig, Adriana. (2005). "Play For Me, Old Gypsy: Music as Political Resource in the Roma Rights Movement in Ukraine." Ph.D. dissertation, Columbia University.

Helbig, Adriana. (2008). "Managing Musical Diversity Within Frameworks of Western Development Aid: Views from Ukraine, Georgia, and Bosnia and Herzegovina." With contributions from Nino Tsitsishvili and Erica Haskell. *Yearbook for Traditional Music* 40: 46–59.

Hooper, John. (2012). "Bosnia's National Museum is latest victim of political funding crisis: Museum to close after 124 year as state government's powers and funding are eroded by antagonistic communities." *The Guardian*, October 2012.

Kalendar, Aida, and Dijana Marjanović. (1996). "Rock Under Siege." http://www.kabi.si/si21/IASPM/aida.html.

Kohlmann, Evan. (2004). *Al-Qaida's Jihad in Europe: The Afghan-Bosnian Network*. Berg Publishers, Oxford.

Kurkela, Vesa. (1995). "Local Music-Making in Post-Communist Europe: Mediatization and Deregulation." *East European Meetings in Ethnomusicology* 2: 105–115.

Laušević, Mirjana. (1996). "Illahiya as a Symbol of Bosnian Muslim National Identity." In *Retuning Culture: Musical Changes in Central and Eastern Europe*, edited by Mark Slobin, 117–135. Durham, NC: Duke University Press.

Laušević, Mirjana. (1998). "A Different Village: International Folk Dance and Balkan Music and Dance in the United States." Ph.D. dissertation, Wesleyan University.

Laušević, Mirjana. (2000). "Some Aspects of Music and Politics in Bosnia." In *Neighbors At War: Anthropological Perspectives on Yugoslav Ethnicity, Culture, and History*, edited by Joel Halpern and Davis Kideckel, 289–301. University Park: Penn State University Press.

Lockwood, William. (1978). *European Moslems: Economy and Ethnicity in Western Bosnia*. New York: Academic Press.

Maners, Lynn D. (2000). "Clapping for Serbs: Nationalism and Performance in Bosnia and Herzegovina." In *Neighbors At War: Anthropological Perspectives on Yugoslav Ethnicity, Culture, and History*, edited by Joel Halpern and Davis Kideckel, 302–315. University Park: Penn State University Press.

Pettan, Svanibor. (1998a). "Music and Censorship in Ex-Yugoslavia: Some Views From Croatia." Paper presented at the First World Conference on Music and Censorship, Copenhagen, November 1998.

Pettan, Svanibor, ed. (1998b). *Music, Politics, and War: Views from Croatia*. Zagreb: Institute of Ethnology and Folklore Research.

Pettan, Svanibor. (1999). "Musical Reflections on Politics and War. An Ethnomusicologist in Croatia in the 1990's." In *Musik im Umbruch: New Countries, Old Sounds?*, edited by Bruno B. Reuer. Munich: Verlag Südostdeutsches Kulturwerk.

Pettan, Svanibor. (2001). "Encounter with 'The Others from Within:' The Case Study of Gypsy Musicians in Former Yugoslavia." *the world of music* 43(2–3): 119–137.

Ramet, Sabrina. (1994). *Rocking the State: Rock Music and Politics in Eastern Europe and Russia*. Boulder, CO: Westview Press.

Ramet, Sabrina. (1996). *Balkan Babel: The Disintegration of Yugoslavia from the Death of Tito to Ethnic War*. Boulder, CO: Westview Press.

Reyes, Adelaida. (1999). *Songs of the Caged, Songs of the Free: Music and the Vietnamese Refugee Experience*. Philadelphia: Temple University Press.

Rice, Timothy. (1994). *May It Fill Your Soul—Experiencing Bulgarian Music*. Chicago: University of Chicago Press.

Scaruffi, Piero. (2003). *A History of Rock Music: 1951–2000*. New York: iUniverse.

Silverman, Carol. (1996). "Music and Marginality: Roma (Gypsies) of Bulgaria and Macedonia." In *Retuning Culture: Musical Changes in Central and Eastern Europe*, edited by Mark Slobin, 231–253. Durham, NC: Duke University Press.

Silverman, Carol. (1989). "Reconstructing Folklore: Media and Cultural Policy in Eastern Europe." *Communication* 11: 141–160.

Slobin, Mark, ed. (1996). *Retuning Culture: Musical Changes in Central and Eastern Europe*. Durham, NC: Duke University Press.

Sorabji, Cornelia. (1989). "Muslim Identity and Islamic Faith in Sarajevo." Ph.D. dissertation, University of Cambridge.

Sugarman, Jane C. (1999a). "Imagining the Homeland: Poetry, Songs, and the Discourses of Albanian Nationalism." *Ethnomusicology* 43(3): 419–445.

Sugarman, Jane C. (1999b). "Mediated Albanian Musics and the Imagining of Modernity." In *New Countries, Old Sounds? Cultural Identity and Social Change in Southeastern Europe*, edited by Bruno B. Reuer, 134–154. Munich: Südostdeutsches Kulturwerk.

Urbain, Olivier, ed. (2008). *Music and Conflict Transformation: Harmonies and Dissonances in Geopolitics*. Tokyo: The Toda Institute for Global Peace and Policy Research.

Zubčević, Edin. (2006). Interview with author. Sarajevo, March 2.

CHAPTER 7

....

THE STUDY OF
SURVIVORS' MUSIC

....

JOSHUA D. PILZER

Mountain pass after mountain pass, though I cli—(laughs)
always one yet remains.
Though I climb over, though I climb over,
this endless road of mountain passes . . .

Han Jeongsun, "(Hot) Pepper"

INTRODUCTION

....

THE last decades of the twentieth century saw the gradual unraveling of the concept of culture, which for many years prejudiced anthropology and ethnomusicology against the particularity of people's experiences, and particular uses of music in the interest of getting by in everyday life. As part of this movement, "practice theory"— the inquiry into the ways that people do this—made its way into ethnomusicology and anthropology. The fields also witnessed the rise of the ethnographic study of violence. In the midst of this atmosphere, a field of study has arisen that can be called the study of survivors' music, the inquiry into and documentation of the musical lives of those who endure or have endured violence and traumatic experiences (see Schwartz, 2012a, 2012b; Shapiro-Phim, 2008; Silent Jane, 2006; Pilzer, 2012).

In the chapter I outline basic characteristics and methods of the study of survivors' music, giving examples from my work and that of others, and from other scholarship, memoirs, and other sources that could be considered part of the literature of survivors' music. I dwell on some of the examples at length, to give an example of the work in practice.[1] My perspective has evolved through 10 years of work with Korean survivors of the Japanese military "comfort women" system of the Asia Pacific War (1931–1945),[2] and through more recent work with Korean survivors of the atomic bombing of Hiroshima and their families.

Music appears again and again in survivors' stories of their traumatic experiences and survival—because it is often a part of those traumatic experiences, because it can be a powerful expressive alternative or contrast to speech or writing, and for a whole host of other reasons. As a result, it has special stories to tell about the nature of those experiences and the means by which people survive. Its documentation, interpretation, and dissemination can therefore contribute much to human history and knowledge.

Simply put, the study of survivors' music is an attempt to document the musical practices of survivors and to understand them as both records of experience and adaptive resources for survival and selfhood, which often tell a very different story about experience than other expressive forms and historical records. The study of survivors' music is a kind of applied ethnomusicology because it is about documenting, interpreting, and making ethically accessible experiences and lifeworks that otherwise would pass from the historical record. It is therefore a species of the work of cultural and historical preservation that is so central to applied ethnomusicology, although its focus on traumatic experience may be atypical.

Scholars and others interested in survivors' music may seek to put the documentary results of the study of survivors' music in the hands of people with similar experiences who can be inspired or helped by them; to make materials ethically available to educators and others who are interested; or to put survivors and educators together for educational projects. Based on what scholars of survivors' music discover, they may play a role in the reorientation of political and social movements, or may become part of these movements themselves. For scholars of survivors' music, perhaps even more so than for other educators, education is often a form of advocacy and activism.

However, like the work of many recordists, yet unlike some kinds of political activism, the study of survivors' music does not need to assume a clearly defined political position. Nor does one necessarily presume to seek to "help" survivors; it has been my experience that survivors help those they address, much more than the other way around. One may seek rather to document and tune in to the complex understandings about the nature of social violence and strategies for survival that people spend their lives cultivating, yet which political movements often neglect in the interest of ideologies or political aims.

Of course, without attempting to grasp the finer points of the experience of sexual slavery, nuclear atrocities, ethnic genocides, domestic violence, or other catastrophic world events, one can know enough to quite legitimately object to them and to organize socially and politically against them. But the study of survivors' music can play an important role in complementing that kind of activism, beginning from the assumption that the deeper understandings that reside in musical practice are important to the record of human history, can benefit the general project of human flourishing, and can provide important guidance to social movements.

This work privileges survivors above all else—genres, ideologies, and, yes, music—and tries to listen carefully to their voices, stories, and the music that they impart to others in diverse circumstances. This *listening perspective* acknowledges that survivors have much to tell and to teach us about the nature and significance of their experiences, about the arts of surviving, mitigating, and preventing the more ugly sides of social life, about ethics, and about the art of human flourishing. "The accretion of marginalized voices transforms experience into collective memory," writes Victoria Sanford (2006: 13) in *The Engaged Observer: Anthropology, Advocacy, and Activism*. Survivors relate understandings that are essential to the revision of collective memory, and to the documentation and rewriting of history. They can help to reorient political movements, both through refining those movements' understandings of history and the present and through refreshing the place of survivors and their welfare on the list of movement priorities; and they can be of enormous value to other people who may be experiencing or have experienced similar traumas, injuries, and other struggles. When survivors speak and sing, they are often engaged in multiple forms of outright and more implicit activism; and from one perspective, the study of survivors' music is a comple-ment to those practices, helping to make them more legible across the many gaps of cul-ture, language, generation, class, gender, sexuality, and ability that separate people from each other.

Why is it so important to keep survivors at the center? Put simply, it is because survivors, their experiences, and their wisdom are routinely marginalized for a whole host of reasons. First, there are numerous survivors who are shunted to the margins of society by the political and social pressures that suppress public awareness of the often-systematic violence and exploitation they suffer or have suffered. The act of listening to such survivors, therefore, is a political act of the most signal importance, capable of inaugurating political movements for social justice, reparation, and reconciliation. The millions of current and past victims of global sex trafficking are one such set of survivors at present; so, too, are the survivors of Japan's most recent nuclear catastrophe.

Second, in cases where such exploitation and violence have been acknowledged, many societies, political movements, and scholars nonetheless tend to overlook survivors' voices in favor of their own, or to domesticate them through various techniques of appropriating others' experiences and voices. Political movements and public cultures may do this in a rush to righteous proclamation, or in pursuit of the transference of ownership of political issues from survivors to bourgeois civil societies, national subjectivities, and so on. Such public, political, and scholarly cultures seek, as intellec-tual historian Dominic LaCapra has put it, identity rather than empathy (1999: 699); in extreme instances we lay total claim to others' experiences of victimization as aspects of our own identities, rather than acknowledging them as something of their own. This is always a threat in the case of survivors of the Japanese military "comfort women" system in South Korea; similar appropriative projects characterize historiographies and public understandings of the mid-century European holocaust, and countless other traumatic events of modern history.

Scholars, as well, are guilty of ignoring or selectively hearing survivors' voices. Of course, for a long time scholars in ethnomusicology (with important exceptions, discussed below) were more preoccupied with rescuing or documenting cultural forms in danger of extinction than with paying attention to particular people and the texture of their experiences, traumatic or not, and the musical cleverness that they bring to bear on the effort to survive those experiences. Often with the best intentions and perfectly good scholarly goals in mind, scholars of music and traumatic experience have treated survivors as receptacles of the past that allow for its reconstruction. Much of the literature of survivors' music falls into this category, and means, ironically enough, that in the interest of learning something about survivors, one has to attempt to sense their imprint on accounts of the past that are based almost entirely in their testimonies. This might be said of Gila Flam's remarkable *Singing for Survival* (1992), a vivid reconstruction of the musical lives of Jews in the Lodz ghetto in Nazi-occupied Poland. This book is created almost entirely from survivors' memories; yet it is not concerned with the role that these songs might have in survivors' postwar lives, or the possibility that processes of traumatic remembering, forgetting, and overcoming could have deeply impacted the songs and stories, and the ways in which they were presented to the researcher. Shirli Gilbert's exhaustive study of *Music in the Holocaust* is another example of a fine scholarly work that relies principally on survivors' written narratives, interviews with survivors, and recordings of their singing, but tells us nothing about survivors' postwar lives and their struggles in the long unfolding of traumatic experience, which leave an indelible imprint on the oral-historical material. Susanne Cusick's powerful work on music and torture in the United States' war on terror (2008) is yet another example, reconstructed from the narratives of survivors, but focusing on the uses of music as torture rather than the experiences of people who have been tortured with music. These are important scholarly works with pressing agendas of their own; I mention them not to criticize them, but to highlight that, despite all of this fine work on the subject of music and violence, a hole remains in our understanding about survivors' lives and musical work. The musical means by which survivors stay alive and come to terms with their experiences are overlooked, and this is certainly a great loss to human knowledge.

The study of survivors' music attempts to address this void. It may draw inspiration from and find precedents in humanist ethnomusicologies like those practiced by Veronica Doubleday in her *Three Women of Herat* (1988), and Judith Vander in her *Songprints: The Musical Experience of Five Shoshone Women* (1988), and in the ethnomusicologies of marginalized social groups, such as those of Adelaida Reyes (1999), Amelia Maciszewski (2006), James Porter and Herschel Gower (1995), and Carol Silverman (2012). This latter category can be considered part of the literature of survivors' music.

The study of survivors' music considers survivors' musical activities as important sites of witnessing, of reckoning and overcoming, and of self-reconstruction. Many survivors have spent large portions of their life cultivating music as a means of survival, an arena of identity and community building, and a site for imagining alternative social formations. They imbue these musical creations and acts with knowledge and wisdom they have acquired through many trials and long processes of struggle and reckoning. Furthermore, survivors often make music in the interest of communicating these different experiences, sentiments, identities, and understandings, and often are actively interested in the kind of receptive and flexible audience that ethnomusicologists can be.

"Survivors' Music"

It is worth spending a moment to discuss the advantages, problems, and issues arising from the appellation "survivors' music." The word "survivor" and its analogues in other languages—*seizonsha* in Japanese, *saengjonja* in Korean, and others—are typically over-burdened in one way or another, variously inspiring shame, guilt, cinematic romanti-cism or liberal triumphalism. Often these positive and negative valences of the word are complexly intertwined. Nevertheless, naming the field of study "survivors' music" rather than "music and traumatic experience," "music and violence," or "music and conflict" seems preferable to me because it refuses to displace people from its center, and it refuses to reduce people and their music to experiences of trauma, violence, and conflict. I have been frustrated by this tendency in much of the scholarship on music and violence, most crystallized in Steve Goodman's fetishistic *Sonic Warfare* (2012). My partner Yukiko coined the term "survivors' music" in Korean (*saengjonja ui eumak*) in 2006, helping me come up with a name for a seminar that wouldn't essentialize people in this way.

My preference for "survivor" emerges from a Northeast Asian context in which many sufferers are deemed "victims," in which this victimhood is spectacularized in popular and political culture, and in which survivors are at times exploited for political ends. The turn toward "survivor" is a corrective to that tendency. That said, the study of "survivors' music" should not ignore or de-emphasize the importance of real victimization experi-enced by different people, or the centrality of the different concepts of victimization and "victim ideologies" that popular and political cultures evolve.

Another issue: the phrase "survivors' music" runs the risk of valorizing survivors and their expressive lives over those who have not survived. I believe it is possible to study survivors' music without doing this, however. Typically, the opposite is true, and the dead are valorized while survivors are viewed with suspicion or taken as walking monuments to the dead. The study of survivors' music seeks to re-establish a balance between the importance of history and historical losses, and the importance of living people.

I use the term to refer to people who have survived violence and traumatic experience, but also to refer to people who are currently enduring such experiences—people living through war, armed conflict, situations of domestic violence, and so on. Such people might not conventionally be called survivors, but it is important to remember that they, too, are engaged in the daily activity of surviving, and their music or musicality may be a crucial part of this effort. Many women worldwide, for instance, are such survivors, living with the constant threat of domestic and sexual violence.

Classical "survivors" are commonly supposed to have lived through something that is over; but it is important to acknowledge that traumatic experiences do not simply end—rather, they unfold over time, and rarely have clear endings. Furthermore, they are often accompanied by regimes of suppression and discrimination, as in the case of many survivors of sexual abuse, or the strategically forgotten victims of war and authoritarianism. Thus the work of survival is ongoing and often treacherous and difficult.

In sum, "survivors' music" is a complex and imperfect moniker, as perhaps all names are. The important thing is to proceed aware of, sympathetic to, and interested in the complexities and contradictions inherent in the name. To be attentive to these is not to split hairs in self-serving academic discussion; it is to strive to rightly orient one's moral and scholarly compass, and the moral compass of the political and social movements in which the study of survivors' music can play a part.

Key Issues

Ethics

There are many ways one might go about the study of survivors' music, and what follows are just some key issues that emerge through a consideration of work in the field. I have already discussed the focus on particular people, rather than music, or culture, or violence, or anything else. The first thing that this requires of a researcher, student, or educator interested in the study of survivors' music is profound thought about how to proceed in a way that is appropriate to one's subject position, that is frank and open about one's goals, that avoids causing harm at all costs, and that above all prioritizes the wishes and interests of survivors over particular scholarly objectives. This generally means that one does not go digging into painful aspects of people's lives unless by the will of survivors who wish to explore their experiences or let others know about them. There are often many publicly available documents that speak to these things already. In any case, we must take care not to violate survivors' privacy or expose them to recriminations and harm. This is not a sort of moral requirement, an "ethics" of scholarship and education that we must get out of the way prior to beginning work: it is rather an opportunity to create a method of scholarship or pedagogy that puts people in the center and prioritizes them over political, scholarly, or pedagogical aims. This has to be done by researchers, students, educators, and survivors together.[3]

But perhaps there are some basic principles, or guidelines. For one, one should attempt to demystify the "informant" and "researcher" relationship, and should base relationships with survivors along the lines of a culture-appropriate friendship between people of certain genders and ages. One should not conceive of research subjects as people one engages with for scholarly ends; rather, the ends are whatever emerges from the relationship. My collaborators and I build relationships fitfully, over long periods of time; and I do not let these lapse once some sort of scholarly goal has been accomplished. Surely this enduring relationship, and the empathy and understanding it produces, are greater gifts to life and knowledge than the conventional relationship between researcher and subject.

The self-importance, arrogance, and class prejudice that abound in scholarly cultures often take the form of bourgeois paternalism when scholarship is "applied." Avoiding this is an ethical issue, a matter of making scholarship about more than reinforcing positions of social power through the doing of "good works." As such, the study of survivors' music begins with the supposition that survivors are generally of more help to scholars and publics than the other way around, and that the student of survivors attempts to learn from survivors first, not to "help" them. In addition, there is a further step to take to avoid this paternalism: the study of survivors' music, a kind of scholarship turned to public good, should not be founded on an exoticized or fetishized notion of survivors as others whom "we" study and teach about. There are many survivors of traumatic experience and violence who are also scholars and activists. Silent Jane documents and probes the relationship between her synesthesia and her experience and memories of childhood sexual abuse in her "Beautiful Fragments of a Traumatic Memory: Synaesthesia, Sesame Street, and Hearing the Colors of an Abusive Past" (2006). Survivors' written narratives and testimonies, when they focus on musical activities or embody musical qualities, are also a precious part of the bibliography of survivors' music, and they, too, are scholars of survivors' music.

Aesthetics

A people-centered study of survivors' music often requires scholars and educators to for-sake evaluative criteria by which we distinguish between "good" and "bad" music, other than those which survivors themselves utilize in the process of making music useful and meaningful in their lives; rather, we are tasked to appreciate music as people make use of it. I was forced to overcome this instinct to aesthetic judgment in my work with many Korean elderly and middle-aged people who are fond of the sentimental Korean pop genre *teuroteu* (a Koreanization of [fox] "trot"). The genre grated against almost every aesthetic preference that I had inherited as a post-punk in late twentieth-century America. It was drippily sentimental; it was vigorously mass-produced; and it was popularized on recordings featuring only synthesized instruments accompanying the singing voice. As the genre overwhelmingly preferred by professional bus drivers in South Korea, it was the soundtrack to many a terrifying interstate bus ride. Furthermore, the genre jarred against my political sentiments, as it was a legacy of the assimilation of Japanese popular music to Korea during the Japanese colonial era (1910–1945). Yet, when survivors of Japanese military sexual slavery began to sing these songs for me, I realized that all of these evaluative criteria were useless to me; they offered no help in understanding how people make this music and make use of it in the daily work of getting by. That ingenuity, the stories that people told me about music, and the sounds of their voices singing these songs were fascinating and indeed profoundly beautiful.

A people-centered field like survivors' music studies must also not go in search of prepared notions of authenticity, or expect survivors to produce certain kinds of music that we believe appropriate to their experience. The point is to attempt an understanding of others' experience and expressive lives, not to animate caricatures of others we have encountered elsewhere. Yet I have heard, on many occasions, people ask survivors to sing and then stop them in the middle of their favorite songs to demand something older, something from the wartime, something of their own composition, something more Korean, something more serious or more sorrowful.

The expectations and demands of others are important because they are part of survivors' experience. But survivors do not often conform perfectly to these expectations. Beginning my fieldwork in South Korea with elderly survivors of the "comfort women" system, I expected to hear them sing songs from childhood and the wartime, and was routinely surprised to find many of them singing songs that were only a few years old. Learning and singing new songs is a way for profoundly marginalized people of whatever age to remain contemporary, and to maintain contact with mainstreams, real or imagined. Learning manifestly popular songs, or engaging in decidedly "mainstream" musical practices, is another way of participating in societies to which one has not been granted full membership. So, in the study of survivors' music, we must be ever willing to relinquish such prejudices against new music, against popular music, and so on.

A Practical Analytics

The study of survivors' music is a practical analytics of music in people's lives. This means that one inquires into the value—strategic, aesthetic, cultural, or social—of particular musical things and actions to particular people in particular settings. This means that a musical event is not interesting in and of itself, either as "great music" or as somehow representative of culture or historical experience. One is typically not interested in what musical behaviors and objects can tell us about culture as a whole, or in finding kinds of musical activity that definitively represent historical experiences of traumatic experience and violence. Experiences of violence and traumatic experience may promote certain kinds of solidarity that make generalizations about culture and experience tenable; but they are just as likely to disrupt social relationships and produce experiences of such singularity that scholarly generalization is not possible, or at least not interesting. We must acknowledge and appreciate this particularity at first if we are going to make our way back to the systematic connections that link people's experiences.

From this perspective, a piece of music, or a fragment of music, or a song or a fragment of song, performed by a survivor or group of survivors in a particular circumstance for a particular reason, is a cultural and historical treasure—it is not necessary that it should be a particular instance of a generic phenomenon. It is precious because it is part of the alchemy through which people survive and make life livable or worth living. In that way, it is as precious as any other great work of art.

It is most important to the people-centered study of survivors' music to consider musical events not primarily as pieces representative of culture or experience broadly, but as part of a survivor's daily life and personal history. Yi Okseon, a friend and survivor of the "comfort women" system, sang a song for me that illustrates this nicely. We were at a party in the summer of 2002 in the living room of the House of Sharing, a rest home for survivors of the "comfort woman."[4] Five survivors sat on the couches in places of honor; the rest of us—guests and staff—sat on the floor around a long table. One by one, people sang songs by way of self-introduction, moving around the circle in rough order of seniority. When the circle came to Yi Okseon, she stood up and sang her show-piece song,[5] the classic colonial-era pop ballad "Tear-Soaked Duman River" ("Nunmul jeojeun Dumangang"):

When I went to China at age sixteen[6] I crossed the Duman River, you know? I didn't realize that, and only afterwards I learned that I had crossed it. So that "Duman River" song, if I forget it I won't lose it, if I die I won't forget it. Because I was dragged away by Japanese across the Duman River . . .

In the blue waters of the Duman River
A boatman works the oars
In the flowed-away long ago a boat took my beloved
And left for somewhere
My beloved, for whom I long,
My beloved, for whom I long,
When will you come back?

The listeners began to clap pre-emptively, assuming she would stop after verse one, as many people do. But Yi Okseon pushed on to the final verse:

On a moonlit night the river's water
Catches in its throat, and it cries
This person who lost (her) beloved sighs.
. . . It left for somewhere . . .
My beloved, for whom I long,
My beloved, for whom I long,
When will you come back?

"Tear-Soaked Duman River" was written by composer Yi Si-u and lyricist Kim Yongho, and debuted by male vocalist Kim Jeonggu in 1938. Yi Si-u wrote the song in the 1930s, when he toured Southwestern Manchuria near the border with Korea, working for a theatrical company that was giving performances for the many Koreans in the region.

There is a widely told colloquial story of the origins of the song: one evening Yi Si-u was staying at an inn, and sat up in the night listening to a woman sobbing in the next room. The next day he asked the innkeeper about her. Her husband, a friend of the innkeeper, was an anti-colonial independence fighter (dongnip-gun), who had been captured by Japanese forces. She crossed the Duman River to seek him out, but by the time she had arrived at the prison to which he had been taken, he had already been executed. The night Yi Si-u had heard her crying had been the evening of her husband's birthday. She had made a small memorial altar to him, and was drinking before it and mourning his death.

Over the course of the colonial era (1910–1945) the song became famous for its political subtexts, which were veiled in obscurity and thus protected from colonial censors. As postcolonial South Korea cultivated both its popular music industry and its national consciousness, founded in the wounds of the colonial era, the song became one of the most famous popular songs in the land, playing a large part in the production of that national consciousness. The woman's tears drop into the Duman River on behalf of an entire people that had lost its national sovereignty, seamlessly welding private grief and a national-cultural sense of woundedness.

Many accounts of Yi Okseon's performance might end here, with the general significance of the song to Korean colonial history, reducing Yi Okseon's experience to an extreme instance of that. But the study of survivors' music privileges the singer, not the song. We ask what the song might mean to Yi Okseon; how she altered it to make it her own; how it bridges the gulf between her experiences and popular culture; how she herself changed in the process of taking it to heart; and why she sang it on this particular occasion for this particular group. In order to discover these things, we must situate the song and the performance in Yi Okseon's life history.

Yi Okseon was born in 1927 in the southeastern port city Busan, the second of six siblings, to a poor family. She wanted to go to school, but the family couldn't afford tuition. When she was 13, a small drinking house recruited her for work, promising to send her to school in exchange. The proprietor, however, took her on as a servant and made no signs of sending her to school. Over the next two years she moved around between drinking houses, often asked to pour drinks and keep customers company, narrowly avoiding being pressed into sex work. All the same, she was glad to be making money to send home.

One day in 1942, while on her way home from a department store, Yi Okseon was abducted by a burly man and put in a truck with other girls in the back. Guarded by a Korean and a Japanese, the girls were loaded into a train. After several days' journey they crossed the Duman River and were offloaded, on July 23, at Yanji, a Manchurian town close to the border. She was raped on the night of her arrival. For the next three years she was held against her will and forced to provide sexual services to soldiers, mostly from the nearby air force base—seven or eight men on weekdays and upwards of 50 on the weekends.

On that night in 2002 when Yi Okseon sang "Tear-Soaked Duman River" at the House of Sharing, she related how she cried for the young self that was taken across that river. So the song records a traumatic wound and a self split in two. One half has been taken; the other half sits on the riverbank and cries for the lost self. So Yi Okseon's version of the song differs dramatically from the original, about a woman by the banks of the Duman River, or an unnamed "I," or the "we" of postcolonial Korean nationhood longing for a lost love object. She has lost a part of herself, and lives in two places at once. Yi Okseon often speaks and sings to me about feeling like a foreigner in South Korea, and about feeling that her heart lives in northeast China. So that feeling of a split self stuck with her throughout her life, finding expression in many of her songs and stories. Yet in adopting this song as her own, she related her experience to the popular story, making her traumatic experience intelligible to others in the room and elsewhere throughout South Korea, and claiming a place for herself in the popular story of the colonial and wartime experience.

Our consideration of Yi Okseon's performance of "Duman River" might easily stop at the end of the war—it is quite typical for scholarly and public interest in the lives of survivors to extend only as far as the so-called end of their infamous traumatic experiences.[7] But the experience of Japanese military sexual slavery was only a part, if the most terrible part, of Yi Okseon's saga of suffering and survival, and as such goes only partway to explaining the significance of the song for her. Three years after her abduction the war ended, and both Manchuria and Korea were liberated from colonial rule. She, however, had no funds to return to Korea. While wandering destitute in Yanji city, she met a Korean man whom she had met previously at the air force base. "I took hold of him and begged him to open a liferoad for me" (to secure my livelihood), she reported in a published testimony (Kang, 2000: 174). They married; but he was denounced for his high status in the pre-liberation Volunteer Labor Corps, and escaped south across the Duman River into Korea. She waited for 10 years for him to return, but he never came back. The river thus had another significance for Yi Okseon, for like the independence fighter in the song, her husband had gone away across the river, never to return.

After that long wait she remarried at the urging of her parents-in-law. In the late 1990s she made contact with a South Korean organization searching for survivors of the "comfort women" system, and relocated to the House of Sharing in 2000, after the death of her second husband. Thus the song and the Duman River obtained yet another sense for her, as she returned to a land that she hardly recognized after her 58-year absence. The song tells us a long story of loss and dislocation—from self, home, and loved ones. But this story is nonetheless Yi Okseon's, a means of making a coherence of self across a tumultuous life. The song is also a means of connecting Yi Okseon's personal history to Korean popular culture and society. For these and other reasons, it has been a tool for her in her survival. Together with many of her other songs, it also documents her long reflection about the nature of home and the passing of time. She told me that although she had returned to the land of her birth, she felt like she had "returned to a foreign country." She had family in northeast China; and she had changed; and home had changed. This is something that diasporic people know about the nature of "home" that people who have never left often never recognize.

Yi Okseon's twisting "Duman River" story is an opportunity for us to learn about the experience of diaspora, the nature of loss, and the nature of identity. As a canonical popular song about displacement, it reveals a paradox of South Korean and many other national identities—a quintessential "Korean" experience is an experience of marginalization. National identity depends on outsiders like Yi Okseon to embody the spirit of modern Korean experience, while it denies them full social membership and considers them broken—speaking imperfect Korean as returnees from abroad, not fully grounded in culture, behind the times. But Yi Okseon, in the coherence of her narrative of fragmentation and loss, is actually several steps ahead of most Koreans in the process of understanding what it means to change in the process of becoming yourself, what transformations the passage of time works on the places we are from, and the scars and traces that the wounds of time's passing leave behind.

If we forget about all of this, and essentialize survivors and their music by constantly referring back to the particular experiences that we consider to have been of paramount importance in their lives, we miss out on the stories of their survival in the wake of such experiences. We also lose out on the opportunity to learn of their wisdom and their hard-won philosophies of life.

Interpretation and Collaboration

This take on Yi Okseon's "Duman River" is of course my interpretation, arrived at over 10 years of talking with her about life and music. What is the place of interpretation in the study of survivors' music? Might it not be better to "let the recordings speak for themselves?" By now in ethnomusicology we know that even the seemingly simple act of recording involves a complex of interpretive moves. One decides what to record, thereby deciding how experience is to be divided and recorded, and what parts of experience are important. The recordist selects how to record these, and how to contextualize that thing that she has newly made or inflected. This is true for any kind of recording: sound recording, writing, drawing, film, photography, and so on.

Since recordings of whatever kind are already interpretations, there is no use in trying to keep one's interpretation out of it; rather, it is important to understand one's interpretive moves and their significance, and to involve others in these processes of interpretation. In the case of survivors' music, one can attempt to understand the interpretive moves of survivors, what they consider important about music and the musical and their relation to it; then one can attempt to document these as faithfully as possible, using technology to imitate these interpretive moves, such as making sound recordings when people habitually close their eyes when singing. When music is accompanied by significant movement, this is because someone has decided that they go together, or conceives of them as a single activity, and the recordist can choose an audiovisual medium. One can then engage in dialogue with others about the significance of these things, listen or watch recordings together, and so on.

Songs and other kinds of music are already, in many ways, recordings of different kinds of experience, places, times, and other things. Many survivors document their own musical lives, and these documents—stories, recordings, illustrations, writing—are of paramount importance. The complex process of making ethnographic inscriptions, recordings, and documents is something that survivors and ethnographers do together, however much or little they acknowledge it. It is a process rife with the most interesting possibilities. This takes time, an ongoing relationship of discovery and making. With Yi Okseon and others, this has involved my recording songs in many different contexts; listening to and discussing recordings together; working together to choose favorite renditions for scholarly examination or public exhibition; and forging relationships that provide a crucial context for interpretation.

Performance

The narrative of Yi Okseon's "Duman River" that I have presented here begins in the present, and works its way back to it along the swath of her life experience. We return to the living room of the House of Sharing to consider another key issue in the study of survivors' music that this song demonstrates. Yi Okseon's "Tear-Soaked Duman River" is a *performance*, at a particular time for particular people. She sang for an audience of political activists and social workers—the staff of the House of Sharing and a cohort surrounding a group of Japanese lawyers who were helping with the struggle for reparations and apology for the "comfort women" in the Japanese legal system. In speech, she related the song only to her experience of abduction during the war. Yi Okseon was a compelling, savvy activist whose performances of wartime victimization were utterly legitimized by experience. She saved other parts of the story for other, equally sincere and equally performative contexts. Considering survivors' music as performance does not mean questioning its authenticity or sincerity; rather, we attend to the social value and the significance of the different kinds of performances, and survivors' performative competence and social power, which they demonstrate. At other times, as she spoke about the song and other ruminations on love, loss, and the nature of home, she related her experience of dislocation to mine, as a foreigner in South Korea. While the experiences are of course dramatically different, the act of relating was a way that she made a connection between us. It was an example of her skill as an educator, building a bridge to teach me about her experiences.

The "Musical"

From the example I have given above, one might begin to think that the study of survivors' music is principally about the search for and interpretation of *pieces* that shed light on the past and survivors' experiences. To the extent that one looks for such musical *things*, as in the discussion of Yi Okseon's "Duman River," one must attend to how they are brought to bear on life and presented in performance. Nonetheless, it is also important not to neglect the "thingness" that people attribute to music—the way they come to possess it, treasure it, use it, exchange it, and so on—which is crucial in order to understand how music is a resource for survival, and to understand people's beliefs about music and its power. Musical talismans can be very important to survivors, whether they be physical objects, songs, or memories. Yi Okseon's song is one example, which she said she would remember beyond death. Another is Daran Kravanh's narrative of music and its role in his survival of the Khmer Rouge period (Lafreniere, 2000): Kravanh relates finding an accordion in the woods and carrying it through his time in the labor camps and the killing fields, and credits the accordion on several occasions with saving his life.

Nonetheless, from Yi Okseon's song and Daran Kravanh's story it is clear that "music" and its material culture are not the sole objects of the study of survivors' music. For one, the things people say about music are also crucial. But the study of survivors' music goes further than this, beyond the duality of music and speech, beyond a world in which there is *music and everything else*, or *music and its context*. In order that the study of survivors' music not displace people from the center of the inquiry and set an artificial notion of music in their place, in order that it not exclude survivors who are not professionally or conventionally musical, and in order that one can understand the important gray areas and connections between different arenas of survivors' expression, the study of survivors' music can fruitfully embrace a generous notion of the "musical."[8] One can pay attention to the musical qualities of speech, writing, sound, silence, and so on, and of the continuities that connect different expressive spheres and sounding to the realm of music. The connectivity between expressive spheres is the key to understanding the practical value of music in survivors' lives. It is the mechanism by which the kinds of voice, identity, resilience, expressive power, and expressive content that people cultivate in music find their way into other realms of life, and vice versa, like the system by which electricity circulates through and out of a batteries. In addition, spaces between can be powerful and productive expressive spaces in themselves.

This is one of the basic perspectives of sociomusicology, although practitioners of that branch of our field, with notable exceptions,[9] tend to focus on particular relations between expressive arenas—particularly music and speech, or music and language, rather than taking the global view that I feel is so essential to the study of survivors' music. The way that people live in silence, or live with sounds and noise; the ways these silences, sounds, and noises produce music, or speech, or written narrative, or other things, in whatever order—the relative connectivity of expressive realms and the content of the interstitial spaces between them tells us about the usefulness of music in human life. In survivors' lives, silence and noise are especially important categories, for survivors often live in political and social conditions that silence them or deem their expressions—linguistic and musical—to be noise.

As such, the study of survivors' music can benefit from carefully listening to the gray areas that connect music to other sound arenas of life for survivors. This is one of the basic perspectives of my book (2012),[10] which provides numerous examples. In my current project on Korean radiation sufferers, I have moved yet further in this direction. Han Jeongsun, a second-generation Korean victim of the atomic bombing of Hiroshima, provides a powerful example of the importance of thinking broadly about "the musical" in order to understand the significance of music in survivors' lives.

One of Han Jeongsun's songs about walking provides the epigraph that begins this article. The song is "Gochu" (pepper), debuted by pop star Yu Ji-na in 2009. In the song the protagonist walks across mountain passes, always finding yet another steep incline before her. The mountain pass is a popular metaphor for struggle in Korea, as it is elsewhere. Since the age of 30, Han Jeongsun has suffered from avascular necrosis of the femoral head—a condition in which interrupted blood flow causes cellular death of bone components in the tops of her femurs. Her condition has thus far required four hip replacements and other sorts of major reconstructive surgery. She told me that songs about walking have literal significance for her due to the trouble she has walking. The text of the song emphasizes this difficulty; but the dotted 4/4 rhythm of the piece lilts along with an effortlessness and energy that makes the endless walking artful and seems to make it possible. When Han Jeongsun sings "Pepper," she often dances, even when sitting down, shifting her weight from side to side and moving her arms alternately up and down in the improvisatory manner of Korean traditional dance. She also sings while walking, borrowing the rhythm of music for daily movement.

My current work with Han Jeongsun connects her songs, her dancing, her walking, and her political testimony by tracing themes and rhythms across her expressive life. We take walks together; she infuses her political testimony with discussions of her ailment and of her difficulty in walking. She sings and dances to songs of walking before and after activist meetings. In the study, I aim to show how in this way she weaves and holds a workable sense of self and world together, draws inspiration from music for her daily physical struggles, and draws on popular culture to find a voice and to claim political rights for herself and her fellow radiation sufferers.

There are a number of advantages to this broad perspective on "the musical." For one, it means that anyone interested in doing fieldwork or reading about survivors' music does not need to wait for people to participate in formal music-making. The ethnographer—whether working with people or historical documents—gets right to work, trying to get a sense of survivors' expressive universes and the techniques, qualities, and thematic material that link formal music-making or the musical facets of daily life and expression with the rest of their expressive lives. This entire network could be thought of as the changeable circulatory system of "the musical" in survivors' everyday life. As we assemble the circuitry, we get a sense of what the musical is good for—what sort of stories people use it to tell, what sort of strength people draw from it and competences they cultivate within it, and what sorts of knowledge it embodies.

I prefer the broad approach to the musical not only because it gets at the core significance of music in survivors' lives, but also because it allows me to make use of manifold documentary resources not focused on music. While primary research and recording are important, there is often a tremendous amount of documentation of survivors' lives already, and within these we find countless evidences of the importance of "the musical" in survivors' lives. This means that plentiful materials are already available, which one can make use of without engaging in firsthand field research. This means that the people who engage in the study of survivors' music need not be scholars with leave and resources to conduct ethnographic research. There are documentaries, published testimonies, and survivors' narratives, recorded collections, and scholarly works that one can consult in search of the musical in survivors' lives. Many of these materials are available online, in university libraries, and for purchase. Sometimes it may feel like searching for a needle in a haystack; but because of the many uses of music and the deep presence of the musical throughout expressive life, usually one does not have to look very long or very hard.

Examples of this are readily available. Claude Lanzmann's *Shoah* (1985), an almost 10-hour-long film documentary about the Holocaust of Jews and others in mid-twentieth century Europe, follows its long, scrolling opening text with survivor Simon Srebnik singing several songs and discussing them. The US Library of Congress website "Voices from the Days of Slavery,"[11] a collection of nearly seven hours of recorded interviews with survivors of the enslavement of African Americans, includes a hyper-linked index of song titles.

Most importantly, the broad approach to "the musical" in survivors' lives also allows the student of survivors' music to work with almost anyone, not only those survivors who have a particular memory for, interest in, or talent for music. We find out about the fragments of song or sound in talk and testimony. We talk about music and sound that survivors encounter in the course of their daily lives. We can even include people who never "make music" themselves or are averse to music for various reasons. Some survivors had their voices partly or completely taken from them—as in the case of the many victims of nuclear radiation exposure who have had to undergo thyroid surgery, or in the case of the severely psychologically traumatized. Some have had experiences of the coercive power of music—for instance, the many women in sex-and-entertainment cultures the world over who are expected to sing or dance or otherwise perform for patrons—and may have forsaken music for this reason, or because they have decided that it is sinful. Often these silences are just as telling about the nature of experience and the place of music in social life as any recordings of musical performance that we might make.

Redemptive Narratives

One might reasonably expect that the study of survivors' music privileges the redemptive powers of music, its power as means of resisting social domination, countering or diffusing violence, healing and overcoming trauma and hardship. Indeed, there is much to learn from survivors about how to survive, and music, at times, is useful in this process in many ways. It can be a means of making or maintaining senses of self and social connectedness; of finding things to live for; of connecting with society from the margins; of consolidating social groups that can resist different kinds of violence and oppression; of communicating in secret; of securing the sympathy of one's tormenters; and of securing the financial means of life, among other uses. But it is also profoundly important to look beyond such notions of the redemptive power of music, just as ethnomusicology has found it important to look beyond beliefs in the transcendental power of music that often hold sway in Western art music circles.

The newly emerging study of music and violence, which has its own special interest group in the Society for Ethnomusicology, is founded on this idea. Shirli Gilbert gives the most powerful scholarly statement of this that I have yet found, in her introduction to *Music in the Holocaust* (2005), calling for a re-evaluation of the place of music in the Holocaust that accounts for its role in manufacturing obedience and inspiring Nazi terror. Survivor Szymon Laks, in his memoir *Music of Another World* (1979), about his term as a member and conductor of the Auschwitz II men's orchestra, explains the role of music in naturalizing suffering, of encouraging fatal conformism, and other pernicious uses of music in concentration camp life. To this we could add the role of music in consolidating social groups which then perpetrate violence against excluded others; the (related) ways in which music helps to naturalize notions of national, racial, gendered, sexual and other sorts of superiority; the role of music in torture (Cusick, 2008; Pettan, 1998); the uses of music in the performance of domination and submission (Pilzer, 2014), and others. And beyond this dark side, upon close examination many uses of music in survivors' experience fill us with neither hope nor despair, and are as ambivalent as so many other things in life.

Leaving people in the center of the study of survivors' music, we set aside these beliefs in the moral goodness or badness of music, just as we forsake our own aesthetic judgments about it, and instead ask how survivors think and feel about music, and how they are musical in the pursuit of life. The result is a much subtler understanding of the role of music in situations of social violence and in survivors' lives. Laks relates in his memoir of Auschwitz II (1979: 65–66):

> One evening. . . I found lying on the ground a crumpled and greasy piece of paper covered with writing that attracted my attention. I picked it up and, after returning to the barracks, unfolded it carefully so as not to tear it. It smelled of herring and God only knows what else. But it was music! Only the melody, written by hand but very legibly, without harmonization, without accompaniment. The title at the top read *Three Warsaw Polonaises of the 18th Century, author: Anonymous.*
>
> I washed the precious document as carefully as possible and hung it up in a discrete place in the music room to dry overnight. During the next few days I harmonized all three polonaises and wrote out the parts for a small chamber ensemble, after which we began to practice the pieces in the barracks when conditions allowed. The pieces turned out to be true pearls of eighteenth-century Polish music.
>
> Some of my Polish colleagues congratulated me on this deed, regarding it as an act of the resistance movement. This surprised me a little, since for me this was an ordinary musical satisfaction, heightened by the Polishness of the music to be sure, but I did not see how its being played in secret could have harmed the Germans or had an effect on the war. In any case, if this episode can be regarded as a sign of resistance, it is the only one I can boast of during a rather long stay in Birkenau. The rest was a struggle for survival.

Laks's colleagues are hungry for tokens of resistance; but he is not so sure. He has seen how the most sincere and devout appreciation of music can live within the most monstrous of men; and is well aware that he survived when so many others did not because of a musical ability that it was his luck to possess, but did not make him any worthier of life than they were.

This is a profoundly complex account of the social power of music in the face of suffering. Laks suspects the redemptive narrative, but his "ordinary musical satisfaction" is no small thing. This moment is one of the few in his narrative when he encounters music that reminds him of his life as a concert pianist and conductor in prewar Warsaw, and of the glories of Western art music. It is a moment that recalls a deep belief in higher things. It is a glimmer of the glories of music that precede and follow Laks's wartime narrative, and which were so important to him in rescuing his life from its Holocaust; but he is reluctant to admit it to the nightmare world that he survived.

Daran Kravanh, in his narrative of playing the accordion and surviving the Khmer Rouge period, relates:

> I cannot tell you how or why I survived; I do not know myself. It is like this: love and music and memory and invisible hands, and something that comes out of the society of the living and the dead, for which there are no words.
> Yes, music, the power within my accordion's voice, saved my life and, in turn, the lives of others.

(Lafreniere, 2000: 3)

So while we are obliged to look beyond redemptive narratives in the appreciation of music in survivors' lives, we must at once be capable of looking beyond the aura of suspicion that surrounds beliefs in the transcendental or redemptive powers of music. These beliefs are held by many people living through violence and traumatic experience or living with the consequences of such experiences, and they form the contexts of many survivors' encounters with music. The study of survivors' music takes these beliefs seriously, seeking to understand their power and their usefulness, while recognizing that there are many stories where such beliefs are nowhere to be found.

Advocacy and Activism

The study of survivors' music, as I have outlined it, attempts to put the interests of survivors first over scholarly arguments or goals. This principle leads us naturally to another set of questions concerning advocacy and activism.

First, is this study advocacy? This is an open question. I have put forward my preference for thinking about the study of survivors' music as a practice of listening, documentation, and learning over political action; but there is an implicit politics in my choice of whom to listen to. More often than not, I choose the underprivileged, marginalized, and ignored, and advocate for the importance of their points of view. I have attempted to do this through writing, teaching, public presentations, and the exhibition of recordings (see below).

Another, related question: Is the study of survivors' music activism? I think the study of survivors' music should seek understanding and prioritize the best interests of survivors, whether or not this understanding or those interests are congenial to political movements; to that extent it is its own kind of activism, of the sort that Svanibor Pettan advocates: the use of ethnomusicological knowledge and understanding "for the betterment of humanity" (2010: 90). Prioritizing the wishes and interests of survivors is not an abstract or legal matter of intellectual property, but of trying to do right by others and ourselves; and it is a political act of the utmost importance, and most certainly a form of activism. But it is a kind of activism that may lead the scholar of survivors' music to guard her autonomy from movements and organizations, while often sharing many sympathies with them and working together.

It is also possible to look at the question of activism from another perspective. Claims that one kind of ethnomusicological scholarship or another are activism run the risk of overlooking the ways in which the people we study engage in different kinds of activism. The survivors of the "comfort women" system and the nuclear bombing of Japan are often multiply engaged as activists, often making political statements in speech or song, often taking to stages and media platforms to testify to their experiences and advocate for social groups. One can learn from survivors about how they go about expressing themselves politically, organizing (or not organizing) into movements, cultivating movement consciousnesses, and so on, and why.

We can also listen to testimony and observe activist culture with an ear for the imprint of the musical. Han Jeongsun's testimonies about walking and living with radiation-related disability are one example of this, as an example of the place the musical facets of life can have in helping survivors to cultivate political voices, and the ways that the content of personal musical expression can become part of political discourse. We can listen to survivors' explicitly musical activities during testimony, or musical presentations meant to be kinds of action and testimony in political spheres or preparatory to such action. The fact that so many Korean survivors of the "comfort women" system sing or reference music during testimony (see Howard, 1995) is what motivated me to study their musical lives in the first place.

One such woman whom I came to know quite well is Yi Yongsu. In her testimony, she relates how at 16 years old she was taken from Daegu by a Japanese businessman and placed on a boat for Taiwan, where she was raped repeatedly by soldiers and others. She was taken to Hsinchu, about 60 kilometers southwest of Taipei, where she was placed in a "comfort station," a military sex camp. The camp was near an air force airport that served as a base for kamikaze pilots. For the next eight months, she was imprisoned and forced to have sex with soldiers, in months which saw a dramatic increase in the number of suicide missions as the war effort turned in the Allies' favor and the Japanese became increasingly desperate. One of these pilots came to visit her many times.

One day he told her that he was leaving for his mission, and wouldn't be coming back. He had brought all of his toiletries with him and gave them to her as a present. He said that he had gotten a venereal disease from her, and he would take this to his grave as a precious gift. Finally, he taught her a song. She sang this song often in testimony; and she related it to me at her home in Daegu in 2004.

That soldier, he was an officer, when he was going away to die, he taught me a song:

> *I take off with courage, leaving Taiwan behind,*
> *Riding and rising above waves of gold and silver clouds.*

There is no one to see me off,
And this little one is the only one who cries for me.
I take off with courage, leaving Shinchiku behind,
Riding and rising above waves of gold and silver clouds.
There is no one to see me off,
And the only one who cries for me is Toshiko.
He gave me the name Toshiko.

The song was "Hikokinori no uta" (Song of the Pilot), a Japanese military song (*gunka*) associated with his particular squadron of kamikaze pilots. He had changed the words, adding his own place of departure and putting in the Japanese nickname he had given her. I discuss this song as part of her wartime experience in detail elsewhere (Pilzer, 2014).

As Yi Yongsu has told her story countless times to the expectant South Korean public and others, and as activists in the "comfort women grandmothers movement" have encouraged the women to standardize their stories of sexual slavery for important legal reasons, her story has become quite formalized. In this process, her "Song of the Pilot" song often has an honored place, dividing the testimony in half. It arrests the flow of time and zooms into that moment, thus becoming the dramatic high point of the testimony.

It is a mechanism of transport; but it is also a disciplined traumatic memory. It is a scene like the disembodied scenes that characterize traumatic memory, but one that Yi Yongsu has taken hold of and placed into a narrative frame in a broad process of self-making. Listening to survivors sing in testimony can allow us to see the artistry by which they put their lives back together and give their lives continuity.

Yi Yongsu explained that she sang this song in testimony because she had discovered, through its lyrics, that she was in Taiwan. Listeners to her testimony realized at this moment that prior to learning this song she did not know where she was. But in recent years she began to add a different reason, as she became more secure in her place in the movement and in society. She said that the man had helped her by giving her hope. Certainly this hope was complicated by the fact that he had such tremendous power over her, and many in the South Korean public and elsewhere would frown at this deeply problematic relation of affection. But nonetheless the relationship and its song played a role in her survival, and became a cornerstone of Yi Yongsu's postwar project of self-reconstruction. And as she became more and more entrenched as a star of the "comfort women" movement, she showed more and more of this sentimental core of her story to South Korean public culture. In interviews and testimonies she began to speak of how important this officer had been to her and of her fruitless attempts to find him in the postwar period, while stating, for the record, that she did not love him. So music in testimony can allow survivors to express unwelcome but important feelings and experiences in public and politicized forums, and can allow deep listeners to hear them and share in them. Of course, by listening to music in testimony, we can also learn about the role of music in projects of social domination and in traumatic memory; a recent article of mine addresses the former issue in the context of the "comfort women" system (Pilzer, 2014). And there are many more things we can learn from listening to music in the context of testimony.

RECORDING AND DOCUMENTING
SURVIVORS' MUSIC

When thinking of the many tragedies of modern life, from genocides, to wars, to sexual and domestic violence—one tends to think, first and foremost, of images or texts. Many have noted that the visual means of representing the Holocaust of European Jewry have long consisted of a codified type of image (Hirsch, 2001: 7, Young, 1988: 163), and this is true for the representation of South Korean survivors of Japanese military sexual slavery as well. In a seminal article in the anthropology of social suffering, Arthur and Joan Kleinman point to the predominance of images in the representation of suffering worldwide, and describe the techniques of their appropriation and commodification (1997). Survivors' narratives are second most popular in the representation of modern atrocities, and are often turned into films—and thus into moving images. Written narratives benefit from the cultural cache accorded to the written word, even taking on a sort of sacral quality.

This dominance of the textual and the visual adds urgency to the study of survivors' music. Many survivors pass from this world without having their voices recorded at all. So the act of recording someone's voice—whether casually speaking, singing, or giving testimony—is very powerful and important. Despite the artificial severing of the world that sound recording accomplishes, the attention it draws to the voice is one reason that it is still an important means of documentation, although other forms are equally important and useful.

It is standard in ethnomusicology to obtain permission from subjects before making recordings. Often this permission is obtained in spoken or written word only, and subjects have very little idea of what will actually be done with the recordings. It is preferable, in the study of survivors' music and in the field generally, to maintain ongoing conversations about the recording process, to listen to recordings together, and to decide together on preferred ones. One must delete recordings when survivors request that this be done. One might think of the process as similar to paging through the photographs on a digital camera, getting rid of some and keeping others, making the process a transparent one and a kind of play.

ARCHIVING, ACCESSING, AND EXHIBITING
SURVIVORS' MUSIC

Once one has made documents of survivors' expressive lives, one must work out what to do with such things. How should one archive and govern access to archives? Not only libraries, but also books, websites, personal collections, and many other things can be archives.

In order for documentary materials to contribute to human knowledge and under-standing, they must be accessible; but the degree of this accessibility should be governed above all by what survivors want—how much they want their voices, names, stories, and music publicized, and in what form. First, recordings should be accessible to survivors themselves should they want them. One also may need to consider any organizations one has worked with in the production of such documents, which may expect copies or may have made this a condition of their assistance. Such organizations may or may not make suitable places for an archive.

One could draw up a form that survivors sign, giving you unilateral permission to use audio visual materials, stories, and so on, in certain ways. However, in general these things should be worked out on a case-by-case basis, because people's feelings about these things and their personal circumstances change over time. Ethically speaking, open access is the most complicated kind of accessibility, because subsequent uses of material become impossible to trace and to square with survivors' wishes.

Of course, since writing is another kind of recording, books and articles are archived as well, and one must decide on what terms this is to happen and how accessible they are to be. Open-access and online journals, which don't require membership in elite ac-ademic institutions, seem preferable to me; and presses capable of making inexpensive books seem an obvious choice. The things one has to do to make a book inexpensive—limiting the number of color images, for instance—can be made up for these days by websites where color images and other materials can be made available. Accompanying websites or online publication make associated recordings available for no extra cost to the reader. Above all, it seems preposterous—no matter how much one is worried about one's tenure case, scholarly reputation, and so on—to publish a book on survivors' music with an elite academic press that favors small pressings of expensive hardback books that only university libraries and the affluent will buy. There are far too many examples of this in the small literature focused on survivors' music.

Another possibility for creating ways of accessing work is exhibition. In the summer of 2004, photographer Yajima Tsukasa and I opened an exhibition of sound recordings and portrait photographs of Korean "comfort women" survivors in one of Seoul's gal-lery districts. It went on to be exhibited throughout South Korea and in Germany. The exhibition was sponsored by the House of Sharing and by the South Korean Ministry of Culture, Sports, and Tourism. At the exhibition, listeners stood before 160 cm-squared portraits of 12 current and former residents of the House of Sharing, listening to recordings of each of the women on headphones. There were two sets of headphones so that people could listen together. I used field recordings, selecting short audio examples excerpted from a wealth of recordings of each survivors' expressive life. I worked with each woman to choose the song she would prefer to have exhibited. Similarly, the women had been asked by the photographer to choose whatever clothing and makeup they liked for their portraits, although they were not invited to choose one photograph over another.

The exhibition ran for two weeks surrounding August 15, Korean Independence Day: the gallery director wanted to take advantage of the upsurge in nationalism and interest in national issues surrounding this day. So visitors to the exhibition were already conditioned to encounter the women as symbols of national suffering. Political contexts of different scales and distributions will frame one's attempt to exhibit survivors' music—in this case, a South Korean national context of the "comfort women" issue and its associated movements.

I attempted to intervene in this political landscape by challenging the overwhelming perception of these survivors as symbols of victimization, creating a space for listeners to encounter them as grandmothers, as women, as philosophers, as talented storytellers and singers. There were songs from the wartime, but there were also prayers, joke songs, and philosophical musings—on life, on the passage of time, and on making peace with suffering and transience. Despite this, however, the symbolic power of the "comfort women" issue in public culture made it very difficult to listen with fresh ears. One man in late middle age told me: "These are not songs. . . they are the sounds of crying." One young girl, in a fever of militarized emotion, wrote in our comment book: "We've really got to do to [Japan] just as they've done unto us!" Another young girl wrote, "This made me think that we've really got to have a war with those Japanese bastards!" The language of victimization and of masculinized militaristic response—the ideological complex of postwar South Korean national identity—rose to the surface and swept away the laughter, the peace, everything but the galvanizing tears and anger.

This experience made me deeply skeptical of the utility of exhibiting survivors' music; one will typically contend with a prefigured political context that governs how people listen, and it will almost always overwhelm authorial intention, the particularity of survivors' voices, the exceptions to popular canonizations of survivors' stories, and so on. However, if the sounds only reach a few people, this is nonetheless of immense importance, for each person carries within them a universe of possibilities. One girl wrote:

Ah~
Grandmother(s)[12]~
Now refreshing Autumn has come and
Let's all of us hold hands
*And go for an Autumn stroll ^_^*
And let's also go
*To look at the changing leaves ^_^*

At the opening of the exhibition the majority of the women were there, and stood listening to their songs, singing along, admiring or critiquing their photographs, and answering questions from reporters and others. Typically audiences listen to survivors to hear of their victimization. But in this instance they were listened to for their speaking and singing voices, their songs and stories; no matter how much the public still rendered those songs as the sounds of crying, the survivors themselves felt a different sort of validation in public, the public recognition of songs they had made their own and selves they had made over the long years of their lives.

Yi Yongnyeo's recording for the exhibition was a medley of pop songs, which she had sung at a New Year's party at the House of Sharing. With Bae Chunhui's *janggo* (hour-glass drum) accompaniment, Yi Yongnyeo had blended three verses from three separate songs—Son Panim's 1955 "Cry, Guitar String," about wandering in a foreign land; another song none of us could identify, which might have been of her own invention; and "Jal itgeora Busan-hang" (Take Care, Busan Harbor), a 1970 pop classic. In the first piece she sang about drifting in a foreign land in search of lost love. In the second piece she sang from a woman's perspective, asking a departing man why he had fooled her into love. In the last verse she assumed the male perspective, bidding a number of women well as he takes his leave in Busan Harbor. Yi Yongnyeo transformed the song, which in its original version bid a fond, wistful, but jovial and inevitable farewell to the man's female conquests, into the bottomless lament of a woman who recalls the words of the one who left. One of the women to whom the man bids farewell is a Miss Lee (Yi). Yi Yongnyeo thus found herself in the song and cried as she sang in her cigarette-scarred voice.

At the exhibition, Yi Yongnyeo listened to her song and sang along, crying, then slowly starting to laugh; when the song was over she walked briskly to the center of the exhibition space and began to sing her breezy version of "The Ballad of the Travelling Entertainer" ("Changbu Taryeong"), which exhorts us: "Life is a one night's spring dream, so we've got to have fun while we can." Media photographers and television crews captured images of Yi Yongnyeo singing, dancing, and laughing in the face of her victimization; not all of them only used the images of her in tears.

Attempts at exhibiting survivors' music must face the general complexity of displaying music and people, and the difficulty of intervening in overdetermined political contexts. They are fraught with ethical quandries and dangers, and can easily become the kind of "conscience pornography" that the Kleinmans describe in their powerful article on images of social suffering (1997). In general, this means that longer and more complex media, such as books and documentary films, are preferable, in the interests of diffusing sensationalism, making sustained political interventions, and cultivating respectful and productive relationships with survivors. This means a step away from the streamlining of ethnographic material for political activism. Again, though, this is itself a kind of activism—on behalf of the people concerned, and on behalf of mutual empathy and understanding.

Teaching Survivors' Music

While most presentations of survivors' music are intended to be educational, class-room and other person-to-person teaching about survivors' music has its own set of challenges and opportunities. Smaller classes are preferable to large lecture courses, because they allow the instructor to stay in touch with students and field their often dramatic reactions to the material: no matter how much one privileges survivors, their music, and their ingenuity over the calamities that they survive in such a course, many students nonetheless encounter many new and shocking social realities, and react in a variety of ways. Some students associate the survivors' experiences they encounter with their own experiences of violence and trauma. Bearing this in mind, it is important to make information available to students about counseling services and emergency resources available to them through their school, government, and nonprofit organizations.

A course on survivors' music may be built around case studies, but there are a number of framing issues to bear in mind and focus in on. There is the fundamental issue of how to listen to survivors' music, and the question of witnessing—for survivors' musical performance is often a kind of witnessing, and the listening subject is also a witness. This topic provides an opportunity for thinking about the politics of listening, the act of witnessing as a recuperative act, and also about traumatic transference and secondary trauma.

Another core issue is the role of music in social domination and resistance. Shirli Gilbert's introduction to *Music in the Holocaust*, which, as discussed above, problematizes notions of the redemptive power of music, is quite useful as a discussion piece here. So, too, is James Scott's *Domination and the Arts of Resistance* (1990), which elaborates a theory of public and hidden transcripts of power, and describes how the performance of submission can be a strategy of resistance, allowing us to understand the complex interrelatedness of concepts such as "domination," "subordination," and "resistance." Throughout, it is useful to juxtapose these scholarly texts with survivors' narratives that variously bear out and challenge these ideas. Regarding the variously destructive and redemptive power of music, Laks's memoir (1977) and Daran Kravanh's narrative of life under the Khmer Rouge (Lafreniere, 2000), both mentioned above, make a compelling contrast. The cumulative effect is to shift focus from abstract arguments about the nature of music and social domination to a consideration of what music means to survivors and how it unfolds in particular situations as people make do in life.

Perhaps the pre-eminent issue to be considered in teaching survivors' music is the role of music vis-à-vis survivors' experiences of violence and traumatic experience. There are a number of different perspectives from which one can consider this relationship: the psychological relations between music and trauma; the music of rituals aimed at healing and overcoming; music and cultural trauma; and the role of survivors' music in political arenas, among others.

All of these issues prepare a mature discussion of case studies, which can be woven throughout the course, along the lines of my suggestions for incorporating the Laks and Lafreniere books above. I have taught case studies in the music of survivors of African-American slavery and the US Civil War; the Khmer Rouge; domestic violence, child abuse, and sexual violence in North America; the genocide of Native Americans; the European Holocaust; the Asia-Pacific War; the Vietnam War; the recent Afghan and Iraq wars; and the Palestinian-Israeli conflict.

One of the core tenets of the study of survivors' music is that survivors themselves are teachers of music and life. Just as the question of whether or not the study of survivors' music is a kind of activism is interestingly answered by shifting focus away from the researcher to the ways that survivors themselves become activists, the teaching of survivors' music can be fruitfully pursued by drawing attention to survivors' teaching activities. An instructor must first find such materials in the written literature, and this may seem difficult; but since most often survivors perform, testify, and write narratives of their experiences at least partly to educate others, there is an abundance of material.

Using survivors' teaching practices as inspiration, one may instigate group learning of pieces of survivors' music in classes. I have found this to be one of the best ways to convincingly demonstrate the pleasure and the hopefulness inherent in the study of survivors' music, and to demonstrate the utility of music in people's lives. Such learning and performance also create bridges across the gulfs that often separate students from survivors, by affecting a transubstantiation of a song, melody, rhythm, or other musical piece or activity from one person to another or to a group. My survivors' music seminar has learned and performed songs and instrumental pieces of survivors of the "comfort women" system, the Holocaust, and African-American slavery.

CONCLUSION

In this chapter I have overviewed some of the primary ethical, intellectual, and practical issues that arise in the study of survivors' music. The overriding issue, in my view, is to find a way to be a scholar, educator, and activist without displacing people from the center of one's intellectual, pedagogical, and political goals. If "the study of survivors' music" doesn't coalesce into a crystal-clear method, this is because so much must be worked out between scholar-educator-activists and the people they work with; that working-out is the fundamental principle of the method.[13] It is a method that stresses listening to and learning from survivors and their music rather than helping them, and facilitating others in similar processes of learning. In this way it hopes to spread the word about the plights of people who suffer and have suffered, to spread appreciation of their artistry, and to disseminate the knowledge they have acquired through their struggles—knowledge that may make life easier for many of us, and may prevent cycles of violence and traumatic experience and repetitions of shameful episodes in human history. As a kind of musical inquiry interested in people and practice over ideas and ideologies in the abstract, which stresses the importance of listening to others, of educational activism, and of forging connections with educators and others outside the academy, it is my hope that the study of survivors' music may make a profound contribution to human history—musical and otherwise—and to the general well-being of social worlds. Many survivors slip away from us every day and take these reservoirs of music and knowledge with them, to our lasting impoverishment. There is much work to do.

Acknowledgments

I would like to express my gratitude to Yi Okseon, Yi Yongsu, Han Jeongsun, and the other survivors of the Japanese military "comfort women" system and radiation sufferers who have inspired this chapter. I am grateful to the students of my seminars on "Survivors' Music" at the University of California, Santa Barbara, and Columbia University. Thanks also to the attendees of a Columbia University Ethnomusicology Center presentation, titled (somewhat hyperbolically) "Survivors' Music: A Manifesto," for their suggestions and questions, and to the editors of this volume for their careful criticisms.

Notes

1. My book *Hearts of Pine: Songs in the Lives of Three Korean Survivors of Japanese Military Sexual Slavery* (2012) puts this method into practice much more thoroughly.
2. A system of organized sexual slavery by which the Japanese military and business provided sexual services for soldiers and affiliated civilians. The system, often called Japanese military sexual slavery, involved between 50,000 and 200,000 girls and young women from across Japan's colonial territories. See Yoshimi (1995: 92–93).
3. My own attempt to sort these things out, and turn them into a method of inquiry and documentation, can be read in the preface to *Hearts of Pine* (2012: ix–xii).
4. www.nanum.org.
5. One's showpiece song, or "number eighteen" (*ship-pal bon*, an expression of Japanese origin) is a kind of personal favorite/best song which many Koreans of older generations often sing voluntarily or by request at parties and other informal social settings. For more on the "number eighteen," see Pilzer (2012: 38).
6. Korean ages are counted from conception, so Yi Okseon was roughly a year younger in European reckoning.
7. Many survivors' written and spoken narratives generally stop at the moment of "liberation," although at this moment survivors have hardly begun to grapple with their experiences. Two nonetheless immeasurably valuable narratives exemplify this: Bree Lafreniere's *Music through the Dark*, about accordionist Daran Kravanh's tale of survival under the Khmer Rouge (2000); and Szymon Laks's *Music of Another World*, about his term as the conductor of the men's orchestra at Birkenau (1979). The fetishization of violence in the historical understanding of modern atrocities and traumatic experience is such that many survivors have come to understand their value as public people to be concentrated in their ability to relate traumatic historical events, and often stop when the most horrific part of their story is finished, before the work of self-reconstruction and healing has begun.
8. One might contrast this adjectival way of thinking about music with Western art music's predilection to foreground musical "pieces" (nouns) or Christopher Small's (1998) emphasis on musical practices (verbs).
9. For instance, Steven Feld's *Sound and Sentiment* (1980), one of the central documents in the small literature of sociomusicology, is notable for focusing on the relations between environmental sound, language, and music.

10. I listen to Pak Duri's musicality in her speech, testimony, and singing, and in her *shin-sae taryeong* (ballad of life's trials), a kind of vocalization between song and speech, attempting to understand how the voice she cultivated in song was useful to her in other expressive realms, among other things (2012: 31–66). I recorded many conversations with survivor Mun Pilgi, and listened for how she "musicalized" her daily life by introducing musical sounds—song quotations, clapping, rhythmic vocalization—and topics while speaking, sitting in silence, and listening to environmental sound (ibid.: 67–104). In this way, Mun Pilgi used music to strive away from her feelings of isolation and toward different senses of togetherness—the togetherness of the shared rhythm of clapping, or shared knowledge of a song, or a fandom, for instance. In one remarkable example, she begins to sing to the pulse of a young woman's casual tapping, establishing a collective pulse which bridges generations and gulfs of experience (ibid.: 102). Such moments of the emergence of music also demonstrated the way that she used "the musical" to weave threads of thematic coherence through her life—peppering her talk with quotations from her favorite songs, for instance.

11. http://memory.loc.gov/ammem/collections/voices/.

12. *It is not uncommon in written Korean, especially when approximating speech, to omit plurals. So it is impossible to know if this refers to one woman or a group, or both.*

13. A remarkable example of another project in the study of survivors' music is Jessica A. Schwartz's work with Rongelapese survivors of American nuclear testing in the Pacific and their descendants. Her attention to the political interests and personal wishes of her collaborators is admirable, and she has evolved her own methods to reflect these interests and desires (see Schwartz, 2012a, 2012b).

References

Cusick, Suzanne. (2008). "'You are in a place that is out of this world . . . ': Music in the Detention Camps of the 'Global War on Terror.'" *Journal of the American Musicological Society* 2(1): 1–26.

Doubleday, Veronica. (1988). *Three Women of Herat*. London: Cape.

Feld, Steven. (1982). *Sound and Sentiment: Birds, Weeping, Poetics, and Song in Kaluli Expression* (2nd ed.). Philadelphia: University of Pennsylvania Press.

Flam, Gila. (1992). *Singing for Survival: Songs of the Łodz Ghetto, 1940–45*. Urbana: University of Illinois Press.

Gilbert, Shirli. (2005). *Music in the Holocaust: Confronting Life in the Nazi Ghettos and Camps*. New York: Oxford University Press.

Goodman, Steve. (2012). *Sonic Warfare: Sound, Affect, and the Ecology of Fear*. Cambridge, MA: MIT Press.

Hirsch, Marianne. 2001. "Surviving Images: Holocaust Photographs and the Work of Postmemory." *The Yale Journal of Criticism* 14(1): 5–37.

Howard, Keith, ed. (1995). *True Stories of the Korean Comfort Women: Testimonies Compiled by the Korean Council for Women Drafted for Military Sexual Slavery by Japan and the Research Association on the Women Drafted for Military Sexual Slavery by Japan*. London: Cassell.

Kang Yonggwon, ed. (2000). *Kkeulyeogan saramdeul, ppae-atkin saramdeul: gangjero jingyongja wa jonggun wianbu ui jeungeon* [People Dragged Away, People Stolen: Forced Conscripts and Military Comfort Women's Testimonies]. Seoul: Haewadal.

Kleinman, Arthur, and Joan Kleinman. (1997). "The Appeal of Experience: The Dismay of Images: Cultural Appropriations of Suffering in Our Times." In *Social Suffering*, edited by Arthur Kleinman, Veena Das, and Margaret Lock, pp. 1–24. Berkeley: University of California Press.

LaCapra, Dominick. (1999). "Trauma, Absence, Loss." *Critical Inquiry* 25: 696–727.

Lafreniere, Bree (Daran Kravanh). (2000). *Music Through the Dark: A Tale of Survival in Cambodia*. Honolulu: University of Hawaii Press.

Laks, Szymon. (1979). *Music of Another World*. Evanston, IL: Northwestern University Press.

Maciszewski, Amelia. (2006). "Tawa'if, Tourism, and Tales: The Problematics of Twenty-First Century Musical Patronage for North India's Courtesans." In *The Courtesan's Arts: Cross-Cultural Perspectives*, edited by Martha Feldman and Bonnie Gordon, pp. 332–352. New York: Oxford University Press.

Pettan, Svanibor. (1998). "Music, Politics, and War in Croatia in the 1990s: An Introduction." In *Music, Politics and War: Views from Croatia*, edited by Svanibor Pettan, pp. 9–27. Zagreb: Institute of Ethnology and Folklore Research.

Pettan, Svanibor. (2010). "Applied Ethnomusicology: Bridging Research and Action." *Music and Arts in Action* 2(2): 90–93.

Pilzer, Joshua D. (2012). *Hearts of Pine: Songs in the Lives of Three Korean Survivors of the Japanese "Comfort Women."* New York: Oxford University Press.

Pilzer, Joshua D. (2014). "Music and Dance in Korean Experiences of the Japanese Military 'Comfort Women' System: A Case Study in the Performing Arts, War and Sexual Violence." *Women and Music* 18: 1–23.

Porter, James, and Herschel Gower. (1995). *Jeannie Robertson: Emergent Singer, Transformative Voice*. Knoxville: University of Tennessee Press.

Reyes, Adalaida. (1999). *Songs of the Caged, Songs of the Free: Music and the Vietnamese Refugee Experience*. Philadelphia: Temple University Press.

Sanford, Victoria. (2006). "Introduction." In *The Engaged Observer: Anthropology, Advocacy, and Activism*, edited by Victoria Sanford and Asale Angel-Ajani, pp. 1–19. Piscataway, NJ: Rutgers University Press.

Schwartz, Jessica A. (2012a). "A 'Voice to Sing': Rongelapese Musical Activism and the Production of Nuclear Knowledge." *Music and Politics* 6. http://quod.lib.umich.edu/m/mp/9460447.0006.101?view=text;rgn=main.

Schwartz, Jessica A. (2012b). "'Between Death and Life': Mobility, War, and Marshallese Women's Songs of Survival." *Women and Music* 16: 23–56.

Scott, James C. (1990). *Domination and the Arts of Resistance: Hidden Transcripts*. New Haven, CT: Yale University Press.

Shapiro-Phim, Toni. (2008). "Mediating Cambodian History, the Sacred, and the Earth." In *Dance, Human Rights, and Social Justice: Dignity in Motion*, edited by Naomi Jackson and Toni Shapiro-Phim, pp. 304–322. Lanham, MD: Scarecrow Press.

Silent Jane. (2006). "Beautiful Fragments of a Traumatic Memory: Synaesthesia, Sesame Street, and Hearing the Colors of an Abusive Past." *Trans: Transcultural Music Review* 10. http://www.sibetrans.com/trans/.

Silverman, Carol. (2012). *Romani Routes: Cultural Politics and Balkan Music in Diaspora*. Oxford: Oxford University Press.

Small, Christopher. (1998). *Musicking: The Meanings of Performing and Listening*. Middletown, CT: Wesleyan University Press.

Vander, Judith. (1988). *Songprints: The Musical Experience of Five Shoshone Women*. Urbana: University of Illinois Press.

Yoshimi Yoshiaki. (1995). *The Comfort Women*. Translated by Suzanne O'Brien. New York: Columbia University Press.

Young, James E. 1988. *Writing and Rewriting the Holocaust: Narrative and the Consequences of Interpretation*. Bloomington, IN: Indiana University Press.

CHAPTER 8

....

MUSIC AND CONFLICT
RESOLUTION

The Public Display of Migrants in National(ist) Conflict Situations in Europe: An Analytical Reflection on University-Based Ethnomusicological Activism

....

BRITTA SWEERS

NATIONALISM and migration have been two central forces in shaping the political landscape of Europe—besides the formation of transregional structures, such as the European Community (e.g., Behr, 2005). This has become particularly apparent in the post-1989 situation (e.g., Fijalkowski, 1993). While the period before 1989 also experienced a strong migrant movement, especially into states like Germany, Austria, and Switzerland that recruited so-called "guest-workers" during the economic boom, the political perception was mostly focused on the divided situation of the Cold War. The fall of the Berlin Wall in 1989 and the subsequent downfall of the Soviet Union and communist governments of the Eastern Bloc countries led to a change of the economic and political systems in Eastern Europe. One could thus observe the formation of new nation-states, including the Baltic states Estonia, Latvia, and Lithuania, along with an increasingly unstable situation that also influenced regions outside the initial conflict zones. This became most visible with the Yugoslavia Wars in the 1990s, but also with new persecutions, for example of Romanian Roma, and relocations of earlier migrant populations, such as the Russian-Germans. The result was a large migration flow, particularly into those Western countries that had started to accept political refugees after the end of the guest-worker recruiting period. The admittance of the modern, partly traumatized migrants and the integration of the earlier migrant groups have been partly highly conflict-laden processes, which partly led to violent escalations, as became apparent in Germany in the early 1990s.

By particularly focusing on three different case studies of so-called "action ethnomusicology" from Germany and Switzerland (cf. Pettan, 2008), this chapter predominantly focuses on the university-based work of public display of migrants through music in time-restricted contexts with limited preceding research data. Based on a general analysis of the impact of applied ethnomusicology in this situation, the chapter addresses the relation between academic research and applied work. All these projects indicate that successful intercultural interaction is not only based on profound ethnomusicological research—such as a cartography of the addressed migrants or musical cultures, an analysis of the specific problem situation, and the role of the music in this context. Rather, a systematic knowledge and management of the projects' key factors is likewise essential—particularly, as most projects require pragmatic compromises with regard to the scientific hard facts. Besides the infrastructural situation, these key factors also comprise a clear knowledge of, for instance, the various target groups, including the needs and interests of the participatory groups and institutions involved—that is, the ethnomusicologist, his or her institution, public institutions, the government, audiences, and, most important, the migrants themselves.

As I will thus argue here, a central condition for successful applied work in this situation is a careful (self-)analysis of the general possibilities of the ethnomusicologist. This systematization of these various steps and factors notwithstanding, the large number of factors involved in this applied work indicate that a generalization and theoretization is difficult. Not only does music play highly different roles in the various contexts, the "human factor"—be it with regard to the target groups and even the ethnomusicologist him- or herself—adds an element that is difficult to calculate and systematize, as the various interests, needs, and assumed role/power expectations often do not correspond with each other.

FRAMING THE INSTITUTIONAL AND POLITICAL CONTEXT

Following this line of argument, it appears essential to first clearly frame the projects with regard to the broader political situation, the general role of music in this context, and the institutional position of the ethnomusicologist. The latter can strongly vary—for example, the specific situation of an ethnomusicologist within the German-speaking countries partly strongly deviates from the US situation and related discourses. I will first focus on the latter aspect, before undertaking a broader political contextualization of the case studies.

THE INSTITUTIONAL CONTEXTUALIZATION OF THE ETHNOMUSICOLOGIST

Unlike the situation as outlined by Harrison (2012: 506–515) and Titon with Fenn (2003), ethnomusicologists were forced to work outside a strictly academic context in the

German-speaking countries from early on. This was not only a result of the extremely marginal situation of ethnomusicology (Sweers, 2008b), but also of Wilhelm von Humboldt's ideal of a comprehensive university education that was favored as a value in itself—yet not as a subsequent and clearly defined job guarantee (ibid.). This has led to a strong(er) tradition of non-academic applied activities (including journalism, the commercial music business, and diplomatic employment), as well as to a much earlier awareness of the discipline's social position than in the United States (cf. Harrison, 2012: 514). Consequently, the work in the commercial sector might be, but is not necessarily viewed as, an area of applied work in German-speaking countries. Rather, it is perceived as a normal or at least inevitable form of subsequent employment—the detachment from more scholarly activities notwithstanding.[1]

With regard to the projects discussed below, it is further important to realize the clear difference of applied ethnomusicology, which is tied to an academic infrastructure (and institutional representation), the situation of ethnomusicologists employed at non-academic institutions (e.g., civil initiatives), and ethnomusicologists active as freelance workers who have little or no access to institutional infrastructures and depend more strongly on comprehensive funding. This chapter will particularly focus on the first group, that is, full-time employed ethnomusicologists who are connected to an academic institution. However, unlike the situation of applied ethnomusicology as depicted by Sheehy (1992) and Seeger (2008), the projects discussed here are not related to preceding research or fieldwork but rather emerged at the request—often on short notice—of the communities in which the ethnomusicological post is located.

THE POLITICAL CONTEXT OF THE CASE STUDIES: MIGRATION IN GERMANY AND SWITZERLAND

Germany experienced several waves of migration since the end of World War II (Bade and Oltmer, 2004; Reißlandt, 2005). From 1955 to 1973, foreign workers were specifically recruited in both Germanys in order to compensate for labor shortage in specific branches of industry. Thus, West Germany established recruiting contracts with Italy (1955), Spain and Greece (1960), Turkey (1961), Morocco (1973), Portugal (1964), Tunisia (1965), and Yugoslavia (1968). In East Germany, these were especially contract workers from Vietnam, Poland, and Mozambique, yet in total much less than in West Germany. In the 1970s (the recruiting of so-called "guest workers" was stopped in West Germany in 1973), this group was succeeded by asylum seekers and refugees, while the 1980s were likewise shaped by the joining of the family members from the former recruiting countries. Finally, the 1990s were shaped by the resettlement of the so-called "Spätaussiedler" ("late repatriates") from Eastern Europe and the former Soviet Union. This historical development is also reflected in the distribution of migrants within the counties at the time of writing with a stronger share in the west of about 12%—in contrast to the eastern counties with an average share of 2%.[2] As a total, the population of Germany comprises a share of migrants (7.289149 out of 82.437995 persons).[3]

Unlike countries like the United States that have been strongly shaped by a clear awareness of migration, political discourses only started to perceive Germany as a migrant country from the mid-1990s on (e.g., Buterwegge, 2005). Within the context of a democratic system, yet also of an increasing number of conflicts, this has, first of all, resulted in a relatively supportive situation regarding intercultural research and institutionalized applied projects in Germany.[4] This is clearly different from what Hemetek (e.g., 2006) depicted in her studies on minorities and what Araújo (e.g., 2010) or Corn (2012) described with regard to indigenous cultures that are strongly shaped by conflicts with governmental structures and might require more hidden acting.

This altered political awareness appears to be in striking contrast to the long-existent presence of migrants especially within (particularly West) German major urban areas that also have established a rich network of intercultural music-related institutions. For example, Berlin not only features public events like the *Karneval der Kulturen* ("carnival of cultures") in early June, visible venues like the *Haus der Kulturen* ("house of cultures"), and world music radio stations like the internet station multicult.fm, but also provides integrative and productive support from the governmental administrative sector (e.g. the *Senatskanzlei* ["senate's chancellery"] Berlin offers sound studio scholarships for world music or migrant music bands). Similarly, Cologne features a strong network of intercultural agencies, such as *alba Kultur* or the *Weltmusik, Klezmer und Ästhetik Akademie, Integration- und Begegnungszentrum e. V.* (including an academy for Klezmer music), as well as cultural and integration centers like *Phönix: Kultur- und Integrationszentrum in Köln*.[5] However, having been a judge for the counties Mecklenburg-West Pomerania, Brandenburg, and Berlin during the world music CREOLE competition in 2008 (see also below), I could clearly observe a difference between Berlin and the more remote, infrastructurally weaker areas in East Germany at that time. Not only was it more difficult to locate suitable bands, but also a comparable visibility of migrants, as apparent in Berlin, was clearly missing in these regions.

However, the long-neglected political acknowledgment of migration has also been paralleled by a large gap in scientific research. On the one hand, one could observe the emergence of the active field of intercultural music education within German school music pedagogy since the 1980. This is reflected in the studies of, for example, Merkt (1983, 1993), Schütz (1997), Ott (1998), Barth (2000), Stroh (2005), and Schläbitz (2007). On the other hand, the situation and the different forms of migrant music have only been marginally researched in (ethno-)musicological studies, including the contexts and spheres of impact (e.g., the role of sound studios and independent CD labels). With a few exceptions, such as the Berlin-based research of Max Peter Baumann (1979) and Brandeis et al. (1990), studies on migrant music have been mostly focused on Turkish communities (e.g., Baumann, 1984; Reinhard, 1984a, 1984b; and particularly Greve, 2003; also Wurm, 2006). Different perspectives such as Schedtler's (1999) analysis of migrant street musicians in Hamburg were long isolated studies until Clausen, Hemetek, and Saether (2009) added a broader perspective that included Germany as well. Yet, with regard to a more comprehensive picture, the analysis of other music cultures is still rare (see, for example, Baily [2005] with regard to Afghan music cultures or Bertleff with regard to the repertoire of Russian-German migrants).[6] This still comparably sparse research output is also the result of the difficult situation of German ethnomusicology, which had only been marginally represented at German universities and music universities until the new millennium (Sweers, 2008b).

. Different from Germany, modern Switzerland has long been shaped by a strong migration (22.4% in 2010). Already in 1914, Switzerland counted an average of 15% migrations (in the cities up to 30%–40%), which, however, led to very early discourses about feared foreign "infiltration" and restrictions, although World War II resulted in another flow of refugees—not least to the neutral position of Switzerland (Wottreng, 2001).[7] In contrast to war-destroyed Europe, Switzerland could revive its industry very soon after 1945, which led to a very early recruiting of migrant workers, particularly from Italy. Furthermore, Switzerland experienced a strong political migrant wave, particularly from Hungary, Czechoslovakia, Tibet, and Sri Lanka. Much earlier than Germany, for instance, Switzerland experienced strong anti-foreigner campaigns as early as the 1970s, which became particularly apparent with the so-called *Schwarzenbach-Initiative*.[8] The economic boom of the 1980s saw an additional recruitment campaign. However, while the country has clearly addressed its integrative problems in public, Switzerland has increasingly likewise been shaped by populist anti-migrant slogans—particularly by the dominant leading party SVP (Schweizer Volkspartei; "Swiss Peoples' Party"). Given the smaller size of the country, as well as the even more strongly marginalized situation of ethnomusicology and a stronger focus on folk music research,[9] the musical background of the migrants in Switzerland has been even less analyzed than in Germany at the time of writing. While there exists a body of research on migrant cultures in general (see, for instance, McDowell [1996] with regard to Tamil cultures), the research on music outside journalism[10] and outside the work of applied institutions like the Geneva-based *Ateliers d'Ethnomusicologie* (ADEM)[11] has again only been covered by occasional university-based projects in the new millennium (e.g., Liechti [2012] on world music groups in Bern).[12]

In summary, these observations indicate that most applied projects addressing migration in these countries ideally requires long-term research. However, particularly in the situations outlined below—projects that emerged at a request of the local communities—time and/ or funding to adequately undertake this step were clearly lacking. The conceptualization of the approaches thus required a broader overview of the role of music within migration contexts. At the same time, the study of especially these relatively small projects allows for a detailed study of the interplay of the multiple factors that contribute to the outcomes.

THE ROLE OF MUSIC WITHIN THE MIGRANT COMMUNITIES

As music has been intertwined with most of the central life contexts, one can observe a highly complex situation in Germany (that can, in parts, be transferred to Switzerland). Just to outline a few selected aspects that should only serve as a framework:

- Many migrants have been continuing their music traditions within their internal cultural networks. This basically occurs in a private sphere—as apparent with the Rostock-based German-Russian choir Nadejda (Sweers, 2011). Many *Spätaussiedler*, for instance, had their own singing clubs, which primarily functioned as a central sociocultural anchor point at the time of the research of the *Polyphonie der Kulturen* ("Polyphony of Cultures") project in Rostock (2004–2006). Public performances and the connection to various intercultural institutions, particularly within the larger urban areas, notwithstanding, these activities occur either on an amateur level or are located within a strongly private sphere. This includes performances within the life cycle (e.g., fertility celebrities, weddings, or funerals).
- As the Rostock case illustrates, even regions with a small share of migrants (in this case, 3.2%) are shaped by a broad range of musical activities. For many migrants, music groups constitute a central contact point into the public sphere and are a central source of income, especially in an illegal situation, as the case of the Togolese migrants in Rostock elucidates (Sweers, 2010a, 2011). At the same time, as is apparent with Schedtler's (1999) study, migrant performers are also strongly present within the street music scenes.
- Music is a central expression of identity, especially for the younger generation. This is often expressed in fusions with modern Western directions. For example, the second and third Turkish migrant generations have created their own music language (Oriental hip-hop) on the basis of American hip-hop, while texts (e.g., of *Shakkah* and *K.S.B. Kanacks with Brain*) often reflect on the contemporary situation of the teenage generation. Something similar could also be observed with the *Spätaussiedler* generation (Sweers, 2008a).
- Besides the presence within the various above-sketched intercultural networks, music can provide a contact point with "official" state-based institutions, which can be described as Slobin's (1993) "supercultural sphere." For example, migrant musicians are increasingly active at the central German *Jugendmusikschulen* ("Youth Music Conservatories"). In Hamburg, which features one of the largest Afghan migrant communities, one can discover an Afghan *tabla* teacher at the state-based *Jugendmusikschule*, while Essen and Berlin already have established local categories in *baglama* playing at the transregional *Jugend musiziert* ("Youth Makes Music") competitions (cf. Baily, 2007).

- Migrant musics are also embedded into global networks. For example, within the Hamburg-based Afghan migrant community, one finds sound studios that have provided a recording infrastructure for the musicians of the entire diaspora. Likewise, as is apparent in Switzerland, music performers of "mother countries" are often booked within migrant communities for concerts, as well as seasonal festivities, and rituals of the life cycle (e.g., fertility festivities, weddings, funerals)—the presence of local musicians notwithstanding.
- The emergence of new music directions through the fusion with the "German"/Western pop culture—for example, within the club scenes, as has been apparent in Berlin's *Russendisko* scene. Named after a novel of the German-Russian author Wladimir Kaminer, *Russendisko* (2000) denotes a genre that has been fusing traditional Russian and modern music genres. Played at a high speed, *Russendisko* was popularized in dance events and radio shows by Kaminer and RotFront musician Yuriy Gurzhy in Berlin in the first decade of the millennium (Eckstaedt, 2005).[13] In a few cases (Turkish music, *Russendisko*) music has become part of the global world music scene—which is likewise the case with a few migrant groups like the Ensemble Kaboul.

These examples not only indicate a broad range of possibilities for applied ethnomusicology projects working with migrants, they again highlight that the conceptualization of each project needs to take the specific musical context into consideration—amateur performances directed at private context have different requirements and interests than, for example, street performers or professional "world musicians." It appears likewise useful to be aware of the chosen general form and related possible impacts of the applied approaches.

STAGING MINORITIES: THE RANGE OF PUBLIC DISPLAY POSSIBILITIES

Given the above-mentioned political support of intercultural education in Germany, this chapter will particularly focus on the applied approach, which I call "public display" or "staging," that is, the presentation of migrants through ethnomusicological work in a visible sphere in order to raise the general awareness of these groups (within other local communities, the broader public, etc.), yet also in order to strengthen the groups' self-affirmation through public affirmation. This includes the support of these groups in locating and facilitating these spaces for themselves (cf. Pettan, 2008). The goals of this approach can also be described as a display of migrant groups in spaces originally not immediately accessible to them, based on the assumption that public notice plays a central role for the conflict resolution. As could be observed during Rostock's *Polyphonie der Kulturen* project, the desire of becoming publicly acknowledged appears to be an important factor of developing further self-esteem among migrant groups—besides economic aspects. As the case of the Russian-German *Spätaussiedler* group Nadejda indicates here, particularly amateur musicians perceive a performance at a state-based music conservatory or university as an essential experience of being noticed. However, as the list below illustrates, there actually exists a broad range of levels of public display through university-based ethnomusicological work—again, that clearly differs from the work of public institutions—with different degrees of control (from the perspective of the migrant groups) and direct interaction with public audiences:

- **Mediatized display**: While the outcome (music, documentary, performance) is ideally based on direct interaction between researcher and interlocutors, a direct interaction with audiences is not necessary; the final form and range of display are often under stronger control of the authors and publishers, less of the migrants.
  - **Visibility through printed documentation** (e.g., in scholarly and journalistic articles). Digital media possibilities—and related media coverage (e.g., through newspapers) notwithstanding—a printed documentation still represents a high form of recognition through its physically comprehensible form, distribution, and interconnection with institutional (especially academic) sides, although the production process can be very slow.
  - **Visibility through audio-visual media** like CD recordings and film documentation (as occurred in the *Polyphonie der Kulturen* project)—which often *symbolizes* a broader perception and—real sale accounts notwithstanding—broader public recognition within the physical mass-media sphere.
  - **Visibility through digital media**, for example, internet platforms that have a wide range of distribution and can be quickly altered, yet are often perceived of having less iconic—physical—visibility.
  - **Other forms of display**, such as the transformation of the knowledge into school teaching material (a large range of Rostock's *Polyphonie der Kulturen* material was transformed into music teaching units).
- **Live display** (which includes an interaction of the migrant group, the ethnomusicologist(s), and the audience), for example:
  - **Public lectures** on and with the migrants (as occurred in the Münsingen Project). This allows a direct reaction of the migrants to their presentation, plus an interaction with the audiences.
  - **Public concerts and events** with the ethnomusicologist as a host and presenter, but mostly in a moderating function between musicians and audiences, for example, *Polyphonie der Kulturen; Musik Festival Bern*.
- **Independent acting of the migrant group, which is in direct control of the interaction with audiences**, with the ethnomusicologist as a mediator at most, for example:
  - **Lectureships and teaching options at schools and universities** (e.g., *Polyphonie der Kulturen, Musik Festival Bern*)—ideally as a regular implementation, yet often just as a one-time event.

- **Network development**, which includes establishing contacts with direct and indirect policy makers, that is, entrepreneurs, marketers, and so on (cf. Lundberg, Malm, and Ronström, 2003: 50) for further concerts, and likewise of the sociopolitical sphere, including civil initiatives, and so on (e.g., *Polyphonie der Kulturen*).
- **Possibilities of access** to recording studios, their equipment, and human knowledge (e.g., of a sound technician)—which is particularly important for amateur groups, who often have little experience on this level, yet also for more professional performers who often lack the financial resources.

While the central aim of the projects discussed below has been to provide the migrant groups with access to public platforms in order to provide more visibility in spheres that had previously not been accessible for these groups, they also reveal that each approach is in fact a complex interaction of Pettan's (2008: 90) fourfold model of *action, adjustment, administrative*, and *advocative* ethnomusicology.[14] Each project offered the migrants space for *action* in public—in spaces where encounter with other, mostly local, groups is at the core (*adjustment*), often including the interaction with institutions (*administrative*), while the ethnomusicologist often served as mediator between the various groups (*advocative* ethnomusicology). In order to analyze the interplay of action, adjustment, advocacy, and administrative ethnomusicology (Pettan, 2008), this chapter will discuss three case studies of migrants in national(ist) contexts in Germany and Switzerland.

THREE CASE STUDIES FROM GERMANY AND SWITZERLAND

As some of the cases presented below have already been discussed in various publications (e.g., Sweers 2010a, 2010b, 2011), I will briefly sketch the projects according to the initial conflict and context, conflict/target groups, involved institutions, and display approach. The German project will be clearly at the focus, yet is relativized by the comparison with two projects in related situations in Switzerland.

PROJECT 1: THE POLYPHONIE DER KULTUREN PROJECT (ROSTOCK, 2005–2008)

The first—and largest—project was stimulated by an event that took place in Rostock (East Germany) in August 1992, when several thousand Neo-Nazis attacked a multi-story building hosting Romanian Roma asylum-seekers and Vietnamese contract workers. After a siege that lasted several days, the first two floors were set on fire. The Lichtenhagen pogrom not only led to a restriction of German asylum laws, but also left Rostock with the stigma of xenophobia. The local population, however, reacted to this situation and subsequent Neo-Nazi threats with the foundation of various private initiatives against intolerance that finally resulted in the foundation of the citizens' group *Bunt statt braun* ("Colourful instead of brown"—the latter color being a symbol of the Neo-Nazis) in 2000.

This conflict situation has been shaped by a strong local xenophobia, which was further fueled by right-wing extremist activism (including right-wing extremist music CDs that were distributed on schoolyards from 2004 on) and a still marginalized situation of the actual victims, and migrants in the region in general. Given Rostock's negative reputation in public media even more than a decade after the events, the *Ausländerbeirat* ("Advisory Board of Aliens")—that had, like *Bunt statt braun*, been founded after Lichtenhagen—suggested setting a more positive emphasis on the present situation and variety through a stronger visibility of the migrant groups, rather than only looking backward at a static picture of the negative past.

The applied ethnomusicological project, called *Polyphonie der Kulturen*, was undertaken between 2005 and 2008 as a collaboration between the *Hochschule für Musik and Theater Rostock* ("University of Music and Theatre Rostock," abbr. HMT Rostock) and the civil initiative *Bunt statt braun* (Sweers, 2010a, 2011), which had approached me with this request. Set in a situation with only few intercultural institutions and limited funding options, it consisted of the production of a CD (released in 2006; Figure 8.1) and a CD-ROM (released in 2008) at its core—thus a form of mediaized display. While *Bunt statt braun*, as producer of the CD, was responsible for organization and finances, the HMT Rostock provided the scientific background (and thereby authorization) of the project, as well as the recording infrastructure. The project also resulted in scholarly articles and the transformation into school teaching material. This mediatized display was further enhanced by live presentations in the forms of accompanying concerts and festivals—that have partly led to a strengthening of independent acting of the migrants, that is, in form of lectureships and further concerts and networks.

The integrative side of this approach was reflected on the CD that not only comprised Rostock-based migrant performers with their own music and Germans playing "world music," but also intercultural music projects. The CD-ROM contains background information on the music and performers, as well as a unit on dealing with Neo-Nazi music in the classroom in order to strengthen teachers/educationalists (as "indirect policy makers," cf. Lundberg et al., 2003) and teenagers. As the latter case indicates, the project thus addressed three target groups:

- At the core were the *migrants* whose visibility was strengthened through public media and concert presentation and the support of independent acting.

FIGURE 8.1 *The Polyphonie der Kulturen* CD cover.

- Regarding the local target groups, one central discourse behind the project could be described as raising tolerance and acceptance through the knowledge of the music of "other" cultures (which was directed at a *teenage audience*—as the central target group of contemporary right-wing extremist groups). This discourse was also stimulated by a situation that differed—with its small number of migrants (2004: 3.2%; 2011: 1.9%)[15]—clearly from that of urban contexts like Hamburg, Berlin, and Cologne), which have been shaped by much larger numbers (2005: Hamburg: 26%; Berlin: 22%; Cologne: 33%).[16]
- A third, likewise important, aim of the project, also with regard to the actual balance of local and migrant population, was a direct confrontation with right-wing extremism (which was particularly targeted at *school teachers* and intended to strengthen their position in the classroom through knowledge).

Case Studies 2 and 3: Switzerland

Project 2: The Münsingen Project (2010–2011)

This small project was conducted at the request of the small city of Münsingen (11,300 inhabitants; share of migrants: 8.5%[17]). Located approximately 20 kilometers southeast of Bern, the local community of Münsingen had set up an exhibition entitled "Alien in the village? No-one has always been living here" ("Fremd im Dorf? Niemand war schon immer hier"). The documentary that was displayed in the castle museum from autumn of 2011 until spring of 2012 highlighted the migrant history of the community since the 1960s. Focusing on the Italian guest-worker migration and modern refugee and immigration history, it likewise reanalyzed the concept of "Swiss" identity by discussing the presence of Celtic and Roman communities prior to the Alemannic tribes in the sixth century, the latter being considered a keystone of Swiss-German identity.[18] Given the strong anti-immigration paroles of the leading political party, SVP, which held a share of 26.6%[19] in the national parliament in 2011, this could also be read as a form of protest— by individuals, but—as became apparent in the opening speech of the town's major—of the larger community as well.

The exhibition was accompanied by public lectures at Münsingen's Adult Education Centre. Within this context, I was requested by Therese Beeri—one of the project leaders and a retired politician who was working for Münsingen's cultural center—to develop a one-night lecture. Again, in a situation in which the political debate had contributed to a strong de-individualization of the migrants, the factor of "visibility" became significant. The idea of this smaller project—a variant of live displaying—was thus to introduce the (Swiss) audience to various "world musics" via the musical interests and contexts of migrant interlocutors (none was an active public performer), thus raising the level of tolerance within the Swiss audience and strengthening the position of the migrants in the communities. The presentation in February 2012 was centered on four similarly structured interviews and was framed by musical sound examples that had been chosen together with the migrants (Figure 8.2). With the migrants likewise sitting in the audience, I presented their life stories through their musical preferences, which was further framed by a general introduction into the music of their region. As a large portion of the local Swiss audience has initially been stimulated by their interest in world music, this presentation resulted in a close interaction between not only myself and the interlocutors, but also with the Swiss audience during the final discussion.

Project 3: The *Musik Festival Bern* (2011)

In contrast to the previous two examples, the third case study was exclusively sited in a professional musical context—the third *Musik Festival Bern*, which was set under

FIGURE 8.2 Excerpt from the exhibition flyer with Mandi Lutumba and Nada Müller. (Transl. of the quotations: "Mandi L.: The possibility of being able to work is important for integration, Paula B.: I was not prepared for Switzerland, I did not know anything. Lorenzo B.: In Italy, dealing with government agencies and craftsmen is madness. Kouano Pierre N.: People are very open in Cote d'Ivoire—which I miss here.")

the motto "Flucht" ("flight/escape") in September 2011. While this theme was mainly directed at music-theoretical aspects, such as fugue structures, it nevertheless also thematized the experience of exile. This led to a collaboration of the Festival organizers with Bern's Institute of Musicology. At the core of this collaboration was the presentation of the Geneva-based Afghan Ensemble Kaboul and its *rubab* player Khaled Arman (b. 1965) (Figure 8.3). Arman's nomination as the festival's Artist in Residence, as well as the presentation of his music as equivalent to Western classical music, was clearly intended as a means of empowerment—in form of stronger visibility within the high art cultural segment—of the exiled performers. My role as ethnomusicologist was to interview Khaled Arman after a film presentation in public (live display), and to facilitate and organize a practical workshop in Indian and Persian music at the Institute of Musicology—in which Arman was presented and strengthened in his role as a teacher authority. As this resulted in a subsequent one-semester lectureship on Indian music at the Institute of Musicology, we can likewise speak of an independent acting approach here.

FIGURE 8.3 Khaled Arman teaching at the Institute of Musicology in Bern.

THE ROLE OF THE ETHNOMUSICOLOGIST: BETWEEN OBSERVER AND ACTOR

Having sketched the projects according to issues such as conflict situation, target groups, output, and so on, the role of the ethnomusicologist—as a representative, yet as an authority—also needs to be taken into consideration, as it strongly influences the course and outcome of the project.[20] Furthermore, the reflection on the ethnomusicologist's own role within the project reveals the clear tension between a theoretically neutral position and the actual interactive situation. With regard to the examples presented above, we can observe three different layers of partly open, partly hidden role perceptions:

- the ethnomusicologist as a representative of an institution;
- the ethnomusicologist as an academic authority; and
- the ethnomusicologist as a private person.

In contrast to the position of an idealized neutral observer that might be paralleled in the ethnomusicologist outside the conflict zones or actual acting initiatives,[21] these situations required the ethnomusicologist to become actively involved. How strongly

the Swiss political situation has been affecting the perception of ethnomusicological work became clearly apparent when my professorship in Cultural Anthropology
of Music was established at the University of Bern in 2009. I and my assistant Sarah
Ross were soon drawn into requests for an active public involvement. As is even more
strongly apparent here, public notice of ethnomusicological work can be a key factor
in the emergence of applied work. In my case, it started with an article in *Der Bund*, a
leading Swiss newspaper, on my work (Mühlemann, 2011), which included a description
of the applied activities in Rostock. This brought me into contact with several representatives of cultural organizations who had apparently been looking for institutional
collaborations. This perception as an authority figure within the wider community is a
good indicator of the different roles attached to the ethnomusicologist, which go far beyond documentation, ranging from collaborator, institutional representative, and active
political actor, to expert and mediator.

My position as an academic was further challenged by my actual personal background. In the context of Rostock's *Polyphonie der Kulturen*, I clearly had an outsider position, because I had not been involved in the conflict from 1992 and was,
moreover, from Hamburg, West Germany (I had moved to Rostock, East Germany,
in 2001). At the same time, I was also acting—being a German citizen—as a representative of the power group, that is, the German institutions, the governmental layer,
and Rostock's population, hereby being in a position to actually criticize the political
situation.

When I moved to Bern, where I undertook the other two projects, I found myself in a
completely different situation. While representing the university—and, thus, seemingly
a neutral academic—I now was a migrant myself and in an inferior situation. This became particularly apparent during my first two months in Bern, which were shaped by
the various campaigns for the *Bundesratswahlen* (Federal Council Elections) in 2009.
The central negative target group of the leading party SVP had been the largest—at that
time—migrant group, the Germans. I was clearly struggling to position myself in this
situation. Not holding a Swiss passport, immediately recognizable by my *Hochdeutsch*
(High-German) speaking (that was clearly opposing the dialect that dominated everyday speaking) and part of the publicly attacked migrant group,[22] my voice seemed to
have lost the power it had held only a few months before.

I thus found that I had to develop a different voice through long-term observation,
which I regained two years later, yet in a different position. As I observed during the
Münsingen Project and the *Musik Festival Bern*, I had moved to a much more restrained
position—more concerned to give both parties a voice, rather than to speak out too
strongly myself. While the Münsingen Project was part of a larger political statement—
set against the anti-migration policy of the SVP—it likewise required a lot of diplomacy,
for example by protecting the interests of the migrants and my own situation. Being a
migrant myself, I had to be careful about making too direct remarks on the complex
political situation. While I still was in a power position (by representing academia) and
while I also reacted to a specific political situation, my statement has shifted to more

general human issues than a direct criticism. My role as ethnomusicologist thus took on different features during the three projects:

- Regarding the *Polyphonie der Kulturen* project, the civil initiative *Bunt statt braun* took the position of the HMT Rostock as a neutral public space, also for staging the cultural festival *Nacht der Kulturen* ("Night of Cultures"). The ethnomusicologist was seen as a collaborator and institutional representative, but not active political actor—rather, as someone who would elevate the project beyond normal recognition, especially due to the academic background. At the same time, the production process was a constant mediation between *Bunt statt braun's* interests and concepts and the resources of the HMT Rostock (e.g., concerning the capacities of the recording studio or the financial interests of provost and dean).
- The Münsingen Project viewed the ethnomusicologist as an official expert who could actually explain the specific situation to not only the organizers, but also the migrants.
- The *Musik Festival Bern* clearly regarded the ethnomusicologist as an important authority figure to adequately present the Afghan Ensemble Kaboul.

From Science to Applied Work: Semi-Calculable Factors

Returning to the initial question of the relation of science and applied work, the analysis of the background, the actual conflict/problem situation, as well as the ethnography of the related music traditions, can be described as the scientific basis. Similarly, there are segments and decisions of the applied project that are based on hard facts and scientifically grounded aspects, that is, systematic factors, including, besides approach and output (e.g., passive display through a CD), the identification of the target groups and involved groups, or the analysis of the infrastructure and financial means. A well-prepared management side clearly enhances the chances for a successful outcome of the project. An ethnomusicologist nevertheless needs to be aware of the transformative process occurring during applied project work, not least due to a number of semi- or even incalculable factors that are the result of the various power interplays that likewise have a strong impact on the original outline. This can be illustrated in the case of the *Polyphonie der Kulturen* project. Figure 8.4 illustrates the results of a statistical survey of Rostock's migrant communities. However, the produced CD featured a different distribution, shown in Table 8.1.

A comparison of the actual share of migrants (Figure 8.4) with the musicians represented on the CD (Table 8.1) reveals clear differences, which indicates that the production process was not only shaped by pre-investigations and statistics, but also

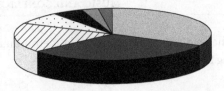

☐ Former Soviet Union (33%) ■ Asia (31%) ☑ European Union (18%)
☐ Rest Europe (8%) ■ Africa (4,9%) ▨ Americas (2,8%) ■ others (2,3%)

FIGURE 8.4 Share of migrant communities in Rostock (2004) [6598 persons = 3.2%].

Statistisches Amt Mecklenburg-Vorpommern, *Statistische Berichte: Bevölkerungsentwicklung. Ausländische Bevölkerung in Mecklenburg-Vorpommern (Ausländerzentralregister)* 2004. http://service.mvnet.de/statmv/daten_stam_berichte/e-bibointerth01/bevoelkerung--haushalte--familien--flaeche/a-i__/a143__/daten/a143-2004-00.pdf.

Table 8.1. Track List of the CD Polyphonie der Kulturen

No.	Group	Background	Country/Region Represented by the Music	Music Style
1	Schoolchildren from Rostock	German (Rostock-based; one Jewish choir)	Germany (political statement)	Latinized hip-hop
2	Halb & Halb	German	Jewish music	Klezmer
3	Students of the *Musikhochschule*	Intercultural	Roma	Improvization in Roma style (Russia/Romania)
4	Percussion Project Rostock	German	Venezuela	Jazz/classical composition
5	Nadejda	Migrant	Russia	Russian choir singing (19th/20th-century style)
6	La Prado Band	Migrant	Latin America	Salsa
7	Los Talidos	Migrant	Latin America	Salsa
8	Zartgesottene Melodealer	German	Germany (political statement)	German-Anglo-American folk
9	InterSquad	Migrant	Russia	Russian-speaking hip-hop
10	Sambucos	German	Brazil	Samba drumming
11	Capoeira Rostock e.V.	Intercultural	Brazil	Capoeira
12	Akanga	Migrant	Africa (Togo)	Traditional drumming/singing
13	Hikmat al-Sabty	Migrant	Iraq	Oriental pop
14	Nyabinghi	Migrant	Ghana/Jamaica	Reggae
15	Bilwesz	German	Mecklenburg-West Pomerania	Regional folk music
16	Agua Flamenca	German	Spain	Flamenco
17	Schoolchildren from Rostock	German (Rostock-based; one Jewish choir)	Germany (political statement)	Latinized hip-hop

by other factors. As Askew and Wilk emphasized in the preface of *The Anthropology of Media* (2002), each media object represents its own ethnographic history—and this is likewise reflected in this CD. As the project had been developed at the request of *Bunt statt braun*, many groups were connected to the activities of the civil initiative, while the track list was also shaped by the orientation of the central target group (a teenage audience), and its political message against right-wing extremism. I will subsequently highlight this decision-making process in more detail—particularly with regard to the infrastructural basis and finances.

INFRASTRUCTURAL BASIS, FINANCES, AND FUNDING

One central factor of the outcome of these projects was the access to infrastructural power. For example, Rostock's *Polyphonie der Kulturen* project could relate to the institutional basis of the HMT Rostock, which was necessary in this situation in which larger intercultural institutions were—in contrast to urban centers like Hamburg, Berlin, and Cologne—rare. This included free

- access to recording studios and time;
- performance spaces, such as the central concert hall (which relieved additional considerations such as room renting, insurances, advertisement, handling of entrance fees, etc.);
- further support of the public affairs office; and
- funded academic publication possibilities.

This infrastructural situation had a strong impact on the application process. Only because the HMT Rostock could provide such a central basis, was it possible to obtain and work with funding from a variety of sources—the only way to conduct such a project in a financially weak region. At the same time, *Bunt statt braun* wrote not only the funding applications (that were more likely to be successful because of its political background), but also provided a network of performers—which was important due to the limited time frame, which did not allow for lengthy research.

In the case of the Münsingen Project, the exhibition organizers provided the presentation infrastructure (lecture hall, advertising) and the interview spaces, or drove the interlocutors to Bern's Institute of Musicology. The latter was highly valued by the interlocutors as they—as private persons—thereby entered a space of institutional (and, thus, assumed societal) power. In the case of the *Musik Festival Bern*, the institute was significant in that it provided financed teaching options and student audiences, while the festival provided the public spaces for the frame program (e.g., for the film documentary presentation and discussion) and advertisement.

This institutional basis situation notwithstanding, additional funding is often essential, not only depending on the intended outcome, but also on the situation of the migrants:

- In the case of the *Polyphonie der Kulturen* project, the mixture of amateurs and professionals was a clear cost factor. While the amateur performers were obviously satisfied just to be part of the project, they could not provide ready-produced tracks for the CD (which had been the initial idea of *Bunt statt braun*), while the professional bands could provide the tracks (which would save studio time) but also expected financial support in some form.
- The Münsingen Project can be described as a relatively easy format. Focused on one presentational event, it required little funding (except for a few travel expenses and a small honorarium) that could be easily covered by both institutions.
- In contrast, the *Musik Festival Bern* presented professional musician(s) living from teaching and performing, who would expect an adequate payment. In the case of the *Musik Festival Bern*, it became only obvious at second sight that the festival organizers who depended on mixed funding expected the Institute of Musicology not only to host Khaled Arman's performances, but also to finance his workshop. This was only possible because I still had some starting money related to my professorship, which had been established in 2009. Otherwise, the combination of conference and concert segments has been a highly difficult mix for Swiss sponsors, as mostly only one component is supported.

Returning to the above outlined deviation of the statistical share and represented performers on the *Polyphonie der Kulturen* CD—the ideal production situation for a CD that accurately represented the statistical data would have been a backing of a large amount of money without any conditions. Quality CD, CD-ROM, or DVD productions are expensive if undertaken professionally and if aiming to reach a broader audience (this includes studio time, sound engineers, packaging, booklet production—and, last but not least, musical copyright fees). In reality, applied projects often have only a limited financial means, which—or parts of it—are also subject to further conditions set by funding organizations, donators, and so on. Finances thus need to be viewed as a likewise decisive factor with regard to the outcome, however carefully planned.

The *Polyphonie der Kulturen* can be described as a low-key project—we acquired approximately 10,000 euros of financial support. Given the lack of major business companies in Mecklenburg-West Pomerania, we could only fall back on smaller or publicly funded sponsors. Yet, the variety listed here indicates the possibilities of gaining financial support for applied projects, even in financially struggling regions. The list of sponsors included the *Landesrat für Kriminalitätsprävention M-V* (a section focusing on criminal prevention of Mecklenburg-West Pomerania's Ministry of the Interior), the *Hansestadt Rostock* ("Hansa City Rostock," i.e., Rostock's city council), the *Norddeutsche Stiftung für Umwelt und Entwicklung aus Erträgen der Lotterie BINGO! Die Umweltlotterie* (a lottery-sponsored foundation that supports environmental and developmental issues), the *Bundesministerium für Familie, Senioren, Frauen und Jugend* (Federal Ministry of the Interior [Family, Senior Citizens, Women, and Young People]), and the *Landeszentrale für politische Bildung Mecklenburg-Vorpommern* (the regional center for political education). While these organizations either supported specific parts of the project or gave general amounts of money, a media storehouse financed the CD packaging, and a media production company supported the CD design and booklet production.

I still regard this project as an example of what is possible with little financial means. However, working with mixed financial sources likewise required awareness of the different deadlines and conditions of each sponsor—also with regard to the musical outcome. For example, the framing piece (nos. 1 and 17) is a Latin schoolchildren's hip-hop recording. The song that emphasizes the positive multicultural side of the city developed out of a request of two sponsors and was recorded with approximately 100 schoolchildren. Given the large number of participants and soloists, we decided to include two versions on the CD. While this track most strongly reflected the spirit of this project and was shaped by pedagogic considerations (we included song sheets and a playback version on the CD-ROM for further work at school), it also created a strong imbalance on the CD, which was initially aimed at a more dance-oriented teenage audience.

SCIENCE MEETS APPLICATION: THE ISSUE OF REPRESENTATION

We thus can discover a strong semi-calculable side by even seemingly clear factors like financial issues. Yet, as we could observe during all three projects, this transformation becomes even stronger in the selective process with regard to representation. As is apparent here, the choice of the performers was actually shaped by multiple interplays of interests and very pragmatic issues that each required the willingness to work with compromises. In order to highlight these processes in more depth, I will subsequently particularly focus on the problematic sides—especially in the case of the successful *Polyphonie der Kulturen* project.[23]

THE SELECTION OF THE PERFORMERS FOR THE POLYPHONIE DER KULTUREN CD

Returning to the *Polyphonie der Kulturen* project, the representative outcome was clearly shaped by the actual situation, time/financial restrictions, and pragmatic decisions. Given the small share of 3.2% of migrants in the broader region of Rostock, the question of representation was highly complex: Should we select the few professional musicians who were likely to have high-quality material at hand, or rather amateurs who might reflect the actual share of migrants more clearly, but did not have any pre-recorded (and, thus, more affordable) material available, which would present a financial challenge and delay the production? Set against the political idea of providing a public platform for migrant performers, we decided to include a much larger share of amateur musicians than initially calculated. In the end, we had to record approximately half of the material—of different musical quality, which contributed to the highly heterogeneous nature of the CD.

A further deviation from the statistical data was a result of pragmatic decisions. As outlined above, many groups were connected to the activities of *Bunt statt braun* as the central intercultural organization within the region. For example, some members of the Russian-German amateur choir Nadejda were part of the Advisory Council for Aliens and were—while again deviating from our teenager target group in age and general taste—the most accessible Russian-German late migrant group. The obvious dominance of Latin-American groups (in contrast to their small share of 2.8%) is not only explained by their involvement in *Bunt statt braun*'s peace festivals, but also by the orientation to dance music. It can be debated whether playing or dancing to Latin music indicates a stance of tolerance. Yet, it clearly mirrored the contemporary taste of German audiences, which explained why some of Rostock's best world music performers were Latin groups at that time. Due to the small size of the migrant communities, we had to work with compromises on other levels as well, and sometimes had to face internal group conflicts:

- The Iraqi *oud* player Hikmat al-Sabty was the best representative of music from the Middle East in Rostock—one of the few professional performers from this region at that time. Yet, being a Mandean, he was not fully accepted by the small, but highly heterogeneous local Islamic community (0.2%).
- The relatively small group of African migrants (325 persons/198,000 inhabitants in 2006) was represented by the group Akanga, which mainly consisted of Togolese performers. The group apparently came together by coincidence, because this band formation offered the only occasion to perform in public. As was apparent here, finding appropriate musical partners within this small musical community with whom one would also be able to get along personally can be challenging. One could clearly observe personal tensions between the performers, which became apparent in that it was already difficult to agree about the recording date, the pieces, length, and line-up. Most of the women had simply decided not to turn up, and it was constantly debated who was actually the spokesperson of the group, which more or less fell apart after the recording session.
- Jewish music presented a specific dilemma, because the older—modern—local community only slowly accepted the growing conservative group of immigrants from the former Soviet Union. We thus decided for a German group playing Klezmer. This might make sense from a political and pedagogic perspective, but also strongly altered Rostock's actual musical picture on the CD.

One could likewise observe "conflicts" with regard to the musical styles. As Adelaida Reyes elaborated in *Songs of the Caged, Songs of the Free* (1999), Vietnamese refugees based in the United States fell back on (past) traditional styles to indicate ties to their home country. In contrast, the present was represented through contemporary (e.g., pop music) styles. One could discover similar tendencies in Rostock, where the migrants on the CD preferred to be represented by modern styles. Hikmat al-Sabty decided to contribute a pop piece, while the Russian hip-hop piece by InterSquad was clearly Anglo-American in style. In contrast to these "urban folk pop" styles, the German performers preferred the older, acoustic styles, that is, they went backward and played "ethnically flavored" music to emphasize their stance of tolerance. This also explained why no Vietnamese piece (as a reference to the Lichtenhagen conflict) was included in the end, because the Vietnamese civil initiative could not find a group that represented a commonly acceptable Vietnamese music identity from their perspective, although we would later include video segments of a dragon dance performance on the CD-ROM.

SELECTING INTERLOCUTORS FOR THE MÜNSINGEN PROJECT

The situation was partly similar with the Münsingen Project. In this case, the issue of representation was related to private persons—who should present an access to their cultures through their biographies and musical experiences—and therefore not performers. Again, the chosen group of interlocutors partly deviated from the statistical data, clearly due to pragmatic reasons. The interlocutors were chosen on the basis of preceding research that had been undertaken by the community of Münsingen. However, the selection—that was basically undertaken by my central partner, Therese Beeri—strongly depended on availability, language skills, and willingness to actually reveal the individual's own biography in public, which thus led to several shifts in the initially intended group.

Three of the four interlocutors were migrants who had married a partner from Switzerland: Nada Müller from Albania, who had left her home country independently from her family soon after finishing school and had also been on one of the refugee ships of the 1990s; Paula Brechbühler, a former biologist from Brazil; and Mandi Lutumba from the Democratic Republic of Congo, who initially came to Switzerland to study law. Only in one case, I deviated from the suggestions of the Münsingen organizers: Given the strong presence of Tamil refugees from Sri Lanka, I insisted on including a Tamil family—although it proved difficult to reach into the close-knit Tamil communities—and to convince someone to participate, something that had already been difficult with the general exhibition. Finally, the Udayakumar family—who had been one of the first Tamil families to migrate to Switzerland—agreed to participate, which was fortunate in that Mr. Udayakumar was one of the religious leaders in the local Hindu temple.

The biographical questions also included themes to which a broader Swiss audience could relate, for example, childhood musical recollections, musical encounters, and observations about Switzerland. Some issues that emerged as patterns and were highlighted during the presentation included the following:

- The central role of music (besides performance and reception) in the home countries as part of a broader experience of life-cycle celebrations and dancing;
- The experience of dictatorship, which became particularly apparent in the experience of media perception;
- The conscious refocusing on the (formerly unconsciously perceived) music of the mother countries in Switzerland (i.e., the situation of migration).

I also asked the interlocutors for personal musical recommendations, which I further contextualized for the audience, thereby putting the interlocutors in an authority position. However, the dilemma of representation came up particularly here, as the interlocutors' musical tastes often very clearly deviated from what has been stereotypically associated with these countries—an aspect which I will take up again with regard to power interplays and expectations (below).

THE REPRESENTATION OF EXILE WITHIN A FESTIVAL CONTEXT: THE ENSEMBLE KABOUL

Similar issues emerged regarding the representation of the Ensemble Kaboul at the *Musik Festival Bern*. While we first discussed the possibilities of having amateur migrant groups, including one of the many well-known street bands, from the region of Bern as performers, this was soon repudiated by the festival direction for organizational reasons—not least because an overview of migrant music groups in Bern was lacking on *ArtLink*—the Swiss Bureau of Cultural Cooperation that was also considered a warrantor for quality. Furthermore, the festival directors regarded the audience expectations as a significant factor for the financial success of the event, and were hesitant to include a more amateurish or street performance band. As the target audience was mainly a group familiar with an art music concert situation and as the time frame was relatively limited, we finally agreed on the Geneva-based *rubab* player Khaled Arman, who appeared professional and prominent enough for this context.

However, what did Khaled Arman actually represent? His father, Hossein Arman, had been one of the leading Afghan folk revivalists of the 1960s, yet Khaled Arman was initially a classically trained guitarist. Born in 1965 in Kaboul, Arman first learned tabla, before his father started to teach him guitar. Khaled Arman was then discovered by a Czech talent scout and studied classical guitar in Prague, which was followed by a 10-year international career as a concert guitarist. Only later, Arman started to play the *rubab*—the instrument for which he had become known in the world music circuit. In 1995, Arman, his exiled father, and further family members founded the Ensemble Kaboul in Geneva. The first CD, *Nastaran*, appeared in 2001, followed by *Radio Kaboul* (2003), which was named "CD of the Month" by the world music magazine *Songlines*. Arman also collaborated with the internationally known viola da gamba player Jordi Savall. Arman's biography is thus clearly set between different cultures and codes that Arman is clearly aware of and which he has constantly been displaying in interviews (e.g., Burkhalter, 2004; Cartwright, 2003).

This biography has been strongly contrasted by outside portrayals of the Ensemble Kaboul, which has been often categorized under "world music." As Baily (2010) elaborated, in the Afghan music productions with fieldwork recordings had emerged in the 1950s. Baily contrasted these "Music for Non-Afghans (kharejis)" with productions in/ for Afghanistan that—centered around the station Radio Kaboul, which was founded in the 1940s—comprised a mixture ranging from Western-influenced popular music forms to classical Persian/ Indian directions. As Baily (ibid.) outlined further, this local multilayered variety notwithstanding, the global focus was particularly set on the "Music for Non-Afghans" since the events of September 11, 2001: "In this context, one particular group of Afghan musicians based in Geneva emerged to take a leading role in what was now becoming established as the 'world music market'" (ibid.: 83). On their first CD, *Nastaran*, the ensemble recorded entertainment love songs from the 1960s, but became particularly known with their second album, *Radio Kaboul*, which featured the formerly popular singer Ustad Mahwash.

Nastaran appeared on the label *EthnoMad*, which is part of the *Ateliers d'Ethnomusicologie* (ADEM) that was founded by the Swiss ethnomusicologist Laurent Aubert in 1983. The policy of ADEM includes the support of the career of professional migrant musicians in the Geneva region who are often in a highly difficult situation. In a personal interview (September 28, 2012), Arman also spoke of the traumatic/ depressive sides of the migration experiences, particularly with regard to the older generation who often have to deal with health problems that limit musical careers further. The lack of public performances of the ensemble is apparently thus particularly caused by the illness of Arman's father—not so much by the decline of world music, as Baily (2010: 84) suggested. The Ensemble Kaboul belongs to the groups that had been produced as a 10-part series by *EthnoMad* between 2001 and 2003. The policy of the label—another example of the impact of further, partly pragmatic factors into the applied independent acting approach—not only includes retrospectives, but also the search for innovative concepts (for example, Arman plays an altered *rubab*) on a highly qualitative musical level. This in particular can become the starting point for public attention and the notice of other labels—but clearly deviates from a strictly documentary approach.

The subsequent success of the Ensemble Kaboul was partly intertwined with the images related to the 9/11 events. While the Ensemble Kaboul was initially a (however highly professional) migrant ensemble which performed in more intimate live contexts, their first CD was noticed as "The record the Taliban wanted to ban" in the online *New Internationalist Magazine*,[24] while interviews in the British world music magazines *Songlines* and *fRoots* particularly focused on the destruction of Afghanistan through the Taliban (e.g., Cartwright, 2003). However, it was not only the film *Breaking the Silence* (2001) by *Songlines* journalist Simon Broughton, but also Baily's articles which contributed to Western awareness of the ensembles. At the same time, the music of the ensemble has not been depicted as revival (such as the Buena Vista Social Club) or individual artistic expression, but as a desperate struggle for survival, "a group of musicians struggling to keep alive a once mighty music, now in danger of being crushed by war and its aftermath" (Cartwright, 2003: 48).

Khaled Arman's highly reflective stance toward his own position, which I also observed during the *Musik Festival Bern*, partly contrasts the representative role he is associated with in journalistic portrayals. Similar to the previous case studies, this indicates that the issue of representation is inseparably intertwined with the power of interplay of the different interest groups involved in these projects.

POWER INTERPLAYS

As becomes particularly apparent in these smaller projects, the outcome of the three examples was also strongly shaped by power interplays of the involved institutions and other makers (Lundberg et al., 2003: 48–49). First of all, with regard to a broader context:

- Rostock: News media (negative descriptions of Rostock), politics (popular interests—also with regard to elections), and *Verfassungsschutz* ("the Federal Office for the Protection of the Constitution," action against right-wing extremist structures), civil initiatives (as representatives of population and migrants), educational sector;
- Münsingen Project: Politics (against migrants) and local initiatives (encounter with the living worlds of migrants);
- *Musik Festival Bern*: Established cultural business (*Musik Festival Bern*, as attached to the art music scene) and academic institution.

These broader interactive layers shaped, for instance, the decisions on a broader level. For example, the *Polyphonie der Kulturen* was not only a documentary of the migrants, but also included a CD-ROM teaching segment against right-wing extremism; it was furthermore accompanied by news media and politicians during the production process (Sweers, 2010a: 210–211). As is apparent on a more focused level, for example during the recording, these different intentions result in interplays of different powers (and interests) into which the actual project is embedded (cf. Lundberg et al., 2003: 44–52). I will subsequently highlight the interplay of the various perceptions and expectations, which also highlights different forms of negotiation.

REPRESENTATION, AUTHORITY, AND NEGOTIATIONS DURING THE PRODUCTION PROCESS OF THE POLYPHONIE DER KULTUREN CD

How strongly the question of representation is also intertwined with authority issues became clearly apparent during the production process of the *Polyphonie der Kulturen* CD. For example, it had been very important for us to include the group of Russian-German late migrants in the CD production, which were represented by the male hip-hop group InterSquad and the female choir Nadejda. Counting 2.7 million people, this group had surpassed the Turkish-speaking migrants (1.7 million) in Germany and counted as a problematic, yet long overlooked group at the time of the CD production (cf. Sweers, 2011). It was often depending on state support and thus also often socially marginalized (ibid.). It was obvious from the very beginning that this group (and especially the older generation) had the smallest self-confidence and self-esteem among the migrants at that time.

Particularly for Nadejda, the recording process, the interaction with the sound engineer, and further CD-related performances became central experiences, which were at least as important as the finished object. Named "hope for the integration into the new home country," Nadejda was founded in 1988. The choir's central organizer, Adelia Engel, came to Germany in 1966 to work as a planning engineer for economics on the island of Rügen. Having worked as linguistic mediator at the University of Rostock since 1974, she later established an integrative project for late migrants by founding the organization "Friends of the Russian Language." As she recalled:

> The central idea was to set up a context for Russian migrants and German-Russian late migrants where they could establish social contacts. Arriving in Germany, many migrants and late migrants lack a stable social network, in which they can identity outside their former home area. . . . Yet also the Russian culture should be mediated to other people—in order to avoid misunderstandings and to diminish prejudices.
>
> (Interview with Matthias Räther; in Fassnacht and Sweers [2008])

As Adelia Engel elaborated further (ibid.), Nadejda developed from the sheer joy in singing: "The women always liked to sing Russian *Schlager* and folk songs during events and festivities of the organization—and so I had the idea to found [our] own choir." As is apparent from the following interview example, choir singing played an essential role in the everyday life of the members:

> The central part of the eleven active members is unemployed or lives on a pension. The singing in the group is a central alternative for the women. For me, creating a

good atmosphere, which evolves during the singing in a group, is most essential. You can nicely relax, forget about your daily worries and whole stress that built up during the week. . . . The successful public performance in the group and the ap-plause afterwards is, especially for the women, an essential confirmation of their achievements. It gives them an opportunity to present themselves to the outside, get accepted and to strengthen their self-confidence.

(ibid.)

Thus, this approach is very similar to what Pettan (2008) described as action and advocative ethnomusicology. According to our recording policy, the groups them-selves could decide which piece to include—which also gave them a position of power in the project. Nadejda took its repertoire mostly from a choir tradition that emerged in the early twentieth century, that is, traditional Russian melodies that were set to late-romantic arrangements. However, these popular Russian songs did not really match our target audience (youth groups, school classes). When discussing possible tracks with the choir, we—here taking on a power role as producers—therefore suggested not including their show-piece ("Kalinka"), as this well-known piece was immediately associated with a different, older target group. While the choir (here in a decisive power role) still chose a similar piece ("Kadril"), this was lesser known and allowed for open associative space.

A further concern was thus how to turn the performance of an amateur choir into a track that could stand side by side with the professional Reggae and Iraqi pop musicians. Having never been in a professional recording studio (which likewise represented an institutional power situation), the singers were understandably nervous. They not only had to get used to the carefully positioned microphones, but also refused to be separated by dampers. The interplay of different representative ideas became likewise apparent when I announced that I wanted to document the recording session: The singers liter-ally jerked up, raced to the nearest bathroom, added makeup—or, much to the horror of the university technicians, hair spray within the sensitive setting of the performance room—but appeared suddenly much more relaxed.

At one point during the recording, Carsten Storm, the recording engineer of the HMT Rostock, took me aside. He found the performance rather lifeless from his Western art background experience. Musically, he was right. However, the spokes-person of *Bunt statt braun* was concerned: The women had little self-confidence and could panic—a discussion topic that turned up several times and reflected the policy of *Bunt statt braun*—the almost over-protective attitude toward the migrant groups. Given the Neo-Nazi attacks in 1992, this appeared reasonable, yet became musically restricting. Regarding Nadejda, the opposite happened—much to our amazement. When Carsten Storm stopped the recording and asked the group, very charmingly, to emphasize the beats stronger and to display "a bit more emotion" (while the musically problematic, yet highly adored accordionist was moved into a less visible corner), the group sud-denly came to life and gave one of its most vivid performances I had ever experienced. Furthermore, the singers apparently fully integrated Carsten Storm's suggestions during subsequent performances—to an extent that one could argue that we altered the group's performance practice in the course of the applied project, yet to an extent that it gave them more stage presence and self-control.

This issue of classical recording ethics versus protective considerations and different musical attitudes could also be observed with the African group Akanga, with whom the recording engineer saw much more musical potential than he was allowed to evoke through more direct interaction with the performers. Similarly, we were warned by *Bunt statt braun* that these performers would have trouble with turning up on time and would need some time to get adjusted. This was problematic due to the limited studio time that had been granted by the HMT Rostock, which did not allow us time for adjustment or experiments. However, most performers were actually quite punctual. Moreover, while we could indeed observe a constant negotiation between Storm's classical recording ethics, which were focused on exact timing versus improvisation, the musicians very quickly found an easily solution by, for example, helping themselves with an occasional peek at the visibly displayed mobile phone.

All the groups became further tied to the CD through the booklet and subsequent CD-ROM production, for which we conducted interviews. Also here, we had to negotiate between the interests and authority of our interlocutors and our perspectives and academic background knowledge. For instance, Nadejda perceived their repertoire as "traditional" in the sense of rural Russian music—which I actually contradicted, as the choir tradition represented a completely different layer from what was elsewhere recorded in the villages (cf. Olson, 2004). Rather than opting for one version, I and *Bunt statt braun* thus decided to elaborate these different perspectives on the CD-ROM, which combined Adelia Engel's interview with a broader background text, which contextualized the choir's repertoire. Yet, although we had thought to have represented the choir with high respect—by also outlining the repertoire as a specific tradition in its own right—we later found that Adelia Engel was not completely satisfied with this outcome. This example in particular indicates that academic knowledge also needs to be taken into consideration when reflecting the power interplays, here with the self-perception of the interlocutors. Should we have hidden this knowledge? However, as this was also the basis for school-teaching material, this gap would have led to an incomplete or even wrong perception of Russian music traditions.

THE MULTILAYERED INTERPLAY OF POWER AND EXPECTATION: THE MÜNSINGEN PROJECT

In the case of the Münsingen Project, this interaction of different powers became particularly apparent during the interview process, which was strongly shaped by the interplay between the ethnomusicologist, the local representative, and the interlocutor. The perception of authority was likewise a strong factor. Just to highlight a few key interaction points that have been contributing to the outcome of this project:

The role of the community representative versus the actual ethnomusicological approach: As I was an outsider to the community, Therese Beeri offered to select the interlocutors and to help me with translations of Swiss-German and Swiss-French during the interviews. I thus not only integrated a communal representative into the research process, but also gave Beeri a strong power role in the selection process. This, however, meant that Beeri, highly educated, preferably chose interlocutors according to linguistic fluency and education, that is, those whom she deemed to be best to talk about music. This is not necessary problematic, but was even rather advantageous, as Beeri's presence contributed to an interview situation of trust, in which the interlocutors very quickly opened up to me as the outsider. Yet it is nevertheless an important transformative factor of the representative outcome of the project from a scientific perspective.

The interlocutors' realities and expectations of the community representative: Given the urban-based, middle-class background, the interlocutors rarely referred to distinct music traditions. Instead, they mostly revealed their preferences of popular *Schlager*, both Italian and Albanian (Nada Müller), modern Tamil *kollywood* music (Udayakumar family)—or indicated that music played only a marginal role in family life (Mandi Lutumba). This took Terese Beeri much by surprise, who had hoped for more traditional, that is, iconic, references. This, like the previous observation, clearly calls for a clear awareness of the expectations of community representatives, which is also a form of power within an applied project that aims at public display.

Anticipated interview expectations of researcher and interlocutors: As these migrants were no musical experts (or performers), we often had to remind the interlocutors *that it was especially their personal musical experiences* that were important for us—not any scholarly book knowledge on which they would be evaluated. As Nada Müller pointed out in retrospect, she had been very nervous about her lacking knowledge about what she considered proper Albanian traditions—thus indicating a fear of evaluation of her tastes (my preceding interview outlines and intentions notwithstanding) and hereby putting me, as the assumed knowledgeable academic, into a high power position. For example, I had avoided any remarks about musical associations with the regions. However, both Beeri and the migrant interlocutors had both almost automatically linked the migrant identities with rural traditions, not with actual individual preferences.

Particularly from this perspective, the interview with the Tamil family Udayakumar turned out to be the most complex one: The 17-year-old daughter had been chosen as the most linguistically fluent spokesperson by the family and was thus in a power position with regard to her parents, who had been at our initial focal interest. At the beginning of the interview, she thus presented mostly material she had researched on the web—to Beeri and myself who were assumed authorities, not equal talking partners. Yet it became apparent that this family—among the first to arrive in Münsingen in the 1980s—remained strongly embedded in religious Hindu and *popular* Tamil music traditions—aspects that we only slowly brought out during the interview process.

The presentation, that is, audience expectations/background and reality/research interests: These observations were also significant for the final public lecture, which was geared at presenting the migrants as powerful representatives of their cultures. I thus put the musical preferences into the center of the presentation, yet without relativizing the material too strongly by "proper traditional music"—of which our interlocutors often had little knowledge. We likewise had to consider an audience that could easily be threatened by musical presentations that were too theoretical. The emphasis on the interlocutor's personal reflections therefore played a significant role here, as the Swiss audience could relate to experiences (childhood, weddings, yet also the migrants' reflections on Swiss music life). The planned interaction was further enhanced by having invited the interlocutors to the presentation. After each short portrayal they had the chance to answer questions from the floor, which again put them into a power situation.

THE ENSEMBLE KABOUL: ROLE-PERCEPTIONS IN A WESTERN POLITICAL AND ART MUSIC CONTEXT

The examples from the Ensemble Kaboul at the *Musik Festival Bern* particularly highlight the power interplays during the displaying process. I will subsequently relate to fieldnotes taken during two situations—the soloist stage performance of Khaled Arman during the Festival opening, and an ensemble concert with traditional or popular Afghan music in the opera house, with further additions from observations from the film documentary with subsequent public discussion at the opera house.

SITUATION I: KHALED ARMAN AT THE FESTIVAL OPENING (SEPTEMBER 8, 2011)

It is Thursday evening, we are inside Bern's old Town Hall. A highly varied audience is assembled for the opening of the Festival: politicians, journalists, political and intercultural activists. Khaled Arman, who carries a rubab, and his tabla player Siar Hachimi, both clad in the traditional Afghan shalwar costume, enter the small, platform-like stage. They sit down, tune their instruments carefully, and start an improvisation. The improvisation starts out like a raga introduction and progresses to increasing levels of virtuosity. At some point I wonder about the similarities between Afghan-Persian music and the music of Johann Sebastian Bach (Arman still maintains his initial posture of a rubab player), until I realize that Arman has indeed moved into a Bach-like guitarist improvisation, which becomes even more obvious when Arman moves into a more guitar-like posture (fieldnotes).

As I observe further, the audience appears surprised, as it obviously expected to hear Afghan musicians in a traditional concert setting to play non-Western Afghan music—due to the stage setting, the clothing, the initial tuning procedure—and the political context. At the same time, the audience maintains the habitus of a Western classical concert audience: silent, almost immobile, and nearly separated from the musicians (who are, however, on the same level as the audience, not elevated, as with a Western-classical stage) and applauding. During the unfolding event, it becomes apparent that the audience has adapted to Arman's fusion approach—for example, by reacting physically to Arman's improvisation cascades.

Situation II: Arman at Bern's Stadttheater (Opera House) (September 8, 2011)

A few hours later. It is 10 p.m., and we are inside Bern's opera house. A small, platform-like stage with carpets and microphones is standing in the foyer, ready for the night concert of the Ensemble Kaboul. The group plays a selection of light classical/popular Afghan music. The situation is very intimate; a part of the audience is sitting or standing next to the musicians. The audience is very perceptive, but mainly observant. It appears slightly detached, especially at the beginning, maybe also because of the lacking background knowledge of the related music tradition. Some are sipping at their drinks, others communicate physically with their neighbors, but appear unsure about how to interact in direction of the musicians who are perceived as "stars." Some remark later that they would have liked to see them on an opera stage (adequate for the star-like status of the artists). However, it is also apparent that the audience needs time to adapt to the inner time of the concert (fieldnotes).

As these roughly sketched examples indicate, the musicians performed in a variety of contexts, which are each shaped by different expectations and acting codes, for example, during the opening concert, which can be described as a collision with the political context (and the related audience expectations), which wants to perceive the musicians stronger in the role of "victims"—which Arman denied through his posture. The audience expectation is "authentic" (i.e., traditional acoustic regional) Afghan music, not an artist who plays self-confidently with the codes of different music cultures. Particularly here, parallels to the above-described associations of the ensemble with the events of 9/11 become apparent. This ambivalent situation is a returning trope for Arman in personal communications during the festival. On the one hand, this contributed to his popularity; on the other hand, it does not allow the artists to keep an individual artistic identity. This also relates back to the acting of *Bunt statt braun*, which, like other civil initiatives, has often been emphasizing the "victimized" side in order to help, but thereby reduces the multilayered identity of the artists to one limited imagery.[25]

The migration side of the identity became especially apparent during the public interviews, for example during the film presentation on *L'Ensemble Kaboul en Exile* (2002) on Friday, September 9, 2011, which displayed Arman as a political person who can speak for himself. Especially here, Arman strongly interacted with the audience from the very beginning. Arman's extremely eloquent expression might be unusual, yet it indicates the necessity of creating situations in which equal encounters are possible, even though the organizers might then have to step back. However, we also encounter Arman here as a representative of a specific direction of classical Afghan music, whose performance practice collides with the specific room, the specific audience-musician-relationship, and the codes of an opera house.[26]

This thus raises the question of how we can create—with regard to the highly varied different individual situations—functioning production and active arenas. The Ensemble Kaboul might have other expectations than a rock or electronic group—which raises further questions with regard to migrant groups and the role of public institutions: Which spaces are available here—and how can we negotiate between the different performance expectations?

Long-Term Effects: Developments from the Finished Projects

All the above-discussed projects led to further developments—in some cases, indeed from mediatized and/or live display toward independent acting. As might become obvious from the sketched project results, the above-discussed issues of representation and power interplay strongly influenced the subsequent outcomes, which were not always obvious at the beginning. Also, the long-term impact on a financial level—including the open and hidden expectations of the various partners—should not be underestimated.

The *Polyphonie der Kulturen* Project

The physical result of the *Polyphonie der Kulturen* project is a CD/CD-ROM with a colorful cover, which, however, avoids any references to any direct event. The highly heterogeneous object does not fit well into any sale category (it does not fully work as purely background, dance, chill-out, or political CD). Yet it worked extremely well as a *symbolic object and as a marker of a specific period*—of a political situation, a music scene, and a specific interaction between different groups, institutions, and persons. However, reflection on the outcome indicates that the project was embedded into a large number of different expectations by all groups involved. The public presentation of migrant performers might have been central from an applied ethnomusicological perspective. Yet, given the ongoing problems with Neo-Nazis, the didactic teaching aid against right-wing extremism raised the strongest attention by local teaching institutions, political institutions, the county parliament, and so on, to the *Polyphonie der Kulturen* project at that time. And while I would have liked to have the migrants standing in their own right within this project, it was particularly through the interest in (or rather fear of) addressing the right-wing extremist threat that the migrants were likewise noticed on a supercultural level.

From the perspective of the migrant performers, the CD and the subsequent release concert presentation at the HMT Rostock in February 2007 constituted an important *local public platform* (for live displaying) which had previously not been accessible. The CD thereby not only added a more professional side to their musical work, but the performers subsequently also received several bookings for gigs and parties. Several migrant performers hoped to relate to the HMT Rostock as a public institution with a strong focal role within the city's cultural life. Their reasons were related not only to finances, but also to their desire to be heard within the larger community. This particularly applied to the Russian-German amateur choir Nadejda, which subsequently became a regular member of the annual *Kaleidoskopnacht* ("Kaleidoscope Night")—an annual concert event during which the international students present music from their own countries (cf. Sweers, 2006, 2010a). Likewise, members of Akanga have been performing at various events of the HMT Rostock. Yet, some project participants also moved toward independent acting. For example, a Ghanaian drummer—who additionally performed as an accompanist for a German-African dance group at the CD release concert in February 2007—was subsequently invited to teach a drumming workshop, as part of the practical world music segment of the school music curriculum, in 2008. Furthermore, one member of the German-Russian hip-hop band InterSquad became an internee in the sound studio—and could, in return, teach some hip-hop recording techniques to the students.

Another outcome was the formation of a new music group. My colleague, historical musicologist and cello player Hartmut Möller, who was documenting the Iraq oud player Hikmat al-Sabty, teamed up with his interview partner (on electric cello), plus a Syrian E-bass player and a German tabla player, in the band Ourud Elmahabbe. Having started out with the existent repertoire of Hikmat al-Sabty, the band increasingly started to write new material, such as arrangements of Johann Wolfgang von Goethe's *West-Östlicher Divan* ("West Eastern Divan"). Ourud Elmahabbe was awarded a prestigious prize from the *Deutsche Musikrat* ("German Music Council") in 2007.

The CD also became a strong marker within the broader national context, specifically the German-wide world music contest CREOLE,[27] which attempts to give migrant music—in this case fusion world music—a broader public platform.[28] The CD led to the inclusion of the county Mecklenburg-West Pomerania into the 2008 contest, as it had demonstrated the existence of world music even in this sparsely populated region. In the end, four groups from the CD—the Klezmer band Halb & Halb, Hikmat al-Sabty's band Ouroud Elmahabbe, the instrumental fusion band Chiara, and the folk band Bilwesz—went to the highly competitive regional Berlin contest (with Bilwesz having managed to succeed to one of the three final competition concerts).

While the public display of the migrants' cultures had been the central goal from the ethnomusicological side, it was very obvious that *Bunt statt braun*—which had been struggling financially—had hoped to *secure its work financially* through the CD/CD-ROM production. Yet, a major financial drawback became copyright issues. It had been relatively unproblematic to sort out and pay the recordings to the German society for musical copyright enforcement, GEMA.[29] However, *Bunt statt braun* received an un-expected additional bill for the video material after the CD-ROM release. Although completely self-filmed and produced, and solely used for educational means, the CD/CD-ROM was nevertheless put into a very expensive category. At the same time, *Bunt statt braun* hired the ethnomusicologist Christine Dettmann on a project-base to un-dertake further promotional work. Given the tight time frame of the civil initiative and the HMT Rostock, only this extra research work enabled us to apply for possible awards, for instance. This solved the financial problems in the end, when the project was awarded a prestigious prize from the *Bündnis für Demokratie und Toleranz* ("Alliance for Democracy and Tolerance") in early 2009. The award was combined with a prize that allowed not only payment of the outstanding dues, but also further support of *Bunt statt braun*. Moreover, the project was included in the equally prestigious *Stiftung Bürgermut* ("Foundation Civil Courage") in 2009.[30]

Some Results from the Münsingen Project

The Münsingen Project also highlights a broad variety of impact layers, particularly on the level of live displaying:

- *Setting up a dialogue between interlocutors and community*: Due to the excellent advertising by Therese Beeri, the presentation had been extremely well-attended. According to the feedback, this combination of personal experiences/stories and music indeed had a strong resonance—and we could also observe that the audience enjoyed the dialogical situation.
- *Personal empowerment of the interlocutors* who had been the "stars" of the evening without, however, having been exposed too strongly on a stage (they remained sit-ting in the audience). Furthermore, as Nada Müller reported afterward, the presen-tation of her own life through different lenses had helped her to (re-)focus herself as a personality through music. As she pointed out further, she clearly also enjoyed learning more about her music and broader context, which she experienced as an additional process of authorization of herself.
- I likewise gained some *valuable research data*, which has cast a critical thought on the dilemma of presenting migrants through traditional music. While traditional/folk music has taken on an iconic role within the world music sphere and educa-tion, we might be careful to respect the background of interlocutors who are not always from traditional communities. How do we deal with this on a public level?

Outcomes from the *Musik Festival Bern*

The collaboration of the *Musik Festival Bern* led to a subsequent one-semester lectureship for Khaled Arman at the Institute of Musicology. Located in a more theoretical university context with little performance options, the Institute was in demand of practical workshops. Arman thus developed a class on Indian music—which became a testing ground for further classes. Having basically taught music students, Arman now had to deal with academic students with limited or highly heterogeneous practical background, which required him to develop compromising strategies and new pedagogical concepts. This was possible, because Arman could fall back on a Western institutionalized training and professional career. Yet, these practical workshops were often more difficult with performers who had little experience with institutionalized education and the specific needs of, in this case, more theoretical university-based students. This not only indicates a further challenge for the future, but also the problem that Arman's employment at the university could not be repeated on a regular basis, due to the university's limited finances. As became particularly apparent here—even more strongly than with the *Polyphonie der Kulturen* project—the move toward independent acting within the public sector likewise requires a profound rethinking of established structures. While this is indeed difficult in financially tight situations, it is also a challenge for future applied work.

OUTLOOK

Each of the small-scale examples discussed here indeed indicates that applied work directed at the public visibility of migrant groups is a constant struggle with compromises that lead toward the creation of artificial realities, for example with regard to the selected groups or the recorded material presented on CDs. However, as the reactions to the newspaper article on my ethnomusicological work indicate, there exists a larger public demand for ethnomusicological engagement in local communities. This reflects that the ethnomusicologist is not viewed as a detached academic, but rather as an authority figure of whom instantaneous applied work of any kind is almost expected. Returning to the issue of representation and power roles, these requests in particular confront the ethnomusicologist with a situation that is not necessarily embedded in preliminary research or related to his or her own field of specialization (as depicted by Sheehy [1992] and Seeger [2008])—and requires fast action, often toward an imbalance regarding the research element. However, an awareness of the relation of scientific data and strategic planning, on the one hand, and knowledge of the nature and processes of power interplays, on the other, can lead to a scientifically informed approach of public displaying. The field of ethnomusicology could thus even more strongly contribute to the solution of conflict situations related to migrants in national(ist) contexts.

NOTES

1. Attempts to reconnect both sides are particularly evident within world music journalism, as is apparent with the Swiss world music network *Norient* (Network for Local and Global Sounds and Media Culture (http:www.norient.ch), which was founded in 2002.

2. West German counties like Baden-Württemberg (11.9%), Bremen (13.7%), Hamburg (14.2%), Hessen (11.4%), Nordrhein-Westfalen (10.7%), and Berlin as capital (13.7%) are shaped by a high share of foreigners—in contrast to the East German counties (Brandenburg (2.6%), Sachsen-Anhalt (1.9%), and Mecklenburg-Vorpommern (2.3%), which is the focus of the first project.

3. See also the *Bundeszentrale für politische Bildung*, which provides extensive background data on migration in Germany on its webpage, http://pdp.de/themen. Statistical data can be found on http://auslaender-statistik.de/bund/ausl_3.htm; http://www.statistic-portal. de/Statistik-Portal/de:jb01_jahrtab2.asp; http://www.agaenda21-treffpunkt.de.

4. See *MusikForum* (January–March 2010), entitled "Über Grenzen hinaus: Multikulti ade—Wege in transkulturelle Welten" ("Multicultural goodbye—ways into transcultural worlds") edited by the *Deutscher Musikrat* ("German Music Council") that is a clear reaction to this situation.

5. Further details can be found on the following websites: Berlin: Karneval der Kulturen: http://www.karneval-berlin.de/de/; Haus der Kulturen: http://www.hkw.de/de/index.php; multi-cult.fm: http://www.multicult.fm; Senatskanzlei Berlin, Kulturelle Angelegenheiten: http://www.berlin.de/sen/kultur/foerderung/musik/rock-pop-welt/index.de.html; Cologne: alba Kultur: http://www.albakultur.de/sites/index.htm; Weltmusik, Klezmer und Ästhetik Akademie, Integration- und Begegnungszentrum e.V. www.klezmerakademie.org;Phönix: Kultur- und Integrationszentrum in Köln: http://www.phoenix-cologne.com.

6. See the project description of Ingrid Bertleff, "Russlanddeutsche Lieder: Popularlieder in transkultureller Lebenswelt," Universuität Freiburg (2012–2014). http://portal.uni-freiburg.de/osteuropa/Forschung/Russlanddeutsche Lieder.

7. For further details see Bundesamt für Migration, *Migrationsbericht 2010*, http://www.bfm.admin.ch/content/dam/data/migration/berichte/migration/migrationsbericht-2010-d.pdf. Wottreng (2001).

8. This name relates to the Swiss nationalist politician James Schwarzenbach (1911–1994). Founder of the Republican Party in 1971, he had started a campaign aimed at restricting the number of migrants to 10% in each canton (Geneva: 25%) and the expulsion of the superfluous numbers. While the motion was rejected in the 1970 referendum (with 54% countervotes), it also started a highly emotional debate on migration in Switzerland at that time.

9. Local folk music research (that is often also undertaken by performers and amateur collectors) is separated from ethnomusicology in Switzerland. With a few exceptions, folk music collecting has been mostly undertaken by institutions outside the university-based musicology context.

10. As is, for instance, apparent in the rich publications on the *Norient* platform.

11. *Ateliers d'Ethnomusicologie* (http://www.adem.ch).

12. See also Hannes Liechti, "Eine Stadt voller Menschen, Kulturen und Klänge: Musik der Welt in Bern." *The Fretless Blog* (23.2.2013). http://www.fretlessblog.ch/musik-der-welt-in-bern/.

13. See Kaminer's extensive website, "Russendisko": http://www.russendisko.de.

14. "1. Action ethnomusicology: any use of ethnomusicological knowledge for planned change by the members of a local cultural group. 2. Adjustment ethnomusicology: (. . .) that makes social interaction between persons who operate with different cultural codes more predictable. 3. Administrative ethnomusicology: (. . .) for planned change by those who are external to a local group. 4. Advocative ethnomusicology: (. . .) by the ethnomusicologist to increase the power of self-determination for a particular cultural group" (Pettan, 2008: 90).

15. Cf. Statistisches Amt Mecklenburg-Vorpommern, Statistische Berichte: Bevölkerungsentwic klung. Ausländische Bevölkerung in Mecklenburg-Vorpommern (Ausländerzentralregister) 2011. http://service.mvnet.de/statmv/daten_stam_berichte/e-bibointerth01/bevoelkerung—haushalte—familien—flaeche/a-i__/a143__/daten/a143-2011-00.pdf.

16. Cf. *Bundeszentrale für statistische Bildung*, "Statistik: Migrantenanteil in den deutschen Großstädten wächst." http://www.bpb.de/gesellschaft/migration/148820/migrantenanteil-in-deutschen-grossstaedten-waechst.

17. Statistik Schweiz—STAT-TAB: Ständige und Nichtständige Wohnbevölkerung nach Region, Geschlecht, Nationalität und Alter: http://www.pxweb.bfs.admin.ch/Dialog/varval.asp?ma=px-d-01-2A01&ti=St%E4ndige+und+Nichtst%E4ndige+Wohnbev%F6lkerung+nach+Region%2C+Geschlecht%2C+Nationalit%E4t+und++Alter&path=../Database/German_01%20-%20Bev%F6lkerung/01.2%20-%20Bev%F6lkerungsstand%20und%20-bewegung/&lang=1&prod=01&openChild=true&secprod=2.

18. See Einwohnergemeinde Münsingen/Kommission Ortsgeschichte, *Münsingen: Geschichte und Geschichten*. Münsingen. Fischer Print AG and Museum Schloss Münsingen, ed., Ausstellungsdokumentation "Niemand war schon immer da" (Münsingen, 2011): http://www.geschichte-muensingen.ch/fileadmin/user_upload/ortsgeschichte_muensingen/dokumente/BeglHeftMigrat_V3_web.pdf for a detailed reflection.

19. Bundesverwaltung Schweiz. *Nationalratswahlen: Übersicht Schweiz 2011*. http://www.politik-stat.ch/nrw2011CH_de.html.

20. Cf. Lundberg et al. (2003: 44), hereby meaning "who are directly engaged with thematically related activities," which includes the whole range of active involvement from managing to production, etc. (ibid.: 50).

21. Cf. Seeger (2008) for a deeper reflection on this dilemma.

22. One classical headline from that period that exceeds the actual date of the elections is, for instance, "Deutschen-Hass: 'Ach geh doch wieder heim ins Reich'" (Runa Reinecke) in the public newspaper *20 Minuten*. http://www.20min.ch/news/kreuz_und_quer/story/31228033. Dec. 20, 2009.

23. Cf. Kisliuk (2008) and Barz (2008) with regard to the complex role of situation and conflicts during fieldwork.

24. N.a. 2003. Review *Nastaran* (Ensemble Kaboul). http://newint.org/features/2003/04/05/mix/.

25. This one-sided dominance is also apparent with fusion recordings, e.g. with the *viola da gamba* player Jordi Savall. On recordings like *Orient-Occident*, it was Savall who determined how the ensemble had to realize and to improvise the "orient" musically (cf. Sweers, 2012).

26. This also within broader world music contexts. Arman was apparently angry about the prize awarding of the BBC Radio 3 Awards where the ensemble played in front of a half-drunk audience, which had little interest in acoustic chamber music, but rather expected

electronic music (Cartwright, 2003: 49)—which casts doubt on the relation of mediaized presence, live contexts, and the related audience/ hearing expectations.

27. See also http://www.creole-weltmusik.de.
28. CREOLE particularly addresses professional groups experimenting with fusion projects, but also those who develop styles like Tango or Klezmer further with their own composition. See also http://www.creole-weltmusik.de.
29. GEMA: "Gesellschaft für musikalische Aufführungen und mechanische Vervielfältigungsrechte."
30. The *Stiftung Bürgermut* has collected various projects with regard to civil courage in order to publish these as exemplary in a printed and online collection. See also http://www. buergermut.de.

REFERENCES

Araújo, Samuel, with Grupo Musicultura. (2010). "Sound Praxis: Music, Politics, and Violence in Brazil." In *Music in Conflict: Ethnomusicological Perspectives*, edited by John Morgan O'Connell and Salwa el-Shawan Castelo-Branco, pp. 217–231. Chicago: University of Illinois Press.

Askew, Kelly, and Richard R. Wilk, eds. (2002). *The Anthropology of Media: A Reader*. Malden, MA, and Oxford: Blackwell.

Averill, Gage. (2003). "Ethnomusicologists as Public Intellectuals: Engaged Ethnomusicology in the University." *Folklore Forum* 34(1–2): 49–59.

Bade, Klaus J., and Jochen Oltmer. (2004). *Normalfall Migration*. Bonn: Bundeszentrale für politische Bildung.

Baily, John. (2005). "So Near, so Far: Kabul's Music in Exile." *Ethnomusicology Forum* 14(2): 213–233.

Baily, John. (2007). *Scenes of Afghan Music. London, Kabul, Hamburg, Dublin*. DVD. London: Goldsmiths, 97 min.

Baily, John. (2010). "Two Different Worlds: Afghan Music for 'Afghanistanis' and 'Kharejis.'" *Ethnomusicology Forum* 19(1): 69–88.

Barth, Dorothee. (2000). "Zum Kulturbegriff in der interkulturellen Musikerziehung." In *Kultureller Wandel und Musikpädagogik*, edited by Niels Knolle, pp. 27–50. Essen: Die Blaue Eule.

Barz, Gregory. (2008). "Confronting the Field(note) In and Out of the Field: Music, Voices, Texts, and Experiences in Dialogue." In *Shadows in the Field: New Perspectives for Fieldwork in Ethnomusicology* (2nd ed.), edited by Gregory Barz and Timothy J. Cooley, pp. 206–224. Oxford and New York: Oxford University Press.

Baumann, Max Peter, ed. (1979). *Musikalische Streiflichter einer Großstadt. Gesammelt in Berlin von Studenten der Vergleichenden Musikwissenschaft*. Berlin: Freie Universität Berlin.

Baumann, Max Peter, ed. (1984). *Musik der Türken in Deutschland*. Kassel: Bärenreiter.

Behr, Hartmut. (2005). "The Myth of the Nation and Legacies of Nationalism: Immigration Politics and the Creation of Identity in the European Union." *Political Economy* 2: 1–18.

Brandeis, Hans, Edda Brandes, Maria Dunkel, and Schu-Chi Lee. (1990). *Klangbilder der Welt—Musik International in Berlin*. Frankfurt am Main: Network-Medien-Cooperative.

Burkhalter, Thomas. (2004). "Ich spiele Rubab mit einer westlichen Gitarrentechnik." http://norient.com/de/stories/khaledarman/.

Buterwegge, Carolin. (2005). "Von der 'Gastarbeiter'-Anwerbung zum Zuwanderungsgesetz: Migrationsgeschehen und Zuwanderungspolitik in der Bundesrepublik." *Bundezentrale für politische Bildung*. Dossier Migration. http://www.bpb.de/gesellschaft/migration/dossier-migration/56377/migrationspolitik-in-der-brd?p=all.

Cartwright, Garth. (2003). "Kaboul Rebirth." *fRoots* 245: 49.

Clausen, Bernd, Ursula Hemetek, and Eva Saether, eds. (2009). *Music in Motion: Diversity and Dialogue in Europe. Study in the Frame of the "ExTra! Exchange Traditions" project.* Bielefeld: transcript.

Corn, Aaron. (2012). "Now and in the Future: The Role of the National Recording Project for Indigenous Performance in Australia in Sustaining Indigenous Music and Dance Traditions." *MUSICultures* 39: 231–250.

Eckstaedt, Aaron. (2005). "Russendisko, Balkangroove, Klezmer. Ansätze einer interkulturellen Musikpädagogik zwischen Ost und West." In *Musik und Musikpädagogik zwischen den Kulturen. Okzident und Orient)*, edited by Jaroslaw Chacinski, pp. 149–162, 163–176. Slupsk: Pomorska Akademia Pedagogiczna.

Fassnacht, Lena, and Britta Sweers, eds. (2008). *Polyphonie der Kulturen: CD and Hintergrundmaterialien zur CD.* CD and CD-ROM. Rostock: Bunt statt braun/HMT Rostock.

Fijalkowski, Jürgen. (1993). "Aggressive Nationalism, Immigration Pressure, and Asylum Policy Disputes in Contemporary Germany." Washington, DC: German Historical Institute. Occasional Paper No. 9. http://www.ghi-dc.org/publications/ghipubs/op/op09.pdf.

Greve, Martin. (2003). *Die Musik der imaginären Türkei. Musik und Musikleben im Kontext der Migration aus der Türkei in Deutschland.* Stuttgart, Weimar: Metzler.

Harrison, Klisala. (2012). "Epistemologies of Applied Ethnomusicology." *Ethnomusicology* 56(3): 505–529.

Hemetek, Ursula. (2006). "Applied Ethnomusicology in the Process of a Political Recognition of a Minority: A Case Study of the Austrian Roma." *Yearbook for Traditional Music* 38: 35–57.

Hickmann, Ellen. (1987). "Musikethnologie in der Schul- und Hochschulunterweisung." In *Musikpädagogik und Musikwissenschaft*, edited by Arnfried Edler, Siegmund Helms, and Helmuth Hopf, pp. 270–290. Wilhelmshaven: Noetzel.

Hofman, Ana. (2010). "Maintaining the Distance, Othering the Subaltern: Rethinking Ethnomusicologists' Engagement in Advocacy and Social Justice." In *Applied Ethnomusicology: Historical and Contemporary Approaches*, edited by Klisala Harrison, Svanibor Pettan, and Elizabeth Mackinlay, pp. 22–35. Newcastle upon Tyne, UK: Cambridge Scholars Publishing.

Kaminer, Wladimir Kaminer. (2000). *Russendisko*. Munich: Goldmann.

Kisliuk, Michelle. (2008). "(Un)doing Fieldwork: Sharing Songs, Sharing Lives." In *Shadows in the Field: New Perspectives for Fieldwork in Ethnomusicology* (2nd ed.), edited by Gregory Barz and Timothy J. Cooley, pp. 183–205. Oxford and New York: Oxford University Press.

Liechti, Hannes. (2012). *Eine Stadt voller Menschen, Kulturen und Klänge.* Masterarbeit: Universität Bern.

Lundberg, Dan, Krister Malm, and Owe Ronström. (2003). *Music, Media, Multiculture: Changing Musicscapes.* Stockholm: Svenskt Visarkiv.

McDowell, Christopher. (1996). *A Tamil Asylum Diaspora: Sri Lankan Migration, Settlement and Politics in Switzerland.* Oxford: Berghahn Books.

Olson, Laura J. (2004). *Performing Russia: Folk Revival and Russian Identity*. New York: Routledge.

Merkt, Irmgard. (1983). *Deutsch-türkische Musikpädagogik in der Bundesrepublik: Ein Situationsbericht*. Berlin: Express Edition (Ph.D. dissertation).

Merkt, Irmgard. (1993). "Das Eigenen und das Fremde—Aspekte interkultureller Musikpädagogik." In *Möglichkeiten der Interkulturellen Ästhetischen Erziehung in Theorie und Praxis*, edited by Reinhard C. Böhle, pp. 141–151. Frankfurt: Verlag für Interkulturelle Kommunikation.

Mühlemann, Marianne. (2011). "Die Ankunft in der Schweiz war für mich ein Kulturschock." *Der Bund*. 15(3): 29–30.

O'Flynn, John. (2005). "Re-appraising Ideas of Musicality in Intercultural Contexts of Music Education." *International Journal of Music Education* 23(3): 191–203.

Ott, Thomas. (1998). "Unsere fremde Musik. Zur Erfahrung des Anderen im Musikunterricht." In *Systematische Musikpädagogik oder: Die Lust am musikpädagogisch geleiteten Nachdenken*, edited by Martin Pfeffer et al., pp. 302–313. Augsburg: Wißner.

Pettan, Svanibor. (2008). "Applied Ethnomusicology and Empowerment Strategies: Views from Across the Atlantic." *Muzikološki Zbornik/Musicological Annual* 44(1): 85–100.

Reinhard, Kurt and Ursula. (1984a). *Musik der Türkei*, Vol. 1: *Die Kunstmusik*. Wilhelmshaven: Heinrichshofen's.

Reinhard, Kurt and Ursula. (1984b). *Musik der Türkei*, Vol. 2: *Die Volksmusik*. Wilhelmshaven: Heinrichshofen's.

Reißlandt, Carolin. (2005). "Migration: Migration und Integration in Deutschland." http://www.bpb.de/themen/ToP083,0,0,Migration_und_Integration_in_Deutschland_html.

Reyes, Adelaida. (1999). *Songs of the Caged, Songs of the Free: Music and the Vietnamese Refugee Experience*. Philadelphia: Temple University Press.

Schedtler, Susanne. (1999). *Das Eigene in der Fremde*. Münster, Hamburg: Lit Verlag.

Schläbitz, Norbert, ed. (2007). *Interkulturalität als Gegenstand der Musikpädagogik*. Essen: Die Blaue Eule.

Schütz, Volker. (1997). "Interkulturelle Musikerziehung. Vom Umgang mit dem Fremden als Weg zum Eigenen." *Musik & Bildung* 5: 4–8.

Seeger, Anthony. (2008). "Theories Forged in the Crucible of Action: The Joys, Dangers, and Potentials of Advocacy and Fieldwork." In *Shadows in the Field: New Perspectives for Fieldwork in Ethnomusicology* (2nd ed.), edited by Gregory Barz and Timothy J. Cooley, pp. 271–288. Oxford and New York: Oxford University Press.

Sheehy, Dan. (1992). "A Few Notions about Philosophy and Strategy in Applied Ethnomusicology." *Ethnomusicology* 36(3): 323–336.

Slobin, Mark. (1993). *Micromusics of the West*. Hanover and London: Wesleyan University Press.

Stroh, Wolfgang Martin. (2005). "Musik der einen Welt im Unterricht." In *Musikdidaktik: Praxishandbuch für die Sekundarstufe I und II*, edited by Werner Jank, pp. 185–192. Berlin: Cornelsen.

Sweers, Britta. (2006). CD Booklet, *Polyphonie der Kulturen*. Rostock: Bunt statt braun/Hochschule für Musik und Theater, Rostock (LC 01795).

Sweers, Britta. (2008a). CD-ROM, *Polyphonie der Kulturen*. Rostock: Bunt statt braun/Hochschule für Musik und Theater Rostock.

Sweers, Britta. (2008b). "Ethnomusicology at Germany's *Musikhochschulen*." *European Meetings in Ethnomusicology* 12: S125–145.

Sweers, Britta. (2010a). "Music Against Facism: Applied Ethnomusicology in Rostock (Germany)." In *Music in Conflict: Ethnomusicological Perspectives*, edited by John Morgan O'Connell and Salwa el-Shawan Castelo-Branco, pp. 193–216. Chicago: University of Illinois Press.

Sweers, Britta. (2010b). "Interview Perspectives in Historical Reconstruction Insights From Two German Totalitarian Systems." *Musicology Today* 7: 55–82.

Sweers, Britta. (2011). "*Polyphonie der Kulturen*: Conceptualization and Consequences of an Applied Media Project." In *Historical and Emerging Approaches to Applied Ethnomusicology*, edited by Klisala Harrison, Svanibor Pettan, and Elizabeth MacInlay, pp. 214–232. Cambridge: Cambridge Scholars Publishing.

Sweers, Britta. (2012). "Early Music and the Mediterranean World: The Exploration of Hypothetical Worlds." *Journal of Mediterranean Studies* 21(2): 235–260.

Titon, Jeff Todd. (1992). "Music, the Public Interest, and the Practice of Ethnomusicology." *Ethnomusicology* 36(3): 315–322.

Titon, Jeff Todd, with John Fenn. (2003). "A Conversation with Jeff Todd Titon." *Folklore Forum* 34(1–2): 119–131.

Wottreng, Willi. (2001). *Ein einzig Volk von Immigranten. Die Geschichte der Einwanderung in die Schweiz*. Zürich: Orell Füssli.

Wurm, Maria. (2006). *Musik in der Migration: Beobachtungen zur kulturellen Artikulation türkischer Jugendlicher in Deutschland*. Bielefeld: transcript.

INDEX

Note: Tables and figures are indicated by t and f following the page number